Looking After
ANTIQUES

First published 1987 by Pan Books Ltd,
Cavaye Place, London SW10 9PG

9 8 7 6 5 4 3 2 1

ISBN 0 330 29374 5

Phototypeset by Input Typesetting Ltd London SW19 8DR
Printed and bound in Italy by New Interlitho

To Brian, have a wonderful Christmas now and always.

All the best,

Steven

LOOKING AFTER
ANTIQUES

ANNA PLOWDEN
& FRANCES HALAHAN

**Foreword by Dr Ashley-Smith,
Keeper of Conservation at the Victoria and Albert Museum**

Photographs by Christina Gascoigne
Drawings by Karen Daws

A Pan Original
Pan Books London and Sydney

CONTENTS

FOREWORD

The conservators at the Victoria and Albert Museum receive a constant stream of telephone calls and letters from people who want to know how to care for their possessions, or how to repair them if care has been lacking. The problem for the conservator asked to give advice is whether in the wrong hands a little knowledge could accelerate the deterioration rather than prevent or reverse it.

The care and repair of historic objects is the conservator's job but not exclusively so. It takes several years of learning and practical experience to become a conservator, but there are parts of the necessary knowledge that anyone can learn very quickly. The common causes of deterioration form an easily encompassed subject. Textiles fade in light, furniture cracks in a dry environment, metals corrode in a wet one. Once these causes are known, common sense and a little expert guidance will allow the correct preventive measures to be taken by someone without qualifications or practical experience. Caring for historic objects is mostly a question of attitude. With the correct attitude time is found for the necessary planning and preparation before any action is taken. When historic objects are accorded the right priority, the psychological hurdle of covering the cost of preventive conservation can be overcome.

Giving advice on practical treatment can be more difficult and the temptation is always to tell the enquirer to take the object to a trained conservator. There are many reasons why this is not practical, the shortage of trained conservators being one. Most households have too many items of sentimental value which need cleaning or repair to be able to afford professional help for all of them. There are certain jobs that must be left to someone with the right training and the book explains which they are. Some simpler tasks can be attempted by the untrained person who must be aware of the differences between a professional working in a studio and an amateur working at home. The specialist conservator will have built up skills from doing the same task many times. It is unlikely that an inexperienced person who will face the particular problem only once or twice will achieve anything better than a serviceable appearance. It is therefore important to be aware of the constraint of ethical conservation, especially the idea that any action by a conservator must be capable of being reversed at a later date. A professional working in a studio will have a greater variety of materials and equipment which allows a greater subtlety in the approach to particular problems than is possible for someone who buys in the minimum necessary to deal with one specific job. The well equipped studio will also be able to cope with the hazards to health and safety which practical conservation work inevitably presents. The home conservator must be aware of the hazards of using certain materials and must take seriously the warnings in this book about following the manufacturers' instructions and wearing gloves, goggles and protective clothing where appropriate.

If the owner of objects in need of care and repair understands these differences and is prepared to make time and space, the guidance in this book, written by experienced conservators, will enable them to improve the appearance and increase the life expectancy of their possessions.

Dr. Jonathan Ashley-Smith
Keeper

INTRODUCTION

USING THIS BOOK

A great deal of the looking after of objects is commonsense but it is always surprising how easy it is not to think ahead. Most people are familiar with that terrible sinking feeling when some disaster occurs and the thought 'if only I had . . .'

This is not a book on restoration but one about preventive care and how you can ensure that your objects will survive longer. It is divided into groups of materials and within each group it is divided again into individual materials. There is, for example, a chapter on METALS which is then sub-divided into Aluminium, Brass, Bronze, etc. We have tried to make the information on each material as complete as possible so that you do not have to turn from one part of the book to another. Inevitably, however, it has been necessary to repeat information throughout the book and in some cases to refer to another chapter.

Each section on a material has seven basic headings – **Inspection, Handling, Cleaning, Display, Storage, Ideal Conditions** and **Repair**. Before you handle, clean, display or store an object you need to know its strengths and weaknesses. In **Inspection** we have tried to indicate some of the things you should be aware of that could be potential weaknesses. If, for example, you plunge a ceramic figure into hot water to wash it without carefully examining it first, you could well be left with a handful of bits because you have not noticed an earlier restoration. By inspecting objects regularly you will be able to detect any deterioration before it becomes acute. A great deal of conservation and restoration can also be avoided if an object is closely inspected.

In an ideal world, all objects should be cleaned, conserved and restored by a fully trained conservator. In real life this is not practical. You cannot 'send for a conservator' every time you want to clean your silver teapot nor when the fringe of a carpet is worn through. Conservation is also a costly business. We have therefore tried to give the safest ways of cleaning objects and undertaking minor repairs, and to explain the dangers and problems involved. The methods we have given may not give the most dramatic results but they are least likely to harm your objects. If you do have an object that is especially old, rare, fragile or precious, however, it should always be cleaned, conserved and repaired by a conservator.

CONSERVATION AND RESTORATION

Throughout the book we have referred to conservation and restoration. Both terms refer to the looking after of objects. Conservation is the science of preserving what is already there without adding anything new and leaving the appearance of the object much the same. Restoration is the next stage and involves renewing or replacing some or all missing parts or surfaces.

An example of the difference between conservation and restoration can be given by a chair with an arm riddled with woodworm. If the chair is to be conserved, the arm will be treated for woodworm and, if it is weak, the wood will simply be consolidated. If the chair is to be restored, the woodworm would be treated after which the fragile worm eaten part would be cut out and a new piece of the same wood let into the arm. This new piece of wood would then be finished to match the rest of the chair.

Often, the same person can both conserve and restore objects but the quality of the work, whether conservation or restoration, should be of the highest standard and should not jeopardise the future of the object. Both conservation and restoration work should be reversible. That means that materials used such as adhesives and consolidants should be removable in the future if further work becomes necessary. For example, a broken piece from a Staffordshire figure should be stuck back with an adhesive which is easily reversible (HMG or UHU All Purpose Clear Adhesive) and not with an epoxy resin adhesive (Araldite). The easily reversible adhesives dissolve with acetone while the epoxy resin adhesive is almost impossible to dissolve.

It should always be possible to differentiate between the original and any restoration, even though it may not be immediately obvious.

Curiously enough, by tradition, conservators and restorers working within some fields are only known as restorers. This particularly applies to furniture and painting restorers.

DETERIORATION

In time all objects deteriorate because the materials that are used in their manufacture gradually wear out or break down. How fast this process happens depends on a wide range of factors, including the materials used in the object, how it was manufactured, how the object is handled and the environment (light, heat, relative humidity and pollution) in which it is kept. Some materials are much more resistant to breaking down than others, for instance stone is much tougher than wood. However, within each type of material there is also a difference, for example, alabaster is a softer stone than granite. The process of manufacturing a material can also affect its life – cheap paper like newsprint will not last as long as that of good quality.

Although it may seem obvious, the way an object is used and handled will affect the length of its life. If a pair of silver candlesticks is polished too often or is frequently knocked against other objects the silver will dent and wear away.

Objects are altered more insidiously by the environment in which they are kept. The main factors which affect materials are light, temperature, humidity and air pollution. If the conditions are right for the materials in the object it can last for a very long time, if not, it will deteriorate rapidly. Unfortunately, different materials require different conditions and it is seldom possible to achieve perfect conditions which suit all objects. The process of deterioration is inevitable and irreversible and is merely slowed down by controlling the environment.

LIGHT

Light can have a surprisingly severe effect on the condition of objects. Most people have noticed how curtains become faded where the sun shines on them but what is not always as obvious is that the light also makes the fibres themselves break down. They become very weak and brittle and eventually split. Although direct sunlight is the most damaging, any light, including artificial, will have the same effect though the rate of deterioration may be slower. Sunlight is doubly harmful as it will also heat up the air and the object.

The objects most sensitive to light are watercolours, photographs, dyed or embroidered fabrics, miniatures and wood and other organic materials. Organic materials are those that have been made from living matter such as leather, wood, textiles, paper, feathers, hair and ivory. Any material that has been coloured with a dye or pigment is also sensitive to light. Some materials such as ceramics, stone and metal are not usually harmed by light, although silver may tarnish faster in strong light.

Ordinary daylight (white light) is made up of different coloured light. This is most usually seen when a rainbow is formed, the light divides into its different colours with red one end of the spectrum and blue at the other. What makes the colours different from each other is that they have different wavelengths. Red light

has a longer wavelength and blue a shorter one. Light is also made up of radiations which we cannot see. Beyond the red end of the spectrum is infra-red radiation and beyond the blue end is ultra-violet (UV) radiation. Ultra-violet light and light at the blue end of the spectrum are the most harmful to objects. Yellow and red light are less destructive but they can raise the temperature of the air which can be damaging to the object. If the ultra-violet light can be cut out and the blue light levels reduced, less damage will be caused. You should remember that tungsten bulbs, fluorescent tubes and other artificial light sources also contain ultra-violet light.

It is not only the intensity and the wavelength which are harmful but also the length of time an object is exposed to light. If a watercolour painting is in a low level of light for twelve years the amount of damage done in that time will be the same as for a watercolour kept in light twice as strong for six years.

Not only can light cause damage but some light can affect the appearance of an object. Dyes and pigments can appear to be slightly different colours under different lights. This is particularly obvious in shops where the lighting can make buying cosmetics and clothing difficult. In daylight, for example, two blue colours may look similar but under fluorescent light they can look completely different from each other. When displaying objects you therefore need to choose lighting which will not harm the objects and which will show them to their best advantage.

MEASURING LIGHT LEVELS

Light intensity is measured in lux. Fifty lux is a low light level and is that recommended for light-sensitive materials. Light can be measured using a light meter. For accurate readings you will need a purpose-made light meter but approximate readings can be made using a 35 mm single lens reflex camera with a built-in light meter.

MEASURING LIGHT WITH A CAMERA

You will need a sheet of white board 30 × 40 cm (12 × 16 in) as well as the camera.

Place the board in front of the object where the light is to be measured. Set the film speed adjustment on the camera to ASA/ISO 800 and

adjust the shutter speed to 1/60 second. Position the camera so that the field of view is filled by the board. Adjust the aperture so that the light meter indicates the correct exposure. Note the aperture reading.

The aperture readings will approximately represent the following light levels in lux

f4	represents 50 lux
f5,6	represents 100 lux
f8	represents 200 lux
f11	represents 400 lux
f16	represents 800 lux

PROTECTION FROM LIGHT

Objects which are sensitive to light should be protected from it as much as possible. The difficulty in a house is that people do not want to live in the low light levels that are recommended for some materials. It should be remembered, though, that eyes can adapt quite quickly to low light levels and the lack of light is most apparent when you go from a bright area to a darker area.

There are a number of simple measures you can take to help protect your objects. One of the easiest methods is to keep curtains drawn or shutters closed when a room is not in use. Another is to install blinds as they are very effective at reducing the light levels within a room. Roller blinds made from a pale material such as a natural colour calico can be pulled down to cut out some of the light. It may only be necessary to pull them down a little to block out the sun or a bright sky. Pale material also allows some light to filter in so that the room is not plunged into total darkness.

In a room painted in a pale colour the light is reflected off the walls and this reflected light will illuminate the objects. If the walls are dark they will absorb the light and additional lighting will be required.

Objects which are very sensitive to light can be placed on the window wall, on the side of a room, or in a passage where they will not be in direct light. If you hang objects on a window wall make sure that it is not damp. You may need to insulate the object from the wall (see WATERCOLOURS). Watercolours, textiles and other light-sensitive objects are better displayed in a north-facing room or a room such as the dining room which is not used as much as others.

Ultra-violet absorbing filters can be placed over windows and fluorescent

outside the case, even then it is better to have the light itself outside the case for security and maintenance.

RELATIVE HUMIDITY

Relative humidity refers to the amount of moisture in the air. The quantity of moisture that the air can hold alters according to the temperature. Cold air will hold much less moisture than hot air so if the temperature drops the air can no longer hold the same amount of water and droplets may form on cold surfaces.

The term 'relative humidity' is used as a measure of the moisture content of air. Relative humidity relates the amount of moisture in a given quantity of air at a certain temperature to the maximum amount of moisture the air can hold at that temperature. It is given as a percentage, thus 0 per cent relative humidity (RH) means the air is completely dry while at 100 per cent it is saturated and dew, condensation or rain will fall if the temperature is lowered.

Organic materials (i.e. those made from animals or plants such as leather, wood, cotton, ivory, feathers or paper) contain a certain amount of water in their structure. This amount alters according to the amount of moisture in the atmosphere. If the air is very dry they will give up moisture and if it is damp they will absorb it. Leather and paper become brittle if the air is dry and ivory and wood will crack and warp. When the air is damp most organic materials swell, although canvas and other textiles made from a twisted thread will shrink and become taut. If the amount of moisture in the air frequently fluctuates the dimensions of the object will alter. This continuous change puts a strain on the structure of the material and it may start to break up. The strain is greater if there are several different materials combined together in one object as they change dimensions by different amounts. For example, paint will flake off a painting because it does not move as much as the canvas which will stretch and shrink with changes of relative humidity. Veneer will lift off a piece of furniture because the veneer and the wood of the carcass swell and shrink different amounts in different directions. Moisture in the air also encourages mould to grow.

Some inorganic materials (i.e. not organic, such as metal, ceramic, stone and glass) are also affected by the

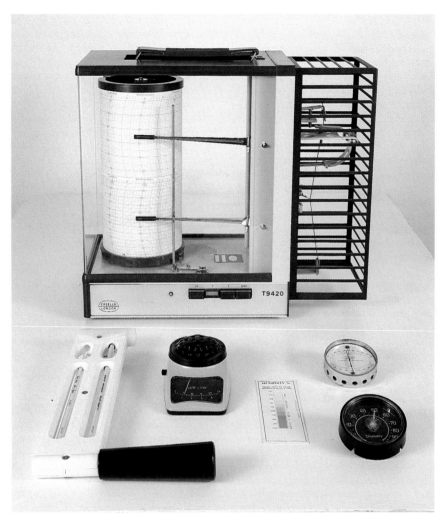

Instruments used for measuring light levels, relative humidity and temperature. Back: *thermohygrograph; left to right, front: whirling hygrometer, light meter, strip of relative humidity-indicating paper; bottom: hygrometer; top: thermohygrometer*

tubes. This does not affect the quality of the daylight. Windows can also be coated with an ultra-violet absorbing film or varnish. The film or varnish should be applied by the supplier and the varnish needs to be applied on a dry summer's day. After some time the filters become ineffective and will need replacing. The manufacturers often say that the filters will last ten years but they frequently stop being effective before this. These filters should never be applied to stained glass, leaded or old glass windows. If the windows are prone to condensation this may harm an ultra-violet absorbing filter; in cases like these you should use a sheet of ultra-violet absorbing acrylic sheet (Perspex or

Plexiglas) which can be placed in front of the windows. This acrylic sheet can also be used for double glazing. Ultra-violet absorbing sleeves are available to place over fluorescent tubes.

Do not shine spotlights directly on to objects and if you use them for general lighting in a room make sure that they do not dazzle. Tungsten-halogen lamps emit a small amount of short-wavelength ultra-violet light which can be very damaging. A piece of glass should always be placed in front of the bulb to absorb some of the ultra-violet light and heat. You will need extra protection against the UV light.

All electric lights give off heat as well as light and as this can be harmful make sure that they are not too near objects nor placed inside showcases. Fluorescent lights have a control unit to start them and to prevent them from flickering; this unit gets quite hot. Fluorescent lights should not therefore be used inside showcases unless the control unit can be placed

amount of humidity in the air. Some metals will corrode if the air is damp and some glass will 'weep'.

In winter central heating can be harmful as it heats up cold air which holds very little moisture, thus making the relative humidity drop right down. In addition, when the heating goes off in the evening the room gets cold again and the relative humidity rises causing condensation to form on objects as they cool off. This condensation, along with the repeated changes in temperature and relative humidity, can cause a great deal of damage to most types of object.

Ideally, objects should be kept in a steady relative humidity. Different materials require different levels of relative humidity but a compromise can often be reached by keeping the relative humidity between 50 and 60 per cent, preferably 55 per cent. Above 65 per cent mould will grow and metals will corrode, and below 45 per cent organic materials become brittle and shrink.

MEASURING RELATIVE HUMIDITY
The relative humidity is measured with an instrument called a hygrometer. The most accurate type of hygrometer is a whirling or wet-and-dry bulb hygrometer. There are less accurate hygrometers available where the relative humidity is indicated by a needle on a scale. Although easier to read, these hygrometers have to be calibrated regularly. There are now thermohygrometers available which measure the temperature and the relative humidity and give a digital readout. These also need calibrating regularly. There are also strips of indicating paper which show the approximate relative humidity of the surrounding air.

CONTROLLING THE RELATIVE HUMIDITY
It is not easy to control the relative humidity in an ordinary house. Most damage is caused during the winter when the central heating goes on and off. If you have very sensitive objects it would help if the heating was left on low at night and was not allowed to get too hot during the day. House-plants give off moisture and can help raise the relative humidity a little, as can bowls of water placed near radiators or containers of water hung on radiators. In general, the effect is negligible because of the large amount

of water necessary, but every little helps.

Good air circulation in a room is essential to help prevent mould forming and to try to maintain a steady relative humidity. You can help the air to circulate by opening windows and doors regularly on dry days and by using a fan heater without heat. Little used rooms should be regularly aired.

It is possible to buy humidifiers and dehumidifiers to help control the relative humidity. These can be very effective and use less energy than keeping the heating at a constant level. They need to be checked and maintained regularly.

SILICA GEL
A small enclosed area can be kept dry by using silica gel. Silica gel is granules of a moisture-absorbing material. It is often coloured with an indicator which changes colour when the silica gel is saturated. When dry the silica gel is blue and when damp it turns pink. The silica gel can be re-generated by drying it out in a moderate oven until it changes back to blue. New cameras and binoculars are often packed with small bags of silica gel.

Some objects need to be kept in a very low relative humidity until they can be dealt with by a conservator. These could be bronzes with bronze disease or ceramics suffering from problems of salts. Place the object in a sealed container such as a polythene box or bag with some silica gel granules in an open container. Make sure that the granules do not touch the object.

TEMPERATURE
The deterioration of a material is caused by chemical reactions taking place in it. If the room temperature is high these reactions will take place much faster. Mould and fungi flourish in warm temperatures and stagnant air.

All materials expand and contract with changes of temperature but they do this to different degrees, for instance metals expand and contract a considerable amount while ceramics change dimension to a much lesser extent. Thus, if different materials are used together in one object the change in dimension can cause problems. For example, some miniatures are painted on a copper sheet and if the copper expands and contracts with the

changes of temperature the paint will begin to flake as it does not move with the copper; the same thing can occur with enamels on copper. The temperature of a room can affect an object more indirectly by altering the humidity of the air.

CONTROLLING TEMPERATURE
Objects are safer if they are kept cooler rather than hotter. The temperature should be as constant as possible throughout the day and night. It is better for the object if you keep the room temperature low and wear more clothes than keep the temperature very high and wear nothing but a cotton shirt.

Do not use direct heat such as fan heaters or electric fires near objects because the heat is intense in a small area and will dry out or scorch the object. Do not place objects where they are in a cold draught as the fluctuations in temperature will be very great. Similarly do not place objects near an outside door where blasts of cold air will rush in on winter days. Gas fires and Calor Gas fires give off water vapour as well as fumes which will tarnish metal.

Heat and draughts carry dust upwards which is why we recommend throughout the book that objects should not be placed on mantelpieces over fires, radiators, storage heaters or other heat sources. Not only is the heat harmful but dust and soot will be deposited on the object.

AIR POLLUTION
Few of us live in air that is free from pollution and city air is particularly bad. Pollution can come from car fumes, factories, fires and gas heating as well as many other sources. It consists of fine dust and gases. Some gases such as sulphur dioxide, nitric oxide and nitrogen dioxide form acids with the moisture in the air which can harm materials such as marble, iron, silver, leather and textiles. Sunlight mixed with car fumes makes ozone which will destroy photographs, degrade textiles and cause some pigments to change colour. Dust can be acidic as well as making an object dirty and dingy. Many objects can also be damaged by too much cleaning and a tarry dust can be hard to remove.

There is also internal pollution generated from materials or objects within the house or office. For instance, rubber flooring and some dyes in textiles give off sulphur compounds which will tarnish silver; photocopiers produce ozone which is harmful to photographs; acetic acid, better known as vinegar, is used in the kitchen and can harm most materials. Many composite woods such as block-board and chipboard give off formaldehyde.

It is not easy to control these harmful effects of the environment. Even museums, whose job it is to look after objects, can seldom afford perfect conditions. Air conditioning can correct the relative humidity, pollution and the temperature but it is expensive to install and maintain.

VULNERABILITY OF MATERIALS

When objects are made from a mixture of different materials we recommend that the cleaning, display and storage conditions 'should suit the most vulnerable material' but the difficulty is in deciding what is the most vulnerable material.

Although light can damage a number of materials, darkness does not harm anything, so if one component of an object is light-sensitive it is unlikely to harm the other components if the object is kept in low light. However, too high or too low relative humidity can adversely affect most materials.

Generally speaking, organic materials are more vulnerable than inorganic, that is materials made from plants or animals such as leather, cotton, wool, ivory and wood are affected more by the environment in which they are kept than inorganic materials such as stone, metals, ceramics and glass. Conditions should therefore suit the organic materials first, but they should not be detrimental to the inorganic materials. For instance, an Art Nouveau figurine can be made of ivory and silver. If the object is kept where the relative humidity is low (*i.e.* 40 per cent) the silver may tarnish slightly but the ivory can crack. If the relative humidity is too high (i.e. 70 per cent) the silver will tarnish slightly faster but the ivory could swell, warp or grow mould. So the figurine should be kept in conditions where the ivory will survive best (i.e. about 55 per cent RH).

It is important that you always check the relevant chapter for all the materials that the object is made of before you make a decision about display and storage conditions. Under each material the **Ideal Conditions** are given. From this you can work out which is the most vulnerable material and therefore which conditions are the most suitable. Generally speaking, 55 per cent relative humidity will not do much damage to anything.

CHOOSING A CONSERVATOR

Throughout the book there are times when we suggest that you consult a conservator or get conservation or restoration work done by a conservator. This is because there are many areas of conservation and restoration which require specialist knowledge and where the amateur can cause a great deal of damage because he is not aware of all the problems that are involved. However, there is not yet a professional institution of conservators that could supply a comprehensive list of conservators nor is there any form of accreditation to help the customer differentiate between an enthusiastic amateur and a well-trained or experienced conservator who will carry out the work with the correct method and materials and to the highest standard. To make the consumer's job harder there are very few registers of conservators and those that do exist have used arbitary methods of selection.

These days conservators often work in a specialist field. There are those who specialize in the conservation and restoration of ceramics and glass, and others who specialize in oil paintings, works of art on paper, books, wallpaintings, objects made from stone and wood, furniture, metals, gilded objects, stained glass and ethnographical objects and other fields. Some may combine more than one specialization but few individuals now work on all materials. There are, however, some conservation firms who employ several specialist conservators and who can therefore conserve and restore a wide range of materials.

FIRST FIND YOUR CONSERVATOR

The Museums and Galleries Commission and the United Kingdom Institute for Conservation (UKIC) should be able to provide you with the names of some conservators. It should be emphasised, however, that, at the moment, being included on these lists is not a recommendation of the standard of work. Similarly, if a conservator is not included it does not mean that their work is not of a good standard.

An antique dealer who is a member of the British Antique Dealer's Association (BADA) may be able to recommend a conservator and some conservation training institutions may provide names of past students. You can also ask at your local museum or a national museum. Although they are usually reluctant to recommend an individual they may supply you with a list of conservators or restorers working in your area. Otherwise *Yellow Pages* or *Thomson's Local Directory* may list conservators under the heading of Antiques or Restorers. A personal recommendation, however, is probably the best method of selection.

HOW TO EVALUATE A CONSERVATOR

Having found your conservator you will have to try to evaluate his standard of work. If you are unfamiliar with conservation this is difficult but consider the following points.

1. Ask for his training and experience. Lack of formal training does not necessarily preclude someone from being a good conservator but lack of experience may.
2. Ask for names of some clients who would be prepared to vouch for his work.
3. Ask to see before and after photographs of other similar work he has done. He should also have records of past work.
4. He should be prepared to talk in detail about the methods he would consider using for the conservation and restoration of your object.
5. He should be willing to give an estimate of the cost of the work and an approximate date when the work will be finished. You may have to pay for a written estimate. Do not expect to be given an estimate on the spot as it takes time to examine an object carefully and evaluate the work that will be necessary.
6. He should be prepared to give a written report at the end of the work but you may have to pay for it.
7. The workshop or studio should be orderly and clean.

8. Ask the conservator if he has adequate security and what his insurance arrangements are for your object. Be prepared to have to arrange insurance cover for your object on his premises. It would be prohibitively expensive for a conservator to have insurance which covered his clients' objects.

9. If you have several objects to be conserved or restored leave the least important object to start with and only leave the others if you are satisfied with the results.

Remember that conservation and restoration is a skilled and time-consuming business. Any reputable conservator is likely to be very busy and have a waiting list. Be prepared for it to be some time before work can be started on your object. Most conservators charge for their work by the hour and not by the value of the object, this means that the cost of conservation is not usually related to the worth of the object. It takes just as long to put together a broken cheap vase as it does a similarly broken Ming vase.

HEALTH AND SAFETY

A great many materials that people use in their houses can be dangerous if mishandled or used carelessly. Kettle descaler is formic acid which is poisonous and can cause severe burns. Household bleach, caustic soda, spirits of salts and household ammonia are all extremely dangerous. They are poisonous, corrosive and can cause burns. Solvents such as methylated spirits, white spirit or even nail varnish remover and adhesives which contain solvents can cause dermatitis if handled carelessly and give off fumes which are toxic if inhaled in large quantities or if the solvent is used in an unventilated area. In addition they are all flammable.

In this book we have recommended the use of a number of materials, some of which, if handled carelessly, can be dangerous. All chemicals should be treated with respect and you should follow these simple safety precautions as they will minimize the risk:

- Do not eat or drink near chemicals nor mix chemicals in eating and cooking pots or with cutlery.

- Always wash your hands after handling chemicals and objects.

Never smoke when using chemicals, particularly solvents. Not only are they flammable but some of their fumes form poisonous mixtures with the smoke.

- Never apply make-up in a workshop environment and always wash your hands after using chemicals and before you do your make-up.

- Wear rubber gloves to protect your hands from strong or drying chemicals such as paint remover or metal cleaning products. Wear goggles to protect your eyes from splashes or dust. If you get any chemical in your eye wash it in copious amounts of water. Wear an appropriate mask (i.e. a dust mask or a respirator with the appropriate cartridges) particularly when using paint remover or when producing dust.

- If you have paint or adhesive on your hands do not 'wash' them with solvents, use a cream or gel hand cleaner (Swarfega, Tuppix) and then wash them in soap and water. A barrier cream may help protect your hands.

- Solvents and detergents remove oils from your skin and dermatitis can develop. Most domestic rubber gloves will soften in solvents apart from alcohol so if you are going to be using any quantity of solvent use Neoprene gloves for acetone and Nitrile gloves for white spirit and dichloromethane.

- Always work in a really well-ventilated room or outside if possible.

- If you are using solvents or paint stripper and begin to feel peculiar or develop a headache, stop, go outside, take some deep breaths of air and do not continue to work until you have improved the conditions. We recommend that you put used cotton wool swabs in a lidded container and then put them outside to evaporate. This is to prevent the solvent in the swabs from continuing to evaporate into the room.

- If a room has been treated for woodworm, is newly painted or you have been using solvents in it make sure that it is well aired and

that the fumes have gone before sleeping or sitting in it.

SECURITY AND INSURANCE

It is now accepted that all houses should have more security than just a Yale lock on the front door. Even if you do not have a lot of valuable possessions it is worth fitting strong mortice locks on doors as well as locks on windows, including upstairs windows, particularly if your house has drainpipes or a flat roof. You may feel it necessary to fit bars on windows and an alarm. The local police station will give advice on the most effective way of securing your home.

There are a few things you can do to help assist the police recover your objects should they be stolen:

- Make a list of the objects in your house giving a good description of each item, including any identifying features such as chips, cracks or dents. It is sensible to leave a copy of the list with a relative or solicitor in case your house is burnt.

- Take clear photographs of each object, front, back and underneath if there are any identifying marks on the base such as factory marks on ceramics or hallmarks on silver. If you have a collection of small objects such as jewellery and coins you can take a photograph of several objects at once. It is important that the photograph shows the objects clearly.

- If you move house it is wise to pack and move small objects, such as watches, yourself.

- If you intend to take an object to be conserved or restored always inform your insurance company and do not assume that the conservator will have insurance for your object. Get the insurance settled before you leave the object.

ARMS, ARMOUR AND WEAPONS

Arms, armour and weapons encompass a vast range of different types of objects and materials. Included in this group are swords, crossbows, arrows, cannons, pistols, guns, maces, axes, cutlasses, daggers, spears, knives, bows, clubs, armour, helmets, javelins, lances, shields, chain mail and many others. Almost all of these have one thing in common and that is that part of the object will be made of metal and that there is usually some other material used as well. This can be wooden butts of guns and pistols, ivory and jade handles of daggers, leather straps and textile padding of shields and armour, wooden carriages for cannons, beaded handles for native weapons and leather and textile on wooden scabbards for swords.

Arms and armour are frequently highly decorated. This can take many forms from gold, silver or brass inlay to precious stones inlaid into jade and ivory dagger handles and mother of pearl and bone inlaid into wooden gun stocks. The surface of the metal may also be intricately engraved, silvered, browned (sometimes known as russetting), blued or damascened.

INSPECTION

Because of the complexity of the construction of arms and armour the range of things that need to be known about the objects is so great that people who seriously collect arms and armour should not attempt to conserve or restore their collection themselves. The conservation and restoration of arms and armour is a very specialist subject and only a conservator with a particular interest in this field should be allowed to touch the objects. The damage that can be done in a very short time is great and irreparable. It is better to leave arms and armour alone than to have an inexperienced person deal with them.

That being said, many people have small collections of weapons that they have acquired over the years. These can range from old muskets and daggers, to possibly a sword or two or perhaps a pistol. The most usual firearms that people have are simply constructed flintlock or early percussion weapons. The later the gun the more complicated its construction and the more highly decorated it is likely to be.

If you buy or are given an old

Arms and armour are often highly decorated with gold, silver or brass inlay. Opposite *Most will be made of metal and usually some other material such as lapis lazuli or wood (Photograph by courtesy of the Trustees of the Royal Armouries)*

14

firearm it is most important, before you begin any work on it, that you make sure that it is not loaded. Even ancient gun powder can explode. To find out if a muzzle loading firearm is loaded take a wooden dowel and carefully insert it into the barrel. When it will not go any further along the barrel, mark the position of the end of the muzzle on the dowel with a pencil. Remove the dowel and place it along the outside of the barrel with the pencil mark by the muzzle. If the other end of the dowel does not reach the touch hole or nipple then the firearm may be loaded. If it does reach the touch hole or nipple the firearm is not loaded. If the gun appears to be loaded do not attempt to clear it yourself. Take it to a gunsmith.

Wooden stocks of firearms and handles of weapons should be examined to see that they are not splitting and that there is no evidence of active woodworm. Look for woodworm in the scabbards of swords and daggers and any other wooden parts of weapons. Also check blades and barrels of weapons for rust and lifting inlay and the wooden shafts and handles of weapons for lifting inlay or loose decoration. Check any textiles for moth or mould and see that the leather is not dry and cracking. For more information refer to the chapter appropriate to the material.

HANDLING

Cocking an antique firearm can break a weak main spring. If it is not your gun never do this without first asking the owner's permission and be prepared for him to refuse it. Pulling the trigger on a cocked flintlock that has no flint can create enough force to snap the metal.

The salts on your hands will attack the metal surface on arms, armour and firearms, so always wipe the metal over with an oily rag after you have handled them to remove corrosive finger marks. When handling a collection of arms and armour always wear clean cotton gloves.

Sheathed swords and daggers should be removed from their sheaths carefully while holding them pointing downwards. Old scabbards can split as you take out the weapon which may still be razor sharp so never hold the sheath by the edges. Always hold the scabbard at the top where it meets the hilt.

CLEANING

Always consult a conservator before attempting any conservation or restoration on weapons that may be rare or precious or about which you are unsure. Do not dismantle firearms in the expectation of being able to clean and reassemble them. If you do dismantle them and then cannot reassemble them do not expect someone else to be able to do it for you. Most weapons are assembled in different ways and the person who is to reassemble the weapon *must* be the person who takes it apart and ideally that person should be a weapons' conservator. Amateurs should not dismantle firearms but if you feel compelled to do so make sure that you label the pieces and record the order in which you take them apart with drawings or photographs.

When weapons are in bad condition it is very difficult to recognize the different materials and surface finishes that may have been used in their construction. If you clean in ignorance you may well lose decoration that is hidden by the corrosion. It only takes a matter of moments to ruin a beautiful object, particularly a blade, by inappropriate cleaning.

Any dusting of fine steel surfaces should be done with an artist's soft paint brush. A duster can grind the dust into the surface of the metal and mark it.

Some tribal weapons have handles and scabbards decorated with beadwork and shells. Clean these as for Beadwork (page 182).

If there is evidence of active woodworm infestation this should be treated (*see* Wood page 198).

Raw linseed oil can be put on the stock of firearms if the wood appears dry. It can also be used on the handles of weapons such as native spears. Apply the linseed oil very sparingly on a clean, soft cloth. Wipe off any excess oil and leave it to dry.

Oil the lock mechanism of fire arms occasionally with a light machine oil (3-in-1 oil).

If any part of a weapon is leather on a wood base, treat the leather as described in Leather (page 74).

A common method of protecting the iron and steel in arms and armour

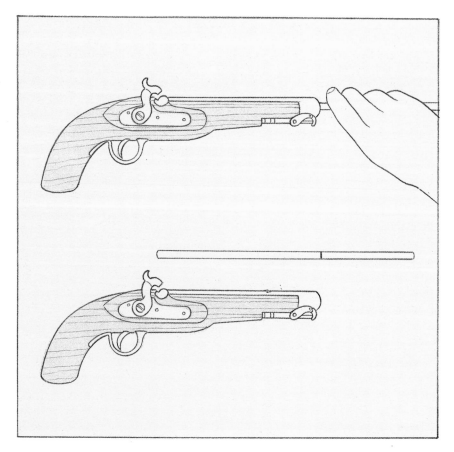

To find out if a muzzle-loading firearm is loaded, take a wooden dowel and carefully insert it into the barrel

from rust is by applying a light machine oil (3-in-1) or petroleum jelly. The disadvantage of this is that dust settles on the oil and absorbs it. This either leaves an object covered in unsightly grey fur or, if enough dust settles, it dries up the oil, falls off and leaves the metal unprotected. Micro-crystalline wax is more effective than oil and as it is not sticky the dust does not adhere to it. The problem with the wax is that it is harder to apply so that the complete surface is covered. Apply the wax evenly with a bristle brush and polish it off with a plate brush or a similar soft brush.

The most perfect sword blades are thought to be Japanese. These are patterned by a method which involves the metal being folded and twisted when it is being forged. If these blades are allowed to become rusty they will be ruined and if you try to remove the rust you will cause even more damage. Never touch the clean blade with your bare fingers as sweat will mark the finely polished surface. These swords are often extremely sharp so take great care when handling them. They should be dusted using an artist's soft paint brush and then very lightly waxed with microcrystalline wax. It is important that there is only a light coating of wax so that the dust will not stick to it. If dust does stick to the blade it could scratch the surface when it is being taken in and out of its scabbard.

Damascened blades have a pattern like watered silk which can only be achieved with steel of a particular carbon content and involves heating, reheating and then light forging. Damascening was originally practised in Damascus, hence its name. This finish is very easily damaged and should be treated in the same way as Japanese sword blades.

Nowadays, the word damascene is commonly used to describe the method of decorating steel or iron by inlaying it with gold or silver which is beaten into undercut grooves. It is extraordinarily easy to damage this inlay work by catching it with a duster or by careless handling. Never use a duster, always use an artist's soft brush to remove the dust and do not clean it at all if you think that the inlay is lifting. Ask advice from a metal conservator.

DISPLAY

Arms and armour should be displayed in a dust-free room where the relative humidity is constant. The conditions will need to suit all the materials included in the construction of the object. Although metals corrode, organic materials such as leather and wood are even more sensitive to the relative humidity.

Never display arms and armour above open fires, radiators or other heat sources. It is not advisable to display arms and armour on outside walls which may be damp but if you have no choice corks should be fixed to the back of the objects to hold them away from the wall. All metal fixings used to support arms, armour and firearms should be covered with poly-thene tubing or chamois leather. Wooden dowelling cantilevered into the wall and facing slightly upwards is a useful way of supporting guns and spears. Remember that oiled weapons will stain wallpaper and paintwork.

Ideally, swords and long firearms should be displayed in a glass-fronted case which will help to protect them from dust. Stand firearms on their butts on a pad of foam plastic with the trigger facing forward. Support the barrels with a rack fixed to the back of the cupboard. The rack should be made from a strip of wood about 2 cm (¾ in) thick. Cut a line of half moons along the front of the wood and cover the edge with chamois leather or baize. Fix the wood into the cupboard.

STORAGE

Store arms and armour in a cool, dry, clean, well-ventilated area that is free from pests. Make sure that the conditions suit the most vulnerable materials included in the construction of the object.

One way of storing ethnographical weapons is to fix a wooden frame to an inside wall and stretch heavy-duty garden nylon netting across it. Attach the weapons horizontally to the net using white cotton tape. Do not use metal wire to fix them as it may rust.

Keep arrows in shallow drawers. Make sure that they do not rattle about and damage each other by using

strips of expanded polystyrene with grooves cut into them to keep them in place. Acid-free card can also be used. Fold a strip about 7.5 cm (3 in) wide in half and cut notches about every 7.5 cm (3 in) along the folded edge.

Long firearms, swords and ethno-graphical weapons can be stored in wooden or steel storage cupboards using wooden racks. An ordinary metal cupboard like an office stationary cupboard can be used. The cupboard must have adequate venti-lation to allow air circulation to prevent condensation and must stand at least three inches away from the wall, particularly an outside wall, to allow the air to circulate round the cupboard. No part of the weapon must touch the metal of the cupboard. The guns can be supported in a rack as described in Display. A sword should be supported by its hilt with the blade hanging free and the scab-bard should hang from a hook beside the sword. Do not store swords in their scabbards particularly leather scabbards, as they tend to absorb moisture which will encourage corrosion. Always make sure that a sword and its scabbard are kept toge-ther, however.

IDEAL CONDITIONS

Household: Normal household conditions. Keep dry and dust free.

Exhibition: Relative humidity 50–60 per cent, constant. Temperature about 18°C (65°F) no higher. Light levels not critical unless wood, leather and other organic materials present.

Storage: Relative humidity 55 per cent, constant. Temperature about 15°C (59°F). Low light levels.

Check: Ideal Conditions with all relevant chapters.

REPAIR

Arms, armour and firearms should not be repaired by an amateur. For fixing small pieces of loose inlay see the relevant chapter.

CERAMICS

Ceramics are made by firing a mixture of clay and fillers such as ground shell, bone or flint in a kiln. The higher the firing temperature the less porous and tougher the ceramic produced. Stoneware and porcelain need to be fired at a high temperature; a lower temperature makes earthenware such as terracotta and tin-glazed ceramics.

Glazes are applied to ceramics both to decorate them and also to make them non-porous. Glazes can be transparent or opaque and colourless or coloured. The surface of the glaze can also be painted with enamel colours and gold. Not all ceramics are glazed. Other ways of decorating ceramics of all types include the application of different coloured clays, pigments, applied relief decoration and incised lines.

There are four main types of ceramics:

Pottery or earthenware which is soft and porous, includes Greek and Roman pottery, Italian maiolica, English delftware and terracotta.

Stoneware which is non-porous and includes the celadons from China, English salt-glaze stoneware and jasper ware pioneered by Wedgwood.

Soft-paste porcelain which is almost non-porous and usually white. It was made in an attempt to copy Chinese porcelain. The English factories which produced it include Chelsea, Bow and Worcester and Derby. Parian ware is unglazed soft-paste with a white matt surface.

Hard-paste porcelain which is non-porous and whitish. It was first made in China in about 900 AD, then copied by the Japanese followed by some European factories. These factories included Meissen, Vienna, Vezzi and Plymouth. Biscuit ware is hard-paste porcelain which is unglazed and matt.

Bone china is produced now in many English factories and comes somewhere between soft- and hard-paste porcelain. It is softer than hard-paste and more durable and cheaper to produce than soft-paste porcelain.

INSPECTION

If the object is glazed, check first to see whether the glaze is crazed or flaking. The glaze on Staffordshire figures is particularly prone to flaking. If an object is unglazed and decorated with powdery pigments, make sure that the colour does not come off on your fingers. Some objects may develop white powdery or needle–like crystals on the surface or along the cracks in the glaze.

Look for hairline cracks by holding the object up to the light or by tapping it gently with your fingernail. If it gives a good 'ring' it probably means that it is not cracked, although well-restored pieces can ring as well.

Old adhesives and overpainting in previous restorations may have discoloured to yellow or brown and may be brittle. Look for metal rivets which may have loosened. New restoration is usually harder to see.

HANDLING

Handle ceramics with great care as they are very vulnerable. Before picking up anything, check for repairs or for pieces which could easily be knocked off. If the glaze is crazed or flaking, or powdery pigment is coming off an unglazed object, handle it with particular care. Never lean over an object to pick up another one and make sure that long necklaces, lockets and objects hung around the neck such as spectacles and pens do not catch the

Glazes are applied to ceramics both to decorate them and also to make them non-porous

object. Never pick up objects by their handles, knobs or rims as they may be weak or the adhesive or rivets in an earlier repair may fail.

Use both hands to carry a piece. Place one under the base and use the other to support the object about two-thirds of the way up. Support large plates from underneath the centre, not the rim. Always put an object down carefully because if it has a hairline crack it could break if dumped down with a sudden jar.

Never carry more than one object at a time. If you need to move several at once, pack them carefully in a box or tray, making sure they will not damage each other. It is better to make several journeys than risk damaging pieces by cramming too many into a box at one go.

Where possible remove lids and loose pieces before turning an object upside down. If you cannot take the lid off always support it with one hand. A loose lid should be wrapped separately.

Many figures have a lot of leaves and flowers as decoration, which is known as bocage. These snap off very easily. When you handle such figures hold them under the base.

If the gilding on an object is badly worn it indicates the gilding is very fragile and should be handled with particular care as it comes off very easily. Any gilding which was applied before the twentieth century is likely to be vulnerable.

Always have clean hands, particularly when handling unglazed objects as they pick up dirt easily. Never wear gloves to handle ceramics as you can not get a grip.

When lifting a heavy object get help. Plan where you want to put it and make sure there are no obstacles in your path. Have any doors propped open before you set off.

Unpack ceramic objects over a table which you have first covered with a thick cloth or thin foam rubber.

CLEANING

Do not clean rare, old, fragile or precious ceramics; they should be cleaned by a conservator. Most other ceramics can be washed by immersing them in water but do not immerse unglazed earthenware and terracotta, glazed earthenware such as cream-ware, delftware and maiolica, objects with deteriorated glazes, gilded objects, objects with metal or ormolu mounts or objects which have been restored. These can be harmed if they become very wet, for instance stains in creamware and pearlware may spread wider under the glaze and many earthenwares contain iron in their body which can cause staining. Old adhesives in previous restorations can come apart and overpainting may be damaged. Metal and ormolu mounts will corrode if they get wet.

Never wash old ceramics in a dishwasher nor any ceramics which have gilding on them even if they are modern and claim to be 'dishwasher proof'. Heat and chemicals in the washing will bleach some colours and remove the gold.

To clean all ceramics brush off the dust with a soft paint brush or an artist's hogshair brush, holding the objects steady with one hand. Take care not to brush dirt into any cracks or it could become trapped. Ceramics must always be dusted before washing.

WASHING

Only wash one object at a time. Wrap the taps with cloth or foam plastic to prevent the object being chipped by them. Chose a plastic bowl large enough to hold the whole object. Place a folded towel or some foam rubber at the bottom of the bowl. If you do not have a bowl large enough and you have to put the object directly into a metal or porcelain sink, always pad the bottom. Fill the bowl with warm, not hot, water and a few drops of a non-ionic detergent (Synperonic N) or a mild household detergent (Fairy Liquid). Use an artist's hogshair brush to remove dirt from any crevices. Rinse the object well in clean warm water. Remove the object from the bowl before you throw the dirty water away and refill it. Having rinsed the object well remove the surplus water with paper towels or a soft cloth and allow it to dry in a warm place or with a hairdryer set on *Cool*.

CERAMICS REQUIRING SPECIAL ATTENTION

Some objects which cannot be cleaned by immersing in water can still be washed successfully by using cotton wool swabs or cotton buds. However, objects with a flaking glaze or surface or loose pigments should not be cleaned in this way.

Cover a table or flat surface with a

Use both hands to carry a ceramic piece, supporting the weight from underneath

thick towel or thin foam rubber (0.5 cm or ¼ in thick). Do not use a very thick covering or the object will be unstable and could easily fall over. Support the object with one hand and brush off the dust. Wipe with cotton wool swabs or cotton buds dampened with the warm soapy water. Use both sides of the swabs and discard them when they are dirty. To clean intricate areas use a cotton wool bud or twist a few fibres of cotton wool around a wooden cocktail stick. An artist's hogshair paint brush is also useful for cleaning ornate decoration. If the surface of the object is rough use a hogshair brush instead of cotton wool to avoid fibres getting caught. Always work from the bottom of the object upwards. If you wash from the top down, dirty water runs on to the dirt lower down. As the water dries the dirt sets very hard and becomes almost impossible to remove. Change the water frequently so that it does not get too dirty. Rinse the object with clean swabs moistened with clean water. When cleaning large or porous objects clean a small area at a time and rinse as you go.

Pat the object dry with paper towels or an old, soft tea towel. Take care not to snap off the bocage. Then leave it in a warm area to dry completely. Very ornate pieces can be dried with a hairdryer set on *Cool*.

CERAMICS WITH METAL AND ORMOLU MOUNTS

Do not get the metal or ormolu mount wet. Dust the mounts with a soft brush. (*See Ormolu, page 102.*) If the ceramic is very dirty clean with cotton wool buds as above. Dry it immediately with a soft dry cloth or a hair-dryer set on *Cool*.

CERAMICS WHICH SHOULD NOT GET WET

Unbaked clay or very soft objects should not be washed or made wet. Use a hogshair brush to get rid of dirt and dust, and a wooden cocktail stick to pick off any soil or debris.

OBJECTS WITH FLAKING SURFACES AND LOOSE PIGMENTS

Some earthenware objects are decorated with pigments which come off easily when touched. These objects could be ancient or ethnographical ceramics or vases and figures brought back from holidays. The surface of some can be powdery, flaking or may even peel off. Do not try to clean them and handle these objects as little as possible. It is possible to consolidate the surface, but this should be done by a ceramic conservator.

DETERIORATED GLAZES

Because of the composition of the glaze or the burial conditions the object may have been exposed to, some glazes deteriorate. At first they become cloudy on the surface but, as the deterioration gets worse, thin layers like onion skins are formed. These layers of deteriorated glaze are usually iridescent and whitish. Very often the iridescence is attractive but sometimes it obscures the original design. The iridescence should not be removed. Frequently unattractive iridescence can be consolidated so that it is less obvious and the true colour of the glaze shows through, but this should be carried out by a ceramic conservator.

People often wet deteriorated glaze to show off the underlying colour better. Do not be tempted to do this as repeated wetting and drying can make the situation worse. Do not wash objects that have iridescent layers. Gently clean off any dust with a soft brush, taking care not to remove the iridescent layer. If the layer is very flaky handle the object as little as possible. Never wrap objects with deteriorated glazes in cotton wool as the fibres may stick and pull off the flaking layers.

STAIN REMOVAL

Some stains can be removed from ceramic objects but *never* use domestic bleach or chlorine-containing bleaches as they can change the colour of the object and cause long-term damage. The stains on many objects can be made worse by inappropriate cleaning. Never attempt to remove stains from any ceramic object other than soft- or hard-paste porcelain where it is in good condition but do not try to remove the stains from these if there is any gilding on them or they have a lustre surface or decoration.

The stains may be bleached out by using hydrogen peroxide with a strength of twenty vols. Always wear rubber gloves. Pour the hydrogen peroxide into a lidded glass or ceramic container and add a few drops of ammonia. Pull some strips of cotton wool off a roll, about 1 cm (½ in) wide, and dampen them with the hydrogen peroxide. Place the damp strips over the crack or stain and leave in place for about one hour. If the stain is still there, replace with new dampened strips. Continue to do this until the stain has disappeared. This may take several days and is not always successful. You should not let the cotton wool dry out on the object, so if you leave the strips on overnight put the object in a polythene bag. Once the object is as clean as you can get it, rinse it in clean water and leave it to dry.

If this method does not remove the stain or your object is not suitable for this type of stain removal take it to a ceramic conservator.

SALT REMOVAL

Sometimes ceramics develop salt-like crystals on the surface or in the cracks of the glaze. This may be because the object has been buried and excavated, or it is an object with a crazed glaze being used as a flower vase or it has been inappropriately cleaned in the past. If you allow these salts to grow the glaze can eventually be pushed off the surface.

The salts can be washed out by leaving the object to soak in clean water for about two days. Change the water every two hours. Alternatively, place the object in a washing-up bowl in a sink. Do not put the plug in the sink. Fill the bowl with water from the cold tap and place the object slowly into it. Do not put the object into the water too fast or air bubbles may blow off some of the surface. Then turn on the cold tap very slowly and allow the water to trickle into one corner of the plastic bowl. The water in the bowl will overflow over the other edge. Do not allow the water to run directly on to the object. Leave the object with the water running for up to twenty-four hours. Take out the object and allow it to dry.

If you want to continue using a vase which you have washed free of salt crystals you should use a jar inside or have a liner made. Do not attempt to remove salts from ancient, rare, valuable or fragile objects. These should be treated by a ceramic conservator.

DISPLAY

Ceramic objects are not usually harmed by light so they can be placed in sunlight but restored objects should be kept out of direct sunlight otherwise the adhesives may become brittle and the restoration may discolour. Try to avoid putting objects in a position where they will get dirty quickly such as on mantelpieces or radiators and other heat sources. Dust and dirt rise with heat and are deposited on the objects.

Make sure ceramics are placed towards the centre of a table where they cannot be knocked by passing people. Some floors are quite springy and when walked on make the furniture move up and down slightly. This can cause objects on tables or in display cabinets to move around and work to the edge of a shelf or table and fall off or rub against each other. One way to stop them moving is to fix a piece of chamois leather underneath the object with a little easily reversible adhesives (HMG or UHU All Purpose Clear Adhesive).

The bases of many ceramic objects are rough and can easily scratch wooden and marble surfaces. To prevent this make some pads from chamois leather or felt cut to size and, if necessary, stick them on to the base with an easily reversible adhesive (HMG or UHU All Purpose Clear Adhesive). Use brown felt rather than other colours as the colour may bleed into the furniture. Flower vases should always be put on waterproof mats in case water spills or seeps out.

Do not place objects directly beneath pictures hanging on the wall as picture wire breaks surprisingly often. Keep objects far enough away from flapping curtains or from heavy doors that could slam.

Plates and tiles can be hung on the

wall with metal hangers but make sure the hanger is the correct size. If it is too small the plate will chip and possibly break from strain and if it is too large the plate can easily drop out. The metal of the hanger should be covered with a softer material which will not chip or scratch the plate. You can wrap some chamois leather around the hooks, or slide some soft plastic tubing over them. Alternatively, the hooks can be dipped in silicone bath sealant and allowed to harden. Slip a sheet of thin card behind the plate so no damage is caused to the foot rim. If the plate has a hairline or travelling crack it is not safe to display it in this way as it could break under the stresses.

Glass-fronted cabinets are very good for displaying ceramics. Plates can be propped up at the back of the shelf. There should be a groove or ridge in the shelf to stop the plates sliding forward. Metal, wood or plastic plate stands are available from stores or antique shops and can be used provided they do not put any strain on the plate.

It is not advisable to hang cups by their handles for display but if you insist, make sure that the handle has not been repaired.

STORAGE

Keep ceramic objects in a clean, dry area. Very fragile or crumbling objects should be stored in a constant relative humidity. Ceramics, particularly earthenware can be stained by mould growth if they are kept damp for too long.

Try to keep the dust off objects. Cover them with perforated polythene bags. Do not use cling film. Wrap smaller objects in acid-free tissue and keep them together in a labelled box. Dry objects well before putting them away. Do not wrap ceramic objects in cotton wool or other fibrous materials.

To store ceramics it is better to have more fairly narrow shelves close together than fewer, wider shelves. This means that the objects only stand one or two deep and that you do not have to stack great piles of plates and bowls for the space. If you only have a few wide shelves you can help increase the space by using plastic covered wire shelves which stand on or hang from the existing shelves.

It is important to avoid stacking cups and bowls because they

frequently break from the weight. They can also stick together and the glaze can be worn away. Do not stack too many plates in one pile, keep the same size and shape in each pile and never stack larger plates on top of smaller ones. Put acid-free tissue folded at least double or thick paper between each plate or bowl to stop the pattern or glaze from being worn away.

Do not put too many objects on one

shelf. Try to put the smaller ones at the front. A bar running across the front of the shelf will stop any objects from falling off or being inadvertently knocked off. Do not place pieces so that they are jutting over the edge of the shelf. If they are being stored in a cupboard make sure that they will not be damaged when the door is closed. The cupboard should have good ventilation. Metal hangers or any other attachments should be removed from the objects before they are stored.

If an object has ormolu mounts it should be stored in dry conditions (*see* Ormolu).

IDEAL CONDITIONS

House: Normal household conditions.
Exhibition: Relative humidity 50–65 per cent, Temperature about 18°C

(65°F) or room temperature. Light levels not critical unless there is restoration (200 lux). Avoid spot lights.
Storage: Relative humidity 55–60 per cent. Temperature about 18°C (65°F). Ceramics which have flaking glazes or problems caused by salts in the body should be kept at a constant relative humidity of about 40 per cent.

REPAIR

If you break an object which you might want to have professionally restored do not try to stick it together yourself. Collect all the pieces and wrap them up individually in acid-free tissue so that the edges do not knock against each other and become further damaged. Keep them altogether in a labelled box until you can get them to a conservator. Restoration is not as

Left *A soft-paste porcelain candlestick heavily decorated with bocage.* (Above) *Never wash ceramics in a dishwasher.* Right *A tin-glazed earthenware bust. Chips of missing glaze are a characteristic feature of tin-glaze*

easy as some people believe and if you have any old, rare, fragile or precious ceramics it is worth getting them restored by a ceramic conservator.

Small repairs can be made using an easily reversible adhesive (HMG or UHU All Purpose Clear Adhesive).

TYPES OF CERAMIC WARE

BISCUIT WARE, PARIAN WARE

Biscuit ware is unglazed white porcelian with a texture similar to marble. It was used mainly to make statuettes and, in the mid eighteenth century, it was used widely to imitate antique sculpture. Parian ware is also a white porcelian resembling marble. Introduced in the nineteenth century, it was cheaper to make than biscuit ware. From about 1844 it was used for busts and figures, some dishes, shirt studs and jewellery and even life-sized statues.

It is particularly important not to allow the surface of these wares to become dusty nor to handle the objects with dirty hands nor to get paint or grease on to the surface as they are very difficult to clean. Try to display these objects in a glass-fronted cupboard.

Dust the object with a soft brush before washing in warm soapy water (*see* Ceramics). It may help to remove the dirt to brush the surface with a stencil brush. If washing does not clean the object you may be able to remove the dirt by using a mild abrasive (Solvol Autosol) applied with an artist's stencil brush. Do not let the metal ferrule on the brush scratch or mark the surface. Wipe the abrasive off with cotton wool swabs dampened with acetone or white spirit. Do not be tempted to use household abrasives (Ajax and Vim) as they will scratch the surface and the chemicals they contain can eventually cause severe damage.

Ingrained grease may be removed by using a water soluble dichloromethane-based paint remover (Nitromors in the Green tin) (*see* Marble).

DELFTWARE, FAIENCE, MAIOLICA

Delftware, faience and maiolica are all tin-glazed earthenware. They tend to chip easily and the glaze may flake off. The term faience is also used in archaeology to refer to the turquoise blue Egyptian objects made from glazed powdered quartz.

Do not wash tin-glazed earthenware objects by immersing them in water, clean them using cotton wool swabs as described in Cleaning.

Do not put houseplants directly into tin-glazed earthenware containers as the ceramic may absorb chemicals from the water which will eventually push the glaze off.

Chips of missing glaze on the edges are a characteristic feature of old tin-glazed earthenware so if you have a piece restored it is not necessary to have every chip made good. The glaze sometimes comes away from the body. If this happens consult a ceramic conservator.

UNGLAZED EARTHENWARE

Unglazed earthenware is porous and often has a coarse texture. It is fired at a relatively low temperature and can be very soft. It is usually the colour of earth pigments, browns, reds and greys. This group includes archaeological, Greek, Roman and ethnographical ceramics.

Earthenware is often more fragile than other ceramics so handle it even more carefully. If there is a friable surface or loose pigment avoid touching it with your fingers and carry it by holding the base and the rim. Do not allow oil, grease or wax to get on the surface. Keep earthenware objects as free from dust as possible.

Never immerse unglazed earthenware objects in water. If the surface is sound, clean them with cotton wool swabs (see Cleaning). If the surface is very rough and absorbent do not attempt to wash it, just lightly brush off the dirt. If the pigments come off or the surface is flaking remove the dust very carefully with a soft brush. Do not wash it. If necessary get the object treated by a conservator.

GLAZED EARTHENWARE

Glazed earthenware includes creamware, pearlware, much Staffordshire pottery, glazed Tang figures, green glazed medieval pottery and Islamic ceramics, as well as many others.

If the glaze is damaged or flaking, handle it carefully. If the glaze is parting from the body have the object treated by a ceramic conservator.

Do not immerse these objects in water. If glazed earthenware gets very wet dirt can be carried in to the body which may cause further staining. You can also get staining from impurities in the body such as iron. Frequently this staining does not show until the object dries out. Glazed earthenware takes a very long time to dry if it is allowed to get wet.

LUSTRE WARE

Lustre ware is produced by using metal ores in the glaze which either give a thin subtle iridescence or can produce a thick layer that looks like burnished copper, gold or silver. Depending on the metals used the iridescent colours can range from yellow to red. Lustre decoration has been used on Islamic pottery, Hispano-Moresque, some maiolica, Staffordshire pottery and Beleek.

Do not use bleaching agents on these objects as they can cause the lustre to revert to the mineral form which removes the lustre effect.

Lustre ware is very difficult to restore as it is virtually impossible to simulate the lustre effect.

OUTSIDE TERRACOTTAS

Terracotta statues, plant pots and containers can stand up to being exposed to the weather quite well but freezing conditions can cause spalling, cracking and even breaking. Spalling occurs when the water that has been absorbed by the terracotta freezes and expands. Breaking happens if the pot contains damp earth or water which also expands on freezing, pressure from the ice causing the container to split. If possible move terracotta objects to a shed, garage or greenhouse before the onset of winter. Do not stand terracotta objects directly on a stone, brick or concrete floor. Protect them from rising damp by placing them on polythene sheeting, wooden slats or cork and if necessary cover them with a dustsheet.

Do not keep a terracotta statue of any significance outside if the climate is such that the temperature is likely to drop below freezing.

If a terracotta pot cracks it may be possible to continue using it provided it is not moved, but when you pick it up it will fall apart. Repairs to terracotta objects which are kept outside are seldom very successful. You could try repairing spalling with an epoxy resin adhesive (Araldite) when the terracotta is dry. The repair may not last very long.

Damaged terracotta statues should be dealt with by a conservator.

CERAMIC TILES

Ceramic tiles are collected individually or found loose on floors or walls. Tiles have been made since the first ceramics were made and are used as decoration for floors and walls both inside and outside buildings. During the Art Nouveau and Art Deco periods they were used widely to decorate fireplaces and front porches.

WALL TILES

Dirty wall tiles should be cleaned by brushing off as much dust and grime as possible with a stiff bristle brush. They should then be washed using a cloth or sponge dampened with warm water containing a few drops of a non-ionic detergent (Synperonic N) or a mild household detergent (Fairy Liquid). Rinse with clean warm water and wipe dry. Do not let the washing water become very dirty, change it as often as necessary. Always work from the bottom of the tiles upwards. If you wash them from the top down, dirty water runs on to the dirt lower down. As the water dries the dirt sets hard and becomes almost impossible to remove. When you wash the tiles from the bottom up the surface of the lower tiles is damp so the dribbles of dirty water can be wiped off easily.

Do not scrub the tiles with household abrasive powders such as Ajax or Vim as they can scratch the surface of the tile and the bleaches and chemicals they contain can cause problems in the tile at a later date. If the tiles are very dirty and do not clean with washing you can try using paint remover as described in Stone (page 102) or gently rubbing with a mild abrasive (Solvol Autosol). The abrasive should be wiped off with white spirit on a cotton wool swab. (See Biscuit Ware).

The shine on dull or scratched glazed areas can be revived by applying a very little microcrystalline wax and polishing with a soft cloth.

Tiles have often been painted over. You can remove the paint by applying a water soluble dichloromethane-based paint remover (Nitromors in the green tin) and carefully scraping off the softened paint. Once the paint is off, wash and rinse the tiles. Do not try to burn the paint off because the tiles will crack or break with the heat.

If any tiles are damaged or loose, carefully remove them. Get rid of all the old grouting and regrout the tile in position. Use a tile adhesive. Never fix tiles in place with ordinary adhesives such as epoxy resin adhesives.

Damp walls can cause tiles to deteriorate so that the glaze may flake off and white crystals can occur in the tile or grouting. Check that the damp course has not been broken or bridged and that gutters and drainpipes are not leaking. The salts and flaking surface can take a long time to occur but the effect can be dramatic once the damage starts. If the damp problem is not rectified the deterioration will continue. Do not attempt to stick down pieces of glaze on to the tile without solving the problem or before the tiles dry out completely as this will eventually make the situation worse. If the source of the damp cannot be stopped the tiles may have to be removed and mounted elsewhere. This should be carried out by a conservator.

When the cause of the damp is eradicated allow the tiles plenty of time to dry out. Occasionally brush any crystals off the surface with a soft brush, taking care not to dislodge any glaze. If the damage is quite severe or if the tiles are antique, rare or precious, a conservator should be called to check, clean and consolidate them.

If only small sections of tiles are damaged, leave them to dry out thoroughly. Then wipe them with a sponge or swab barely dampened with water to remove any salts on the surface. Take care not to remove any loose glaze. Stick loose pieces of glaze or tile into position with an easily reversible adhesive (HMG or UHU All Purpose Clear Adhesive). If the damage is more severe or you feel unable to cope, ask a conservator for advice.

You can sometimes find similar tiles in antique shops to replace any missing ones or you may be able to persuade a potter or tile manufacturer to make you some new ones. Make sure any replacements, particularly new replacements, match well. If you cannot replace them a conservator or restorer could make some replicas out of plaster or resin. Alternatively, you could fill the gap with dental plaster and paint the design in with acrylic paint.

Repair broken tiles with an easily reversible adhesive (HMG, UHU All Purpose Clear Adhesive).

FLOOR TILES
Floor tiles should be cleaned in the same way as wall tiles. Remove and regrout loose ones before they get damaged. See also Cleaning Marble Floors.

The main problem for floor tiles is wear. They can be protected by covering them with rugs or rush matting but make sure that the tiles are not so slippery that the mats will slide. Move the furniture from time to time so that the tiles do not always wear in the same place. Some polishes help protect the tiles but do not use

too much and do not allow the polish to build up to a thick layer. Do not use modern silicone floor cleaners and sealers on antique floor tiles because they build up a layer which is virtually impossible to remove. Do not wash or polish the tiles so vigorously that they wear away.

EXTERNAL TILES
Tiles on the outside of buildings are damaged by damp and frost. If water soaks into the tile and then freezes the tile may spall and disintegrate. Normally tiles are quite robust provided water cannot get in through breaks, bad grouting or from behind. If the tiles are valuable or in danger they should be removed and brought inside. This can be done by a conservator. Keep the grouting in good condition and replace it when necessary. Broken tiles are difficult to mend but sometimes they can be held together with grouting or with epoxy resin (Araldite) but never use epoxy resin to stick a tile into position.

Clean and repair as for wall tiles.

INDIVIDUAL TILES
Individual tiles are often collected from all parts of the world and hung on walls. Some have perforations in the back through which you can thread some picture wire, but if not, it is possible to buy hangers for displaying them. There are two types of hangers, ones with springs like plate hangers or ones which stick on to the back of the tile. Avoid the latter type as the adhesive eventually weakens and the tile will fall off. When using the hangers with springs make sure that they are neither too large nor too small and never use them on tiles that are cracked or have been repaired.

You can also display tiles by mounting them on a board. You will need a board made of chipboard or plywood slightly bigger than the tile. Either paint it a suitable colour or cover it with a material such as linen or hessian. (*See* Textiles (page 179) for covering a board.) You will also need plastic covered right angled square cup hooks. The length of the hook will need to be about the same as the thickness of the tile. You will need about five or more for each tile depending on the size. If you cannot find plastic covered cup hooks of the appropriate size you can cover brass ones with plastic tubing or you can dip them in silicone bath sealant and allow them to dry.

Place the tile on the board in the centre or in the desired position and mark round it with a pencil or chalk. Remove the tile. Using a bradawl, make holes in the board near the edge of the tile where the hooks will go. Often you need two cup hooks at the bottom, evenly spaced apart, one at the top and one at either side in the centre.

Screw the hooks in but not too tightly. Turn them so that the hooks face towards the outside of the board. Place the tile in position. Screw the hooks in further so that they hold the tile firmly but not too tightly. The tile must not be under pressure.

If the tile is very out of shape, it is advisable to place some soft padding such as polystyrene, cork or rubber behind the tile to level the back.

Use strong fixings and brass picture wire at the back of the panel.

If you have a number of tiles which make up a pattern they should be mounted by a ceramic restorer or conservator. It is a skilled job to mount panels evenly and safely.

MOSAIC
Mosaics are made from small pieces of glazed or unglazed ceramic, glass or stone, particularly marble, which are set into mortar or cement. The pieces, or tesserae, are often placed so that they form a design or picture. Mosaics are frequently on floors but walls and ceilings can also be decorated with them and small fragments of a mosaic can be hung like a picture.

Before cleaning, check that the tesserae are all securely fixed. If any are loose, remove them from the mosaic, clean the back of the stone and the hole to remove any old mortar and refix them in position with a tile adhesive as described for tiles.

Clean a mosaic in good condition in the same way as described for Wall and Floor tiles. It may be more effective to use a soft bristle brush or a stencil brush rather than a soft cloth to clean the mosaic. The surface of a mosaic is often uneven and the edges of the tesserae can hook on to the cloth.

If you find a lot of tesserae in your garden or even part of a mosaic inform your local museum and ask them for advice.

Fragments of mosaic can be backed and mounted on a wall but this should be done by a conservator.

CLOCKS AND WATCHES

CLOCKS

The first mechanical clocks are thought to have been made at the end of the thirteenth century somewhere on the continent of Europe. They were made of iron or steel, probably by the local blacksmith and had no dial or hands but would strike a small bell at certain times. The timing could be out by several hours but apart from knowing when to eat and pray, time was of little importance as most people were governed by sunrise, sunset and their stomachs. The phases of the moon told people what month it was. No more accurate time was needed except for the monks who needed to know when to go to prayer.

The most simple clocks tell the

below *An English painted tin clock from around 1911*

right *A clock and urns made from bluejohn and ormolu. The dial revolves while the snake 'hands' remain stationary*

approximate time with only one hand, but more sophisticated clocks give the time in hours, minutes and seconds, as well as the day, seasons, year, month, phases of the moon, the stars and the sun. Clocks quite quickly developed to a high level of sophistication. There were two main reasons for this. One was their use by astronomers in observatories to track the stars and planets, and the other was that they were essential for the navigation of ships. Early electrical clocks began to be made at the end of the last century and were a mixture of a mechanical movement driven by electricity. The majority of modern clocks do not have a mechanical movement but are driven by electricity or a quartz movement.

The movement or working parts of clocks are usually made from brass and steel but can include wood, silk and other materials. The movement is a series of gears of toothed wheels and pinions meshing together. The wheels and pinions are pivoted between brass plates known as the back plate and the front plate. The movement is usually made up of a 'going train', which is the part which makes the clock keep time, and the 'striking train', which makes the clock strike a bell or chime.

What makes the clock actually work is that power is applied to one end of the system. This power comes from either weights or a wound up spring. The power is geared through the movement to make the hands turn and the clock or watch strike. The power has to be controlled or regulated so that the hands move evenly and accurately. The power is allowed to 'escape' at the finial wheel tooth by tooth and this is regulated by a pendulum or balance wheel.

A clock case can be made of most materials including wood, marble, glass, alabaster, ceramic, tortoiseshell, metal and plastic and may be very ornate or merely functional. The case is there mainly to protect the movement from dust and dirt but it also makes the clock more decorative. Cases are generally cared for in the same way as a piece of furniture or an object made from the same material. However, the care of the clock case must take into account the movement.

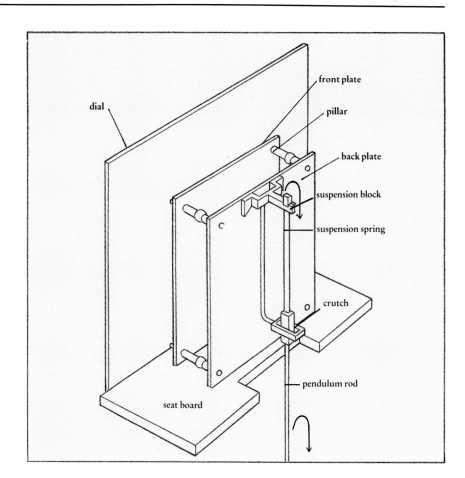

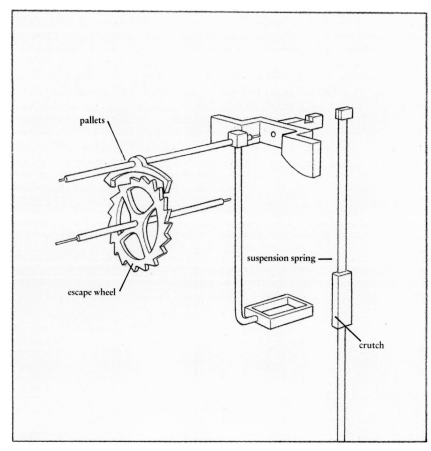

Above *The parts of a pendulum clock*

Right *An escape wheel and the top of the pendulum*

INSPECTION

Once you know what the clock case is made of and have checked its condition, look for loose veneer or moulding, cracked marble or broken porcelain. Refer to relevant chapter.

Check to see if the movement of the clock is very dusty or rusty.

To be accurate, the clock must run 'in beat', the tick and the tock should be even. Check that the clock keeps good time and make sure that it chimes properly and at the right time.

Check that the hands are pointing at the right time, and that when the clock chimes the minute hand is on the hour and the hour hand is pointing directly at the hour numeral.

HANDLING

Clocks should be moved only when necessary (*see below*).

WINDING

Each clock should have its own winding key. You should only use a key that fits the winding square or arbor closely, not one that is too big. Clock keys should be labelled and kept in a safe place. You may be able to keep them in or under the clock. Never put keys from a number of clocks into one bunch. The dangling keys can damage the face and hands as you wind the clock.

When winding a clock hold the case steady with one hand. Put the key on the arbor securely and wind clockwise

A fusee is a conical-shaped spindle. A fine chain is wound round the fusee and attached at the other end to the spring barrel

The length of the pendulum is changed by moving the bob at the end

in a slow deliberate manner (not short rapid turns). Before letting go of the key for the next turn make sure it clicks, which means that the rachet is properly engaged and will not fall back. Never wind an old clock anti-clockwise. Clocks that are wound from the back will be wound anti-clockwise which is actually clockwise when looked at from the front. Confusingly, some modern clocks are wound anti-clockwise.

Wind spring-driven clocks until the spring feels tight but do not force it. It is better to underwind a clock than overwind it. Clocks with a fusee have a stop which prevents them from being overwound. (A fusee is a conical shaped spindle attached to the great wheel. A line of gut or fine chain is wound round it and attached at the other end to the spring barrel.) Some French carriage clocks also have stops.

If the clock is weight-driven, wind it until the pulley touches the seat-board (the board on which the movement sits) but go slowly as the weight nears the top so that you do not bang it against the seatboard.

Spring-driven clocks should be wound regularly as this helps them keep better time. For instance, an 8-day clock should be wound on the same day each week. If you have more than one 8-day clock wind them all at the same time. Regular winding is not as important for weight-driven clocks as the weights give a constant power, but try not to let a weight-driven clock unwind fully as the movement can be damaged if the pendulum swings with no power.

Many clocks have two or three winding holes. These are for different mechanisms such as the going train, the striking train and the chimes. Wind these when you wind the clock.

If you do not know a great deal

about clocks do not attempt to wind turret, tower or stable clocks. Many clockmakers will care for such clocks under contract or give advice.

SETTING HANDS

Early clocks had only one hour hand but most clocks now have an hour, a minute and sometimes a second hand. To set the hands at the right time move only the minute hand by pushing it with your fingers in a forward or clockwise direction. Never more the hand anti-clockwise. If the clock strikes or chimes do not move the hand on until it has finished striking. Do not move the other hands.

If the hands move with difficulty or jam do not force them. Try very gently moving the minute hand backwards a fraction, about one minute, but not back past a time when it strikes, such as the hour or half hour. This may free whatever is jamming the hand. If this does not loosen the hand do not push it any further backwards. If the hand will not move backwards do not force it. Take the clock to a clockmaker.

REGULATING

Whether a clock runs too fast, too slow or just right depends on the length of the pendulum. The shorter the pendulum the faster the clock will run and the longer the pendulum the slower it runs. The length of the pendulum is changed by moving the bob at the end. There is usually a nut for fine adjustment below the pendulum bob, although sometimes it is in the middle of the bob or above it. Turn the nut to the left (clockwise, looking down) and the clock will run slower. Turn it to the right and it will run faster. If the clock is still not running to time even after moving the nut to its limit, take the clock to a

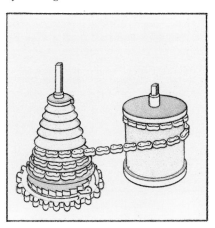

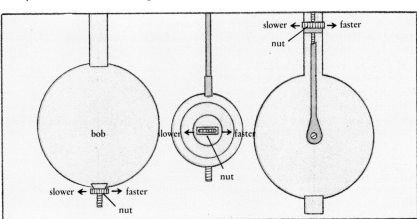

clock restorer as it probably needs cleaning.

Some pendulum clocks, particularly French ones, are regulated using a small watch key through an area on the dial. Turn the key anti-clockwise to reduce speed and clockwise to make the clock run faster.

Clocks with a platform escapement, i.e. those that do not have a pendulum, should be regulated by a clockmaker or restorer.

Some clocks have a lever at the back which can be moved either to the left or right to regulate the clock. The lever is often marked with a + or − to indicate faster or slower.

MOVING CLOCKS

Most clocks should be moved as little as possible and only when absolutely necessary. The whole mechanism can be disturbed and sometimes never runs as well again. Never move antique clocks which have a pendulum in order to dust underneath them. To remove the dust from underneath a clock brush it out with a thin brush.

Clock cases often have handles but these are very unreliable as they are more for ornamentation than practical use. Do not lift a clock by the handles but support it from underneath.

SPRING-DRIVEN CLOCKS

Spring-driven clocks have no weights. If they have a platform escapement with balance wheels (such as a carriage clock) they do not have a pendulum. This type of clock can be moved without damaging the movement but carry them carefully.

Clocks with pendulums must have the pendulum tied down or removed so that it does not swing when the clock is carried. Many spring-driven clocks with pendulums, particularly English ones, have a clip on the backplate for securing the pendulum. There are three main types; either a hook or a clip into which the pendulum is placed or there may be a brass block on the backplate into which the pendulum can be screwed. The threaded knob used to secure the pendulum is often kept screwed into one of the case brackets.

If there is no securing device the clock should only be moved very short distances. Stop the pendulum from swinging by leaning the clock forward so that the pendulum rests against the backplate.

If the clock is to be moved any

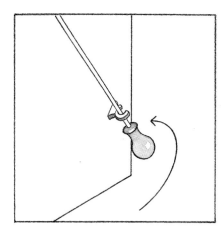

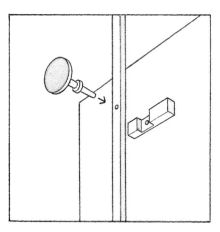

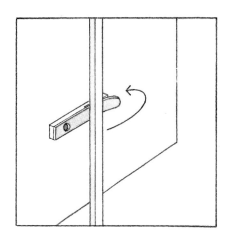

The three main types of fixing used to secure the pendulum: a hook or clip, a brass block on the back plate with a threaded knob

distance the pendulum must be removed. If there is a bell on the backplate take this off first by unscrewing it. Then unhook the pendulum from the suspension block. The clock will run fast or trip if it is not run down when the pendulum is taken off. This will not do any harm but allow it to run down completely. It is sometimes

recommended that you wedge the crutch through which the pendulum fits with paper. Do not do this. It can damage the mechanism and the paper may absorb oil making the clock run dry when it is set up again.

The suspension spring at the top end of the pendulum is very fragile so the pendulum should be carried and stored with great care. If you put the pendulum in the car take care not to close the door on the suspension spring as it will snap off. On some French clocks the spring is attached to the movement rather than the pendulum. Make sure it is not damaged.

WEIGHT-DRIVEN CLOCKS

Longcase, lantern, cuckoo and Act of Parliament clocks are all usually weight-driven. Allow these clocks to completely run down before moving them. The pendulum will have to be taken off the clock and, in the case of longcase clocks, the movement must be removed from the case as well.

The movement of a longcase clock is covered with a hood or cover. This is the part of the clock with the glass door opening on to the dial. The hood will have to be removed to reach the movement. The hood is usually held on by a swivelling catch or vertical bolt which is found below the bottom of the hood or on the backboard. The hood usually slides forward but, on some early clocks, it lifts up.

Then unhook the weights from the chain or rope.

Hold the movement steady with one hand or even better, get someone else to hold it for you. Carefully lift the pendulum off the suspension block by lifting it up and then slightly away from you. Lower it gently so that the spring can slide through the crutch. Make sure you do not damage the delicate suspension spring.

After removing the pendulum from a clock without a case such as a lantern clock, lift it down from its bracket or wall and pack it.

Dial clocks (tavern, school, station or Act of Parliament clocks) do not need to have the movement removed from the case. After removing the pendulum and weights pack or carry the clock carefully.

It is easy to remove the movement

Opposite A tower clock with a mechanical figure which strikes the hours

from some weight-driven longcase clocks such as 30-hour clocks. After you have removed the pendulum just lift out the movement using one hand to lift the rope or chain.

Other longcase clock movements are usually fixed to the seatboard and after removing the pendulum and weights they can be lifted off the case by this board. The board may be screwed to the case so check that it does not need unscrewing first. Take care that the rope or chain does not snag on the case when pulling it through.

Place the movement in a strong cardboard or wooden box well padded with acid-free tissue. Make sure the movement does not rattle around in the box. Lay down the weight lines carefully so that they do not get tangled with each other or the movement. Carry the weights and pendulum separately. If you are moving more than one clock, label the weights and pendulum to stop them getting muddled up.

The bell on lantern clocks can be removed for moving but it is probably easier on all clocks to pad the bell and hammer with acid-free tissue to stop the noise, which is irritating rather than harmful. Some elaborate clocks have moving figures – wedge these carefully with acid-free tissue so that they will not move.

Move the case as you would a piece of furniture or an object.

SETTING UP CLOCKS

Weight- and spring-driven clocks are both set up in the same way. This is a job that should be done by two people.

Place the clock case so that it is vertical and not tilting backwards or forwards as the pendulum needs to swing freely. If necessary, screw the case to the wall or hang it on suitably strong hooks.

Pass the weight lines through the hole in the seatboard and replace the movement in position. Make sure it is central in the case and that the crutch does not touch the back of the case. Where necessary, re-screw or secure the seatboard with its fastenings. Make sure that the weight line is properly over the pulley. Replace the weights on the pulley. Do not worry if the movement trips or goes faster. Carefully replace the pendulum by passing the suspension spring up through the crutch and sliding it

through the slot in the suspension block.

TO GET CLOCKS 'IN BEAT'

To run properly the clock must be in beat, i.e. the tick and tock must be even. It is often recommended that you should carefully bend the crutch by the top of the pendulum to get the clock in beat. This can be harmful as the crutch may break, particularly if it has been restored in the past, and the mechanism can be strained. To even out the beat try putting a coin or a piece of card under the seatboard or under the foot of the clock. If the clock hangs on the wall slightly adjust it by moving it from side to side. If the clock is so out of beat that the case looks crooked when the beat is corrected get the clock checked by a clock restorer or maker.

Clocks are complicated and very delicate pieces of mechanism so do not tamper with them unless you know what you are doing. It is better to get a clockmaker or restorer to help if you are unsure of how to move them than to cause expensive damage.

DISPLAY

Place clocks where they are not likely to be moved, where there are no great changes of temperature and humidity, and where they will be free from dust. Do not place clocks in direct sunlight and avoid windowsills, radiators shelves, mantelpieces and places near heating vents. All clocks should be on a stable base which does not move with the floorboards as people walk past. Longcase clocks should be on a firm position and, where necessary, secured to the wall, particularly if they are standing on a carpet. The wood or other materials of the clock case may need different conditions from the metal of the movement so compromise by not letting the clock get too damp or too dry.

CLEANING

It is not advisable to clean or oil clock movements yourself as to do the job well the movement needs to be taken apart. If this is not done only certain areas will be well oiled and others will run dry which can harm the movement. Never spray a clock movement with spray can oils (WD40) as this gets into areas which should not be lubricated. Too much oil causes dirt and

grime to collect and the mixture will behave more like an abrasive than a lubricant.

Dust the case with a soft duster or an artist's hogshair brush. Hold the clock steady and do not catch loose veneer, moulding, decoration or small nails on the duster. If any pieces of the case becomes loose keep them in a labelled envelope until you or a restorer can replace them.

Cases are made from many different materials. How they are cleaned depends on what they are made of. See the appropriate section.

Metal skeleton clocks should be cleaned by a restorer. They should not be lacquered.

Do not clean the glass of a clock case with a commercial glass cleaner as the chemicals in the cleaner can harm the metal or wood. The glass should be cleaned by polishing it with a clean, dry, soft chamois leather. Protect the surround by holding a piece of thin card against it. A little spit on a cotton wool bud will help remove fly blow and other marks from the glass.

If the glass is very dirty clean it with a swab of cotton wool dampened with warm water containing a few drops of a non-ionic detergent (Synperonic N). A few drops of methylated spirits in the water may remove greasy dirt. Rinse the glass with a clean swab dampened with clean water then polish with a lint-free cloth or soft chamois leather. It is very important that the cleaning fluid should not touch the surround or run into the movement.

DIALS

Never clean a dial unless the whole clock is being restored. Do not polish metal dials. If the dial is very dirty and you cannot resist doing something to it, first check that the numerals or any writing on the dial will not come off. Never clean silvered dials as the silver will come off.

If the numerals and writing do not come off with water wipe the surface of the dial with a swab of cotton wool barely dampened with water containing a few drops of a non-ionic detergent. (Synperonic N). Rinse with a clean swab dampened with clean water and pat dry with a soft cloth or paper towel. Do not allow water to get into the movement. Take care not to catch the hands as you wipe round them.

If the dial is very dirty it will probably mean that the movement is as well, so have the whole clock cleaned by a clock restorer.

Enamel dials are usually white with black numerals and, possibly, the maker's name. Frequently, writing is not fired on to the enamel and may even be written on with ink. Never wipe over an enamel dial as the maker's name may come off, as will any restoration of the numerals.

Enamel is brittle and can break and chip easily, particularly when putting the key into the key hole to wind the clock up. Enamel dials are difficult to restore well and you should not have the enamel dials of old, rare or precious clocks or those made by well-known clock makers restored. If the dial of a less important clock is very badly damaged it can be replaced with a new one identical to the original but always keep the original.

Some enamel dials are repaired by re-enamelling the old dial. This involves stripping off the original enamel and should only be done if the dial is in extremely poor condition. Some restoration can be done without refiring the dial. This is sometimes carried out by ceramic conservators. If the dial is cracked have it consolidated so that the cracking and flaking do not get any worse rather than have it completely restored like new.

Do not clean painted dials. If the paint is flaking and peeling get the dial restored by a dial or painting restorer.

Paper dials, often found on Vienna and similar clocks, are very fragile and are often coated with varnish. Remove any dust with an artist's soft paint brush but do not attempt to clean them further.

STORAGE

Store clocks in a cool, clean, dry, dust-free area. Do not store them in a damp basement or loft.

Always take account of the materials of which the case is made and store the clock in conditions which will suit the most vulnerable material.

Any loose pieces of the clock such as weights, pendulums, keys and pieces of moulding should be kept with the clock or, if boxed separately, clearly labelled as to which clock they came from.

Remove any batteries from electric clocks. If the batteries are antique and you want to keep them, store them away from the clock as they can leak and cause a lot of damage.

Small clocks can be protected from dust by covering them with a rigid, clear plastic container with the top cut off, such as clean sweet jars or large soft-drink bottles. Cut the top off and turn them upside down over the clock. Make sure there is some ventilation to prevent condensation causing mould or corrosion.

IDEAL CONDITIONS

Household: Normal household conditions. Take into account what material the case is made of.

Exhibition: Relative humidity 50–60 per cent, constant. Temperature about 18°C (65°F), constant. Light levels and conditions according to the materials of the case.

Storage: Relative humidity 50–60 per cent, constant. Temperature about 15°C (59°F), constant. Low light levels. Always take into account the materials of the case before deciding on the conditions.

REPAIR

The restoration of clocks is very specialized and you should only entrust the cleaning and repair of rare, old or precious clocks to an experienced clock restorer. There are many people restoring clocks who do not have a full understanding of the problems involved. Bad or inept restoration or repair can turn out to be very expensive when it all has to be put right.

If a clock does not keep good time or behaves erratically leave it stopped until you can get it checked by a clockmaker or restorer. Some clock restorers may visit your house to look at a clock. If they need to take it away they will usually take it down and put it up again for you. They generally charge for this.

Even if a clock is running well it should be serviced regularly by a clock restorer.

Some cases are made with panels of brass fretwork with velvet behind. The velvet protects the movement from dust so if it is missing or very deteriorated it should be repaired or replaced.

ELECTRIC CLOCKS

Electric clocks are a specialist area and not every restorer will accept them. Problems can be caused by loose connections rather than mechanical failure. Some early electric clocks are started by turning them upside down. If they are battery run do not pass too high a current through them. Most early electric clocks need no more than 1.5 amps.

Glass domes for electric clocks and skeleton clocks can be purchased from specialist suppliers. Unfortunately, they do not always produce the domes of exactly the same size as the original, but there is a good range of sizes.

WATCHES

Watch movements are made from brass and steel but they often have a few small jewels, such as rubies, in them and, very occasionally, other materials. The cases can be made from metal or metal alloys, particularly silver and silver gilt, although sometimes copper and copper alloys or gold

are used. The cases can also be made of enamelled metal, plastic and shagreen.

Watches are very similar to clocks, the main difference being that they are made to be carried on one's person and therefore they must have a movement which will work whichever way up the watch is. For this reason watches are not regulated by a pendulum but by a balance wheel.

HANDLING

Keep watches in good working order. A watch which is not being used should be wound and allowed to run occasionally to keep the movement running free. Watches that are used should be wound regularly a set number of turns to prevent overwinding. The hands should be set by turning them clockwise. Do not try to move the hands backwards. To regulate a watch use the screw or lever at the back, although not all watches have either of these. Usually a + or

– or arrows indicate which way to move the screw or lever. If you move it towards the + it will run faster, towards the – it will run slower. Adjust the lever until the watch is running correctly. If the watch will not regulate take it to a watchmaker or clock restorer.

If you have a collection of watches wear cotton gloves when handling

Watch movements are made from brass and steel. Often the back plate was elaborately decorated. Left The interior of a pocket watch showing the fusee and hand-made chain

them to prevent fingermarks from being left on the case.

Watches are very easy to steal so it is always advisable to pack and transport them yourself when moving house. If

The mechanism of this automaton is worked by winding the handle

you are packing a collection of watches for moving wrap them well in acid-free tissue. Label any keys and chains and pack them carefully with the watch. Make a list of what is in each box so that when you unpack them nothing gets left in the wrapping. Do not leave watches packed for

long, particularly if you have used bubble wrap for the packing as the packing can retain damp and cause the steel in the watches to rust.

CLEANING

Do not attempt to clean or oil watch movements. They are delicate and damage easily.

It is very easy to damage a watch dial so do not attempt to clean it.

Do not polish the case too often as this will wear off any decoration or metal coating. Never wet the watch or case. If the case is silver lightly polish it with a Long Term Silver cloth. Do not use polish, powder or water on a watch case as they may get into the movement. If the case is gold, polish it very lightly with a very soft cloth. Gold is extremely soft and the decoration will wear off quickly if roughly handled. Never polish silver gilt.

To clean cases made from other materials see the relevant chapter.

DISPLAY

Display watches in a dry room where there are no great changes in humidity or temperature. Keep watches away from direct sunlight, windowsills, open fires, radiators or heating vents.

Watches are more secure if they are locked in a display cabinet, this also helps keep the dust away. Display tables are a very effective way of exhibiting a collection of watches.

STORAGE

See Clocks.

Keep watches dry and dust-free. Ensure that you know how many watches you have and where they are as they are easily lost or stolen. A collection of pocket watches can be stored in specially-made drawers similar to the type used for coins and medals. A container of a corrosion inhibitor or some tarnish resistant cloth in the drawer will help keep silver watchcases free from tarnish.

To help keep watch straps in good condition you can roll up some acid-free tissue to form a cylinder and put the watches on this so that the straps are supported by a 'wrist' of tissue. It is now possible to buy rolls or supports on which you can keep wrist watches.

IDEAL CONDITIONS

Household: Normal household conditions. Take into account the material from which the case is made.

Exhibition: Relative humidity 50–60 per cent, constant. Temperature about 18°C (65°F), constant. Light levels according to the materials of the case. Always take into account the material of the case before deciding on the conditions.

Storage: Relative humidity 50–60 per cent, constant. Temperature about 15°C (59°F), constant. Low light levels. Always take into account the material of the case before deciding on the conditions.

REPAIR

Only an expert should repair, clean or oil the movement of watches.

MUSICAL BOXES

In a musical box a tune is played on the teeth of a metal comb which are twanged by tiny spikes fixed into a revolving cylinder. In elaborate musical boxes there are also bells which are played by being struck by small hammers, often in the shape of butterflies. Antique musical boxes usually have a choice of tunes.

The mechanism of a musical box is very similar to a clock movement except that musical boxes are often more delicate. The mechanism is generally housed in a wooden box, although the box can be made of glass, ceramic, leather, tortoiseshell, metal and other materials.

INSPECTION

Musical boxes need the same care and treatment as clocks. The case must be checked for the normal problems of wood (*see* Furniture page 20) such as woodworm, cracks and raised inlay. Some boxes have moving or dancing figures. These figures are often made of, or dressed with, textiles, leather or paper, *see* the appropriate chapter.

There may be lists of the tunes that the musical box plays written or printed on paper. This is likely to be on the inside of the lid but is often torn or foxed (*see* Paper page 138).

If the musical box does not play the tune evenly or it makes other odd noises, it could be that the mechanism

is corroded or dirty, or that some of the teeth, spikes or butterflies are missing. Do not play a musical box if it is in this condition. Do not attempt to clean, repair or treat the mechanism yourself.

HANDLING

Do not play a musical box unless you are sure it is in good condition. The handling of musical boxes is similar to clocks (*see* Clocks).

Never stop a musical box in mid-tune. You should always allow it to run on to the end of the tune otherwise the spikes on the cylinder will be engaged with the teeth of the comb and if the musical box is moved or jolted the teeth and the spikes could break off. A musical box should be run down as much as possible before moving it but again make sure that you stop it at the end of a tune.

When the musical box is played the release of energy is controlled by a 'governor' which is a thin piece of metal which whirls round like a fan. To prevent the movement from starting while the box is being moved fold some acid-free tissue and place it in the fan blades of the governor.

The paper with the list of tunes will be damaged if you fix it to the lid with drawing pins or self-adhesive tape. The best thing to do is to place the paper in a clear polyester envelope and fix this to the lid with drawing pins.

CLEANING

Do not clean or touch the mechanism of an old, rare or precious musical box as the movement is very complicated and can easily be damaged or ruined. Do not oil or spray the mechanism with spray oil (WD40). To oil it properly, the mechanism has to be taken to pieces and therefore it should be carried out by a musical box restorer. If this is not done only some areas are lubricated and the rest are left running dry.

See the appropriate section for information on cleaning and care of the case.

DISPLAY

See Clocks and relevant material for the case for display. Make sure an antique musical box does not get hot or the shellac cement in the cylinder will melt.

STORAGE

Keep musical boxes in a cool, dry, clean room but make sure that the area does not become too dry. Store musical boxes with the mainspring run down and the tunes stopped at the end of the tune. *See* Clocks and relevant material for the case.

IDEAL CONDITIONS

Household: Normal household conditions. Take into account the materials from which the case is made.

Exhibition: Relative humidity 50–60 per cent, constant. Temperature about 18°C (65°F). Light levels and conditions according to the materials of the musical box case.

Storage: Relative humidity 50–60 per cent, constant. Temperature about 15°C (59°F). Low light levels. The conditions should suit the materials of the musical box case.

REPAIR

Musical boxes should be cleaned and repaired by a musical box restorer. Some clock restorers also restore musical boxes although there are restorers who specialize just in musical boxes. For the repair of the case see the appropriate material.

AUTOMATA

Although there are earlier examples of automata, they appear to have reached their peak in the sixteenth century when very elaborate automata were made throughout Europe. Since the nineteenth century, automata have become universally popular with both adults and children.

The mechanism of an automaton is usually worked by winding it with a key, by hand cranking it or by putting a coin in a slot. The mechanism is normally made up of wheels, springs and metal armatures, often with pieces of leather or rubber as washers and connections. The cases were frequently made from roughly hewn wood covered with paper or textile but they can be made from a large range of materials from painted metal sheet to plastic. The figures were often made from fur, feathers or leather or fabrics stuffed with newspaper.

Automata should be cared for according to the materials from which they are made. If they are kept too damp iron will rust and other metals such as brass will corrode; mould will grow on materials such as leather, paper or wood. If automata are kept too dry some materials will become brittle. If the temperature and humidity fluctuate too much, paint will flake off and many materials will deteriorate very rapidly.

Avoid placing automata in direct sunlight and keep them as dust-free as possible. If the mechanism winds up allow it to run down before moving or storing the object.

Clean automata according to the different materials included in it and make sure that the cleaning fluids from one material do not run on to another. Remove the dust with a soft brush or photographer's puffer brush.

Do not attempt to take apart and clean the mechanism of a rare, old or precious automaton and do not take apart any automaton unless you are absolutely sure of what you are doing. If you do take it apart photograph and draw the mechanism well and label all the parts so that you know exactly where each belongs. *See* Clocks and Scientific Instruments for the care of the moving parts.

These objects are difficult to restore and should be dealt with by a restorer specializing in this field. *See also* Scientific Instruments, Musical Boxes.

Decorative Objects and Materials

Amber

Amber is the resin of pine trees which has been fossilized. Occasionally, pieces of amber are found with insects trapped in them. Amber can be translucent or opaque and can range in colour from pale yellow to a dark red. It has been used since the Middle Ages for jewellery, for decorating furniture and for small objects such as vases.

There are many false ambers made from glass and synthetic materials as well as Ambroid which looks like a real amber but is made from chips of amber that are heated and pressed together. It is difficult to distinguish between the real thing and copies without sophisticated equipment. However, genuine amber is warm to the touch and if you rub it on a piece of wool material it may give off a faint smell of pine trees.

HANDLING

Amber is brittle and will crack and chip if knocked. Amber jewellery should be kept in a jewel box or roll or wrapped in acid-free tissue so that pieces do not bang against each other. Do not leave amber jewellery on a dressing table where it will be in direct sunlight as this can affect the appearance of the amber. Hairspray and perfume can affect the surface of amber and make it dull.

CLEANING

Never use any spirit solvent or alcohol to clean amber as they will dissolve the surface and leave it matt. Do not soak amber in water to clean it as this may make the surface go cloudy. If amber is dirty, wash it using cotton buds dampened with a solution of warm water containing a few drops of a non-ionic detergent (Synperonic N) or a mild household detergent (Fairy Liquid). Rinse with cotton buds dipped in clean water and dry immediately with a soft cloth. Polish with a chamois to restore the shine. If amber is very scratched and the surface is matt, polish it with a little mildly abrasive chrome cleaner (Solvol Autosol) on a cotton bud. Polish off with a soft cloth. If necessary, use a little microcrystalline wax to give a lustre. To clean amber necklaces *see* Jewellery.

DISPLAY

Amber vases or objects should always be kept out of direct sunlight and placed away from radiators, open fires and other direct heat sources. Cleaning amber objects exposes them to potential harm so if possible, keep them in glass-fronted cabinet.

STORAGE

Wrap in acid-free tissue and store in a cool, dry area. For extra protection, amber objects should be stored in boxes. Roll necklaces diagonally across the sheet of paper and lay as straight as possible so as to minimize the strain on the thread (*see* Jewellery).

IDEAL CONDITIONS

Household: Normal household conditions. Avoid direct sunlight.

Exhibition: Relative humidity 50–60 per cent. Temperature about 18°C (65°F). Light levels 150 lux.

Storage: Relative humidity 50–60 per cent. Temperature about 15°C (59°F). Light levels 150 lux. Low light levels.

left *Antlers used to decorate a baronial hall*

right *Feathers can be free and frothy and almost any colour of the rainbow*

REPAIRS

Rare, old or precious objects or jewellery should be repaired by a conservator. Minor repairs can be carried out using an easily reversible adhesive (HMG or UHU All Purpose Clear Adhesive). Do not use epoxy resin adhesives.

Ancient and Archaeological Amber. Consult a conservator for handling, cleaning, display and storage.

ANTLER

Antler is a modified form of bone. It is the extra growth on the skulls of stags, reindeer, elk or moose and other species of deer. The outer layer of the antler is usually dark and somewhat rough. If antlers are mounted they are usually backed on to shaped boards using part of the deer's frontal bone or complete with the head and possibly part of the neck. Antler has been used for making decorative items such as buttons and knife handles and more recently ashtrays and spoons. The Victorians used antlers for making furniture especially sofas and chairs, chandeliers and coat stands.

HANDLING

Antlers mounted on full heads should be handled as little as possible to prevent damage to the fur and skin, *see* Taxidermy.

CLEANING

Smooth antlers or objects made from antler can be dusted with a soft clean duster but rough surfaced antler should be gently brushed with a clean domestic paint brush or other soft bristle brush. Catch the dust with a vacuum cleaner held in the other hand. If the antler is very dirty, wipe the surface with a soft cloth or cotton wool swabs dampened with warm water containing a few drops of a non-ionic detergent (Synperonic N). Do not use household detergent. Rinse with a clean cloth or swab and clean water. Clean and dry a small area at a time and do not allow the surface to be damp for longer than half a minute.

For antlers attached to heads, *see* Taxidermy.

Knives with handles made from antler should not be immersed in hot water or placed in a dishwasher.

DISPLAY

Display antlers where the relative humidity and temperature remain constant. Avoid hanging antlers in direct sunlight or directly above radiators, open fires or other heat sources as heat can damage antler and rising dust will settle on the head or antlers. Do not hang antlers on a damp outside wall. Although antler is not as sensitive as ivory it still needs care.

STORAGE

Store antler in a cool, dry and dark area. If the antler is attached to a head and it is to be stored for a long time, hang an insect repellant strip (Vapona) in the storage area. Objects made from antler should be examined periodically for insects and mould. Wrap small objects in acid-free tissue. To protect large objects from dust cover them with a clean dustsheet or drape acid-free tissue over them, *see* Taxidermy.

IDEAL CONDITIONS

Household: Normal household conditions.
Exhibition: Relative humidity 50–60 per cent constant. Temperature about 18°C (65°F) constant, never above 25°C (77°F). Light levels low, 150 lux. If antler is painted or dyed, 50 lux.
Storage: Relative humidity 50–60 per cent constant. Temperature about 15°C (59°F) constant. Low light levels.

REPAIR

Small repairs to antler can be made using polyvinyl acetate emulsion adhesive (Evostik Resin 'W').

BASKETRY

Basketry is one of the oldest of all crafts and objects were made in basketry before they were made in pottery or woven. Baskets have been made since about 5000 BC and, in Europe, since about 2500 BC. The process of making basketry is very similar to weaving but the materials used can be varied. These materials may be grass, rushes, willow or other natural fibres. Woven mats and hats, as well as actual basket containers are all made in a similar way.

INSPECTION

Basketry is sensitive to extremes of relative humidity – mould will grow in damp conditions and the materials will become brittle in dry conditions. If the relative humidity fluctuates damage is caused by the expansion and contraction of the basketry.

Dyes will fade in bright light and light also harms the basketry itself.

Look for unravelling or protruding pieces of fibre. Check carefully for woodworm.

HANDLING

With time, basketry will become brittle and it is easily damaged by bad handling. Never lift baskets by their rims or handles. Use both hands to carry an object and support it under its base.

CLEANING

Dust is abrasive and encourages mould and insects. It can be removed from basketry by lightly brushing the surface with an artist's hogshair brush. If the object is very dusty, hold the nozzle of a vacuum cleaner in your other hand to catch the dust. Cover the nozzle with some nylon net to stop any bits being sucked up.

It may be possible to remove ingrained dirt by wiping the surface of the basketry with a cotton bud moistened with water containing a few drops of a non-ionic detergent (Synperonic N); do not use household detergent. If the basketry is coloured, test all the colours in an inconspicuous area to make sure that they will not come off with the water. Rinse with a clean swab dampened with clean water. Do not get the basketry too wet or it may expand or shrink depending on the materials used. Never immerse a basket in water.

Old and ethnographical baskets are often stained from their previous use. These stains should not be removed if you are interested in the objects' history.

DISPLAY

Basketry should be displayed out of direct sunlight and away from spotlights in a room where the relative humidity remains constant. Avoid placing basketry over fireplaces and other direct heat sources otherwise they will become dry and dusty.

STORAGE

Store basketry in a cool, dry, dark, clean area. Soft basketry should be supported by lightly stuffing them with crumpled, acid-free tissue. Try not to stack baskets inside each other but, if it is absolutely necessary, separate each one with layers of acid-free tissue. Do not place basketry directly on a stone, brick or concrete floor. Protect them from rising damp by placing on wooden slats, cork or polythene sheeting. Cover with a clean dustsheet, cotton sheet or drape acid-free tissue over them to protect basketry from dust. Hang dichlorvos strips (Vapona) in the storage area to protect against woodworm and other insects.

IDEAL CONDITIONS
Household: Normal household conditions, avoid bright lights and fluctuating relative humidity.
Exhibition: Relative humidity 50–60 per cent constant. Never below 40 per cent nor above 65 per cent). Temperature about 18°C (65°), never above 25°C (77°F). Low light levels 50 lux.
Storage: Relative humidity 50–60 per cent constant. Never below 40 per cent nor above 65 per cent. Temperature about 15°C (59°). Low light levels.

REPAIR
Any loose or unravelling pieces can be secured by tying them down with a neutral coloured cotton thread. Do not tie the thread too tightly and do not use nylon thread or fishing line as it will cut through the fibres.

CORAL

Coral is made up of the skeletal remains of tiny marine creatures. It is usually dark pink in colour but can range from almost white to a dark brown colour or even black. It is used for jewellery either in its natural branch like form or as polished beads. It may be set into precious metals or ivory and jade. Coral can also be carved into small animals and figures. Coral usually has a polished surface except in its branch form. It is imitated in plastic and it is sometimes difficult to recognise the real thing.

CLEANING
Always dust coral before you wash it using an artist's hogshair brush or a soft, clean cloth. Do not soak coral in water. Wash it with cotton buds dampened with warm water containing a few drops of a non-ionic detergent (Synperonic N) or a mild household detergent (Fairy Liquid). Rinse with cotton buds and clean water and dry it with a clean, soft cloth.

If areas on the surface of the coral are badly scratched or will not clean with washing, polish it with a little mildly abrasive chrome cleaner (Solvol Autosol) on a cotton bud. Polish off with a soft cloth. Use a little microcrystalline wax if necessary to give a lustre.

Necklaces made from branch coral are awkward to clean as the string will rot if it gets wet. Clean 5cm (2in) of the necklace at a time by using an artists' paint brush dipped in the warm soapy water. Rinse using clean water on the brush. Absorb any excess water on to a paper towel. Finally dry the area with a hairdryer set on *Cool*. Repeat the process for the next 5cm (2in). To wash coral beads *see* Jewellery.

Specimens of branch coral should have the dust removed before washing in a similar manner to a necklace. Use a photographer's puffer brush.

DISPLAY
Do not place coral in direct sunlight or over a fireplace, radiator or other heat source. Specimen coral should be kept in a glass-fronted cabinet or be covered with a glass dome to protect it from dust and physical damage.

Coral survives well in a damp atmosphere such as the bathroom but if it is used in conjunction with other materials the conditions should suit the most sensitive material.

STORAGE
Wrap coral objects in acid-free tissue and store in a cool, dark area. Roll necklaces and bracelets diagonally across a sheet of paper and lay as straight as possible in the drawer to minimize the strain on the string, *see* Jewellery. Do not store coral in cardboard boxes or oak furniture as they give off acidic fumes which can affect the coral, *see* Shell.

For additional information on handling, display and storage *see* Glass.

IDEAL CONDITIONS
Household: Normal household conditions.
Exhibition: Relative humidity 50–65 per cent. Temperature about 18°C (65°F). Light levels about 150 lux.
Storage: Relative humidity 50–65 per cent. Temperature about 15°C (59°F). Low light or dark.

REPAIR
For small repairs to coral, use an easily

reversible adhesive (HMG or UHU All Purpose Clear Adhesive).

FEATHERS

Feathers have been used to make head dresses, costumes, exotic cloaks and fans. They have also been used for collages. They can be very small or large, stiff and tight or free and frothy, and they can be almost any colour of the rainbow either naturally or by being dyed.

Feathers should be protected from sunlight as they fade very quickly. They also need to be protected from dirt which not only looks nasty but damages the feathers and encourages moths which are voracious feather eaters.

HANDLING
Feather objects are usually fragile so handle with extreme care. Always have clean hands.

CLEANING
Feather costumes, ethnographical feather objects and rare and precious objects should only be cleaned by an experienced conservator. An amateur should not attempt to clean this type of object as a great deal of damage can be done.

However, if you want to freshen up a feather boa or a feather fan, gently remove the dust from the feathers with an artist's soft paint brush. Alternatively, you can brush over the feathers with a clean feather or gently blow them with a hairdryer set on *Cool*. Make sure that the hairdryer does not cause any damage and take care not to break any of the 'spines' of the feathers.

If the colours do not come off in water the feathers can be cleaned using foam from a non-ionic detergent (Synperonic N). Test a small area first (*see* Textiles). Place the feathers on a sheet of clean white blotting paper placed on Formica, glass or polythene. Add a little non-ionic detergent to warm water; on no account use ordinary household detergent. Agitate the water with your hand to make a froth and moisten an artist's paint brush with the foam, though do not get it wet. Gently brush the foam into a feather working from the quill or spine outwards. Do not press so hard with the brush that you separate the feather.

It is also possible to clean feathers

with white spirit. Lay one feather at a time on white blotting paper which is on glass, Formica or polythene and lightly brush it with white spirit on an artist's soft paint brush. Do not swamp the feather with white spirit and change the blotting paper if it gets too wet. This should be done in a well-ventilated room and you should wear rubber gloves (*see* Glossary). Test a small area before cleaning to make sure the colours do not run (*see* Textiles).

Gently tease the feathers back into position with a tapestry or knitting needle.

DISPLAY

Display feathered objects in the same conditions as textiles. Costumes and headdresses should be supported for display and storage, using acid-free tissue to pad them out. *See* Textiles.

Ivory and bone are often combined with other materials. These figures are made of ivory, bronze and marble.

Small feather objects should be displayed in glass or acrylic sheet (Perspex, Plexiglas) cases or deep frames.

STORAGE

Store feathers in a cool, dry, clean, dark, well-ventilated area. Wrap the object loosely in acid-free tissue or cover it with a perforated polythene bag. Make sure the feathers are not squashed. Use paradichlorobenzene crystals in the storage area to discourage moths and mould but do not let the crystals touch the feathers. *See* Textiles for more information.

IDEAL CONDITIONS

Household: Normal household conditions. Keep dust-free and away from direct sunlight.
Exhibition: Relative humidity 55–60 per cent. Temperature 15°–18°C (59°–65°F). Low light level 50 lux.
Storage: Relative humidity 55–60 per cent. Temperature about 15°C (59°F). Low light levels, dark.

Keep dust and vermin free.

REPAIR

Feathers are extremely difficult to repair. Old, rare and precious objects should be repaired by a conservator.

If you resew feathers onto a backing use cotton thread and take care not to pierce the feather with the needle.

HORN

Horn is a tough, versatile and long-lasting material although it will eventually weaken with time. It is the same sort of material as hair, hooves and fingernails and it comes from cattle, sheep, buffalo, goats and even from rhinoceros, while antler only comes from deer. Horn can be steamed, cut and moulded or used in flat sheets. It can also be hollowed out to make drinking or powder horns. Sheets of horn are translucent and were used for lanterns. Horn is still used to make spoons, particularly salt, mustard and egg spoons because they

do not tarnish. It has also been used for jewellery and spectacle frames and dagger handles.

HANDLING

See Ivory and Bone.

Although horn is rather tougher than ivory or bone it should still be handled with care, particularly if it is splitting and peeling. If horn is decorated with paint avoid touching the surface as much as possible. Horn contains oils which prevent the paint from adhering to the surface well. Thin sheets of horn such as in lanterns should be kept well away from water otherwise they will soften and distort.

CLEANING

Remove the dust from a horn object with an artist's hogshair brush or photographer's puffer brush. Never immerse old horn objects in water. To clean horn in good condition wipe the surface with a cotton wool swab or bud dampened with warm water containing a few drops of a non-ionic detergent (Synperonic N). Do not use household detergent. Rinse with clean cotton wool swabs or buds and clean water. Do not allow the object to become very wet. Dry with a soft cloth.

If horn is painted it should be carefully dusted. Do not get it wet. The paint layer comes off very easily.

If horn is very scratched and the surface is matt, polish it with a little mildly abrasive chrome cleaner (Solvol Autosol) on a cotton bud. Polish off with a soft cloth. Use a little microcrystalline wax if necessary to give a lustre.

Thin sheets of horn should not be washed. If they are dirty wipe the surface with a cotton swab or bud dampened with isopropyl alcohol.

DISPLAY

You should not place horn objects in direct sunlight or over a radiator or fire. Neither should you place them in very damp or dry conditions or where the relative humidity fluctuates. Horn will delaminate, i.e. split and peel, crack, shrink or warp under these conditions.

STORAGE

Store horn objects in a cool, dry, dark area. Wrap smaller objects in acid-free tissue. Horn will readily grow mould if kept in a damp atmosphere or where there is inadequate ventilation. It is

also attacked by the larvae of the carpet beetle and clothes moths, so check stored horn objects regularly. Hang an insecticide strip (Vapona) in the storage area to discourage insects.

When horn is used in conjunction with other materials the storage conditions should suit the most vulnerable material.

IDEAL CONDITIONS

Household: Normal household conditions. Avoid direct sunlight.

Exhibition: Relative humidity 50–60 per cent constant. Temperature about 18°C (65°F) constant. Light levels about 200 lux. If painted 50 lux.

Storage: Relative humidity 50–60 per cent constant. Temperature about 15°C (59°F) constant. Low light levels. Check regularly for insect attack.

A japanned piano and mirror frame. The panels on the piano are inlaid with mother of pearl

REPAIR

See Ivory, Bone and Tortoiseshell.

IVORY AND BONE

Ivory and bone are fairly similar materials.

Ivory is essentially tooth material. True ivory is the tusk of an elephant but 'ivory' often refers to any similar hard, white or cream coloured substance such as the tusks of hippopotamuses and walruses. Ivory is dense and close grained and can be very finely carved, etched, stained, painted, gilded, inlaid with metals and with precious and semi-precious stones or used to inlay wood and metal and other materials. It can be highly polished and when cut into sheets it is translucent. Ivory has been used for caskets, for figurines and panels, for domestic articles such as seals and mirror cases, for bedheads and chair legs, hunting horns and powder flasks. It has been made into handles for daggers and table knives, and used for the decoration on saddles and harnesses and as an inlay for furniture. Ivory has also been used for jewellery, piano keys and billiard balls.

Bone has a spongy central portion of marrow from which blood vessels extend into the more solid areas of the bone. These blood vessels may be seen as small dark flecks all of which run in the same direction as opposed to the onion skin rings that can be found on ivory. Bone is lighter and softer than ivory and, with the exception of whale and elephant bones, bones are a great deal smaller than tusks. Because of this and because the solid part of a bone is thin, bone objects are always quite small unless they are made up of sections of bone.

Bone is used to make small carvings, decorative boxes, knife and corkscrew handles and buttons. It is also used for inlay in furniture, particularly escutcheon plates round keyholes. In the past, bone was used for needles, combs and other domestic objects. Prisoners of war also used bone to make models of ships and figures.

Ivory is denser and heavier than bone and has a finer structure. A series of darker, intersecting lines or striations are often visible on the surface of elephant ivory, particularly on the underside of an object where it has been cut across the tusk. Sometimes these lines are quite clear and sometimes they are very fine like machine tooling lines. These lines show the original circumference of the tusk – rather like tree rings. You do not find the black flecks on ivory that you find on bone.

Nowadays, ivory is banned from being imported into this country and a great deal of fake ivory ('ivorine') is on the market which is made of modern synthetic resins. Poor quality imitation ivory is not difficult to detect as it seldom shows the fine lines. However, good quality imitation ivory is extremely difficult to detect and requires the use of a high powered microscope, *see* Plastic.

On ageing, and with handling, ivory and bone acquire a yellow and then a brown patination which can be very attractive. The surface of ivory can be stained artificially to stimulate this patination. This was done particularly by the Japanese on netsuke.

INSPECTION
Ivory is very susceptible to moisture and heat. Changes in temperature and relative humidity may result in warping, cracking and the breaking up of the surface. Ivory will tend to crack along the grain giving rise to onion-ring-like splits. When ivory becomes very dry it shrinks, cracks and distorts.

Bone is less susceptible to cracking than ivory but is still sensitive to changes in relative humidity and temperature and may react by warping and splitting. Some bone is quite porous and will absorb dirt.

HANDLING
Always have clean hands before handling ivory and bone. Never pick up an ivory object by the decoration, limbs, knobs, rims or edges. For handling ivory and bone objects *see* Ceramics.

Always check any wrapping paper to ensure that no fragments of ivory are left in it and if any are found put them immediately in a safe place. Care must be taken when packing or unpacking objects that contain ivory or bone inlay that the inlay has not warped, shrunk or fallen out. Never use coloured packing materials as they can stain the ivory or bone. Do not leave ivory or bone objects packed unless they are in storage.

Do not move ivory or bone objects directly from a cold, damp area to a hot, dry room as the ivory may split.

CLEANING
Rare, old, painted, fragile and precious ivory and bone objects should be cleaned by a conservator.

Before cleaning ivory and bone always brush off any dust from the surface. Use a photographer's puffer brush or an artist's hogshair brush.

Never immerse ivory or bone in water. To clean ivory or bone in good condition wipe the surface with a cotton bud or small swabs of cotton wool dampened with warm water containing a few drops of a non-ionic detergent (Synperonic N). Do not use household detergent. Rinse with clean buds or swabs dampened with clean water. Do not allow the object to become very wet. Dry with a soft, white cloth. Do not use a coloured cloth as it can stain the ivory and bone. Clean and dry a small area at a time and do not allow the surface to be damp for longer than half a minute.

Figurines, including netsuke, often have colour applied to the surface. This may come off very easily so beware. Never use water on these objects, just brush the dust off.

Do not bleach ivory or bone.

When ivory or bone is used in conjunction with other materials make sure that the cleaning solutions used on the other materials do not get on to the ivory or bone and stain it. Equally, ensure that the cleaning solution for ivory or bone does not harm the other materials.

Cutlery with ivory or bone handles should never be immersed in water or put in a dishwasher.

Ivory and bone inlay Ivory and bone were often used for inlay in boxes, guns and furniture. Over long periods, especially when the object has been kept dry, the inlay shrinks and distorts, will no longer fit and may fall out.

Ivory and bone inlay on furniture and other objects can become discoloured over the years from a build up of wax which has been applied to the surrounding wood or from general handling. Clean the inlay by using cotton buds moistened with white spirit. Discard the buds as they become dirty. Take great care not to get the cleaning fluid on to the surrounding wood. If necessary, make a shield round the inlay out of stiff card (*see* Brass).

Ivory inlaid into silver can become obscured by a build up of old polish. Gently loosen the deposit using a wooden cocktail stick and blow it off. Remove the remainder of the polish with a cotton bud dampened with white spirit. Wipe the object dry with a clean, dry cotton bud. Take care not to scratch the silver or loosen the inlay.

DISPLAY
Although ivory is more sensitive than bone to light and to fluctuations in relative humidity and temperature, both materials need to be displayed under similar conditions.

Thin pieces of ivory such as ivory miniatures are particularly sensitive to their environment. These objects must be displayed in ideal conditions.

Never display ivory and bone in direct sunlight and try to keep them in a room where the relative humidity and temperature remain fairly constant. Do not place ivory or bone objects over a fireplace, radiator or other direct heat source. Light will cause the ivory and bone to discolour and the heat may make them split and warp. Watch out for spotlights, as they generate quite a lot of heat. If you display ivory or bone objects in an illuminated display case use lights that give off as little heat as possible, *see* Introduction – Light. Do not place ivory and bone objects near damp outside walls or close to plants and flowers where water may come into contact with them. Do not place them directly on to coloured material as they can absorb the colouring.

Elaborately carved ivory or bone objects should be displayed under glass to protect them from dust.

Ivory and bone are often used in conjunction with other materials so display conditions must suit the most vulnerable material.

STORAGE

Store ivory and bone in a cool, dry, dark area. It is important that it is neither too damp nor too dry. The relative humidity and temperature should not fluctuate. Wrap small objects in acid-free tissue. If they are placed in a lidded box make perforations in it to allow the air to circulate and prevent condensation. Do not wrap ivory and bone objects in cotton wool or cloth as these can absorb moisture and the fibres can become lodged in the carving of a piece. Never wrap ivory or bone in coloured materials as they may stain them.

Protect large objects from dust by covering them with a clean, white dustsheet or by draping acid-free tissue over them. Do not stand them directly on to stone, concrete or brick floors. Stand them on wooden slats, cork or polythene sheeting to protect them from rising damp.

The objects should be examined periodically for insects and mould.

IDEAL CONDITIONS

Household: Normal household conditions. Avoid direct sunlight.
Exhibition: Relative humidity 50–60 per cent constant. Temperature about 18°C (65°F) constant. Never above 25°C (77°F). Light levels low 150 lux. If bone is painted or dyed 50 lux.

Storage: Relative humidity 50–60 per cent constant. Temperature about 15°C (59°F) constant. Low light levels, dark.

REPAIR

Small repairs to ivory or bone can be made using polyvinyl acetate emulsion adhesive (Evostik Resin 'W') or an easily reversible adhesive (HMG or UHU All Purpose Adhesive). On no account use epoxy resin adhesives.
Cutlery handles Cutlery handles are usually stuck on with animal glue or shellac. Over a period of time the glue softens and breaks down and the handles become detached. Hot water dissolves animal glue and softens shellac very quickly.

To refix the handle, remove the blade and with a long, slender skewer such as a barbecue skewer, clean out all the old glue from the inside of the handle. Wipe round the inside of the handle with isopropyl alcohol to remove any grease or remaining glue. Remove any glue which is left on the shaft of the blade and then wipe the shaft with isopropyl alcohol to remove any grease which may be on it.

Mix up some epoxy resin adhesive (Araldite) and with a long, thin object such as a knitting needle or bamboo

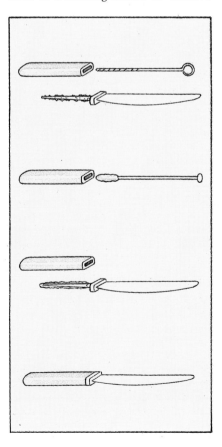

skewer, put as much adhesive as possible down the hole in the handle. Put a little adhesive around the spike and then push and turn the spike slowly down into the handle. The twisting motion will help to release any air trapped in the handle. The handle should be hard against the guard of the blade. If the handle does not settle into place, gently move it up and down the spike to help release any more trapped air. Wipe off any excess adhesive with alcohol on a cotton bud. Leave the adhesive to set for at least twenty-four hours with the knife held vertically with the handle downwards.
Archaeological ivory and bone Ancient ivory and bone are extremely delicate and easily damaged. Take particular care of ivories which have detailed carving. Never wrap them with cotton wool or any soft material which may allow particles to become lodged in the carving and crevices. Move ancient ivory or bone as seldom as possible. It is a very fragile material. If it is in a fragmentary or fossilised condition ivory or bone should be dealt with only by a conservator. When storing or displaying ancient ivory or bone it is particularly important that the temperature and relative humidity should not fluctuate.

JAPANNED AND LACQUERED OBJECTS

There are two categories of lacquered objects. The first is genuine oriental lacquer or Urushi. The second is the European answer to oriental lacquer which is called japanning. They are both made from natural resins but from different ones.

Oriental lacquer is made from the gum of trees into which is mixed the required colour. By the fourth century BC, small exquisite lacquer objects were being produced in China and slightly later in Japan, but it was not until the sixteenth century AD that lacquer work began to be imported in any quantity into Europe. It is still being produced today.

The lacquer is applied in many thin coats, sometimes as many as thirty or forty, and each coat is dried and rubbed down before the next one is applied. Eventually, a beautiful smooth, hard surface is built up. Lacquer can be applied to wood, leather, fabric and other materials and

Refixing cutlery handles

it is used to make vases, boxes, cups, bowls, chests, screens and some furniture. Sometimes the lacquer layer is thick enough to be heavily carved in relief. The lacquer can also be coloured and sometimes different coloured layers were applied and cut through to give a cameo-type effect.

Japanning is made from shellac or gum lac, and it is not possible to build it into as thick layers as oriental lacquer. It is much used for decorating wooden objects such as furniture, brush handles, trays, small boxes and sewing boxes. Japanning is usually dark green, black or occasionally yellow. The English speciality was a sealing wax red. A great deal of japanning was decorated with chinoiserie scenes in gold and other colours.

Another type of japanning was applied to metal, (*see* Toleware).

INSPECTION

The surface of japanned and lacquered objects is brittle and cracks easily, particularly if the basic wooden structure moves. For this reason it is very important to keep lacquered objects in a room where the relative humidity is constant. Japanned and lacquered surfaces can crack, lift and flake.

Lacquered and japanned objects can be ruined by light, heat and water.

HANDLING

Handle japanned and lacquered objects carefully and do not knock them as they chip very easily. Lacquered objects can be easily and permanently marked by finger prints. Always wear cotton or fine rubber gloves when handling these objects but take care that they do not slip from your grasp. *See* Ceramics.

CLEANING

Rare, old or precious japanned or lacquered objects or those that have a cracked or flaking surface should only be cleaned by a conservator.

Japanned and lacquered objects in sound condition should be dusted regularly but make sure that the duster does not catch on broken edges and pull the surface off. If an object has carved decoration remove the dust with an artist's hogshair paint brush. Objects with a highly polished surface should be cleaned with only an artist's soft paint brush or a photographer's puffer brush.

If the lacquered or japanned surfaces do have cracks or lifting areas dust them with an artist's hogshair brush. If necessary, hold a vacuum nozzle in the other hand to catch the dust but take care not to knock the

surface with the nozzle.

If, after dusting, the surface is still very dirty it may be possible to clean it by wiping it with a cotton wool swab or cotton bud barely dampened with warm water containing a few drops of a non-ionic detergent (Synperonic N). Do not use household detergents as the chemicals they contain can cause long-term damage.

It is very important to test the surface first to make sure that the lacquer is not harmed by cleaning. This applies particularly to japanned objects as the decoration may come off. Test in a small inconspicuous area first.

After cleaning the object rinse the surface with a clean cotton wool swab barely dampened with clean water and dry with a clean cotton wool swab. Make sure you do not leave fibres on the object and that you do not catch rough edges with the cotton wool.

The surface can be waxed lightly with microcrystalline wax.

Oriental lacquer with a highly polished surface should never be washed or waxed. Clean only with a very soft brush.

DISPLAY
Japanned and lacquered objects should be displayed only where the relative humidity remains constant. Do not place them in direct sunlight or in any bright light or near any direct heat source such as fires or radiators or where plants and flowers can drip on to them. Take care that chairs and other objects are not pushed back hard against lacquer screens.

Both japanning and oriental lacquer are affected by light, heat and water. Always mop up any spills and do not put any hot or cold objects directly on the surface and keep lacquered objects in as dark an area as possible.

STORAGE
Japanned and lacquered objects should be stored in a clean, dry, dark, well-ventilated area where the relative humidity remains constant. *See* Wood.

IDEAL CONDITIONS
Household: Normal household conditions, temperature and relative humidity must remain constant. Keep out of direct sunlight and bright light. Temperature about 18°C (65°F).

Exhibition: Relative humidity 50–60 per cent, ideally 55 per cent. Never below 45 per cent or above 65 per cent. Relative humidity must be constant. Temperature about 18°C (65°F) constant. Light levels below 100 lux.

Storage: Relative humidity 55 per cent constant. Temperature about 15°C (59°F). Dark.

REPAIR
If the surface of a japanned or lacquered object is flaking or crumbling do not attempt to repair it yourself. Ask a conservator specialising in lacquer work for advice.

Small, loose pieces of lacquer can be replaced using an easily reversible adhesive (HMG, UHU All Purpose Clear Adhesive).

VERNIS MARTIN

Vernis Martin is the name for the brilliant translucent lacquer work perfected in France in the eighteenth century by four brothers of the Martin family who had begun life as coach painters. It was used on extremely elaborate and valuable pieces of furniture, carriages, sedan chairs and numerous small decorative objects such as fans and snuff boxes. It has a beautiful surface and can range in colour from pearl grey, pale green, or lilac to a Prussian blue. Sometimes gold dust was applied beneath the

surface giving a sparkling effect.

Genuine Vernis Martin objects are rare and therefore if they are in good condition they are likely to be valuable. Apart from careful dusting they should be cleaned and conserved by a conservator.

MOTHER OF PEARL

Mother of pearl comes from the lining of mollusc shells and is the same type of material as pearl. It can be cut, carved and engraved, made into jewellery, buttons, knife handles and fans. Mother of pearl can also be sliced into thin sheets to cover small boxes, to make mah-jong counters or inlaid into furniture, silver, lacquer, ivory, leather and papier mâché. Imitation mother of pearl is made from synthetic

above Sea shells have been used to make this elaborate picture

opposite Mother of pearl can be cut, carved and engraved.

materials. This is not usually as hard and cold as mother of pearl.

HANDLING
Mother of pearl is quite brittle so it should be handled with care. Take care also not to spill oil or strong solvents on it as they will stain.

Do not lift bowls or large objects made from leaves of mother of pearl by the rim or edges; support the weight by placing a hand underneath the object.

Surprisingly, mother of pearl does not like getting wet so shells do not last very long if used as soap dishes.

CLEANING

Old, rare, fragile or precious objects made from mother of pearl should be cleaned by a conservator.

Mother of pearl should not be cleaned with solvents such as acetone, methylated spirits, isopropyl alcohol, ammonia, or acids. Never soak mother of pearl in water. Often the most effective way of cleaning mother of pearl is to rub it with your finger, this should remove the dirt and give the surface a shine. If this cannot be done or is ineffective, try cleaning the surface with a cotton wool bud moistened with spit.

Extremely stubborn dirt can be removed by gently rubbing the mother of pearl with a mildly abrasive chrome cleaner (Solvol Autosol) on a cotton wool bud. Remove the cleaner with a clean, soft cloth.

The mild abrasive can also be used for cleaning mother of pearl inlay but make sure that it does not get on to the surrounding material. If the cleaner remains in cracks and crevices it should be removed using a dry cotton wool bud or even a wooden cocktail stick.

Old wax sometimes accumulates on mother of pearl inlay in furniture. This can be removed with a cotton wool bud dampened with white spirit. Turn the cotton bud as you go and discard it when it is dirty. Make sure the white spirit does not run on to the surrounding surface.

Cutlery with mother of pearl handles should not be immersed in hot water nor placed in the dish washer.

See: Tortoiseshell: Pique work.

DISPLAY

Mother of pearl will flake in a very dry atmosphere so do not place objects in direct sunlight or over radiators and fires. A bathroom is ideal for displaying individual shells.

Shell pictures, which may include mother of pearl, should not be displayed in a bathroom or damp atmosphere. This is because the glue used to stick the shells on to the backing may dissolve in the damp atmosphere or it may grow mould. *See* Shellwork.

Mother of pearl is often used in conjunction with other materials, it should be displayed in a constant relative humidity which should suit the most vulnerable material.

STORAGE

Store mother of pearl in a cool, dry, dark area. Wrap individual objects in acid-free tissue. If you use polythene boxes for storing smaller objects, pierce holes in the lid or sides to prevent condensation. Use boxes made from acid-free card rather than ordinary cardboard.

Keep the dust off larger objects by draping them with acid-free tissue.

IDEAL CONDITIONS

Household: Normal household conditions.

Exhibition: Relative humidity 50–60 per cent, constant. Temperature about 18°C (65°F). Light levels 200 lux.

Storage: Relative humidity 50–60 per cent, constant. Temperature about 15°C (59°F). Low light levels.

REPAIR

Small repairs can be made using an easily reversible adhesive (HMG or UHU All Purpose Clear Adhesive).

To replace small pieces of mother of pearl inlay *see* Wood: Furniture Repair and Silver: Inlay Repair.

For refixing mother of pearl handles on to cutlery *see* Ivory and Bone.

PAPIER MÂCHÉ

Papier mâché is a light but tough material that is prepared from pulped paper or layers of paper, glue and fillers. It is shaped in a mould, baked and then either varnished or japanned both for protection, as it is easily damaged by water, and for decoration. Papier mâché can also be decorated by painting and gilding, or inlaid with mother of pearl or semi-precious stones and decorated with metal foil.

Papier mâché was introduced into England from France in the seventeeth century and was used extensively during the nineteenth century to make almost every sort of object from painted panels for coaches and bedheads to bookcases, screens, tables, trays, chairs, mirror and clock frames, miniature chests of drawers, work boxes and small domestic objects such as pen boxes.

INSPECTION

With time, the protective surface of the object begins to crack and become damaged and the papier mâché itself begins to be affected by humidity and rough handling.

Papier mâché is often attacked by woodworm. Check for signs of bore holes and active drilling. Do not use proprietary woodworm killers as the spirit base can affect the finish. If evidence of woodworm is found try to get the piece fumigated. It may be possible to kill the woodworm by sealing the object in a polythene bag or container containing dichlorvos strips (Vapona). The number of strips needed varies according to the size of the object. An object about the size of a sewing box will need roughly four strips. Leave the object in the bag for about four to six weeks. Unseal the bag in the open air and leave the object in the open for a few hours as the concentrated vapours can be toxic to humans. Do not let the strips touch the object.

The paint or the lacquer may be cracking or lifting, particularly on trays and table tops where hot liquid or dishes have been put directly on to the surface. The papier mâché layer is very prone to damage from damp.

HANDLING

Papier mâché is surprisingly brittle and will chip or bruise if it is knocked or dropped. It is mostly affected by heat and water.

CLEANING

Papier mâché should be dusted regularly but take care that the surface is not cracked or lifting or the duster may catch on the edge and pull it off. If the surface is cracking carefully brush the dust off with an artist's hogshair brush.

To remove sticky marks, wipe the surface of the object with a cotton wool swab or soft cloth barely dampened with warm water containing a few drops of a non-ionic detergent (Synperonic N) or a mild household detergent (Fairy Liquid). Rinse with clean swabs or a cloth and clean water and dry immediately with a soft cloth. Do not let the papier mâché get very wet. Take care that the cleaning solution does not remove any paint or surface decoration.

Lightly wax the surface with microcrystalline wax applied evenly with a soft cloth and polish off with a soft clean cloth. The wax will give some protection against spills of liquid.

Do not clean papier mâché objects with solvents such as acetone, white spirit or alcohol as they may remove the paint or lacquer and any decoration.

DISPLAY

Papier mâché should never be placed in direct sunlight or where plants and flowers can drip on it as the light, heat and water will very soon affect the surface and cause the lacquer layer to crack and lift. Table tops and trays are easily damaged by hot dishes and any liquids, either hot or cold, being spilt on them. Always use mats. Never place papier mâché furniture close to radiators or fires.

STORAGE

Papier mâché objects should be stored in a cool, dry, clean area where the relative humidity and temperature will remain constant. Do not keep objects in attics or basements or in the boiler room. Hang an insect repellent strip (Vapona) in the storage area to help prevent woodworm infestation. Cover the surface with a clean cloth to protect it from dust. Do not wrap objects in sealed polythene bags or cover them with polythene sheeting. Do not stand papier mâché objects directly on a stone, brick or concrete floor. Stand them on wooden slats, cork or polythene sheet to protect them from rising damp.

IDEAL CONDITIONS

Household: Normal household conditions.
Exhibition: Relative humidity 50–60 per cent, constant. Temperature about 18°C (65°F), constant. Light levels about 150 lux.
Storage: Relative humidity 50–60 per cent constant. Temperature 15°C (59°F). Low light levels. Insect-free.

REPAIR

Small repairs can be made using a polyvinyl acetate emulsion adhesive (Evostik Resin W) or an easily reversible adhesive (HMG or UHU All Purpose Clear Adhesive).

CARTON PIERRE

In the middle of the nineteenth century papier mâché was used for internal architectural decoration. It was patented under the name of carton pierre and was used extensively for the moulded decoration of roofs and walls and also for dolls' heads and other toys. Treat as for papier mâché.

QUILLWORK

Quills come from feathers and animals such as the porcupine. Porcupine quills are cream and brown in colour. Quills are made of the same material as hair. They have been used to decorate boxes such as jewellery and writing boxes and other small objects. The quills are cut into short lengths and held in position by a band of wood. The wood is often inlaid with ivory.

In North America, quills were used to decorate clothing and furniture and were also used to make jewellery. Quills can be dyed or used in their natural colour.

INSPECTION

Although quills are basically quite tough, they become very brittle as they age, particularly if they are kept in unsuitable conditions. Fluctuating relative humidity, too much light, dust and insects all work together to weaken quillwork.

HANDLING

Handle boxes with care and make sure that the wooden banding is not loose; if it is the quills will fall out. Clothing decorated with quillwork must be handled gently. The object should be carried so that the weight is supported, otherwise the stitching holding the quills may tear or be distorted. The points or broken ends of quills can catch on fabrics and tear them.

CLEANING

Remove any dust with an artist's soft paint brush. Brush the quills from the base towards the sharp tip. If the quills are dirty, wipe them in the same direction with cotton wool buds barely moistened with warm water containing a few drops of a non-ionic detergent (Synperonic N). Do not use household detergent. Rinse with cotton buds rinsed in clean water and leave the object to dry. Do not get the quills very wet. If the quills are dyed do not wash them, only dust them with the soft brush, as the colour comes off very easily.

DISPLAY

Do not display quillwork in direct sunlight or near spotlights, particularly if it is dyed. It should be displayed in a constant relative humidity and temperature. This is most important for quillwork used for clothing or backed on to another material. Do not display quillwork over a fireplace, radiator or other heat source.

STORAGE

Quillwork should be stored in a cool, dry, dark, dust-free area. Quillwork is readily attacked by the larvae of clothes moths and carpet beetles so hang dichlorvos strips (Vapona) in the storage area to discourage insects. Check quillwork regularly for insect attack. Protect the objects from dust by wrapping them in acid-free tissue.

IDEAL CONDITIONS

Household: Normal household conditions.
Exhibition: Relative humidity 45–55 per cent, constant. Temperature about 18°C (65°F), constant. Low light levels. 50 lux if quills are coloured.
Storage: Relative humidity 45–55 per cent, constant. Temperature about 15°C (59°F), constant. Low light levels or dark.

REPAIR

Quills on boxes are usually held in place by the wood and should not need fixing. If you do need to use an adhesive use an easily reversible adhesive (HMG or UHU All Purpose Adhesive). North American quillwork should be repaired by a conservator.

SHELL WORK

Shells have been used to decorate ethnographical costumes, weapons, figurines and musical instruments. Since the late eighteenth century sea shells have been used to make elaborate pictures and three-dimensional works of art as well as to cover clock cases, boxes and other ornaments.

Objects made from shell are difficult to clean so protect them as much as possible from dust. Pictures made from shell should be displayed in deep frames and three-dimensional objects should be under a glass dome or bell jar or in a glass case. If the original glass dome is missing or broken it should be replaced as soon as possible as it is essential for keeping out the dust.

Clean shell objects by brushing off the dust with an artist's soft brush or with a photographer's puffer brush. If the shells are dirty wipe them with a cotton wool swab or bud barely dampened with warm water containing a few drops of a non-ionic detergent (Synperonic N) or a mild household detergent (Fairy Liquid). If the shells are very small use a few fibres of cotton wool wrapped round a wooden cocktail stick instead of a bud. Rinse the shells with a clean swab or bud dampened with clean water and allow to dry. Do not get the shells very wet or the water may dissolve the adhesive fixing the shells in position.

The delicate colour of shells will fade in light so they should be protected from strong light and displayed away from direct sunlight radiators or open fires. Make sure a spotlight is not shining on the object. *See also* Watercolours.

If shells are kept in very dry conditions they eventually become brittle and flake but they are generally quite resistant. However, if shells have been used for pictures or to cover boxes, the adhesive used will most likely be affected by heat and damp. If the air is damp the adhesive may soften or if it is too dry the adhesive will become very brittle. Heat will also soften the adhesive and cause it to break up very quickly.

Acids will harm shell so do not display or store them in cupboards and boxes that may give off organic acid fumes, such as oak and cardboard boxes.

If many shells become loose or fall off or the object is badly damaged it should be restored by a conservator but if you want to replace one or two shells use an easily reversible adhesive (HMG or UHU All Purpose Clear Adhesive. Do not use epoxy resins (Araldite) to replace loose shells.

See also Taxidermy: Shells.

IDEAL CONDITIONS
Household: Normal household conditions. Keep dust free and out of direct sunlight.
Exhibition: Relative humidity 50–60 per cent. Temperature about 18°C (65°F). Low light levels, 50 lux.
Storage: Relative humidity 50–60 per cent. Temperature about 15°C (59°F). Low light levels, dark.

STRAW MARQUETRY OR STRAW WORK

Straw work is the decoration on small boxes, mirror frames and small pieces of furniture which was formed by cutting lengths of bleached and coloured straw and forming geometric patterns or landscapes. It was found in Europe from the seventeenth century onwards and in France particularly in the late eighteenth century. It is still being made today.

Do not place straw work in direct sunlight or the colours will fade and do not place over direct heat sources such as fires or radiators or the rising heat will deposit dirt and dust. Do not place in very damp areas as the adhesive sticking the straw to the base material will soften. Mould can also grow in these conditions.

Clean the straw by removing the dust with an artist's soft paint brush. Never use a duster which will catch the end of the lengths of straw and pull them off. Avoid wetting the straw as the colour will come off and the straw will go soggy.

TORTOISESHELL

Tortoiseshell comes from the shell of sea turtles and the highest quality shell comes from the Far Eastern hawksbill turtle. The part of the shell that is used to make tortoiseshell is the top layer of the upper surface. This part of the shell is divided into regular shapes, as

anyone who has owned a tortoise will know, with the result that the size of the pieces of tortoiseshell is limited by the size of the sections.

Tortoiseshell is a hard, brittle, translucent material. It is usually mottled yellow and brown or black but sometimes it has a red tint. When tortoiseshell is gently heated either by immersing in hot water or heating with smokeless charcoal, it softens and can be shaped and moulded. While the tortoiseshell is soft its edges may be joined and when it cools down these joins are invisible. Tortoiseshell can be polished to a high shine.

The Romans used tortoiseshell as a veneer for furniture and since then it has been used extensively by furniture makers. A. C. Boulle is famous for using it as a veneer in conjunction with brass, *see* Boulle furniture. Tortoiseshell can also be moulded into small boxes and cut into combs and Spanish mantilla combs, buckles, fans, pen nibs, shoe-horns and buttons. It can be used as a veneer for dressing table sets, caskets, mirror and picture frames and can be inlaid into other materials such as wood and silver. Gold and silver are also sometimes inlaid into tortoiseshell, *see* Piqué work.

A lot of objects that appear to be tortoiseshell are, in fact, made from stained horn, celluloid and, more recently, other synthetic materials. It is not always easy to differentiate genuine tortoiseshell from imitation.

Sheets of tortoiseshell can never be very large because of the size of the

opposite *The design of straw work is made by cutting lengths of bleached and coloured straw to form patterns or landscapes*

left and above *The Victorians modelled wax into exotic displays of fruit. This object was displayed for some time in full sunlight, causing the wax to melt*

HANDLING
Handle tortoiseshell carefully.

CLEANING
Brush off dust with an artist's hogshair brush or photographer's puffer brush. Clean with swabs of cotton wool or cotton buds dampened with warm water containing a few drops of non-ionic detergent (Synperonic N). Do not use household detergent. Rinse with clean swabs or buds and clean water. Pat dry with a soft cloth. If the object is inlaid, dry it with dry cotton wool buds and take care not to catch the inlay. Do not soak tortoiseshell objects in water or get them very wet.

If the surface of tortoiseshell is scratched or dull, polish it with a mildly abrasive chrome cleaner (Solvol Autosol) on a cotton bud. Polish it off with a soft cloth or bud.

A little almond oil rubbed into the surface of tortoiseshell with your fingers will revive the colour and shine. Wipe off any excess with a clean, lint-free cloth. Alternatively, wax very lightly with microcrystalline wax. If tortoiseshell has been exposed to sunlight for a long time and become

sections of the turtle shell, so it can never be ordered by the yard like Formica. However, because tortoiseshell can be invisibly joined together, large objects can be covered in what appears to be a single sheet of tortoiseshell.

It is now illegal to import turtles, tortoises or their shells into this country, with the result that new, genuine tortoiseshell should disappear.

Tortoiseshell is thinner, more translucent and usually more flexible than horn which has been coloured to look like tortoiseshell. It can be difficult to tell celluloid or other plastics from

tortoiseshell although celluloid sometimes smells of camphor and other plastics sometimes have a resiny smell which is not a characteristic of tortoiseshell.

INSPECTION
The surface of tortoiseshell is easily scratched. It can develop a grey, milky appearance if it is exposed to direct sunlight or other bright lights. Fluctuating or extremes of relative humidity and temperature will make tortoiseshell distort, crack and peel off any backing or out of any inlay.

very grey and opaque, it is unlikely that you will be able to revive the colour and translucency.

When dusting larger objects covered with tortoiseshell take care not to catch any pieces with the edge of the cloth or duster.

Take care when cleaning boulle furniture not to pull off the metal or the tortoiseshell. Do not polish the metal on boulle furniture. *See* Furniture.

Clean silver inlay using Silver Dip on a cotton wool bud as described in Silver. Take care that the Dip does not get on to the tortoiseshell.

DISPLAY

Do not display tortoiseshell in direct sunlight, in windows or over radiators or fires. Take particular care with objects on dressing tables. Display where the relative humidity remains constant. This particularly applies to any wooden object which is veneered with tortoiseshell as otherwise the tortoiseshell will separate from the wood base and flake off. If tortoiseshell is used in conjunction with other materials the conditions should suit the most vulnerable material.

STORAGE

Wrap tortoiseshell objects in acid-free tissue and store them in a cool, dry, well-ventilated place away from bright sun. Do not store tortoiseshell objects in sealed polythene bags or cling film. If placed in a sealed polythene box make perforations in the lid to allow the air to circulate and prevent condensation.

IDEAL CONDITIONS

Household: Normal household conditions. Avoid direct sunlight.

Exhibition: Relative humidity 50–60 per cent constant. Temperature about 18°C (65°F) constant. Light levels about 200 lux.

Storage: Relative humidity 50–60 per cent constant. Temperature about 15°C (59°F) constant. Light levels low or dark.

REPAIR

Loose tortoiseshell inlay or veneer can be relaid as described in Furniture: Repair.

PIQUÉ WORK

Piqué work is the art of inlaying tortoiseshell, and sometimes ivory and mother of pearl, with gold and silver. The metal can either be inlaid vertically as small rods which give a dotted effect or it can be inlaid horizontally as flat shapes and strips. Both techniques can be used singly or together to form patterns and decorative scenes. Piqué work was used for small decorative objects such as candlesticks, clock cases, boxes, cigarette cases, spectacle cases, jewellery and dressing table sets.

The tortoiseshell was heated and while it was soft, gold and silver were inlaid into its surface. When the tortoiseshell cooled down and became hard again it trapped the metal. It is occasionally possible to find plastic 'tortoiseshell' boxes with so called piqué work on them but this metal-work will usually be stuck on to the surface and not inlaid into it.

Tortoiseshell may shrink over the years and metal does not. This will cause the metal to lift out of the surface. It is very difficult to relay this metal and restoration should only be undertaken by a silversmith who has experience in this type of work.

Piqué work should be cleaned by gently brushing the surface with a soft artist's paint brush. Never dust it with a duster because if the metal is lifting it will catch on the fibres of the duster and be pulled out. If the silver is very dirty clean it by wrapping a few fibres of cotton wool round a cocktail stick and barely dampening them with Silver Dip. Turn the stick as you go and discard the fibres as they become dirty. Rinse by wiping over with a cotton wool bud moistened with water and then dry immediately with clean, dry cotton wool buds. Take great care not to get any Dip on the tortoiseshell or catch any lifting metal.

WAX PORTRAITS AND SCULPTURE

Wax has been used as a modelling material from the earliest times. The ancient Egyptians made wax models of their gods to be used in funeral rites, the Greeks made wax dolls for their children, noble Roman families had wax masks made of their ancestors and the Spaniards made beautiful wax figures of the saints.

Towards the end of the eighteenth century the modelling of wax medallion portraits and relief groups became all the rage. In Florence they made anatomical models showing the workings of the body for teaching medicine. Marie Tussaud modelled the heads of the victims of the French revolution. Throughout the nineteenth century, English doll makers excelled in producing wax dolls' heads. The Victorians also modelled wonderfully exotic displays of fruit and flowers.

Waxes were coloured either by mixing a dye or pigment with the wax or by rubbing dry pigments into the surface of the wax – dolls were often coloured in this way. Sometimes the surface of the wax was painted. The colour on waxes can easily fade if kept in the wrong conditions.

INSPECTION

Although beeswax is one of the ingredients used in the making of most waxes it has, over the years, been mixed with an amazing variety of fillers including lard and flour. This means that although beeswax itself is comparatively stable, when mixed with the other ingredients the combination is usually not, with the result that waxes can be very unpredictable. The surface of waxes can craze and then the slightest vibration can cause them to disintegrate. They can also sweat or develop a brown film or a white bloom on the surface.

Many wax models have internal iron armatures supporting them or a backing of some sort such as glass.

Any extremes of temperature can affect a wax. Heat will make it droop alarmingly, then melt and finally, if hot enough, vanish away. Age and cold will make wax brittle. Light can fade colours and dust and dirt will settle on the surface and be absorbed by the wax. Changes in humidity can affect oval wooden frames causing shrinkage which in turn can break glass backings and the wax itself.

HANDLING

Apart from heat, the greatest danger to waxes is from physical damage. Any sort of sudden jolt or strong vibration can cause a wax to crack or break. Only ever move one wax at a time and make sure you know where you are going with it and where you are going to put it when you get there. Put it down extremely gently, preferably on to a padded surface.

Never move wax objects from a hot room to a cold room or vice versa.

CLEANING

The cleaning of wax models, dolls, tableaux, portraits or any other sort of wax object is an extremely skilled job and should only be carried out by a conservator with experience in dealing with wax objects. Old wax is exceptionally brittle and even brushing with an artist's soft brush can cause it to shatter.

DISPLAY

Objects made from wax are very difficult to clean so protect them as much as possible from dust. Wax portraits and other wax objects should be displayed in deep frames and three-dimensional objects should be under a glass dome or bell jar or in a glass case. The frame or case should be sealed. If the original glass dome is missing or broken it should be replaced as soon as possible as it is essential for keeping out the dust.

Wax should be displayed in a room where the temperature and humidity throughout the year remain constant. *Never ever* place a wax object where direct sunlight can fall on it. Even in winter sunlight through glass can be hot enough to melt a wax. Electric lights, particularly spotlights, can also produce enough heat to melt a wax. Do not place a wax object near any heat source. Never think you may get away with it, a melted wax object is a sad sight and wax melts horribly quickly. If you have a room that is not heated in winter do not use it to display waxes in as low temperatures will make the wax brittle. Conversely do not display them in a room that is kept very warm in winter.

STORAGE

Wax objects should be stored in a clean, dry, dark area where the temperature and relative humidity remain constant. Waxes in frames should be carefully and individually wrapped in acid-free tissue and placed into individual containers so that they do not get knocked or jolted. Label the container on the outside so that you do not have to unpack it to see what is inside.

Never wrap a wax object in cotton wool. When the cotton wool is removed it can pull delicate fragments off the wax and if it is left in contact with the wax for any length of time the fibres can be 'absorbed' by the wax and it is virtually impossible to remove them. If unframed or unboxed waxes are going to be stored for any length of time any wrapping must not be left in contact with the wax surface. Place the wax in a polythene container without any packing, but first perforate the lid to prevent condensation forming in the container.

Wax Seals. Wax seals made from beeswax, resin and fillers should be treated as any other wax object. Seals are very brittle and are easily broken. If a seal breaks it is important to make sure that all the fragments are collected and put in a safe place until the seal can be repaired. Documents with seals attached should be framed by a specialist framer, *see* Paper.

IDEAL CONDITIONS

Household: Not in direct sunlight. Away from heat sources. In constant temperature and relative humidity. Dust-free.

Exhibition: Relative humidity 50–60 per cent constant. Temperature 15°–18°C (59°F–65°F). Low light levels max 150 lux, preferably 50 lux, ensure lighting does not generate heat.

Storage: Relative humidity 50–60 per cent constant. Temperature about 15°C (59°F), constant. Never below 13°C (45°F) nor above 20°C (68°F). Low light levels, dark. Do not store in packing materials. Dust-free.

REPAIR

The repair of wax objects is a highly skilled and very delicate job. If you have a wax object which is broken it must be dealt with by a conservator specializing in wax conservation. Sticking wax silhouettes back on to glass backgrounds should be left to an expert. Synthetic adhesives will not securely stick wax for any length of time.

GLASS

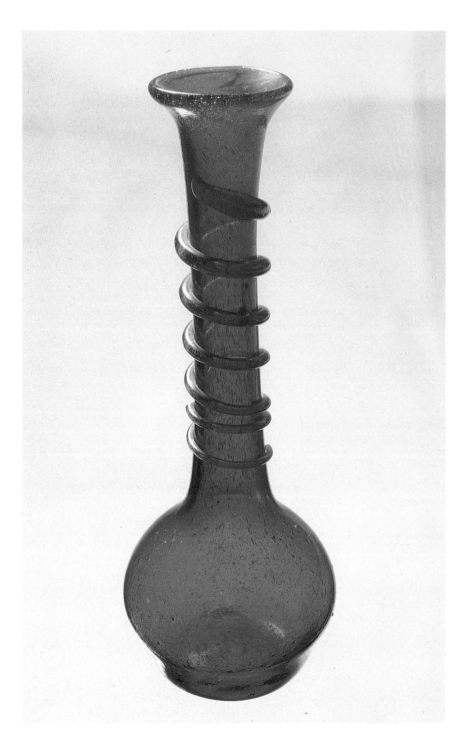

Glass is made by fusing together silica in the form of sand, flint or quartz with potash or soda at a high temperature. They form a clear liquid which, on cooling, forms a transparent solid. In the seventeenth century lead was introduced into the manufacturing process giving flint glass or crystal; this was easier to cut and was ideal for producing highly decorated cut glass items.

The first glass was probably made in Egypt in about 2500 BC and was used as a substitute for semi-precious stones. Once people discovered how to blow glass in about the first century BC, it was mainly used to produce bottles, jars, bowls and other vessels. Glass has also been used to make drinking glasses, walking sticks, chandeliers, windows, mirrors, jewellery, paperweights, vases, goblets, candlesticks and other decorative and utilitarian objects.

Glass is frequently coloured by adding metal oxides such as cobalt which turns it blue and copper and iron which can give it a greenish tinge. Tin and antimony turn the glass white and opaque.

Glass can be decorated by engraving, by firing on enamel colours, by applying oil- or water-paint, by cutting with wheels, by etching with acid or by sand blasting and by moulding. It can be formed into cased or cameo glass or millefiori and can have silver or gold applied to the surface. Glass is also used for glazing ceramics and making enamels.

INSPECTION

Most antique glass which has survived so far will probably be quite stable, the greatest danger being from

left *Glass is frequently coloured by adding metal oxides such as cobalt which turns it blue*

54

breaking and chipping. However, differences in composition make some glass unstable. This glass may deteriorate very quickly in the damp or when it is hot or dry. Venetian glass is particularly vulnerable.

Unstable antique glass may either 'weep' or crizzle. Weeping occurs when the glass absorbs water from the air. It may develop a soapy feel and even small tears of liquid can form on the surface. Early lead glass and Venetian glass often weep. Crizzling occurs when some unstable glass is too dry. The surface can become covered in small cracks and some small pieces of glass can fall off. Buried glass or badly stored glass can form iridescent layers like onion skins which flake off.

Very occasionally glass becomes stained – this happens particularly to decanters. A white cloudiness forms inside a decanter which has been left damp with the stopper in. Occasionally, if alcohol is left in a decanter a white deposit or even a dark stain can appear. These stains are difficult or impossible to remove.

Check glass objects for previous restoration – old adhesives may have discoloured to yellow or brown, new restoration is harder to see. Look also for cracks, flaking enamel or paint and loose gilding.

HANDLING

Handle glass with great care as it is very vulnerable. Before picking up anything check for pieces that can be easily knocked off and for repairs which may come apart as adhesives do not always hold. Never lean over objects to pick up another one and make sure long necklaces, and objects hung around the neck such as spectacles do not knock anything.

Do not pick up glass objects by their rims, handles, knobs or projecting parts. Do not pick up drinking glasses with the finger and thumb on the rim. Use both hands to carry an object, place one under the base and cradle the body with the other.

Set down glass very carefully so that it does not jar and break. Take particular care with glasses on stems such a wine glasses as it is easy to misjudge where the foot is.

Only carry one object at a time. If you need to carry several at once, pack them carefully in a box or tray with a lot of padding between them. Make sure they do not damage each other. It is better to make several journeys than risk damaging the objects.

Where possible remove lids and loose pieces before turning an object upside down. If you cannot take the lid off always support it with one hand. A loose lid should be wrapped and packed separately.

Some glass objects are very elaborate and have a lot of projecting decoration. This snaps off very easily. When you handle such objects hold them under the base and do not grasp the decoration.

Glass with iridescent layers, gold or silver decoration or flaking enamel should be handled as little as possible. If either the layers or the metal decoration come off easily on your fingers, pick up the object using a piece of tissue paper to hold it. Make sure you support the object securely by the base so that the glass does not slip out from between the paper.

Do not move objects quickly from a cool, dry place to a warm damp one as the glass could crizzle, particularly some seventeeth-century glass.

Unpack glass objects over a table which you have first covered with a thick cloth or thin foam.

CLEANING

Most glass objects can be washed in water but do not immerse those which are 'weeping' or crizzled or glass with applied decoration, archaeological glass, restored glass or glass with metal or ormolu mounts. Old adhesives in previous restorations can come apart and metal and ormolu mounts will corrode if they get wet.

If you carry several glass objects at a time pack them carefully in a box or tray with a lot of padding between them

Never put antique glass in a dishwasher. It is also best not to put modern lead crystal in dishwasher as it tends to chip and can get a bloom on the surface which is hard to remove.

Glass that can be washed should be dusted first. Brush off the dust with an artist's soft paint brush holding the object steady with one hand.

Wash only one object at a time. Wrap the taps with cloth or foam plastic so that the object will not chip or crack if knocked against them. Choose a plastic bowl large enough to hold the complete object and place a folded towel or some foam plastic in the bottom. If the bowl is not large enough and you have to put the object directly into a metal or porcelain sink, always pad the bottom of the sink. Fill the bowl with warm, not hot, water and a few drops of a non-ionic detergent (Synperonic N) or a mild household detergent (Fairy Liquid). Use a hogshair brush or a soft cloth to remove dirt from any incised decoration. Do not put undue pressure on any one part, particularly the rim. If you wear rubber gloves take care that the glass does not slip out of your hands. Do not leave glass in a bowl unattended as someone else may not see the glass and put something else into the bowl breaking the glass. Rinse the glass well in clean warm water. Always remove the object before you throw the dirty water away.

Having rinsed it well, place the object to drain on a tea towel or paper towel which will stop the glass sliding around on a wet surface and help absorb the excess water. Dry the object with a linen cloth or paper towel. Do not use cotton or a fluffy material as fibres will be left on the surface. Polish the glass well. Rims of bowls and stems break easily so do not put too much pressure on them. Wine glasses often break when they are held by the base of the stem and the bowl is dried using a twisting movement. Hold the bowl and not the stem and dry it by wiping up and down the glass rather than round it. Keep your working area from becoming overcrowded otherwise the glasses may knocked against each other and chip or break. Do not leave glasses damp as they may stain.

Restored glass, glass decorated with applied decoration which is in sound condition, or glass with metal or ormolu mounts can still be washed with using cotton wool swabs or buds.

Cover a table or flat surface with a thick towel or thin foam plastic (0.5 cm or ¼ in thick); do not use a very thick covering or the object will be unstable and could easily fall over. Support the object with one hand and carefully remove the dust with a soft brush or photographer's puffer brush. Wipe the object with cotton wool swabs dampened with warm water containing a few drops of a non-ionic detergent (Synperonic N) or a mild household detergent (Fairy Liquid). Use both sides of the swabs and discard them when they are dirty. To clean intricate areas use a cotton wool bud or twist a few fibres round a wooden cocktail stick. An artist's hogshair paint brush is also useful for cleaning ornate decoration. Work from the bottom up and change the water frequently to keep it clean. Rinse with clean swabs moistened with clean water.

Pat the object dry with paper towels or an old, soft tea towel. Then leave it in a warm area to dry completely.

Never allow weeping glass, glass with layers of iridescence or glass with unsound applied decoration to get wet. These should be cleaned by a conservator. Layers of iridescence or a thin opaque layer of deterioration should not be removed. If you scrape it off you are removing actual layers of glass and you will be left with a nasty rough surface. Mud or dirt can be carefully picked off glass that has an iridescent surface using a wooden cocktail stick.

GLASS WITH ORMOLU MOUNTS

Do not get the ormolu mount wet. Dust it with a soft brush (see Ormolu, Page 102). If the glass is very dirty clean it with cotton wool buds as above.

DECANTERS

Decanters should be washed and rinsed and allowed to drain upside down overnight. Make sure the decanter is stable and not likely to topple over by placing it in a high sided bowl or saucepan. If necessary, dry with a hairdryer set on *Cool*, never *Hot*. Do not leave a clean decanter with the stopper in (see Storage).

STAIN REMOVAL

It may be possible to remove cloudy or dark stains from a decanter with either a sodium hexametaphosphate water softener (Calgon) or vinegar. Try one and if it does not work try the other.

Put one teaspoonful of the water softener into a jug and pour on about one pint of warm water. Stir the solution until the water softener has completely dissolved. Fill the decanter with the solution and leave it to stand for twenty-four hours. Empty out the solution, rinse the decanter thoroughly and leave it to dry.

If the water softener does not remove the stain pour some clean colourless vinegar into the decanter. Leave it for no longer than twenty-four hours. Pour away the vinegar, rinse the decanter thoroughly and leave it to dry. If neither of the solutions removes the staining it may be that the glass surface has become etched from the decanter being left damp. This damage is irreparable.

DISPLAY

Glass objects are not usually harmed by light but do not put them in direct sunlight because the heat could cause them to craze or crizzle. Glass should be washed and handled as little as possible, therefore avoid places such as mantelpieces and shelves over radiators and other heat sources. Heat can aggravate unstable glass.

Make sure glass is placed towards the centre of the table where it cannot be knocked by passing people. Some floors are quite springy and when walked on make the furniture move up and down slightly. This can cause objects on tables or in display cabinets to move around and 'walk' to the edge of a shelf or table and fall off or rub against each other.

For obvious reasons do not place objects directly beneath pictures hanging on the wall. Keep objects far enough away from flapping curtains or heavy doors that could slam.

Early hand-blown glass may have a sharp edge where it was broken off the iron rod or pontil during manufacture. This 'pontil mark' can scratch furniture, so make a felt or cork mat to go under the glass.

Glass-fronted cabinets are very good for displaying glass. Engraving shows up well when the glass is placed in front of a dark colour. Diffused lighting from above or below shows off cut glass, and back lighting shows up engraving. However, 'cool' lights should be used when displaying glass as the heat given off by tungsten bulbs and ordinary fluorescent tubes can make some glass crizzle. Take care that spotlights, which can generate a lot of heat, do not heat up an object.

Unstable weeping glass must be kept in a controlled relative humidity. This can be done by putting it in a display cabinet with pre-conditioned silica gel. The silica gel can be hidden underneath a small plinth which must have some holes in it to allow the air to pass through.

Restored glass should be kept out of direct sunlight or else displayed in cases with ultra-violet-absorbing filters. This will lengthen the life of the restoration as adhesives and fillers often fail and discolour in sunlight.

STORAGE

Keep glass objects in a clean, dry area. Weeping and crizzled glass should always be stored in a constant relative humidity. Decanters or bottles with stoppers should be stored without the stopper in. Cover the decanter with a handkerchief, piece of muslin or acid-free tissue held on with string or cotton tape to keep out the dust. Make sure you keep the stopper with the decanter or bottle. Store wine glasses upside down on their rims. Dry objects well before putting away.

Keep the dust off objects. Cover them in perforated polythene bags. Do not wrap glass objects in cling film or sealed polythene bags. For extra protection wrap them loosely in acid-free tissue. Tissue paper can hold the damp so do not wrap the objects too tightly. Label any wrapped pieces so that you do not have to unwrap them whenever you are looking for some-

Unstable glass can be displayed in a display case kept dry with silica gel

a hollow to accommodate the shape. Small wooden wedges will prevent cylindrical objects from rolling over.

Archaeological glass or thin sherds should be stored on a tray or in a shallow box and should be padded with acid-free tissue for support.

IDEAL CONDITIONS.

Household: Normal household conditions.

Exhibition: Relative humidity 45–60 per cent. Temperature about 18°C (65°F). Light levels not above 300 lux. Painted glass should be displayed at no more than 100 lux. Weeping glass should be kept at a relative humidity 40–42 per cent, no lower. Crizzled glass should be kept at a relative humidity of 55 per cent.

Storage: as Exhibition.

REPAIR

If you break an object which you might want to have professionally restored do not try to stick it together yourself. Collect all the pieces and wrap them up individually in acid-free tissue so that the edges do not knock against each other and do further damage. Keep them together in a labelled box until you can get them to a conservator. Restoring glass is very difficult and pieces of any value should be restored by a glass or ceramic conservator.

Some decorative pieces that are not going to be handled or used, or archaeological glass can be stuck with an easily reversible adhesive (HMG or UHU All Purpose Clear Adhesive).

Adhesives do not stick glass strongly or reliably so it is not wise to use restored glass.

STUCK STOPPERS

If a stopper is stuck in a decanter or other stoppered bottle try putting a penetrating oil (WD40) round the crack. The oil should penetrate the crack and allow you to turn the stopper out. Always turn the stopper, never pull it. It is easy to break the neck of a decanter so be very careful.

thing. Do not pack glass objects in cotton wool or other fibrous material.

Place small objects at the front so that they can be seen. Do not stack the glass or overcrowd the shelves, the objects should not touch each other. Make more narrow shelves if necessary or use plastic covered wire shelves which can stand or hang from the existing shelf. A bar running across the front of the shelf will stop any objects from falling off or being inadvertently knocked off. Make sure glass objects are not jutting over the edge of the shelf. If they are in a

cupboard make sure that they will not be damaged when the cupboard door is closed. The cupboard should have good ventilation.

Any metal hangers and other attachments should be removed from the objects before they are stored.

If objects are stored lying on their side make sure their weight is evenly spread and that not too much weight is on the rim, also make sure they will not roll over. A glass object can be supported on foam plastic or even an egg tray. Expanded polystyrene can also be used but you must cut out

TYPES OF GLASS OBJECTS

BOTTLES

BURIED BOTTLES

Bottles which have been dug up from the ground can be cleaned by soaking them for no longer than two or three hours in warm water containing a small amount of a sodium hexameta-phosphate water softener (Calgon) and a little biological washing powder (Ariel, Biotex). This solution should help loosen the dirt. You may need to use a bottle brush to get at some of the dirt on the inside. Wear rubber gloves but take care that the bottles do not slip through your fingers. Rinse thoroughly in clean water and dry. Sometimes the contents of bottles are interesting and need not be removed.

If this cleaning solution is not successful, try using a solution of borax. Put 25 gm of borax in 600 ml (1oz in 1 pint) of water. Leave the bottles to soak for two hours in the solution and then rinse them thoroughly in changes of clean water. Borax is poisonous so make sure that you wear rubber gloves and do not breathe in the dust.

The surface of bottles which have been buried sometimes deteriorates leaving an iridescent layer. The iridescence is often attractive and should not be removed. Take care when cleaning and handling the bottle as the layer will come off easily.

When transporting doctor's chests and similar objects the bottles should be removed and wrapped separately otherwise they will jangle against each other and probably break.

PERFUME BOTTLES

Clean old and stale perfume out of perfume bottles with alcohol (methylated spirits or isopropyl alcohol). Leave the alcohol in the bottle for an hour or so and then rinse with changes of alcohol. You may need to repeat the process several times to remove all the old perfume. If necessary, wash the bottle afterwards with warm water and a few drops of a non-ionic detergent (Synperonic N) or a mild household detergent (Fairy Liquid), rinse the bottle with clean water and allow it to dry thoroughly, before replacing the stopper or adding more perfume. If the bottle does not dry out pour a little acetone or alcohol into it, swill this around and pour it away. This should help to dry the bottle.

Metal attachments such as stoppers should be cleaned as appropriate. If the metal gets wet make sure it is completely dry before you put it away.

SNUFF BOTTLES

Chinese snuff bottles are frequently painted on the inside. Do not wash them out. If they are very dirty clean them with a cotton wool bud as described in Glass (page 56). Sometimes snuff bottles have very elaborate carving on the outside. If necessary, use an artist's hogshair brush to get the dirt out of the carving.

CASED OR CAMEO GLASS

Cased or cameo glass is made by fusing a coloured layer of glass on to a clear base glass. A design may then be cut or etched into the outer layer revealing the layer below. This type of glass cracks and chips particularly easily so handle it with great care. Cameo glass should not be confused with shell cameo.

PAINTINGS ON GLASS

Paintings on glass often come from countries in the Far and Middle East such as China, Iran and India, although some types of furniture and American clocks have painted glass panels. The picture is painted on the reverse side of the glass so that you look through the glass to the painting. The paint often crizzles and flakes off and it will scratch easily. It is difficult to re-lay the paint or to restore it well if the glass is broken.

Do not place painted glass pictures where they are likely to get hot or where there are changes in temperature and relative humidity. Do not hang them near a fireplace or radiator or any other heat source, nor in the kitchen or bathroom where the steam will damage the paint.

Paintings on glass are usually framed like pictures. Make sure that nothing is pressing against the painted surface. There should be a fillet around the edge of the glass so that the backboard does not touch the glass directly. Make sure that the frame fits well and the glass does not move around in it. Check that the fixings on the frame are secure.

When handling or packing an unframed painting on glass do not touch the back. Make sure the paint is not rubbed by any packing material.

Clean the front of the glass by brushing off any dust and wiping it with a swab of cotton wool barely dampened with water. Protect the side of the frame by holding a piece of thin card against the inside edge of the moulding to keep the swabs away. If the glass is very dirty add a little methylated spirits to the water. Polish the glass lightly with a dry swab or soft cloth. Do not allow any liquid to get behind the glass. Do not clean the glass with commercial glass cleaners as the chemicals they contain can harm the paint and the frame. Do not attempt to clean the back or painted side of the glass.

If the paint is flaking or has mould spots or the glass is broken it must be restored by a conservator specializing in this type of work. Do not attempt this restoration work yourself.

CHANDELIERS

Chandeliers, lamps and candlesticks which have lustres (glass drops or prisms) hanging from them quickly loose their sparkle if they are allowed to become very dirty but cleaning them can be time-consuming.

A chandelier hanging in a room which is not being used can be kept clean by covering it with a muslin or calico bag or one made from a clean, old sheet.

Chandeliers can be dusted from a step ladder or tower scaffold but to clean the whole object effectively it should be taken apart. Before dismantling a chandelier take some black and white photographs of it. Glass shows up better in black and white photographs than in colour. The photographs will be a good record of where all the lustres go. It is very easy to forget how the chandelier goes back together and it will be too late to do anything about it once it is in bits.

While you are dusting or taking down a chandelier check the ceiling fixing and the wiring. If the wiring has

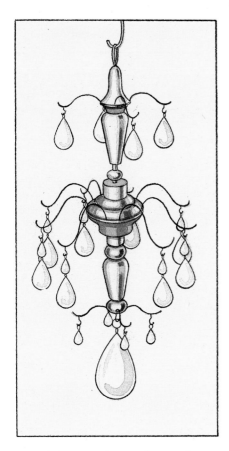

Chandeliers are often made up in layers. Record the layers before you dismantle the chandelier

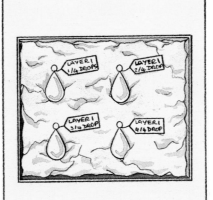

Identify each drop with a tie-on lable. Try to keep the lustres from each layer together

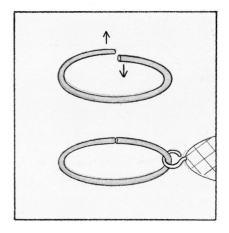

If you need to open the metal links open them sideways

not been checked regularly turn the electricity off at the mains before you begin. If you do not know how long the wiring has been there have it checked by an electrician.

Two people should be available to take down even small chandeliers. The lustres usually unhook very easily. When dismantling large chandeliers it is a good idea to identify each drop with a tie-on label and waterproof ink. This helps prevent muddling up the different layers. You can easily work out a simple system of, say, lettering each layer but numbering the drops in each layer. Lay the lustres in boxes or baskets with acid-free tissue padding. If the chandelier is in layers try to keep the lustres from each layer together.

Wash the lustres in warm water and a few drops of a non-ionic detergent (Synperonic N) or a mild household detergent (Fairy Liquid). Rinse in warm water and drain on a tea towel or paper towel. Make sure the lustres are dry, particularly the hooks as they corrode easily. If necessary use a hair-dryer on *Cool* to dry the hooks. Polish the lustres with a soft, lint-free cloth.

While taking down and washing the lustres check that the metal hooks are in good condition. The lustres need to hang freely so that they can spin and reflect the light but they also must be safe. Any open rings can be closed by squeezing the wire gently with a pair of pliers. Poorly repaired or corroded hooks should be replaced.

REPLACING LINKS
When replacing any metal links use metal wire of the same colour and thickness as the original. Silver or

silver coloured wire can be purchased from craft shops, jewellery suppliers or even jewellers. Fuse wire can be useful as it is silver coloured and is available in various thicknesses. You can get copper wire by stripping an electric cable or from model shops and craft suppliers. Brass wire is available from model shops, craft shops or jewellery or clock suppliers. Use fine tapered or needle-nosed pliers to bend the wire to the right size ring or hook. If you need to open the rings do not pull them directly open as this will ruin the circle. It is easier to open them sideways (*see* Jewellery page 66).

It is sometimes possible to find replacement lustres from specialist shops. You can also find them in antique and junk shops.

To move large chandeliers you need a specialist packer who has experience in this type of work. If you are moving objects with only a few lustres, such as candlesticks, take off the lustres, label them and pack them carefully in acid-free tissue paper with plenty of padding.

MIRRORS

The earliest mirrors were made of highly polished metal, although the Romans occasionally made them of glass with a lead backing. By the mid sixteenth century Venetian glass mirrors had spread throughout Europe and metal ones went out of fashion. Mirrors have been made in all sorts of different shapes and sizes and are usually enclosed in a frame. The frames can be very simple but, like picture frames, they can also be immensely ornate. The size and shape of mirrors made to stand on dressing tables changed according to the size and shape of wigs and hairstyles.

INSPECTION

Check that the chains, wires or cords used to hang the mirror are strong and not frayed or corroded. Check also that the fixings in the wall and on the frame are strong and robust (*see* Frames page 211).

Backing boards used with mirrors, which are usually made of soft wood, are very prone to insect attack. Check regularly and if necessary replace them.

Check antique mirrors to see that the silvering is not peeling off the back.

HANDLING

Remember that mirrors are a great deal heavier than the equivalent sized picture. *See* Oil Paintings.

CLEANING

Small mirrors should be taken off the wall for cleaning but mirrors are very heavy so large ones should be cleaned *in situ*. You will need someone to hold the mirror steady while you are cleaning it.

Do not clean mirrors with commercial glass cleaners as the chemicals they contain will harm the frame and the mirror.

A mirror should be cleaned by polishing it with a clean, dry, soft

---

below *Small boxes were often decorated with painted enamel.*
opposite *Stained glass can be seen in the front doors of many town houses*

chamois leather. Protect the edges of the frame by holding a piece of thin card against it. A little spit on a cotton wool bud will help remove fly blow and other marks.

If the mirror is very dirty clean it with a swab of cotton wool dampened with warm water containing a few drops of a non-ionic detergent (Synperonic N). A few drops of methylated spirits in the water may help remove greasy dirt. Rinse with a clean swab moistened with clean water, then polish with a lint-free cloth or soft chamois leather. Make sure you do not touch the sides of the frame as the gilding, paint or varnish will come off.

It is very important that the cleaning fluid should not touch the frame or run behind the mirror.

See Frames for cleaning the frames.

DISPLAY

See Oil Paintings and Frames.

STORAGE

Keep mirrors in a cool, dry area. Do not let them become damp as the silvering will peel off the back. Although it is possible to re-silver a mirror it is not a good idea to do this on an antique as modern techniques of re-silvering are different and the silver will be a different colour from the original.

See Oil Paintings and Frames.

STAINED GLASS AND WINDOW GLASS

Stained glass was first used in churches and by the eleventh century it was already quite sophisticated. Some of the most magnificent stained glass in churches was made in the twelfth and thirteenth centuries and continued until the seventeenth century. After the mid seventeenth century the art began to decline as the production of large panels of clear glass for windows became possible. In the mid nineteenth century, however, the art of stained glass was revived and stained glass became popular as a feature in houses and other secular buildings as well as in churches and it is still commonly seen in the front doors of many town houses. Around this time it was also used to make lampshades and other decorative panels.

Basically there are two ways in which the colour is added to glass, both when it is in its molten state. With the first technique, colours are

added to the molten glass giving a fairly uniform colour throughout. With the second, a layer of coloured glass (commonly red) is fused on top of a clear sheet of glass. The colour can then be etched out with acid giving two colours on one sheet of glass.

The applied surface decoration of stained glass also falls into two categories. They are enamel colours and stains, which are both fired on to the surface of the glass. The different methods used for applying and firing the various colouring materials give different appearances and colours, ranging from a thin wash to a thick, dark line. The detail on stained glass is usually outlined in black enamel.

Sometimes the side of stained glass that has had the decoration 'painted' on it will have a slightly matt surface. This surface is very easily scratched. The other side will be smooth.

On doors or window panels made in the last hundred years or so the coloured border glass is usually coloured throughout and the main design is applied on only one side.

INSPECTION
Window glass, whether coloured or clear, suffers from the same problems as other glass but to a greater extent as it is exposed to the elements. Window glass gets hotter, wetter and colder, and more light shines on it than other glass, all of which causes it to deteriorate faster. The glass becomes discoloured and brittle, it also builds up layers of weathering, soot and general grime.

Stained glass and leaded windows are made up of three different components: putty, lead and glass. The putty usually deteriorates fastest. The lead normally remains in good condition when in the window as the frame of the window keeps it in shape. When leaded glass is stored unframed, however, the lead often deteriorates as the window is unsupported and the lead bends and buckles. When the lead begins to deteriorate the window will begin to bow out of its vertical shape. There is very little that you can do about this as the window needs to be re-leaded. A stained glass conservator or manufacturer should be able to advise you.

Church windows should never be touched by an amateur but should always be dealt with by a stained glass conservator.

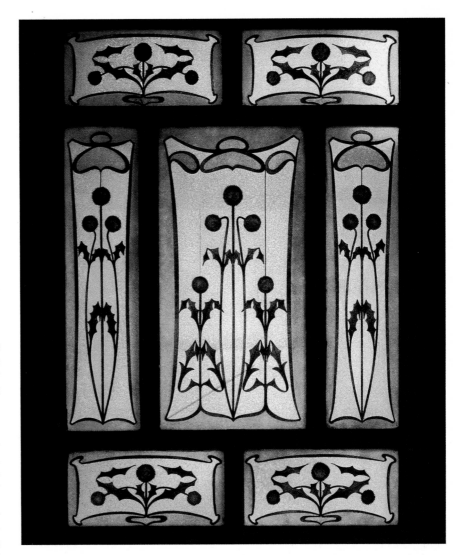

CLEANING
If stained glass is badly corroded it is unsafe to clean it. It should be dealt with by a conservator.

Glass which is coloured on the surface and not throughout should be cleaned with care as the colour comes off easily. If the glass was made after 1850 the colour comes off even more easily. Heraldic designs and other ornate decoration are particularly vulnerable.

Never use commercial window cleaners for cleaning stained glass or leaded windows as the chemicals they contain can affect the glass, the lead and the putty.

Remember with all leaded windows that they have very little strength so do not rub them very hard.

To clean glass where the colour or decoration has been applied to one side you should begin by cleaning the non-decorated side. To clean this side of the glass and glass that is coloured throughout, brush off any dust with a hogshair brush or clean household paint brush. Wipe the surface with a swab of cotton wool barely dampened with warm water containing a few drops of a non-ionic detergent (Synperonic N). Do not use household detergent. A few drops of methylated spirits in the water may help remove greasy dirt. Use both sides of the swab and discard it when it is dirty. Rinse the window with a clean swab moistened with clean water and then polish with a lint-free cloth or soft chamois leather. Work from the bottom of the window upwards rinsing as you go and do not allow the cleaning solution to get on to the decorated side of the window or behind the lead.

To clean the side of the glass to which the colour or decoration has been applied, first remove any dust that may be on the surface, but check that you are not brushing off any decoration. Do not attempt to clean the glass if this happens. Next you will need to test each colour on the coloured surface in an inconspicuous spot to see if they will withstand washing. Using a cotton bud dampened with the washing solution above, but without any methylated spirits, wipe a small area of each colour gently with circular movements. If any colour comes off you should stop immediately and not attempt to clean the glass. If the colour does not come off use the same method for cleaning the glass as described above. Keep an eye open to check that none of the decoration is coming off. If the coloured layer comes off, clean only the other side.

Clear leaded windows should be cleaned in the same way as coloured glass.

If you have a lampshade made of stained glass it should be removed from the lamp and washed in the same way as described above.

DISPLAY

Pieces of unframed stained glass should be framed for additional support before they are displayed. Never use oak for the frame as it will attack the lead (*see* Lead, page 100). Use a metal frame. Do not place glass in direct sunlight or near any form of heat source as this could soften the lead. Ultra-violet-absorbent varnish or film which is recommended to protect objects on display in a room should not be put on stained glass or old leaded windows. If ultra-violet protection is necessary use UV-absorbing acrylic sheet (Persex, Plexiglas) fixed in front of the window.

STORAGE

Sound panels can be stored vertically. Keep them in a cool, dry place and away from organic acid fumes (*see* Lead page 100).

Bowed and distorted panels should be stored horizontally with padding underneath to support the bow and prevent it from dropping any further.

REPAIR

Rare, old, fragile or precious stained glass or window glass should be restored by a stained glass conservator.

If your stained glass is not very valuable it is possible to consolidate a broken or cracked piece yourself. Choose a dry, cool day, as if it is very hot the adhesive will dry too quickly.

Fix the pieces of glass into their correct position using a few thin strips, about 0.5 cm (¼ in) wide, of self-adhesive tape. Turn the strips over at one end so that you have an unstuck end to hold on to when you come to pull them off. Make sure that the adhesive tape is on the glass side and not on the side with the colour.

To consolidate the cracks in the glass squeeze a little easily reversible adhesive (HMG, UHU All Purpose Clear Adhesive) into a clean, aluminium baking cup (suitable for mince pie, tarts) or a small glass container. Mix the adhesive with acetone using a wooden cocktail stick or something similar until the mixture has the consistency of single cream. Take an artist's fine paint brush (no. 0 or 1) and, on the glass side, not the decorated side of the panel, run the diluted adhesive along the cracks. Capilliary action will pull the dilute adhesive into the cracks.

You will not need a great deal of adhesive. It should only just come through to the other side. Allow the adhesive to dry for at least twenty-four hours. Scrape off any excess adhesive on the glass side with a razor or scalpel blade. Do not push on the glass. Should any adhesive have gone through to the decorated side of the glass it may be possible to remove it with acetone but test first in an inconspicuous area that the acetone does not remove the colour. Then, using a cotton wool bud moistened with acetone, gently wipe over the excess adhesive. Turn the bud as you go and discard it as it becomes sticky. If any colour at all comes off stop at once. A little extra adhesive will not look as unsightly as a bare piece of glass. Leave the glass to dry for a further twelve hours before removing the adhesive tape. Do this by pulling it at right angles to the direction of the tape.

ENAMEL

Enamel is used for making jewellery, plaques, miniatures, boxes, picture frames, clock dials, candlesticks and other decorative items. It is made by fusing powdered glass coloured with metal oxides on to a metal base which is usually silver, gold, copper or copper alloys. The enamel can be transparent or opaque.

The four most common forms of enamelling are:

Basse taille; a transluscent enamel is applied over silver or gold reliefs so that the colour of the enamel is strongest where the engraving is deepest.

Champlevé; designs are cut into the metal which is usually silver or copper and these are then filled with enamel and fired. The enamel is then polished down so that the enamel surface is flush with the metal,

Cloisonné; the enamel is put in *cloisons* or compartments made by a network of metal barriers. The top surface of the metal shows, dividing one enamel colour from the other. *Plique à jour* uses the same technique although there is no metal backing so that the light can shine through the enamel giving a similar effect to stained glass.

Painted enamels; a prepared plain coloured enamel base has scenes and portraits painted on to it with enamel colours and the whole thing is then refired.

INSPECTION

Enamel can suffer from the same problems as glass but the main cause of damage is due to the stress between the metal and the glass. Both expand and contract at different rates. Rapid fluctuations of temperature can cause the enamel to separate from the metal base and even slight changes of temperature can cause the enamel to crack or craze.

Enamel is very brittle and shatters easily when knocked or jarred. Once the enamel is broken it continues to come off the base very rapidly. There have even been cases when enamel has appeared to blow up for no apparent reason.

The metal base can corrode and this will push the enamel off. A copper or bronze base will produce green spots and lumps, a silver base usually goes black but if it contains a high proportion of copper it may also get green spots. A base made of copper or copper alloys is more likely to corrode than one made of silver or gold alloys.

Ancient enamels contain an opaque red enamel which oxidises to green with time. Sometimes the red colour can be brought back but this should only be attempted by a conservator.

In the past, flaking enamels have been consolidated with animal glue or gelatin. These consolidants can be attacked by mould causing black stains to appear in the enamel.

Examine objects for cracked, crazed, broken or chipped enamel and check that metal fastenings like hinges and clasps, and teapot and box lids are secure. Look also for small black spots in case any previous restoration has become mouldy.

HANDLING

Always handle enamels with care, particularly if they are damaged. Make sure they are not hit or jarred and that they do not rub against each other. Never lift enamel objects by handles, rims or other projections. Plates in particular should be picked up by placing a hand under the centre and not by grasping the rim. Also make sure that all lids or loose pieces such as sconces on candlesticks are secure before moving or turning the piece.

Only carry one enamel object at a time. If you need to carry several objects at once pack them carefully in a box or tray with a lot of padding between them, making sure they cannot damage each other.

Do not move enamel objects quickly from a cold area to a hot area or vice versa because sudden temperature changes will cause cracks.

CLEANING

Dust rather than wash enamel objects whenever possible and never immerse them in water.

Remove the dust with an artist's hogshair paint brush. Do not use a duster as any raised areas on the enamel can get caught on the cloth and also the dust in the duster can scratch the surface. If the object needs further cleaning and it is not damaged, wipe the surface with swabs of cotton wool barely dampened with warm water containing a few drops of a non-ionic detergent (Synperonic N); do not use a household detergent. Use both sides of the swabs and discard them when they are dirty. Rinse with clean swabs dampened with clean water. Pat dry with a paper towel and leave in a warm area to dry thoroughly.

If the enamel is cracked or crazed, it can be cleaned with a cotton wool bud dampened with acetone or isopropyl alcohol. Make sure that the fibres of the bud do not pull off any enamel. Check also that the object has not been restored and that none of the decoration is ink or paint as it will be affected and can even be removed by the solvent.

Never clean enamel clock dials. They should be cleaned by a clock or dial restorer as some of the decoration, numbers and maker's name are frequently in ink or paint.

Any restoration on an enamel object may well come off with solvents, so always carefully check an enamel piece before you clean it.

The base metal of enamel objects can be polished with a soft clean cloth or, if it is silver, a Long Term silver cloth. Do not polish silver gilt. Do not use metal polish as it can run behind the enamel and eventually cause damage. If the metal is badly corroded it should be cleaned by a conservator.

DISPLAY

Enamel objects should not be placed in positions where the temperature fluctuates widely or frequently, so avoid displaying them over open fires, radiators and other heat sources. If you use display cabinets do not use ones with internal lights as there will be a wide fluctuation in temperature when the lights are switched on and off. You should also avoid places where direct sunlight can fall on them. Although sunlight is not harmful to the enamel the heat from the sun can cause crazing and cracking. Displaying enamel objects in glass topped display tables helps to keep them clean.

Do not display enamel objects in a damp atmosphere because the metal base could begin to corrode. When choosing a display area always take the base metal into account as well as the enamel.

STORAGE

Enamels should be kept in a clean, dry area with a steady temperature. To protect them from dust, cover them with a perforated polythene bag or wrap them loosely in acid-free tissue, this will allow the air to circulate. Never use cotton wool or other fibrous material. Do not use cling film or sealed polythene bags.

Objects should be stored on shelves, but do not overcrowd them or allow the objects to touch each other. Place small objects to the front so that they can be seen. Tiny objects like thimbles and small eggs should be stored separately in specially made trays similar to the type used for coins, with compartments for each object. This ensures that the pieces do not get damaged, lost or roll around. The tray can be covered in velvet with the divisions made from pieces of wood covered in velvet.

IDEAL CONDITIONS

Household: Normal household conditions but with a steady temperature.

Exhibition: Relative humidity 45–55 per cent. Temperature about 18°C (65°F), constant. Light levels not above 300 lux, watch out for heat from lights, particularly spot lights.

Storage: As Exhibition.

REPAIR

Heat normally has to be used to repair metal work and as this can damage the enamel repairs to the metal work of enamel objects such as hinges and clasps should be carried out by an experienced silversmith who is familiar with this type of work.

Missing enamel can be repaired with synthetic materials. Many ceramic restorers also restore enamel objects.

When the metal base is dented or misshapen, the enamel will flake off. The object should be repaired as soon as possible. Small flakes of enamel can be fixed back using an easily reversible adhesive (HMG or UHU All Purpose Clear Adhesive). *Never* use epoxy resin adhesives for repairing enamel.

Always check the restoration method that will be used before leaving an object for restoration. Some restorers will strip off the remaining enamel, pickle the metal base and re-enamel the object. This method destroys all the original enamel and it should not be carried out on rare, antique or precious pieces.

JEWELLERY

People have always made jewellery to decorate themselves or secure their hair and clothes and a vast range of materials have been used, ranging from gold, silver and precious stones to plastic, paper, hair, glass, leather, quills, beads, feathers and seeds. All jewellery should be treated with care as it was never intended to be robust.

INSPECTION

Check jewellery that has precious or semi-precious stones with a magnifying glass to see that all stones are present and not loose. Look for broken fittings, settings and clasps. Make sure the clasps and catches are secure. If rings have stones set into them make sure that the claws or the bevelled edges are not pulled up or wearing away. If a stone is held in place with an adhesive check that the adhesive is still effective and has not softened. Check the strings of necklaces, particularly those that have stone or glass beads. Look for frayed

string or sharp edges on the beads.

Check chains for wear at the end of links and particularly check the chains on cuff links as well as the links on pendants and charm bracelets. Gold will wear through faster than silver and if a gold chain is worn regularly the links can wear through surprisingly quickly. Check rings to make sure that the ring itself has not worn thin and is not in danger of breaking.

HANDLING

All jewellery should be handled with care. Make sure the objects do not rub or knock against each other. Precious and semi-precious stones are easily chipped and diamonds in particular will scratch other objects.

When wearing jewellery make sure it is securely fastened. It is always advisable to have a safety chain fitted to necklaces, bracelets and brooches. Earrings for pierced ears are safer than clip-on earings. Make sure that clothing does not damage nor is

damaged by jewellery. Keep jewellery away from perfume sprays, hair lacquer, make-up.

Many stones and enamel decoration shatter easily, so do not drop, knock, or expose them to rapid changes in temperature. Always remove rings before washing your hands or doing domestic work. Tap water temperature can shatter emeralds, sapphires and opals as well as other stones. Do not leave jewellery lying on a dressing table where it could be in direct sunlight.

Valuable jewellery should be kept and transported in individual cases.

Do not stick self-adhesive labels or tape on to jewellery as they can harm the metal and other materials. Use labels attached with thread.

Ancient jewellery may look very strong but is frequently badly corroded and can break easily. Before wearing ancient jewellery check with a metal conservator that the piece is actually tough enough to wear. If there is any doubt don't wear it. Do not open and close clasps more than is essential. Ancient gold jewellery that is wearable today was usually made from almost 24-carat gold. This is softer than modern gold and marks, scratches and bends very easily.

CLEANING

Rare, ancient or precious jewellery should be cleaned by a jeweller or metal conservator.

Before cleaning jewellery yourself, always check that any stones are secure and that the mount is safe.

POLISHING JEWELLERY
Tarnished metal jewellery can be cleaned by buffing gently with a chamois leather. This is often safer

left   *A fine collection of tie pins displayed on a* petit point *cushion*

than washing it but take care that you do not catch a claw mount. Some materials such as pearls, turquoises and opals and some glass beads and enamel decoration must not get wet. Check under the appropriate heading for washing and cleaning.

WASHING JEWELLERY

Some jewellery can be cleaned by washing but it should never be done over a sink. Work on a tray with raised edges covered with a towel or drying-up cloth. The tray will stop beads or stones from rolling on to the floor if the string breaks and will catch any stones that drop out of the object if you drop it. Use a saucer or shallow bowl to hold warm water containing a few drops of a non-ionic detergent (Synperonic N) or a mild household detergent (Fairy Liquid).

Pieces of jewellery which have stones with an open back (claw type) setting can be washed using a small bristle toothbrush (a bristle brush off an electric toothbrush is ideal) or stencil brush to remove the grime. If the object is very dirty immerse it in Jewellery Cleaning Dip for about one minute. Use a bristle brush to help loosen the dirt. Then wash the object in warm soapy water, rinse it well and pat dry with a soft lint-free cloth or kitchen towel.

CLEANING JEWELLERY THAT CANNOT BE WASHED IN WATER

Jewellery with stones in an enclosed setting should not be immersed in water or Dip. Any adhesive may become loose and the liquid may get trapped behind the stone, setting off corrosion. Clean the piece of jewellery with a cotton wool bud moistened with isopropyl alcohol. Wipe the surface, turning the bud as you go. Dry it with a clean cotton bud.

VERY DULL OR DIRTY JEWELLERY

Some jewellery that is very dull or dirty and will not clean up satisfactorily with any of the above methods can be polished with a mildly abrasive chrome cleaner (Solvol Autosol). Apply the cleaner on a cotton wool bud and gently polish the surface. Polish off the cleaner and wipe away any traces of the cleaner from the crevices with a soft bristle brush dipped in isopropyl alcohol.

Never scrape at jewellery with a pin or needle to remove dirt as you may scratch the metal or stone. If picking is

essential use a wooden cocktail stick.

After cleaning a piece of jewellery gently buff it with a chamois leather.

NECKLACES

Immersing strung necklaces in water will eventually cause the string to rot or shrink. Pearls, opals and turquoise should not get wet (*see* Pearls). Branch coral necklaces are awkward to clean (*see* Coral). Most other beads can be cleaned with a cotton wool bud moistened with the same soapy solution as used above. Rinse using a clean bud moistened with clean water. Pat dry with a paper towel. Avoid wetting the string. *See* Repair for restringing a necklace.

DISPLAY

When you take off jewellery put it away in a box or hang chains up to prevent them getting knotted. All jewellery whatever its worth will look better if it is carefully looked after and not just thrown on the dressing table. If you do not have a suitable jewellery box, brooches and earrings can be stuck into a cork noticeboard and rings, bracelets and chains can be hung from 'trees' which are now widely available from large stores.

If you have a display of jewellery at home such as ethnographical jewellery do not put it where direct sunlight will fall on it or over open fires, radiators or other heat sources. If possible, keep jewellery in glass-fronted cabinets or display cases. Keep silver jewellery away from tarnish-inducing materials (*see* Silver) such as rubber adhesives, household paints and coal and gas fires.

Velvet is a good backing to use for a display as it comes in many colours, is soft and protective and durable. Cover a cork or polystyrene board and hold the jewellery in place with stainless steel pins. Some dyes used on textiles contain sulphur which will tarnish silver. If the velvet is going to be used in a showcase first test it as in SILVER.

See the appropriate chapter for the different materials that your jewellery is made from.

STORAGE

There are many purpose-built jewellery boxes, cases and rolls on the market. These are a good idea, they prevent rings from knocking against

each other and earrings and chains from becoming tangled. Chains and necklaces that are worn infrequently can be rolled diagonally across a sheet of acid-free tissue and stored flat in a drawer.

Jewellery stored for the long term should be wrapped individually in acid-free tissue, a soft cloth or chamois leather or small bags made from soft cloth or chamois leather (*see* Silver Jewellery, page 70). Never wrap jewellery in cotton wool. Store jewellery in a cool, dry area.

IDEAL CONDITIONS

Household: Normal household conditions.
Exhibition: Relative humidity 50–60 per cent. Temperature about 18°C (65°F).
Light levels depending on the materials involved.
Storage: As exhibition.
For the ideal conditions of different

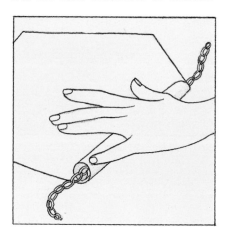

Roll chains diagonally across a sheet of acid-free tissue

materials included in jewellery see the appropriate chapter.

REPAIR

Ancient, valuable, rare or precious jewellery should be repaired by a reputable jeweller or silversmith. *See* Introduction: Finding a conservator (page 12).

A jeweller may be able to strengthen worn links on a gold chain by adding a little more gold to thicken them. If the links are too worn it may be easier and cheaper to replace them. If a ring has worn thin it can be thickened or strengthened.

Do not try to reset precious or

semi-precious stones if they become loose. This should be done by a reputable jeweller. Pearls, opals and turquoises can sometimes be stuck into position with a quick-setting epoxy resin adhesive (Devcon, UHU Strong Bond). Remove all the old adhesive first.

RESTRINGING A NECKLACE
Very valuable necklaces should be restrung by a jeweller.

An ordinary necklace, however, can be restrung quite easily. Work over a tray with raised edges just in case the beads drop. If the beads are already loose work out the order in which they should be strung, for instance some necklaces have larger beads in the centre. To stop the beads rolling about sandwich them between the edge of the tray and a ruler or piece of wood.

Use nylon or silk thread. The thread should be at least as thick as half the diameter of the hole in the bead. Many necklaces have knots between the beads, this is partly for effect and partly so that the beads do not all fall to the floor if the string breaks.

Tie a knot in the thread 75mm (3in) from the end. Thread the first bead on the other end of the thread and push

it up close to the knot. Tie the next knot using a needle to move it up close to the bead. Tighten it against the bead with finger or thumb nail. Thread on the next bead and repeat. Once all the beads are threaded tie the final knot.

Thread the thread through the ring of the clasp and then back through the last bead. If it is difficult to pass the thread through the bead use a needle or stiffen the thread by dipping it in adhesive (HMG or UHU All Purpose Clear Adhesive) or by applying a little wax or soap. Pull the thread through so that the clasp is held firmly against the bead. Tie a knot around the thread. Cut the thread leaving about 0.5cm (¼in). Put some adhesive or wax on this end and then push into the second bead. It may be necessary to use tweezers to push the thread through the bead. Fix the other end of the clasp in the same way.

METAL LINKS
Always open metal links sideways, i.e. move the ends sideways using two pairs of pliers to hold each end. Do not pull the ends apart as the links will distort. Close the links by reversing the process until the two ends meet. Some links are safer if soldered closed but this should be done by a reputable jeweller.

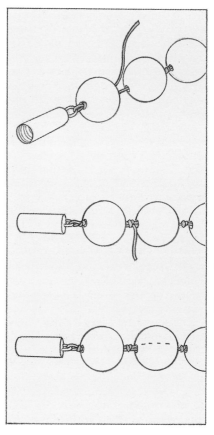

Fitting the clasp to the restrung necklace

TYPES OF JEWELLERY

GOLD JEWELLERY

Gold jewellery is very seldom made from solid gold, it is usually 9-or14-carat gold, but occasionally it is 18 to 22 carat. Some cheap modern 'gold' jewellery is made of rolled gold which is manufactured in a similar way to Sheffield plate. A thin sheet of gold is fused on to a base metal and then the sheet is rolled very thin. Rolled gold is not hallmarked as there are no regulations governing its gold content. Other 'gold' jewellery is made by electrolytically depositing gold on to a base metal. The gold layer is usually thinner than the gold on rolled gold. Gold-plated objects are also not hallmarked although 'gold plated' is often stamped on the object.

See Gold for information on handling, storage and ideal conditions.

Restringing a necklace

CLEANING
Gold jewellery does not tarnish and can usually be cleaned just by buffing with a soft cloth. If it is very greasy clean it in warm soapy water or Jewellery Dip as described in Jewellery, page 68. Gold scratches very easily so do not use a hard bristle or nylon brush. If the gold is decorated with stones see the appropriate paragraph.

The gold on rolled gold and gold-plated jeweller wears off easily so clean these objects very gently and do not polish them. Do not wear gold-plated jewellery for domestic chores such as washing up or gardening.

REPAIR
Gold should only be repaired by a jeweller, goldsmith or metal conservator.

SILVER JEWELLERY

Silver is used a great deal for making jewellery as it is harder, stronger and much cheaper than gold. It can be used on its own, be plated on to a base metal or can itself be the base for gold plating. Silver is alloyed with other metals such as copper or gold for strength. Silver jewellery is often decorated with niello (*see* Niello), particularly jewellery from the Near and Far East and India; this must be cleaned with particular care.

For ideal conditions, handling, display and store *see* Silver and Jewellery.

CLEANING

Polish tarnished silver jewellery with a Long Term Silver Cloth. If it is very tarnished use Silver Dip as described in Silver. If the jewellery is set with stones see Cleaning Jewellery, (page 68).

Modern silver often has colours applied to the surface during manufacture. Make sure you do not remove these by mistake. If some tarnish on a modern piece seems particularly hard to remove it may be intentional.

STORAGE

See Jewellery and Silver. If possible keep silver jewellery in acid-free tissue or tarnish-resistant cloth. Do not wrap it in baize, felt or chamois leather as they will tarnish the silver.

PLATINUM

Platinum does not tarnish. If necessary, buff platinum jewellery with a soft cloth. If it is very dirty wash it in warm soapy water as described in Cleaning Jewellery (page 68).

BRASS, BRONZE AND COPPER JEWELLERY

Bronze and brass are both alloys of copper. Much ancient jewellery was made of bronze but recently brass has been more popular. Modern brass jewellery can be buffed with a soft cloth. If it is very dirty wash brass jewellery in warm water containing a few drops of a non-ionic detergent (Synperonic N) or a mild household detergent (Fairy Liquid). Use an artist's hogshair brush to remove stubborn marks. Rinse in clean water and dry well using a soft cloth or a hairdryer set on *Cool*.

Brass can tarnish and it may be necessary to clean it with a copper or brass polish to restore its shine (*see* Brass). Take care not to get the polish on to other materials used in the jewellery and make sure the polish is all washed off well or it may mark clothing or skin.

On some people brass leaves a green or black mark on the skin, particularly in hot weather, this will easily wash off and is not harmful. However, a coating of microcrystalline wax on the object may help prevent the marks on your skin.

Do not lacquer brass jewellery as the lacquer will soon become scratched with wear and the resulting tarnish is even more unsightly.

Ancient bronze or copper jewellery should be worn as little as possible as it is usually quite fragile. Before wearing ancient bronze jewellery ensure that the metal is not corroded away. Open and close the clasps as little as possible.

For more information *see* Brass, Bronze, Copper and Jewellery.

CHROME JEWELLERY

Some jewellery is chrome-plated, especially modern and Art Deco jewellery, Watchstraps in particular may be chrome-plated, Modern watchstraps sometimes have a black chrome coating. Do not polish chrome too frequently or the metal coating will wear off. If the chrome is badly worn it can be replated by a chrome plater (*see* Chrome).

PEWTER, TIN AND LEAD JEWELLERY

Lead, pewter and tin were used in ancient jewellery and Art Nouveau and Art Deco jewellery. These metals are all very soft so handle this jewellery with care. Do not try to solder or heat the metal or the whole object may melt. *See* Lead, Pewter and Tin for cleaning and care.

STAINLESS STEEL

In recent years stainless steeel has been used to make jewellery. If the jewellery is very dirty wash it in warm soapy water, rinse and dry. If stainless steel jewellery is set with stones in closed settings, do not immerse it in water (*see* Cleaning Jewellery). Stainless steel does not take a high shine so it should only be buffed up with a soft cloth.

GEM STONES

Stones are referred to as 'precious' or 'semi-precious' according to how hard they are on a scale from 1 to 10. A diamond is the hardest at 10 and those stones with a hardness of 9 and 10 are precious; and include rubies and emeralds. Stones below this hardness such as garnets, opals, aquamarines and citrines are all semi-precious.

Stones are 'set' or fixed into a piece of jewellery using different techniques. There are open and closed settings. An open setting (e.g. a claw setting) allows light to shine and reflect through the stone. A closed setting encloses all of the base of the stone. The light does not shine through. In many cases metal foil was placed under the stone to help reflect more light. Adhesives of various types were often used to help hold a stone in a closed setting. If this type of setting is immersed in water or other liquid the adhesive could be dissolved or loosened, similarly water could get trapped under the stone causing the metal to corrode.

There are many different ways that stones are cut. The different cuts are intended to show the stone at its best. However, not all stones will take an elaborate cut as they shatter.

Do not try to reset stones, this should be done by a jeweller. See Jewellery for information on cleaning, handling, storage, etc.

AGATE, CORNELIAN, ONYX, CHALCEDONY AND JASPER

These are translucent stones with a waxy lustre used for making necklaces and pendants and set into rings and brooches. Stones which are in an open setting (i.e. have an open back) can be cleaned by washing in warm soapy water as described in Jewellery. If the stones are encased clean with a soapy solution using a cotton wool bud but do not get this type of setting very wet as water can damage the metal behind the stone. Strung necklaces should not get wet (*see* Beads for cleaning).

Make sure no oil or grease is in contact with these stones as they can stain. If the surface is not very shiny polish with a mild abrasive chrome cleaner (Solvol Autosol) as described in Jewellery.

AQUAMARINE

Aquamarines crack very easily, particularly in warm or hot water so remove rings before washing hands. *See* Jewellery for cleaning (page 68).

DIAMONDS

Diamonds are hard and strong and will scratch and chip all other stones, so store them carefully. Clean as in Jewellery.

GARNETS

Garnets can also be damaged by heat. **Topaz, sodalite** and **turquoise** can change colour if exposed to strong light for any length of time and **lapis lazuli** can fade. Clean as in Jewellery.

MARCASITE

Marcasite should not be exposed to a high relative humidity therefore it should not be washed or cleaned in Jewellery Dip. Clean marcasite with a mildly abrasive chrome cleaner (Solvol Autosol) *See* Jewellery.

RUBIES

Rubies are very hard but they chip more easily than diamonds. Handle them with care. Clean as in Jewellery.

SAPPHIRES

Sapphires are very hard but they can be damaged by heat. Even hand hot water can cause them to crack. Always remove them before washing your hands. Clean as in Jewellery but always use cold water.

SIMULATED GEMS

There are many different types of simulated gems. Many of them are difficult to differentiate from the genuine stone. The stones may well be stuck into their settings with glue so do not wash them in water. Clean them with cotton wool buds dipped in warm soapy water as described in Jewellery. A mildly abrasive chrome cleaner (Solvol Autosol) may be used to polish the surface if it is a little dull.

AMBER JEWELLERY

Amber is used quite widely to make jewellery. It can be affected by hair-spray, perfume, alcohol and other solvents. It can be quite brittle so take care not to knock it (*see* Amber).

BEADS

Beads have been made from almost every material including glass, precious and semi-precious stones, seeds, grasses, papier mâché, amber, metals, wood, pottery, bone, ivory, pearls, shell, teeth, feathers, porcupine quills, stalactites, marble and plastic. *See* under individual headings for more details on handling, cleaning, display and storage.

Never wash a string of beads by immersing them in water no matter what they are made of, as the thread will get wet and rot or possibly shrink. Remove the dust with a brush. Clean each bead with a cotton wool bud moistened with warm soapy water, cleaning about 5cm (2in) of the neck-

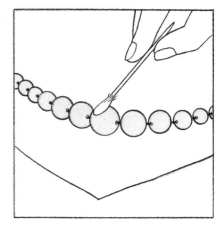

Clean each bead with a cotton wool bud moistened with warm soapy water

lace at a time, then rinse with a clean bud and clean water, dry with a soft cloth or paper towel. Continue cleaning the next 5cm (2in). If the dirt is very stubborn use talcum powder as a light abrasive. Mix it with a little water to a paste and apply on a cotton wool bud and lightly rub the surface. Stop if you are removing any surface decoration or colour.

Pearls, turquoises and opals should be dry cleaned. *See* Pearl.

Glass beads were sometimes treated to make imitations of other materials. Imitation pearls, for instance, can be made from thin glass covered in a pearly substance. Some beads have silver or gold coatings on the inside. None of these should be washed in water as the coating will come off. The colour runs out of some coloured glass beads if washed, particularly those made in the nineteenth century. Brush off the dust and wipe these beads with a barely damp cloth or a cotton wool bud moistened with isopropyl alcohol. Dry them with a soft dry cloth.

Some glass beads have sharp edges which can cut the thread. It may be possible to soften the sharp edges but this should be done by a jeweller. Check the thread regularly to see that it is not frayed. The hole in stone and pearl beads is usually made by drilling from both ends of the bead. Sometimes a sharp edge is formed inside the bead which can cut the string. It may be possible to smooth the hole but this should be done by jeweller.

In the nineteenth century some beads were made from steel which was not stainless. Do not wash these beads, get them wet or store them in

Mexican dancer's seed bells

a damp place as they will rust.

Other beads which should not be washed are made from papier mâché, wood, seeds, straw and lacquer. They may be damaged by water and the colour may be removed. Dust these beads with a stiff brush and wipe with a very slightly damp chamois leather or soft cloth.

Imitation pearls were sometimes made by soaking alabaster beads in hot wax and then dipping them in a pearly substance. Do not get these beads wet or use isopropyl alcohol on them. Polish them with a soft clean chamois leather. They should not be exposed to heat so keep them away from radiators and bright sunlight.

Beads can also be made from rolled beetle wings. These beads can be cleaned with cotton wool buds dampened in water. They may turn brown during the process but they will revert to their original colour when they are dry.

CAMEOS AND INTAGLIOS

Cameos are made from shell which is carved in such a way that the image stands out in relief, exploiting and showing up the different layers of colour in the shell. Intaglios are made from semi-precious stones such as moonstones. The design is cut into the stone so that the image is below the surface of the stone.

They are both usually set in metal frames to make rings, brooches and lockets. Intaglios are often used for family crests on signet rings, and cameos for brooches.

Cameos and intaglios should be cleaned with a cotton wool bud moistened with warm soapy water as described in Jewellery. Any stubborn dirt can be removed using a soft bristle brush. Remember to clean the back as well as the front.

If they are very dirty, particularly intaglios, cleaning with an artist's hogshair brush dipped in white spirit may remove some of the grime and grease. The object should then be washed in warm soapy water as above. Do not use any abrasive material such as metal polish.

Cameos, being made of shell, should not be stored in an acid enviroment such as an oak cupboard. Store them wrapped in plenty of acid-free tissue.

CORAL JEWELLERY

Coral is used widely for making jewellery either as branch coral or polished beads. *See* Coral for cleaning coral necklaces, care and storage.

COSTUME JEWELLERY AND DIAMANTÉ

The metal parts of costume jewellery often have a plastic or coloured metal coating. Sometimes what appears to be solid metal is only a thin coating so it should be handled carefully or the coating will start to peel off. The stones often have a coloured backing. This may come off if it is allowed to get wet. Diamanté stones are often stuck into the settings with adhesive. These, too, should not get wet as the water can soften the adhesive. To clean costume jewellery and diamanté remove the dust with a soft bristle brush and brush the stones lightly with a bristle brush or cotton wool bud dipped in isopropyl alcohol. Remove the isopropyl alcohol immediately by patting the object with a paper towel. After cleaning check the stones to ensure that they are not loose. If a stone becomes loose remove all the old adhesive with alcohol or acetone and refix the stone in place with an epoxy resin adhesive (Araldite).

ENAMEL JEWELLERY

Some jewellery is decorated with enamel. Enamel should not get wet and should be cleaned with a cotton wool bud dipped in isopropyl alcohol and polished with a soft cloth. *See* Enamel for full details on handling, cleaning, storage and display.

If the metal backing is quite thin the object may bend and the enamel crack off. Bangles and rings are particularly likely to do this. Do not squeeze them to get them over your hand. Remove rings and bangles before washing your hands. Store enamel jewellery carefully; use a jewel box. *See* Jewellery.

HAIR JEWELLERY

Hair was used to make jewellery for mourning wear in Victorian times. It was often woven or plaited and placed in a locket. Do not pull or try to tidy the hair as it unravels very easily but is impossible to re-weave. Hair can be attacked by insects and should be kept where it will not get too wet or too dry. Do not attempt to clean hair jewellery.

African elephant hair is often used for bracelets. In the nineteenth century horsehair was also used for making bracelets, necklaces and rings. Clean the hair with warm soapy water and rinse well. Dry by absorbing the water on a paper towel. If the hair feels very greasy rinse it with some white spirit, remove the excess solvent with a paper towel and allow the hair to dry. If the hair appears very dry rub a very little drop of almond oil in with the finger tips.

IVORY AND BONE JEWELLERY

Ivory and bone are used widely for making brooches, bracelets and bangles, rings and beads. Elaborately carved ivory and bone jewellery is very fragile and both ivory and bone are damaged by changes in relative humidity so do not wear rings and bracelets when washing your hands. *See* Ivory for cleaning, handling, display and storage.

JADE JEWELLERY

Jade is quite strong but can shatter or crack if hit sharply so take care when wearing bangles and rings not to knock them *See* Jade for further information.

JET JEWELLERY

Jet is a black stone made from fossilised wood, which when used as jewellery is highly polished. It was very popular in Victorian times, particularly for mourning jewellery. It is very hard and glass-like. A substitute for jet was made from moulded rubber. This is also hard but not as hard and glassy as jet and it scratches more easily.

To clean jet, brush the dust off and wash with a cotton wool bud or a soft bristle brush dipped in warm soapy water as described in Jewellery. Do not wet the strings of beads (*see* Cleaning Beads). Very stubborn dirt can be removed using a mildly abrasive chrome cleaner (Solvol Autosol) on a cotton but as described in Jewellery. Jet can be harmed by organic solvents such as white spirit, acetone or isopropyl alcohol so avoid getting perfume or hairspray on the jewellery.

Jet can be brittle so handle with care. Do not expose it to a low relative humidity, heat or strong light.

Small repairs to jet can be made using epoxy resin adhesive with some black pigment mixed in.

PEARLS, OPALS AND TURQUOISES

Moisture damages pearls, opals and turquoises so they should never be washed but dry cleaned instead using powdered magnesium carbonate. Place the jewellery in a plastic screw-top jar with enough powdered magnesium carbonate to cover it. Shake it gently for a few minutes then leave it in the jar overnight. Remove the piece from the jar and brush the powder off with a soft bristle brush.

If pearls get too dry the surface flakes off so do not keep them in a low relative humidity, leave them in strong sunlight or allow them to get very warm. The sheen of pearls is improved by being worn. If pearls are not worn for a long time they may eventually 'die'. They lose their sheen and can even turn black.

There are many types of imitation pearls, see Beads for cleaning and care.

Opals also should not be kept in a low relative humidity, bright light or heat. Opals chip and crack very easily. Opal rings should be removed before washing hands. Oily liquid will discolour and damage opals and cannot be easily removed. Some opals are dyed, this colour will fade.

Turquoise will also change colour when it is exposed to strong light. Keep turquoise in the same conditions as pearls and opals.

Turquoise and opals should be cleaned in the same way as pearls as they should not get wet.

SEEDS

Some jewellery, particularly ethnographical jewellery is made from seeds. The seeds can be polished, carved, dyed, painted or used in their natural state. In some countries decorative objects are made from large seeds such as coconuts.

To clean seeds remove the dust with an artist's hogshair brush. Wipe the seeds with a barely damp cloth or chamois leather. Do not allow the seeds to get very wet particularly if they have been decorated with paint as the paint may come off. Allow them to dry. Seeds can be protected by brushing them with a light coating of microcrystalline wax.

Do not store seeds in damp or very dry conditions. Seeds require similar conditions to wood so see Wood for handling, cleaning, storage, display.

LEATHER, PARCHMENT AND VELLUM

LEATHER

Leather was the forerunner of nonbreakable materials and has been used widely throughout history for domestic objects as well as for decorative items, including clothing, bags, sandals, gloves, boxes, buckets, jugs, bottles, mugs, wall hangings, hinges, seat covers, book covers, screens and table covers.

Leather is the hide of an animal which has been treated to make it flexible and durable. Without treatment the leather would be brittle and would rot. The part of the skin used for making leather is the middle of the sandwich between the epidermis with hair or fur growing out of it and the tissue of fat or flesh beneath.

Leather objects can be made from the skin of goats, cows, sheep, ostrich, snakes, alligators and almost any other animal. There are many different types of leather and many ways of treating it. A supplier of leather or a leather conservator should be able to identify what type of leather an object is made from. The main types are Morocco, calf, cow hide, sheep and reptile skins.

There are three main preserving processes;

Chamoising, where the skin is treated with oil or fats. It is also known as oil tanning. Chamois leather now has little or nothing to do with the chamois antelope from which the name originally comes. It is used to make soft clothing, jerkins, car washing leathers.

Tanning or vegetable tanning where the skin is immersed in a tannic

left *A painted Javanese puppet*

right *A leather decorated polychrome figure*

solution which used to be made from oak galls or oak bark but which is now done chemically. The leather is then treated with oils, grease or soap to make it supple. It is used to make harnesses, belts, footwear, upholstery, bags and book covers. This is the most usual form of leather preservation.

Tawing or mineral tanning, where the skin is treated with alum, though more recently chromium salts, and produces pale coloured leather, although sometimes the leather is dyed. Water should not be used on leather tanned in this way as the minerals can be washed out and the leather may decay. This type of leather may be used for kid gloves, footwear and some bookbinding.

Sometimes two processes can be combined such as tawing and chamoising.

After preserving, the leather is 'dressed' to make it suitable for the task for which it is intended, for instance shoe soles have to be strong and waterproof.

Leather can be coloured by being dyed or lacquered and can be grained or embossed to give a surface pattern or treated to give a shiny smooth surface.

Leather can be stretched over shapes to make scabbards or sewn or riveted together to make water bottles, jugs and pails. It can be moulded, punched, incised, carved or bruised over a relief of carved wood. Motifs can be applied to the surface with a stamp, gold leaf can be impressed into the tooled decoration, paint can be applied to the surface and metal or glass inlaid into the leather.

Not all leathers can be treated or decorated in the same way, it very much depends on how they have been preserved and dressed.

Suede is the undressed flesh side of the leather rubbed to a nap.

INSPECTION

Check leather for damage caused from use, over cleaning, vermin attack and mould growth. It may have an abraded surface from wear and tear and if it is allowed to become very dry it will feel hard and brittle and may crack.

Leather is frequently used in conjunction with other materials such as wood, metal, textiles and paper. It also often has surface finishes such as gold leaf, varnish, silver leaf and paint. These materials must be taken into account when caring for leather and any treatment applied to the leather should not harm the other materials, similarly the leather must not be harmed by, say, metal polish or woodworm treatment.

Check wooden frames in objects such as trunks, furniture and scabbards for woodworm or decay. Small areas of woodworm can be treated by injecting fluid into the worm holes as explained in Furniture. Make sure that the liquid does not get on to the leather. Objects where the leather is decorated with gold leaf or paint or other applied decoration should not be treated with an insecticide. It may be possible to fumigate this type of object but this must be carried out by a conservator or someone experienced in fumigation. Small objects can be treated for woodworm by sealing them in a polythene bag with an insecticide strip (Vapona), but make sure that the strip does not touch the leather. Leave the object for two to three weeks.

RED ROT
Leather normally deteriorates as a result of poor tanning or atmospheric pollution. The fibres in the leather crumble into a red powder known as 'red rot'. Red rot usually occurs on vegetable tanned leather made in the last half of the nineteenth century, although it can still occur in modern leather.

The rot first has a pinkish colour but, as it gets worse, the colour deepens to dark red. No satisfactory solution has yet been found to reverse red rot but it can sometimes be slowed down by painting on a dilute solution of ammonia. Do not use household ammonia. Ask a chemist for a small quantity of pure ammonia. Take care when handling the ammonia as the fumes are very unpleasant. Use it in a well-ventilated room. Mix one part ammonia with five parts de-ionised or distilled water. Apply the liquid with a paint brush or with a sponge dampened with the solution. Allow the leather to dry. If you are going to clean the leather treat it for red rot after cleaning.

If red rot is found on a rare or valuable object or one with applied decoration such as gold leaf, paint or lacquer

the object should be given to a conservator for treatment.

HANDLING

Frequent use and handling can cause leather to deteriorate. Always handle leather with clean hands and do not get grease, oil or paint on the surface. Old and rare objects should not be used and should be handled as little as possible.

Old leather often looks more robust than it in fact is so always handle it with care. It may tear and split very easily. Do not try to unroll or flatten leather which is hard or brittle as it may break. Ask for advice from a conservator.

Do not stick adhesive labels or tape on to leather, they may pull the top surface of the leather away when you remove them.

CLEANING

How leather should be cleaned and treated very much depends on how it was tanned and dressed. Old, rare or precious objects should only be cleaned and treated by a conservator. Too frequent or too vigorous cleaning can damage leather.

With age leather develops a patina as a result of use, wear, tear and care. The surface may be darker or lighter in some areas and be slightly damaged. Do not try to change this or to over clean an old piece.

When cleaning and treating leather objects care must be taken that the treatment does not affect the base material, adhesives or metal attachments and linings which may be on the object.

Remove the dust from a leather object by brushing it off with an artist's hogshair brush. If the piece is very dusty hold the nozzle of a vacuum cleaner in your other hand to catch the dust. Take care not to damage the leather with the end of the nozzle. A photographer's puffer brush is useful for blowing away dust from cracks and crevices on small objects and from inside hollow objects. After dusting the object wipe the surface with a barely damp cloth to remove any fine particles of dust that remain.

CLEANING WITH SADDLE SOAP
Although most robust leather can be cleaned using saddle soap, it should not be used for ancient, fragile, rare or

precious leather objects. These should only be cleaned by a conservator. Saddle soap also should not be used on leathers which do not have a smooth surface (e.g. suede-like leather) or leathers coloured with a dye or lacquer which will come off with water. Leather tawed with alum should also not be cleaned this way as it will remove the preservative salts. If you are not sure how your leather has been preserved take it to a leather dealer, bookbinder or leather conservator who may be able to advise you.

Test the leather for colour fastness before cleaning. Rub the saddle soap into a small inconspicuous area on a damp cotton wool bud. Check that only dirt and no colour is picked up on the bud. Leave the leather to dry and then check that the appearance of the leather has not been harmed by the soap. If all is well continue to clean the leather.

Make a lather by rubbing a damp sponge over the saddle soap. Gently work the sponge over the surface of the leather using a circular motion. Rinse the soap away by wiping the leather with a clean damp sponge. Do not get the leather very wet. Allow it to dry thoroughly and then lightly polish the surface with a soft, lint-free cloth. If the object is very large, clean and rinse one small area at a time to prevent the soap soaking into the leather.

CLEANING USING WATER AND NON-IONIC DETERGENT
If saddle soap takes off the colour try a small test area using water and a few drops of a non-ionic detergent (Symperonic N) (not a household detergent). If this is successful, apply it on a barely dampened sponge in the same way as the saddle soap and rinse with clean water on a clean sponge. Do not allow the leather to become very wet.

CLEANING USING POTASSIUM OLEATE SOAP
If saddle soap does not clean the leather well or it removes the colour from the object it may be possible to clean the object using liquid potassium oleate soap (Vulpex). Some leather such as tawed leather which should not be cleaned with saddle soap can be cleaned with potassium oleate soap.

Be warned that potassium oleate soap smells quite strong and the odour is persistent. Make the soap into a 1

per cent to 5 per cent solution with white spirit (1:100 to 1:20 parts of soap to white spirit). First test a small area of the leather to make sure that the soap does not remove any colour. If all is well, dampen a sponge with the solution and wipe the surface with a circular movement. Remove the loosened dirt and soap with a clean cloth or sponge dampened with clean white spirit. If the leather surface is very rough a small piece of towelling might be more effective than a sponge. It should be well wrung out.

CLEANING SUEDE OR SIMILAR LEATHER
If the surface of the leather is rough or has a velvet finish such as doeskin, remove any surface dirt with fine granules of a gum eraser (Draft Clean). Lightly rub the powder into the leather surface with your fingertips and either brush it off with a soft bristle brush or vacuum it off. It may be easier to make up a small muslin bag of the gum eraser (Draft Clean) and lightly rub this over the leather.

If the suede is very robust and very dirty try gently brushing it with a brass wire brush. Do not brush vigorously or the suede will be rubbed off.

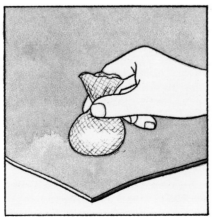

Fine granules of gum eraser can be rubbed into the leather using your fingertips or a muslin bag

Modern suede can be cleaned with proprietary suede cleaners.

STAINS
Stains such as ring marks or oil spillages are difficult to remove from leather. It is often better to leave the stain than to risk getting a paler area where you have tried to remove it. Do not use bleaches as they can damage the structure of the leather.

MOULD
Mould will readily grow on leather in damp conditions. If an object has mould on it take it outside and brush off the mould with an artist's hogshair brush. Wash the brush after cleaning off the mould so that it does not spread mould spores on to other objects.

A 10 per cent solution of thymol or orthophenylphenol in alcohol (industrial methylated spirits or isopropyl alcohol) can be sponged or brushed on to the leather to kill the fungi. Do not use methylated spirits as the purple dye could stain the leather. Alternatively, place the leather object in a sealed container or polythene bag with a small amount of thymol crystals. Warm the container very gently by placing it near a light bulb which is switched on. The fumes given off by the thymol will stop the mould growth. Leave the object for at least an hour. Mould should not recur if the leather is kept in suitable conditions.

If the leather is dry and brittle you can try to make it more supple after you have cleaned it, *see below*.

DRY LEATHER
Brittle, cracked or dry leather sometimes can be revived using a leather dressing such as the one developed by the British Museum (Pliantine). Some leathers should be treated with the water based emulsion of the leather dressing (Pliancreme, Connolly's Hide Food or Bavon). These leathers include those which have very smooth or shiny surfaces or have a lacquer coating such as patent leather or some furniture leather.

First clean the leather as described above then apply the dressing or cream *sparingly* on a soft lint-free cloth or with your fingers. Allow it to dry for at least twenty-four hours and then buff up the surface. If the object is very dry several applications of the cream or dressing may be required but always allow at least twenty-four hours between each application. Use only a very little leather dressing (Pliantine) as it is rather sticky and can attract harmful dust and grit. If the surface feels very waxy or greasy after twenty-four hours remove the excess dressing with a sponge or lint-free cloth moistened with white spirit. Repair leather before applying the dressing as it may prevent adhesives from sticking.

Pale coloured leather is often made slightly darker by leather dressing though as the dressing dries out it may become paler again. However, use only a very small amount of dressing and apply it evenly. The cream dressings have less effect on the colour.

Leather dressing is too thick to be used on thin leather such as brittle gloves, belts or wine or water containers. This leather should be treated with a special leather lubricant for fine leather (ASAK ABP [Bavon]). Apply the lubricant sparingly to the clean leather with a lint-free cloth or your fingers, wipe off any excess with a paper towel or clean cloth.

After cleaning and treating leather objects, lightly buff them with a soft lint-free cloth. A small amount of microcrystalline wax applied on a cloth or soft brush and polished off will help protect the surface. Do not apply a lacquer to the surface.

DISPLAY

Never display leather in sunlight or strong light as light speeds up the deterioration of leather and changes colours. Make sure wall-hangings are not placed where sunlight can fall on them. Keep leather away from houseplants and flowers. Do not leave leather objects in a damp room. Display leather where the temperature and relative humidity are fairly constant. Do not place leather objects over fireplaces or radiators or other heat sources.

STORAGE

Store leather objects in a cool, dark, well-ventilated area which is neither damp nor very dry. Do not lock them away in a cupboard or chest with no air circulation. Put paradichlorobenzene or thymol crystals in a small container with the objects but do not let the leather touch the crystals. The crystals should discourage mould and insects. You can also hang an insecticide strip (Vapona) in the storage area.

Leather is flexible, if it is unsupported it will stretch and distort and if it is folded it will develop creases. Leather clothing and soft leather objects should be stored in a similar manner to Textiles. They should be padded out with acid-free tissue and either hung on padded hangers or laid flat with the minimum of folding. Place wads of acid-free tissue along any folds so that creases do not develop. Bags, hats and shoes should be padded with acid-free tissue to keep their shape.

IDEAL CONDITIONS

Household: Normal household conditions, avoid damp rooms and direct sunlight.

Exhibition: Relative humidity 50–60 per cent, constant. Temperature 13°–18°C (56°–65°F). Low light levels, 50 lux.

Storage: Relative humidity 50–60 per cent, constant. Temperature about 15°C (59°F). Light levels as low as possible. Storage area should be clean and vermin free.

REPAIR

Rare, old, precious or very fragile leather objects should only be repaired and treated by a conservator. However, there are some repairs that you can do yourself to less important pieces.

Do not try to restore the colour to leather. It is nearly impossible to achieve a good colour match and the object usually looks worse than before.

RE-SEWING

Leather is usually stitched together and often the stitching wears out before the leather. The leather can be re-sewn using the existing needle holes. To sew thick leather you should use a strong thread such as button thread or a waxed thread specifically made for sewing leather. Thinner leather will require finer thread. The colour should match the colour of the remaining thread. A thread that is not waxed should be pulled across a block of beeswax to make it easier to work. Do not use thread much longer than

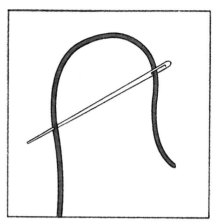

Resewing leather: prevent the thread slipping through the needle

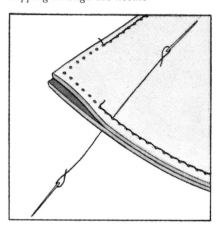

Pull the thread until there are equal lengths on either side of the hole

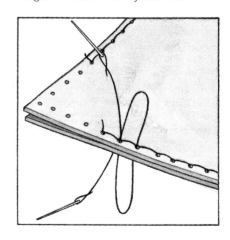

Push both needles through the next hole

60cms (2ft). Thread an appropriate sized needle on each end of the thread. To prevent the thread slipping out through the needle pass the needle through the thread near the end and pull it right through.

Work towards your body. To ensure that no more of the old thread

Sew back over a few stitches and cut the thread

Use a needle to position the frayed edge of a tear

unravels, start sewing a few stitches before the area that needs restitching. Using the holes that are already in the leather, push one needle through a hole and pull the thread half of its length until the hole is in the centre of the thread. Push both needles through the next hole; they will go through the hole from opposite sides of the leather. Keep the right-hand needle on top of the left as they pass through the hole. If both needles cannot go through the hole at once push them through one at a time. Take care not to tear the holes and not to sew through the thread. Pull the stitch tight. Continue in this way to the end of the seam. When you reach the end sew back over a few stitches. Cut the thread. Do not make new holes or the edge of the leather will be weakened. Very thick leather may need to be sewn with a harness needle.

If the leather is split along the sewing holes it should be patched before sewing.

Torn or split leather should be patched not sewn. Leather should be patched from behind. This means that leather upholstery or leather attached to a frame such as a screen would have to be taken off its frame. This restoration work should only be done by a restorer.

Canvas, thin or skived leather, vellum or parchment can be used to patch thick leather. A thin material such as silk or nylon net should be used for thin leather. Cut out a patch slightly larger than the tear. If necessary, colour it a similar colour to the leather so that it will not show as bright white. Use a flexible adhesive such as PVA emulsion (Evostik Resin 'W'). If the adhesive is too strong or inflexible the patch will show and the leather may crack at a later date.

Apply a small amount of the adhesive on the reverse of the leather and on the patch. Place the patch behind the tear and adjust the tear so that it is in the correct position. One edge of the leather may be frayed, use a needle to gently place the frayed edge under the hard edge. Lay the back of the tear on silicone paper and place some silicone paper over the front of the tear. Press the patch with a weight to ensure that the fabric sticks well to the leather. Leave overnight.

ARCHAEOLOGICAL LEATHER
Archaeological leather, whether wet or dry, should always be examined, cleaned, and treated by a conservator.

When leather deteriorates the fibres crumble into a red powder known as 'red rot'

BOOK BINDINGS
See Books.

JUGS, TANKARDS, BOTTLES, FLASKS, BUCKETS, HELMETS, SHIELDS, ETC.
These types of objects are usually made from vegetable tanned cattle hide about 2-4mm thick. They are usually in good condition but may be brittle so handle them with care. Very little can be done to objects such as these. If necessary, clean them with a sponge dampened with warm water containing a few drops of a non-ionic detergent (Synperonic N) as described above and if needed treat the object with the leather dressing (Pliantine).

LEATHER SCREENS
Leather screens were very fashionable at the end of the last century. Unfortunately, a great deal of the leather used is prone to red rot and becomes very brittle. Corners of furniture and backs of chairs will tear the leather if pressed against the screen. If the leather starts to tear, particularly along the frame, it is sensible to get it repaired as soon as possible because this indicates that the whole screen needs help. This is one occasion where a stitch in time really does save nine. Once screens begin to split and tear very little can be done by the amateur.

Dust screens carefully as for Wall-hangings, *see below*. Do not apply any leather dressing.

LEATHER-TOPPED DESKS AND BUREAUX

If the edges of the leather on a leather-topped desk or bureau top are lifting, they can be stuck down using PVA emulsion adhesive (Evostik Resin 'W'). Remove any old glue from the wood and leather. Paint a little emulsion on to the wood taking care not to get glue on the surrounding wood surface. Press the leather down, cover it with a sheet of silicone paper and weight it down until the adhesive is completely set, at least twenty-four hours. Put some hardboard or cardboard between the silicone paper and the weight so that the surface is not marked by the weight. This method can also be used for sticking lifting leather back on to small boxes and other leather covered objects.

The leather should be cleaned and treated in the same way as upholstery, but do not rub the gold tooling with either saddle soap or cream dressing. Take care not to get any on the surrounding wood.

If the leather is in bad condition ask a furniture restorer for advice.

LEATHER WALL-HANGINGS

Never attempt to clean leather wall-hangings. Protect them from direct sunlight. If necessary use blinds at the window to block out the light (*see* Textiles). If the wall-hanging is in really good condition remove the dust by brushing the surface gently with an artist's hogshair brush. If it is very dusty catch the dust with a vacuum cleaner held in your other hand. Do not knock the leather with the nozzle.

Do not attempt any other treatment yourself. Consult a conservator.

OBJECTS COVERED IN LEATHER

Leather is used to cover objects with a framework of wood and occasionally other materials. Take care when cleaning these objects that whatever you do to the leather does not affect the base material.

Before cleaning the leather any loose pieces should be stuck back to the frame (*see* Repair). Then check the object for woodworm and treat it if necessary. Leather objects which have wooden frames or a wooden backing such as chests or scabbards are difficult to repair. If the wood is very

badly attacked by woodworm it may be possible to consolidate it but this should be carried out by a conservator.

In most objects of this type the adhesive used to attach the leather to the frame is likely to be bone or animal glue. This should not get wet as it will dissolve. In this case clean the leather using potassium oleate soap solution (Vulpex) in white spirit.

Paper linings in leather-covered boxes or trunks may be cleaned using Draft Clean. The powder should be lightly rubbed over the surface and vacuumed off, *see* Paper. Consult a conservator if the lining is made from a textile and requires cleaning and repairing.

REPTILE LEATHER

If reptile leather is not very dirty it can be cleaned after dusting by rubbing the surface gently with a little microcrystalline wax on a soft lint-free cloth. Very dirty reptile leather can be cleaned using potassium oleate soap, *see above*.

A leather dressing cannot usually penetrate the scales of reptile leather so wax the object periodically with microcrystalline wax.

Cases and boxes covered in reptile skin are often lined with skiver, which is a very thin leather stuck on to the framework and often varnished for protection. Clean and polish skiver with microcrystalline wax.

Reptile leather has been copied by stamping pig skin to simulate the scales. Usually the size of the scales are more even than they would be on genuine reptile leather. This mock reptile leather should be treated in the same way as ordinary leather.

SHAGREEN

Shagreen is made from the skin of sharks and ray fish. It has been used extensively for covering small boxes, tea caddies, picture frames and other decorative objects. Often the surface has been rubbed flat to give a granulated appearance. It is frequently dyed to show up the granulations. Natural unpolished shagreen is used for the hilts of ceremonial swords.

Shagreen should be dusted and cleaned if necessary using a cotton wool swab damped with water containing a few drops of a non-ionic detergent (Synperonic N). Rinse the shagreen with clean swabs dampened with clean water and dry with a soft

clean cloth. Polish with microcrystalline wax applied on a soft bristle brush. Re-polish occasionally.

SKIN

Skin or untanned hide includes parchment and vellum. They are used for writing on, for covering books and boxes and making percussion instruments such as drums. Rawhide has been used for luggage. These materials have not been tanned and are not true leather. They have been through a preserving process but are still adversely affected by water or damp and can rot if kept in the wrong conditions. They should not be treated in the same way as leather.

Skin should be cleaned and repaired by a conservator. Make sure skin is kept in a controlled environment as too much damp will make it distort and deteriorate and if it is too dry it will crack and shrink. Skin is particularly prone to insect and rodent attack. *See* Parchment and Vellum.

UPHOLSTERY

Leather upholstery should be regularly dusted. Remove the dust from around the buttons or button-backed chairs and sofas with an artist's hogshair brush. Have a vacuum cleaner nozzle at the ready in your other hand to catch the dust as you brush it out. If the leather is very dirty clean it with saddle soap as above. Then apply a very little cream dressing (Connolly's Hide Food, Pliancreme, Bavon) on swabs of cotton wool. Leave the cream to be absorbed for at least twenty-four hours then polish it off with a soft clean cloth. Make sure you remove all the excess cream otherwise it will mark clothing.

The upholstery should be treated with the cream dressing at least once a year but should be cleaned with the saddle soap only where necessary.

VINTAGE CAR UPHOLSTERY

Vintage car upholstery is often restored to pristine condition. Specialist firms such as Connolly's, dye or lacquer leather to match the original. They also supply lacquer for touching up worn leather and will re-sew car seats. This degree of restoration is not normally carried out on other leather objects.

PARCHMENT AND VELLUM

Parchment and vellum are made from skin which has not been tanned. Parchment in usually made from sheep skin, although other animal skins can be used, and vellum is made from calf skin. Calf parchment or vellum is usually harder than sheep parchment and is used more for the binding of books than for the pages. Parchment and vellum have been through a preserving process and their surfaces are prepared for painting and writing. Parchment is used for documents, miniatures, paintings, book covers, box coverings and even on some furniture.

INSPECTION

Parchment is vulnerable to attack by rodents, insects and mould. It can also be badly damaged by inappropriate temperatures, and relative humidity and will distort or become very hard, brittle or even crack. Paint and gilding on the surface will lift and flake if the parchment wrinkles or distorts due to changes in relative humidity. If framed parchment distorts, pushing the paint layer against the glass, the paint may become stuck to the glass. Pastels on parchment are easily attacked by mould so they should be inspected frequently.

HANDLING

Parchment should be handled as little as possible, *see* Leather and Paper.

CLEANING

Old, rare, precious and fragile objects made from parchment should be cleaned and cared for by a conservator.

Dust can be removed from parchment with an artist's soft paint brush. Always check that the paint or gilding is sound before touching the surface. Never allow water to come in contact with parchment. Do not apply any kind of leather dressing.

DISPLAY

Parchment is very sensitive to the environment so that it is important that it is displayed in the correct conditions.

Do not place parchment in direct sunlight or bright lights. Parchment should be displayed where the temperature and relative humidity will remain as constant as possible, so keep it away from outside walls, entrance doors, heating pipes, radiators and fireplaces. *See also* Paper.

Parchment documents should not be out on display unless they are framed or in glass-fronted cabinets.

If parchment objects are framed badly, damage can occur to the paint surface and mould can grow. Use acid-free mounting card to create an air gap in the frame between the surface of the parchment and the glass. The thickness of the card will depend on how flat the parchment is but should normally be between 3–5mm (⅛–¼in). The more buckled the parchment, the thicker the card should be. Parchment objects are difficult to mount; the mounting is often done when the material is damp to prevent it from cockling. This must be done by a framer specialising in this kind of work.

Parchment documents with seals attached have additional problems, for instance the seal will need support so that it does not put strain on the document, these should be mounted by a specialist framer.

STORAGE

Store parchment in a cool, dry, well-ventilated, dark area. The storage area should be kept clean to discourage insects and rodents. Unframed parchment should be interleaved with acid-free tissue and stored horizontally in acid-free boxes. Parchment covered objects should be wrapped in acid-free tissue. Do not leave parchment in a cupboard or trunk where the air cannot circulate. It is very important that the conditions should be carefully controlled. Do not store parchment on metal shelves or in metal safes or deed boxes. If you have to put a parchment document in a metal deed box include a lot of acid-free tissue in the box. This will help reduce the effect of changes in relative humidity. Put paradichlorobenzene or thymol crystals in a small container with the objects to help discourage insects and mould but do not let the parchment touch the crystals. You can also hang an insecticide strip (Vapona) in the storage area. Parchment is a mouse's smoked salmon, so put down mousetraps.

IDEAL CONDITIONS

Household: Normal household conditions. Avoid damp rooms and direct sunlight.

Exhibition: Relative humidity 55–60 per cent, constant. Temperature 13°–18°C (56°–65°F) constant. Light levels 50 lux.

Storage: Relative 55–60 per cent, constant. Temperature about 15°C (59°F), constant. Light levels as low as possible. Keep storage area clean and vermin-free. Good ventilation essential.

REPAIR

Do not attempt to repair parchment.

METALS

It is thought that gold, silver and copper were the first metals to be used by man because they are the only ones that can be found as actual metal in nature. All other metals, apart from meteoric iron, occur as ores which have to be smelted to turn them into metal. Gold, silver and copper are also more commonly found as ores. Few metals are used on their own, they are usually mixed with other metals or materials to make alloys. Copper is mixed with lead and tin to make bronze and zinc to make brass. Iron is mixed with carbon, among other things, to make steel.

Metals try to revert back to their mineral form which is why they corrode. Some metals corrode quicker than others, for instance iron will corrode faster than lead. Some corrosion actually protects the surface of the metal and slows down the rate of corrosion of the rest of the metal. Once copper roofs develop their characteristic green colour they are likely to survive for a very long time. Some types of corrosion are desirable, such as the green or brown patination found on bronze statues. Pure gold does not corrode at all.

Tarnishing is a form of corrosion where the shiny surface of the metal is discoloured by a thin layer of metal compounds. Silver is particularly prone to tarnish and turns brown, blue or black. The tarnish can usually be easily polished off. Corrosion is more disfiguring than tarnish. Layers of corrosion can build up and completely obliterate the original shape of the object.

below *Grazing bronze deer*

right *A Sheffield plate biscuit barrel, the silver worn away by years of polishing*

How much a metal is cleaned often varies from metal to metal and with taste. In some museums silver is left to go black as cleaning it removes a small amount of silver. Bronze is never polished but is admired for its brown or green patina, while brass is often kept bright and shiny. Many people prefer metals not to be sparkling as they look too new but prefer them to develop a patina.

ALUMINIUM

Aluminium is a silvery metal which is very light and malleable. It is alloyed with other metals and does not easily take a high polish. It has been used since the end of the nineteenth century, particularly for Art Deco figurines, modern sculpture, car bodies, garden furniture, and kitchen utensils. The figure of Eros in Piccadilly was one of the earliest statues to be cast in aluminium.

INSPECTION

When aluminium is exposed to the weather it acquires a dull grey tarnish which forms a protective layer against further corrosion. However, it can corrode under certain conditions and small white powdery areas appear which eventually turn into pits on the surface. This occurs particularly when water collects in hollows. Contact with iron and copper can cause aluminium to corrode faster than normal.

HANDLING

Aluminium is soft and will scar easily. Hard objects will nick the surface of aluminium and rough handling will bend and dent it. Handle aluminium objects with care to avoid damage.

CLEANING

Never use abrasives to clean aluminium nor caustic solutions such as caustic soda. When aluminium has been used to make parts of a machine such as a car, old grease and oil can be removed with paraffin.

OUTDOOR SCULPTURE
Outdoor sculptures made of aluminium should be washed to remove dirt using warm water and a few drops of a non-ionic detergent (Synperonic N) or a mild household detergent (Fairy Liquid). If the object is standing on a base this should be protected from the dirty cleaning water by covering it with polythene sheeting. Use a soft cloth or soft bristle brush and lightly clean all over the surface. Rinse the sculpture well with clean water and dry with a soft, clean cloth.

Do not wax the object after cleaning.

SMALL OBJECTS
Aluminium objects which are kept indoors can be cleaned by wiping with methylated spirits. Dampen cotton wool swabs or cotton buds with the methylated spirits. Wipe the surface using each side of the swab and discard it when it is dirty. Dry with clean cotton wool swabs.

If the metal is used in conjunction with other materials such as ivory which could be stained by the colouring in the methylated spirits, use isopropyl alcohol which contains no colouring. Work in a well-ventilated area and wear rubber gloves. Place the dirty swabs into a lidded container. When you have finished, take the container outside, remove the lid and allow the swabs to dry out before placing them in the dustbin. Methylated spirits is flammable so avoid naked flames.

PAINTED ALUMINIUM
Caustic solutions will attack the surface of aluminium so never use caustic soda to remove paint. Acetone and methylated spirits may help soften the paint otherwise paint removers containing dichloromethane (Nitromors in the green can) can be used to remove really difficult paint. Do not leave it on for too long and rinse it off well with clean water. Wear rubber gloves and work in a well-ventilated room.

DISPLAY

Aluminium is very stable and can be displayed virtually anywhere. However, do not display aluminium objects where they can touch iron and copper. These two metals interact with the aluminium and can set up corrosion problems. If aluminium is used in conjunction with other materials the object must be displayed in conditions to suit the most vulnerable material.

STORAGE

Keep aluminium in a dry area and away from other metals. Small objects should be wrapped in acid-free tissue to protect them from being knocked. Aluminium used in conjunction with other materials should be stored under conditions to suit the most vulnerable material.

IDEAL CONDITIONS

Household: Normal household conditions.
Exhibition: Relative humidity 50–55 per cent. Temperature about 18°C (65°F). Light level not critical.
Storage: Relative humidity 45 per cent. Temperature about 18°C (65°F). Light level not critical.

REPAIR

Aluminium needs to be welded if it is broken. This should be done by a welder. Small repairs can be made using an epoxy resin adhesive (Araldite).

BRASS

Brass is a gold coloured alloy of copper and zinc which is familiar to most people unless it is heavily tarnished when it can be brown or greeny black in colour. Brass is used to make a wide range of items, many of which are everyday objects such as candlesticks, coal scuttles and fire irons. It is also used for door furniture, some of which is finely decorated. In churches it is used for memorial plaques, lecterns and the brasses fitted over the tombs on church floors. Brass can be engraved, enamelled, inlaid or embossed.

INSPECTION

Care should always be taken to check that gold-plated objects are not mistaken for plain brass. Gold-plated brass objects will only lightly tarnish no matter how old they are. If the gold on a gold-plated object is rubbed through, the object will have some dull areas where the brass has become exposed to the atmosphere and become tarnished and some shiny gold areas where the plating remains. Gold-plated objects should never be polished.

Brass tarnishes, becoming dull and eventually a greeny-brown colour. If a piece of brass has been badly stored in an attic or cellar the surface will become matt and very dark in colour. This is extremely difficult to remove. Occasionally, some brass objects become very green when the copper in the brass corrodes.

HANDLING

Brass is a soft metal that is easily scratched and dented by careless handling. It also tarnishes easily. The acids and oils in the skin are left on the surface of the brass when it is touched with bare hands. These encourage tarnishing to begin and to accelerate. Once decorative brass has been cleaned and polished try to wear clean cotton gloves when handling it.

Carry candlesticks and other brass objects so that the weight is supported from underneath. Do not pick objects up by protruding decoration.

See that fire tongs are placed so that they do not fall on to the fender or the coal scuttle thereby denting them.

CLEANING

When polishing any metalwork always cover the working surface and its edges with something soft such as an old towel or blanket so the object is not dented or scratched.

Before cleaning any brass object wash it in warm water containing a few drops of a non-ionic detergent (Synperonic N) or a mild household detergent (Fairy Liquid). Rinse the object in clean water and dry with a soft clean cloth. This will remove any grease and dust.

Brass that is only lightly tarnished can be cleaned by rubbing with a Long Term Silver Cloth. Do not use this same cloth on copper or silver.

Domestic objects are normally displayed with a high polish. To clean domestic and utilitarian objects such as fenders, candlesticks and coal scuttles use Long Term Copper and Brass cleaner or a mild abrasive chrome cleaner (Solvol Autosol). Apply the polish with a clean, soft cloth or a wad of cotton wool. Use a circular movement and polish off with a soft clean cloth. Impregnated wadding (Duraglit) used in the same way is also very effective for polishing brass. Always replace the lid of the tin of the impregnated wadding so that the solvent does not evaporate.

Brass objects with engraved, embossed or raised decoration can be cleaned by applying the polish with a soft bristle brush. Never use a nylon toothbrush as the bristles are very hard and will scratch the surface. If you brush too harshly the top surface of the decoration will be worn away. Polish with a clean soft bristle brush. A soft bristle brush can also be used to remove any polish out of incised or repoussé decoration or corners and crevices. Do not use the same brush for copper or silver. Each metal must have its own brush.

Accumulated old polish can be removed using cotton buds moistened with isopropyl alcohol or white spirit. Dip the bud in the solvent and push it along the cracks turning it as you go. Discard the bud when it is dirty. If the old polish and dirt is hard to remove agitate it with a hogshair brush dipped in the isopropyl alcohol or white spirit. Mop up the sludge as you go with a soft cloth or cotton wool.

If you are trying to clean a very small brass object wrap a small amount of Duraglit round the end of a wooden cocktail stick and use as a cotton bud.

HEAVILY TARNISHED BRASS

Use a brass metal polish to remove brown or greeny-black tarnish. Apply using a soft cloth, rubbing hard. Do not use this metal polish for cleaning lightly tarnished objects as it overpolishes. Take the metal polish off with a soft cloth.

If domestic items made of brass such as fenders, curtain rails, coal scuttles are so corroded that no amount of polishing will clean them, it is possible to find commercial firms who will polish them for you. They will chemically strip them and polish them on a polishing mop so they will be very bright and shiny.

Never use steel wool or Scotchbrite to clean brass as it will score the surface, nor use lemon juice or vinegar

When polishing door furniture protect the surrounding wood from the polish by fitting a template

and salt as they can damage the surface of the brass.

Wear rubber gloves when using brass polishes.

FURNITURE FITTINGS

Brass fittings on furniture should not be polished to a high polish. They need to look clean but not bright. Regularly clean them when you clean the furniture. Dust them with a duster and occasionally buff them up with a chamois leather or a clean soft cloth. Never use brass cleaners as they make the brass too bright and can also leave a white deposit on the wood surrounding the brass.

Wax the brass at the same time as you wax the furniture. The best wax for brass is microcrystalline wax but as it is not so good for furniture, brass fittings can be waxed with a good quality beeswax polish.

Door furniture, finger plates, door knobs, key holes covers, wall plates can be buffed up with a Long Term Silver Cloth. If they are very tarnished clean them with a mildly abrasive chrome cleaner (Solvol Autosol). Protect the surrounding surface from the polish by fitting a template of card or stiff paper around the brass. Use adhesive tape to join the card together but do not put tape on the paint or woodwork. Keep the template in position with your hand.

Some door furniture has finely chased or etched decoration. This can be worn away by constant polishing. If possible, protect it by applying a coat of lacquer. Otherwise dust it regularly with a soft duster and occasionally buff it up with a chamois leather.

Brass can be used as an inlay on furniture, grandfather clocks, decorative boxes and many other objects. This inlay should never be cleaned with polishes. Clean the inlay when

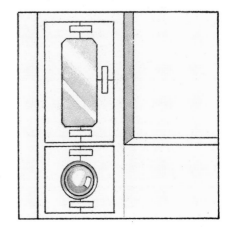

left *People often mistake spelter for bronze. Despite the fact that spelter does not survive well out of doors, many garden statues were made of it.*

above *Brass tarnishes, becoming dull, and accumulated old polish may turn green.*

right *A combination of rain, dust, soot and tar can cause unsightly streaks. Here the wire fixing is ugly and harmful.*

possible, put candlesticks in the refrigerator for about half an hour. The wax should then push off with your fingernail. If it does not all come off easily, scrape off what you can and then remove the rest with white spirit. Never use a metal object to scape the wax off.

LACQUERING
Brass can be protected from tarnishing by a coat of clear lacquer. This is more suitable for decorative objects such as candlesticks, than for utilitarian pieces such as coal scuttles. It is very easy to scratch lacquer and once this happens the exposed areas will tarnish rapidly and the lacquer will have to be removed before you can re-polish the brass. The best lacquer to use on brass is Incralac. To apply and remove the lacquer *see* Laquering in Silver. If you have previously used Long Term Silver Cloth to buff up brass you will have to clean the object very thoroughly before lacquering otherwise the lacquer will not adhere to the surface. If it is possible, wash the object well in warm soapy water. Dry it and then wipe the surface with acetone or alcohol or clean it with impregnated wadding (Duraglit)

you clean the object. Remove dust with a soft cloth, taking care not to catch and lift any pieces of inlay which may be loose and proud of the surface. Where possible stick them down before cleaning (*see* silver inlay). Wax the brass at the same time as you wax the object. *See also* Boulle furniture.

Brass inlay on armour should be attended to by a conservator. However, if the armour is in very good condition, the brass can be waxed with microcrystalline wax for protection.

REMOVING CANDLE WAX
It is best to remove candle wax when it is cold as it is more brittle then. If

followed by acetone or alcohol to remove all traces of polish.

Protection does not last indefinitely, but if the surface is well prepared and the lacquer is well applied and is not scratched or damaged, the brass should not tarnish for several years. Dust the object regularly to avoid a build up of dust and dirt.

DISPLAY

Brass can be displayed almost anywhere, but as heat and light accelerate tarnishing try not to place brass objects on mantelpieces, above radiators or in direct sunlight. Avoid damp areas. Do not put brass objects directly on to stone or brick floors as the damp in the floor can affect them. Stand them on cork mats, wooden slats, or a piece of polythene. If you are using brass bowls as cache pots always place a plastic container or a saucer in the bottom of the bowl so that the water from the plant does not come into direct contact with the brass.

Brass used in conjunction with other materials should be displayed under conditions to suit the most vulnerable materials.

STORAGE

Wrap small items in acid-free tissue to help preserve them from tarnishing. Do not place objects made from different metals touching one another as they can interact with each other, for instance you may get rust spots on a brass object if it is touching an iron object. Keep brass objects in a dry place. Do not stand brass directly on stone, concrete or brick floors as the damp from the floor can cause corrosion. Place objects on wooden slats, cork or polythene sheeting.

Brass used in conjunction with other materials should be stored under conditions to suit the most vulnerable materials.

IDEAL CONDITIONS

Household: Normal household conditions.
Exhibition: Relative humidity 50–55 per cent. Temperature about 18°C (65°F). Avoid bright light.
Storage: Relative humidity about 45 per cent. Temperature about 18°C (65°F). Low light levels if possible.

REPAIR

Do not attempt to repair old, rare or precious objects. This should be done by a metal conservator.

Brass can be repaired with lead solder using a soldering iron or a gas torch. Do not use a corrosive flux. Use a multi-core solder as used in the electronics industry. Clean the edges of the join very carefully before soldering. Make sure the solder does not run all over the surface of the object as it is difficult to remove. Hard solder (Easi-flo) can be used by an experienced metal worker.

Small breaks can be repaired using an epoxy resin adhesive (Araldite).

BRASS BEDSTEADS

Brass bedsteads should ideally be lacquered to protect them from tarnishing. Most of those bought today will probably have been lacquered already, particularly if they are modern but it is unlikely that old bedsteads bought in antique shops or junk shops will have been. It is possible to get bedsteads professionally polished and lacquered by a commercial company. It is also possible to do it yourself, *see* Lacquer. If it is not possible to lacquer your bedstead, wax it lightly with microcrystalline wax after cleaning it. Polish the wax with a soft clean cloth.

BRASS MUSICAL INSTRUMENTS

Modern brass musical instruments are often lacquered. These should be dusted and wiped with a soft cloth dampened with warm soapy water (*see above*). Older brass band instruments such as bugles are often shone to a sparkle, much to the pride of their owners. To polish the brass use impregnated wadding (Duraglit or Silvergilt), *see above*. However, remember that every time you polish the surface you remove a thin layer of brass and the metal will eventually wear thin and decoration will be lost.

Do not polish the brass fittings on woodwind and other musical instruments. *See* Wood, Cleaning Furniture Fittings.

PINCHBECK

Pinchbeck, like brass, is also a copper alloy but with a lower percentage of zinc. It was invented by a watchmaker, Christopher Pinchbeck, in the early eighteenth century and was used for making snuff boxes, watch cases and small items. Some pinchbeck objects were gilded but it is difficult to see where the gilding has worn off on the edges and high spots as its colour is very similar to gold unless the pinchbeck has tarnished.

If you can tell whether the pinchbeck is gilded, handling, cleaning, display and storage are similar to Ormolu.

If the object is not gilded, handling, cleaning, display and storage are similar to Brass.

Use a photographer's puffer brush to blow off dust, holding the nozzle of a vacuum cleaner in your other hand to catch it

BRONZE

Bronze is an alloy of copper and tin, although zinc and lead may also be present. It has excellent casting properties and is ideally suited to making statues. Some of the most wonderful sculpture in the world has been made from bronze and if you take the time and trouble to look after even simple pieces of bronze sculpture they will give a great deal of pleasure.

Bronze has been used from earliest times, since the Bronze Age (1000 – 500 BC in Britain). When bronze is cast it can vary in colour, depending on the composition of the alloy, from a copper to a golden tone. If it is left to tarnish naturally it will eventually darken to a dark brown colour. Atmospheric pollution can turn the surface of bronze to a pale green or even a blue colour. This can also happen when a bronze is buried.

As well as sculpture, bronze has been used for domestic and decorative objects, such as fire dogs, early cooking pots, tables, decorative fittings on furniture, clock mounts, weapons, cannons and coins. Bronze can also be combined with ivory, silver, marble and other materials.

Many modern bronze statues have the surface coloured by the application of chemicals or paint. Most bronzes which are found indoors range from a golden brown to a brownish-black colour, although a few may be green. Ancient bronzes are more likely to be green. The patina on bronzes is highly prized and should not be removed.

INSPECTION

As bronzes usually have an intentional surface colouring there is no need to

worry about tarnishing. However, they can corrode under certain conditions and when this happens the copper in the bronze can turn green. There is a particularly destructive corrosion called 'bronze disease' where small areas can corrode quite quickly, producing pitting on the surface. Bronze disease appears as bright green powdery spots on the surface of the bronze. It is generally a brighter colour than ordinary green corrosion and is usually only found on ancient bronzes. However, salt will cause bronze disease even on modern pieces and this salt can come from your hands, the sea, or many other sources. For this reason it is unwise to keep bronzes outside if you live by the sea or have a chlorinated swimming pool.

HANDLING

Ideally, you should wear clean cotton gloves when handling bronzes as they will prevent the salt from your hands being left on the surface. Always pick up a bronze sculpture by the main part of the object and not by the arms or decorative projections, even though these appear to be convenient handles, as they may bend or break off. Take care that pieces that stick out do not knock into doorways when the statue is being carried – bows, spears, horses tails are particularly vulnerable. Make sure that your belt buckle does not scratch the bronze as you carry it against yourself.

Check that mounted sculptures are secure on their mounts. If the base is not firmly fixed to the object it may well fall off when you pick up the bronze and could cause a lot of damage.

If you are moving a bronze sculpture which you cannot easily lift yourself, use a sack barrow or something similar. Always make sure the barrow is well padded with clean blankets or foam rubber as grit and dirt can damage the patination. When moving large bronzes professional lifting equipment will be required.

CLEANING

Rare, old or precious bronzes should only be cleaned by a metal conservator. The only cleaning that other bronzes should require is a light dusting. If the bronze is very dusty the dust should be blown off as otherwise it acts as an abrasive and may scratch the surface. Use a photographer's puffer brush or you can blow down a straw. Hold the nozzle of a vacuum cleaner in your other hand to catch the dust. Protect the bronze from damage by the nozzle by wrapping foam plastic round the end.

Bronzes that have been regularly cleaned and so are not particularly dusty should be dusted with a soft clean duster. Remove any dust from crevices and decoration with an artist's hogshair paint brush.

Never use abrasive cleaning materials such as metal polish on a bronze. Never use water or methylated spirits or any solvent on an indoor bronze as these may remove any surface colouring.

Avoid rubbing a bronze too vigorously as raised surfaces can become highlighted and dirt can still be left in the depths. To remove caked dirt from crevices and hard to reach areas, take a few fibres of cotton wool and wrap them round the end of a cocktail stick. Dampen them with spit. Gently push the padded cocktail stick along the crevices turning it as you go so that the dirt is not ground into the surface.

If cleaning objects made of more than one material, one of which is bronze, make sure that the cleaning materials used on the other components do not harm the bronze.

WAXING

If a bronze statue has a dull surface from having been in some unsuitable place, such as a conservatory or attic, it may be revived by taking a soft bristle brush and lightly waxing the surface. Touch the surface of the bristles with microcrystalline wax – there should hardly be any wax on the brush – and if necessary wipe any excess off on a clean piece of paper towel. Then, very lightly, brush over the surface of the bronze and lightly polish with a soft clean cloth.

If a bronze has a green patination which has been either chemically induced or painted on, check a small area to see that the wax will not take the colouring off. Make sure you only use a very small amount of wax.

Do not use a brush that has been used for waxing bronze on any object made of a different metal.

BRONZE DISEASE

Bronze disease is usually found on ancient bronzes but occasionally it can be found on more modern bronzes whether displayed outside or inside. If you find a very small area of bronze disease, wax the spot thoroughly and keep a close eye on it. If the bronze disease gets worse, if more spots appear or the existing spots get bigger, ask a conservator for advice.

BADLY DISEASED BRONZES

It is not possible for the layman to treat extensive bronze disease. Keep a badly diseased bronze as dry as possible and ask a conservator for advice.

DISPLAY

Bronzes can be displayed almost anywhere in the house but avoid bathrooms and conservatories or anywhere where there is a very damp atmosphere. Do not place bronzes close to windows which are frequently opened as cool damp air will form condensation on the bronze. Do not place vases of flowers or houseplants that need to be sprayed with a fine mist of water close to bronzes. The spray may drift on to the bronze.

Bronzes which have been painted green should be kept away from radiators or fireplaces. The variations in temperature can make the patina crack.

Bronze used in conjunction with other materials should be displayed under conditions to suit the most vulnerable material.

STORAGE

Store bronzes in a dry area. Avoid damp cellars, outhouses or attics. Where possible, store bronzes in a room or cupboard where the relative humidity will remain constant and as low as possible. Wrap small bronzes carefully in acid-free tissue and put them in a cardboard or wooden box. Alternatively, use a perforated polythene box or perforated polythene bag. Do not use sealed polythene as if the conditions are less than perfect condensation may occur.

Bronzes used in conjunction with other materials should be stored under

above *The shape of a sculpture can affect the way it corrodes. Contaminated water may drain into and remain in crevices such as folds*

right *Some bronzes have internal iron armatures which can rust and expand and eventually split the bronze*

conditions to suit the most vulnerable material.

IDEAL CONDITIONS

Household: Normal household conditions.
Exhibition: Relative humidity 50–55 per cent. Temperature about 18°C (65°F). Light levels not critical. Bronzes with bronze disease and ancient bronzes require relative humidity 40–45 per cent.
Storage: Relative humidity 45–50 per cent. Temperature about 18°C (65°F). Light levels not critical.

REPAIR

A great deal of damage can be done to bronzes by the layman trying to repair them. Always take a damaged bronze to a metal conservator. Small repairs can be made by using an epoxy resin adhesive (Araldite).

OUTDOOR SCULPTURE

Bronze is frequently used for outdoor sculpture. Compared with many other metals and alloys, bronze is reasonably resistant to corrosion but it is not immune to the heavily polluted atmos-

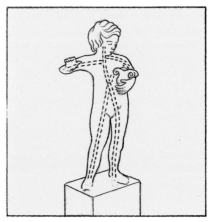

pheres of industrial cities which contain corrosion-inducing chemicals. Corrosion forms on the surface of the bronze and when it rains a fresh surface of bronze is exposed to attack when water soluble corrosion is washed away. The shape of the sculpture can also affect the way it corrodes. For instance contaminated water can drain into and remain in crevices such as the folds of clothing. This water is likely to be strongly corrrosive. The water can also seep into the bronze through pit holes in the surface and the inside of the object can become very corroded. The underneath of a statue can also deteriorate badly.

Examine small gullies, folds of material and the underneath as well as the major part of the statue to make sure that the metal has not completely corroded away leaving holes.

Some bronzes have internal iron armatures. These will rust and expand and can eventually split the bronze, particularly in narrow parts of the sculpture such as legs and arms. Check for orange or brown iron staining on the surface of the bronze and any sign of cracks in the bronze. Keep an eye on the iron staining. If it gets any worse or if the bronze is cracked you should consult a metal conservator sooner rather than later.

The combination of rain, dust, soot and tar can cause unsightly streaks, stains and pitting on the surface of a bronze. Streaks particularly occur on bronzes positioned underneath trees.

CLEANING

Regularly remove leaves and other debris which collect in crevices as they hold water and speed up corrosion.

Old, rare or precious bronze sculptures should only be cleaned by a metal conservator.

If you have a bronze statue outside in good condition, it can be cleaned by washing. Choose a warm, dry day.

If the statue is on a base, protect the base from the dirty cleaning water by covering it with polythene sheeting securely taped into place.

Remove as much as possible of the dust and bird droppings with a dry, medium stiff bristle scrubbing brush. Do not use a brush that is too stiff or you could scratch the surface of the bronze. Then scrub the bronze with a similar brush using warm water containing a few drops of a non-ionic detergent. (Synperonic N) or a mild household detergent (Fairy Liquid). Scrub off any further deposits which did not come off when dry.

Rinse the sculpture really well with clean, warm water and again examine the entire surface of the bronze for any further loose material. Pay particular attention to sheltered parts, including the underside of the figure and to ledges or crevices where water may have tended to collect. If necessary wash the sculpture again, then dry as much as possible with clean, dry cloths or a chamois leather and allow it to dry completely in the sun.

If the sculpture has unsightly green streaks or patches it may be possible to tone them down by mixing ordinary artist's powder colour with microcrystalline wax. Raw Umber, Burnt Umber and Black are the most useful colours. Mix the colours into the wax with a spatula or a knife. Rub the coloured wax well in to the pale streaks and they should go darker. This should be done before you wax the whole sculpture.

After cleaning outdoor bronzes, they should be lacquered or waxed for protection. Unless the lacquer is applied expertly and is regularly maintained it can cause worse damage than not applying it at all. So on balance, it is better to wax, and not lacquer, a bronze sculpture. Waxing should be carried out thoroughly and often.

Waxing a bronze sculpture Make sure that the bronze is completely dry. Apply microcrystalline wax on a bristle stencil brush or, if necessary, a bristle toothbrush. Make sure wax covers the entire surface, including the underneath and all crevices, folds and ledges. Polish the wax with a soft bristle brush or a soft dry cloth. Apply

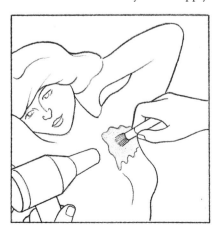

Waxing a bronze: to achieve a better seal, warm the bronze with a hairdryer

opposite *Regular maintenance of outdoor statuary will keep it in good position*

above *Chrome is a hard white metal used as a decorative finish. It has a harder shine than silver*

a second coat of wax in the same way an hour later.

If you warm the surface of the bronze you will achieve a better seal. The heat causes the wax to melt and run into all the pores and crevices. If this is practical to do, apply the wax as above but hold a hair dryer in your other hand about 10 cm (4 in) away. You will see the wax melt on the surfaces. Do not let the wax get too hot as it is flammable. When the wax is set, polish the statue with a soft

bristle brush or a soft, clean cloth. Statues that have been cleaned and waxed should remain in good condition if they are regularly maintained.

Maintenance Once the bronze sculpture has been thoroughly cleaned and waxed it should be re-waxed at regular intervals. It is not necessary to wash the sculpture every time you wax it. Dry brush off any loose dirt and bird droppings and wax two or three times a year. Normally you need only wash the sculpture once a year. This should keep the statue in good condition.

Sculptures in bad condition If a statue

is badly negelected you should ask a metal conservator for advice.

DISPLAY

Sculptures that are going to be newly displayed should have plinths tailor-made for them. A plinth should have a damp proof membrane such as polythene or slate. All plinths should stand square to the statue to prevent the statue leaning and producing unnatural stresses. Keep a space round the plinth filled with small stones to improve drainage and keep the area clear of plants and grass.

Do not place lawn sprinklers near bronze sculpture as the spray is always carried further than one thinks. Do not allow trees and bushes to grow too close to a bronze. Overhanging branches can scratch the surface and if a sculpture is overhung with a canopy of greenery the air around it stays quite damp and this can cause the sculpture to corrode unnecessarily fast. The damp will also cause algae and lichen to grow on the bronze and water dripping off the trees will cause streaks in the patination.

STORAGE

Keep bronze sculptures under cover when they are not on display. If you put them in a garage or a shed cover them with perforated polythene or a tarpaulin to keep off the dust, dirt and bird droppings. Make sure that they are clear of other objects and that they will not get knocked when you are trying to get the lawn mower out or moving other things about. Stand bronze sculptures on pieces of wood or polythene to protect them from being affected by any damp rising from the floor.

BRONZE CANNONS

Bronze cannons are generally kept outside and, with time, a green patination can form on them. Sometimes more active corrosion is set off by atmospheric pollution. When bronze cannons were in use they were allowed to tarnish to a dull bronze colour and were not kept polished. If you have a cannon in this condition maintain the colour by regularly cleaning and waxing. *See* Outdoor Sculpture. Cannon should not be placed directly on the ground. If there is no carriage mount them on wooden blocks.

COLD CAST OR SIMULATED BRONZE

With the advent of modern resins it is now possible to make what are known as cold cast or simulated bronzes. These are cast in a mould and are made of a synthetic resin filled with a bronze powder and then coloured to look like genuine bronze. They can be very like a real bronze. However, they are basically made of resin and can therefore be treated in the same way as plastics. One thing to bear in mind is that a cold cast bronze is not nearly as strong as a genuine bronze and parts like legs, arms and tails are very vulnerable and will easily snap off.

Cold cast bronzes should be cleaned by dusting them with a soft, clean cloth. If they need further cleaning they can be washed in warm water containing a few drops of a non-ionic detergent (Synperonic N) or a mild household detergent (Fairy Liquid). First test a small inconspicuous area to see that the surface colour does not come off. Use a cotton wool swab and dampen with the washing liquid. Carefully wipe the test area. If any colour comes off on the swab do not continue. If the colour does not come off wipe the surface with swabs of cotton wool dampened with the washing solution. Use both sides of the swabs and discard them when they are dirty. Rinse the object by using clean cotton wool swabs dampened with clean water. Dry it with a soft, clean cloth.

Cold cast or simulated bronzes can be displayed and stored under most conditions. Avoid direct heat sources or direct sunlight which could affect any surface colouring.

CHROMIUM

Chromium is a hard white metal with a very high shine as a decorative finish on a variety of metal surfaces. It can also be coated on to plastic. It is mainly found on twentieth-century objects such as Art Deco figurines, clocks, lamps, car mascots and bumpers, furniture, bathroom fittings, as well as on more modern plastic objects, including toys.

INSPECTION

Chromium itself does not corrode. If the chromium plating is broken,

however, the metal underneath will corrode. Where the original layer of plating is thinly applied, tiny air bubbles left in the chrome layer can cause breaks in the surface. The base metal may corrode in these breaks forming small pimples which appear on the surface of the chromium as black or grey discolouration.

HANDLING

The chromium plate layer is very thin so do not scratch it or treat it roughly.

CLEANING

Any loose dust or grit which could scratch the surface should be brushed off with a artist's soft paint brush or a photographer's puffer brush. Grimy, greasy dirt can be removed by washing the chrome with a soft bristle brush dipped in warm water containing a few drops of a non-ionic detergent (Synperonic N) or a mild household detergent (Fairy Liquid). Rinse thoroughly with clean warm water and dry with a soft clean cloth. To make sure all the water is removed dry with a hairdryer set on *Cool*.

On Art Deco objects particularly, chromium was used in conjunction with other materials such as ivory and plastic. Wash the chromium of such objects with a cotton wool bud dampened with the warm washing solution, rinse with a clean bud dampened with clean water and dry thoroughly with a soft clean cloth. Do not allow the cleaning solution to spread on to the ivory or other materials. Do not dry the object with a hair dryer.

Never use wire wool or Scotchbrite on chromium as it will scratch the surface.

To remove areas of discolouration, clean the chromium surface with a mildly abrasive chrome cleaner (Solvol Autosol). Apply the cleaner on small wads of cotton wool and polish with a circular movement. Polish off with a soft clean cloth. If the areas to be cleaned are very small use cotton buds.

Do not try to remove or flatten the pimples as this will break the chromium layer even more. Once they are polished they will not look nearly so disfiguring.

If the chromium layer on ultilitarian objects such as cocktail shakers or car bumpers is badly damaged and cleaning does not improve it sufficiently, it will have to be professionally replated. Art objects should *never* be replated, however.

DISPLAY

Chromium can be displayed almost anywhere but if the chromium surface is damaged the object should be kept dry and clean.

Chromium used in conjunction with other materials should be displayed under conditions to suit the most vulnerable material.

STORAGE

Wrap chromium-plated objects in acid-free tissue to protect the surface from physical damage and store them in a dry place.

Chromium used in conjunction with other materials should be stored under conditions to suit the most vulnerable material.

IDEAL CONDITIONS

Household: Normal household conditions.
Exhibition: Relative humidity 50–55 per cent. Temperature about 18°C (65°F). Light levels not critical.
Storage: Relative humidity about 45 per cent. Temperature about 18°C (65°F). Light levels not critical.

REPAIR

Chromium-plated objects have to be repaired according to the base metal. *See* the relevant chapter. Small breaks can be repaired using an epoxy resin adhesive (Araldite). Do not try to solder chromed objects as any heat will discolour and blister the surface.

COPPER

Copper was the first metal to be used by man. It is occasionally found in lumps which can be worked immediately without smelting but usually it is smelted from ores. Copper is a very soft metal which does not cast well unless it is alloyed. Sheets of it can be cold hammered into cooking pots, jewellery and other objects. Because copper corrodes the food vessels are frequently coated with another metal, usually tin. The base metal of Sheffield plate is copper. Copper has also been used extensively as the base for enamel painting.

Copper is alloyed with tin to make bronze, with zinc to make brass and with tin and other metals to make pewter; it can also be alloyed with gold. It is most often made into domestic objects, kettles, coal scuttles, bed warmers and warming pans, saucepans and engraved printing plates.

When copper is polished it is pinkish in colour but it will tarnish to a brown colour or corrode to green. This green, which can be seen on copper roofs, is often carefully preserved for its appearance. Copper objects are often more attractive when they have been allowed to tarnish slightly.

INSPECTION

Old cooking pots and bowls are often used for holding plants. Check that the seams have not corroded through or split otherwise the water from the plant will come through.

HANDLING

Copper is a very soft metal that is easily scratched and dented by careless handling. Do not set round bottomed copper bowls down hard as they will dent and crack. The salts and oils in the skin are left on the surface of the copper when it is touched with bare hands and these encourage tarnishing. Once copper has been cleaned and polished wear clean cotton gloves when handling it.

CLEANING

Old, rare or precious copper objects should be cleaned by a metal conservator.

When polishing any metalwork, always cover the working surface and its edges with something soft, such as an old towel or blanket, so that it does not dent or scratch the object.

Before cleaning any copper object wash it in warm water containing a few drops of a non-ionic detergent (Synperonic N) or a mild household detergent (Fairy Liquid). Rinse it well in clean water and dry with a soft clean cloth. This will remove any grease and dust.

Copper that is only lightly tarnished should be rubbed with a Long Term Silver Cloth. Do not use this same cloth on brass or silver.

Heavier tarnish can be cleaned off using Long Term Copper and Brass Cleaner or a mild abrasive chrome cleaner (Solvol Autosol). Apply the polish with a clean, soft cloth or a wad of cotton wool. Use a circular movement and polish off with another soft clean cloth. Impregnated wadding (Duraglit) used in the same way is also very effective for polishing copper. Always replace the lid of the tin of the impregnated wadding (Duraglit) so that it does not dry out. If polish accumulates in the corners or cracks use a soft bristle brush to remove it. Do not use the same brush for copper as you do for brass or silver, they must each have their own brush.

Accumulated old polish can be removed using cotton buds moistened with methylated spirits or white spirit. Dip the bud in the solvent and push it along the cracks turning it as you go. Discard the bud when it gets dirty. If the old polish and dirt is hard to remove, agitate it with an artist's small stencil brush and some solvent. Mop up the sludge as you go with a rag or cotton wool.

To remove really stubborn tarnish use a brass or copper metal polish (Brasso). Apply it on a soft cloth, rubbing hard. Do not use a metal polish for cleaning lightly tarnished objects as it over polishes. Polish the metal polish off with a soft cloth.

If domestic items are so corroded that no amount of polishing will clean them, it is possible to find commercial firms who will polish them for you. They will chemically strip and polish the object to a bright finish.

Never use wire wool or Scotchbrite to clean copper as they will score the surface.

Wear rubber gloves when using copper polishes.

Do not polish your copper too often as it is very soft and will wear away. Do not press too hard when you polish thin copper as you could make a dent in the object.

PRINTING PLATES
Printing plates should never be polished as this will soften the lines of the engraving and polish will fill them up. Wash them in warm water containing a few drops of a non-ionic detergent (Synperonic N) or a mild household detergent (Fairy Liquid). Rinse them well in warm water and

pat them dry with a soft cloth.

TINNED COPPER VESSELS
Only polish tinned copper vessels occasionally with a Long Term Silver Cloth. Frequent polishing of any kind will wear away the tin.

COPPER INLAY
Copper can be used as an inlay on furniture and decorative boxes. This inlay should never be cleaned with a polish because the polish will get on to the wood and is almost impossible to remove. Clean the inlay when you clean the object. Remove dust with a soft cloth. Take care not to catch and lift any pieces of inlay which may be proud of the surface. Where possible, stick them down before cleaning (*see* Silver Inlay). Wax the copper at the same time as you wax the object.

Copper is also inlaid into silver and brass. This copper inlay can be polished at the same time as the object itself.

---

below *If the armature in a lead statue corrodes and fails the statue will begin to collapse under its own weight*

opposite *When copper is polished it is pinkish in colour*

COPPER JEWELLERY
See Jewellery.

LACQUERING
Copper can be protected from tarnishing by a coat of clear lacquer. *See* Brass and Silver.

DISPLAY

Copper can be displayed almost anywhere but as heat and light accelerate tarnishing try not to place copper objects on mantlepieces, above radiators or in direct sunlight. Avoid damp areas. Do not put copper pots directly on to stone or brick floors as the damp in the floor can affect them. Stand them on cork mats, wooden slats or a piece of polythene. If you are using copper bowls as cache pots place a plastic container or a saucer in the bottom of the bowl so that the water from the plant does not come into direct contact with the copper.

When copper is used in conjunction with other materials it should be displayed under conditions to suit the most vulnerable material.

STORAGE

Keep copper in a cool, dry area. As copper is very soft, wrap smaller pieces in acid-free tissue, and place large pieces where they will not be knocked. Do not place objects of different metals touching each other since a chemical reaction can take place between them causing corrosion.

When copper is used in conjunction with other materials it should be stored under conditions to suit the most vulnerable material.

IDEAL CONDITIONS

Household: Normal household conditions.
Exhibition: Relative humidity 50–55 per cent. Temperature about 18°C (65°F). Avoid bright light.
Storage: Relative humidity 45–50 per cent. Temperature about 18°C (65°F). Low light levels if possible.

REPAIR

Do not attempt to repair old, rare or precious copper objects. These should be taken to a metal conservator.

Copper can be repaired using lead solder and a soldering iron or gas

torch. Do not use a corrosive flux (Tinman). Use a multi-core solder as used in the electronics industry. Make sure the joints are clean. Take care that the solder does not run all over the surface of the object as it is difficult to remove.

Small breaks can be repaired using an epoxy resin adhesive (Araldite).

ELECTROTYPES

Electrotyping is a method of reproducing an object by depositing metal electrolytically into a mould. Electrotyping was developed in the mid nineteenth century and is a similar process to electroplating. The difference between the two is that in electroplating a surface of gold or silver is plated onto a finished base metal object. In electrotyping the whole object is made by depositing metal into a mould. The metal usually used for electrotyping is copper, although it can be gold or silver, which becomes the body of the object. The deposited copper is very thin so it is often backed with another metal, usually lead, to give it strength.

Most objects made by this process consist of several pieces, backed with the lead and then joined together to make a complete object. With a coin the obverse and reverse would be made separately and then soldered together to make a complete coin. The copper base is often plated with another metal such as gold or silver or chemically patinated. Occasionally electrotyped objects are left copper coloured.

Very fine detail can be obtained by this process and nowadays many reproduction reliefs, medals and small ornaments are electrotypes.

If the surface of the finished object is copper treat it in the same way as copper. If it is gold or silver plated *see* Gold and Silver. Always bear in mind that the body of the object is very thin so handle electrotypes with great care. In addition, any metal plating will be even thinner and will wear through quickly, exposing the copper.

GOLD

Gold is regarded as the most precious metal of all. Very occasionally pure gold objects are made but normally it is too soft and too expensive in its pure state to be used, so it is alloyed with other metals. The amount of gold in the alloy is expressed in carats. Pure gold is 24 carats. The other standards used are 9, 14, 18 and 20 carats. The number represents the proportion of gold out of 24 parts.

The colour of gold varies according to the type and quantity of metal in the alloy. The gold is usually mixed with silver which gives a pale greenish colour, or copper which gives a reddish tinge. If a mixture of copper and silver is used it makes the metal a much yellower colour than the pure metal. Platinum makes it silvery and a 25 per cent platinum 75 per cent gold alloy produced 18-carat white gold.

Gold, like silver, can be decorated by engraving, embossing or enamelling. It has been used for jewellery, decorative objects, coins, medals and statues. Gold can also be coated on to other metals and made into gold leaf for decorating frames, furniture, ceramics and glass and illuminating manuscripts. It is used as an inlay to decorate other materials and is itself inlaid with a variety of materials.

INSPECTION

Pure gold does not tarnish but when it is alloyed with a high percentage of another metal the surface may be tarnished by the corrosion of the secondary metal.

HANDLING

Gold is a very soft metal and even when alloyed with other materials will dent and scratch easily. Gold objects should therefore be handled very carefully and, if possible, to prevent leaving finger marks you should wear clean cotton gloves. *See* Silver for further handling.

CLEANING

Old, rare or precious gold objects should only be cleaned by a metal conservator.

Before cleaning gold objects check that the object is solid gold and not silver gilt, ormolu or gold-plated. These types of object can be severely damaged if cleaned incorrectly.

If possible, gold objects should be cleaned only by dusting them with a soft clean cloth or chamois leather. If the object is very dusty use a photographer's puffer bush to remove the dust and grit so that the surface is not scratched. Grimy, greasy dirt can be removed by washing the object in warm water containing a few drops of a non-ionic detergent (Synperonic N) or a mild household detergent (Fairy Liquid). Rinse the object well in clean warm water and pat dry with a soft clean cloth. Gold is so soft that the more it is rubbed the faster it will wear away.

Gold is frequently decorated with enamel and gem stones or other applied decoration. These should not get wet and should not be cleaned by immersing in water or solvents.

GOLD-PLATED OBJECTS
See Ormolu for cleaning. *See also* Jewellery.

ARCHAEOLOGICAL GOLD
Do not try to clean an archaeological gold. Some ancient gold is covered in green copper corrosion from the copper in the alloy. Do not attempt to remove this. It should be cleaned by a metal conservator.

DISPLAY

Place gold objects far enough back on tables and sideboards where they cannot be knocked off on to a hard floor. Do not leave them in view of the window where they will act as temptation for burglars. Try to avoid putting gold objects over a fireplace or radiator as they will quickly be covered in dust and soot and will need cleaning too frequently.

To display gold-plated objects *see* Ormolu and *see also* Jewellery.

Ancient gold objects with a lot of copper in the alloy must be kept dry.

When gold is used in conjunction with other materials it should be displayed under conditions to suit the most vulnerable material.

STORAGE

Gold objects should be well wrapped in acid-free tissue, which will protect them from physical damage. Gold itself can withstand almost any storage conditions but the other metals in the alloy will corrode or tarnish if the conditions are not suitable. Therefore keep gold dry and away from atmospheres harmful to silver (*see* Silver). Do not wrap gold objects in chamois leather or baize as any silver in the alloy may tarnish. Do not wrap objects in cling film or sealed polythene bags because condensation may form inside.

The objects can be stored in a box or trunk but make sure that the weight of those on top does not squash those at the bottom. Put enough tissue as extra padding to prevent any dents or scratches.

For gold-plated objects see Ormolu.

Gold used in conjunction with other materials should be stored to suit the most vulnerable material.

IDEAL CONDITIONS

Household: Normal household conditions.
Exhibition: Relative humidity 50–55 per cent. Temperature about 18°C. (65°F). Avoid bright light. Avoid conditions harmful to silver.
Storage: Relative humidity 45–50 per cent. Temperature about 18°C (65°F). Light levels as low as possible. Avoid conditions harmful to silver.

REPAIR

Repairs should be carried out by a metal conservator or a goldsmith.

IRON & STEEL

Iron is one of the most common and utilitarian metals. It can be cast, forged or rolled, made into steel or other alloys, or coated with a metal such as tin to make tin plate. It was first used for weapons and domestic utensils and later for decorative objects and has been used for cannon balls and cooking pots, for door hinges and armour, for fire grates and ornamental railings, for garden furniture, for wall lights and farm machinery, for cars and ocean liners. The Japanese also inlaid it with gold and silver to make decorative objects.

Iron and steel are magnetic. Even with heavily corroded objects, if you place a small magnet near the object you will feel the slight 'pull' that indicates that it is made of iron or has an iron base. However, if the metal has completely corroded away leaving no metal the magnet will have no effect.

IRON

There are two types of iron, cast and wrought. Cast iron has a high carbon content making it too brittle to forge and items are made by pouring the metal into a mould. They consist usually of one piece or of several pieces bolted together as cast iron cannot easily be welded together. As it is very brittle, it will not bend and it breaks easily. When cast iron is broken the inside is grey in colour and rather coarse. Iron that has been badly cast will have air bubbles trapped in it giving it an appearance of Aero chocolate. Cast iron objects tend to be more elaborate than those made in wrought iron. Examples of cast iron objects are ranges, fire backs, fire irons and fire surrounds, though it can also be made into small decorative objects and is sometimes inlayed with gold and silver.

Wrought iron has a low carbon content and is malleable. It can be hammered into simple patterns, twisted, curled or flattened. These pieces are then welded or riveted together to form complete objects such as gates, fire screens, wall lights.

INSPECTION

Damp is the main cause of iron rusting. In a damp atmosphere iron and steel will very quickly form a layer of rust and if this is left unchecked the surface becomes pitted and the object will eventually disintegrate. Cast iron rusts more easily than wrought iron. As an iron object rusts, it expands, and flakes of rust will eventually fall off. Iron should always have some kind of surface coating such as paint, wax or oil, or graphite, which was used on kitchen ranges.

Decorative objects kept in the dry may not rust very badly but rust may appear in localized areas. It can be thick in some spots but absent elsewhere.

HANDLING

Most iron, particularly cast iron, is very brittle. If you drop it or set it down hard it will break surprisingly easily. When lifting a heavy piece of iron always have enough people to help move it and make sure the pathway is clear and that you have a prepared place to set it down. Take care not to catch edges on doorways or garden walls. Set the object down on wooden blocks as this makes it easier to relift and means you can set it down square without getting your fingers trapped. Make sure the weight is evenly distributed and do not set it down on one corner.

CLEANING

Rare, old or precious iron objects should only be cleaned by a metal conservator.

Cast iron that has been left outside for some time will have absorbed a considerable amount of water. Make sure that it is thoroughly dry before you begin work on it. This may take several days.

Using a wire brush, brush off any flaking paint and rust. Remove any remaining paint with a paint remover containing dichloromethane (Nitromors in the green tin). Wear rubber gloves, and work in a very well-ventilated room, or preferably outside, and do not smoke while using the paint remover. Take precautions against any remover getting in your eyes. Wash off the paint remover with water and dry the object thoroughly and quickly using an electric fan heater. Alternatively, remove the remaining paint with a blow lamp or hot air paint stripper and scraper. Remove as much of the rust as possible with the wire brush.

Any remaining rust can be removed using a commercial rust remover (Jenolite or Modalene). Follow the instructions carefully. Instead of rust remover you can also use wire wool (grade 00 or 000) and paraffin. Soak the object in the paraffin or paint it on and leave it for a few hours to allow the rust to soften. Scrub off the rust with the wire wool. Remove the slurry with rags and then wipe down the object with clean paraffin. Wipe off the paraffin with a dry cloth and allow the object to dry thoroughly. If rust remover is used the surface will be duller and possibly darker than if you use wire wool and paraffin.

Wear rubber gloves and goggles. Do not smoke.

If the object is movable, it is possible to have it sand blasted. This will clean the surface right down to the sound metal.

Once all the paint and rust has been removed and the surface is clean and dry, coat the object with a rust inhibitor (Jenolite). Always read the manufacturers' instructions carefully. The rust inhibitor will tend to darken the surface colour.

Cleaned iron should not be left exposed for any length of time. Some form of surface coating should be applied within twenty-four hours. When you have cleaned iron, avoid touching it with your bare hands before applying surface protection as fingerprints can cause corrosion to start almost at once. Wear clean cotton or gardening gloves.

The chemical barrier formed by the rust inhibitor is a help but not sufficient to protect the surface completely on its own. Protective coatings need to be applied. These can be paint, lacquer, oil, wax or graphite.

CLEANING SMALL IRON OBJECTS
Small, unpainted objects should be dusted with a soft cloth. Remove any dirt or grime by wiping the surface with cotton wool swabs moistened with methylated spirits or white spirit. Allow to dry thoroughly.

If there are any rust spots these can be removed by locally cleaning with paraffin and wire wool (grade 000 or 0000) as explained above. Dry the object well. If the rust spot is fairly thick remove the top layers with a sharp scalpel. Hold the blade parallel to the surface of the object. Finally wax the object with microcrystalline wax applying it with a soft clean cloth

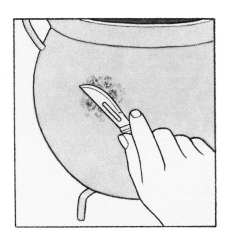

When removing rust spots with a scalpel hold the blade flat against the surface of the object

or soft brush. Polish it with a cloth.

Some iron objects are inlaid with silver or gold. In this case remove any rust spots with a scalpel and polish with a soft brush, not a cloth which could pull up the inlay.

PAINTING IRON
Outdoor iron work must be painted. Having cleaned the object thoroughly and applied a rust inhibitor, paint on two coats of red lead metal primer; always read the manufacturer's instructions carefully. When the primer is dry, paint on two coats of surface enamel paint. It is essential to leave sufficient drying time between applying the coats of paint. Always follow instructions. Make sure the paint is compatible with the primer.

If you wish to paint indoor objects, after applying the rust inhibitor, use one layer of red lead metal primer and at least one layer of enamel paint. Read all instructions carefully.

If an object has been sand blasted, particularly fireplaces or fenders, you may wish to retain the silver-grey colour. Ask the sand blasting company to polish and lacquer them for you, or you can wax them yourself with microcrystalline wax.

Apply the microcrystalline wax with a bristle brush, making sure it covers the entire surface, including the underneath and all crevices and incised decoration. Polish the wax with a soft bristle brush or a soft dry cloth. Apply a second coat of wax an hour later.

If you warm the surface of the iron you will achieve a better seal as the heat causes the wax to melt and run into all the pores and crevices. If this is practical to do, apply the wax as

above but hold a hair dryer in your other hand about four inches away from the surface. You will see the wax melt on the surface. Do not let the wax get too hot as it is flammable. When the wax is set, polish the object with a soft bristle brush or a soft clean cloth.

Any stripped iron object can be waxed if you do not wish to paint it.

KITCHEN RANGES

Remove any heavy rust with a wire brush, using a vacuum cleaner with a brush attachment to collect all loose dust and rust. Remove any remaining rust with a commercial rust remover or wire wool and paraffin as described above. Finally clean the surface with cotton wool swabs dampened with methylated spirits, never use water. Use both sides of the swabs and discard them when they are dirty into a lidded container and then allow them to dry outside before putting them in the dustbin. Methylated spirits is flammable, so keep flames away and

make sure the room is well ventilated.

Old ranges will have absorbed a lot of grease from the cooking over the years which could prevent paint from adhering to the surface. If the range is not going to be used try painting with a thin coat of black paint (Manders Black Ebony paint Finish M757, Joy stove black or other purpose-made paints). Apply the paint to a small area and leave it for at least a week. If the paint does not peel off during this time you can then paint the whole range.

If the paint will not adhere to the surface or if the range is going to be used, the surface should be protected with black lead (Zebrite). Apply this with a black lead brush and polish off with another. Repeat when necessary.

IRON GRATES AND FIREBACKS

If they are covered with old paint and rust clean as for cast iron. If they are purely ornamental protect them with a coat of primer and a coat of black paint for metal. Do not apply the paint so thickly that it obscures the detail.

If necessary, thin the paint with white spirit.

If the fire grate and fireback are going to be used protect them with black lead (Zebrite).

FIRE IRONS AND TOOLS

Fire irons and tools made from wrought iron do not rust very easily. During a period when you do not use the fire, and particularly if the weather is damp or humid, give them added protection by applying microcrystalline wax and polishing with a soft cloth. If any rust does appear it can be removed with steel wool (grade 000 or 0000) and paraffin. Wax well after cleaning.

REMOVING WAX

Accumulations of old wax can be removed with white spirit. Using a cotton wool swab or soft cloth moistened with white spirit, wipe the surface until all traces of wax are removed and dry with a clean cotton cloth and rewax.

CANNONS

Iron cannons were normally painted black when they were made in order to protect them from rusting. Inspect the cannon regularly for signs of rust and if any is detected clean the rust spots off with a wire brush and steel wool and paraffin and when the area is clean and dry repaint it. The bore of a cannon is not normally painted but rainwater can collect in it and should be drained out.

Cannon should not be placed directly on the ground. If there is no cannon carriage they should be mounted on wooden blocks.

IRON AND STEEL SCULPTURE

Iron and steel may be used in modern sculpture. Sometimes it is painted and sometimes the surface is pretreated to protect it. If this coating is removed or broken the object will rust rapidly like ordinary iron, so do not attack it with a wire brush or wire wool. Some modern sculpture is untreated and is meant to rust.

Stainless steel and treated surfaces should be washed from time to time. Painted areas will need repainting every few years. It is important to know the artist's specification for the paint and the colour so that you can duplicate it when necessary. Inspect the condition of iron and steel sculptures regularly.

ARCHAEOLOGICAL IRON

Archaeological iron should be kept very dry and should only be cleaned by a metal conservator. It is surprising what skilful cleaning can reveal from a lump of rust. Gold and silver inlay can easily be lost by careless cleaning.

MACHINERY

Farm machinery, gun carriages, traction engines, pumps and any other machinery should be inspected regularly. The conservation and restoration of these items is not within the scope of this book. Always research the subject before you begin work.

DISPLAY

Well-maintained and protected iron can be displayed almost anywhere.

above left *Outdoor ironwork must be painted regularly*

right *Steel grates and fireplaces often have raised decoration*

However, remember that the damper the atmosphere the more easily the piece will rust.

STORAGE

Keep iron objects as dry as possible. Avoid damp cellars, outhouses and attics, and do not place them directly on a stone, concrete or brick floor. Place them on wooden slats, cork or polythene sheeting. Do not place iron objects in contact with other metals, because they can interact. Small objects should be wrapped in acid-free tissue and kept in a very dry place.

IDEAL CONDITIONS

Household: Normal household conditions. Keep dry.
Exhibition: Relative humidity 50–55 per cent. Temperature about 18°C (65°F). Light levels not critical. Archaeological ironwork requires a relative humidity of about 40 per cent and in some cases lower.
Storage: Relative humidity 45–50 per cent. Archaeological ironwork may require 15 per cent. Temperature about 18°C (65°F). Light levels not critical.

REPAIR

Some metal conservators may be able to do repair work for you or give advice. A blacksmith also may be able to help. Small breaks can be repaired using an epoxy resin adhesive (Araldite).

STEEL

Steel is an alloy of iron, carbon and other metals. It is usually tougher than iron and corrodes more slowly. Stainless steel contains chromium which prevents it from rusting. Steel is used for weapons and cutting instruments, and also for decorative objects and jewellery.

Damascene Steel can be manufactured in such a way that it has a decorative 'watered silk' appearance. This is known as damascening, although the term is now applied inaccurately to the process of decorating steel with gold or silver wires beaten into undercut grooves. This is actually a type of inlaying, *see* Arms and Armour.

Blueing Some steel is treated to give the surface a blue colour. This helps to prevent rust and was mainly applied to guns, small decorative objects and clock hands. It should not be removed.

Unless steel has been decorated by blueing, gilding or any other surface finish it should be left steel coloured, i.e. shiny grey, but it will need surface protection.

CLEANING

Steel grates and fireplaces in particular often have raised and engraved decoration which may be obscured by rust and dirt. There may also be gilding on some areas, particularly on the raised work. Do not attempt to clean a steel fireplace before looking closely for any possible gilding or engraving. Clean small trial areas in places where you suspect there may be engraving or gilding using wire wool (grade 0000) and a mildly abrasive chrome cleaner (Solvol Autosol). Peer very closely at the surface as you clean it and if possible use a magnifying glass. If you find gold or engraving clean these areas slowly and with great care so as not to remove the decoration. If in doubt, consult a conservator. Continue to clean in this manner.

Ideally, steel should have a smooth grey surface. Steel in good condition which has not rusted can be polished with a mildly abrasive chrome cleaner on cotton wool swab. Polish in straight lines, do not use a circular motion as the scratches will show. Polish off the cleaner with a soft cloth. Any remaining cleaner in the crevices can be removed with a soft bristle brush. If it helps, use a little methyl-ated spirits to remove traces of the cleaner. Do not use the brush on any other metal. After cleaning the steel, wax it lightly with microcrystalline wax and polish it with a soft clean cloth. Make sure the surface is completely covered by the wax. *See* Waxing Iron.

If there are any areas of rust on the steel they can be removed with the chrome cleaner and fine wire wool (grade 000 and 0000). Never use patent rust removers as they will discolour the steel and may cause further damage. A wire brush will make deep grooves in the steel so do not use one.

Very rusty steel objects can be cleaned in the same way as Iron.

Stainless steel Never clean stainless steel with wire wool or Scotchbrite or treat it harshly. Wash it with warm soapy water. Rinse and dry well.

Blued steel and damascening Never clean rare, old or precious steel objects. They should only be cleaned by a metal conservator.

Do not strip blueing off the surface. Remove any spots of rust very carefully using a blunt scalpel blade held parallel to the surface. If the spots are only very light remove them with chrome cleaner and cotton wool. Take care not to remove the blueing, or scratch the surface. It is better to under clean rather than over clean. Protect the surface with microcrystalline wax. A blued object with no rust can be cleaned by wiping the surface with methylated spirits on cotton wool swabs to remove grime. Then wax it. If in doubt, consult a metal conservator.

The finish of damascening is important; you can ruin a fine piece in seconds. The cleaning of damascened objects should not be attempted by an amateur. Some books refer to cleaning with dilute nitric acid. This method should never be used.

For further information *see* Iron.

LEAD

Lead is a very soft, dull, heavy, grey metal which has a shiny surface when cut. It was used by the Romans for water pipes and repairs to other metals, for example bronze. More recently, it has been used for garden statues, cisterns, early toys such as soldiers and model ships, seals on documents, drainpipes, roof coverings and coffins. Garden statuary was frequently painted to look like marble, stone or bronze. This paint layer also helped to protect the lead from the atmosphere. An alloy of lead is also used extensively for soldering and repairs as it is very easy to work and has a low melting point.

INSPECTION

Lead is heavier than all other commonly used metals, it is also extremely soft and easy to scratch. Clean lead makes a black mark when rubbed on white paper, tin does not.

Lead is so soft that it cannot sustain its own weight. Most woods, particularly oak and sweet chestnut, are known to be harmful to lead as they give off organic acid fumes which corrode the lead. These fumes can also be given off by materials such as household paint, wood-based boards and cardboard boxes. In a corrosive atmosphere the surface of the lead becomes milky white and if the corrosion continues the object becomes very distorted. The corrosion is white and powdery and expands pushing the lead out of shape.

Most lead sculptures have an iron armature inside to support the weight. Over the years the iron corrodes, expands and disintegrates, and when this happens the statue will begin to collapse under its own weight. The head is likely to loll and the statue can split or may begin to lean alarmingly from the knees or ankles. If this should happen you should send for a metal conservator accustomed to dealing with lead. The conservator should replace the original iron armature with one made of stainless steel.

Toy soldiers and early models are becoming very collectable. If they have stood the test of their original owners they are likely to survive quite a lot longer. The original paint will probably be chipped and small parts like guns and horses' legs may be bent. Do not repaint them. It is not advisable to try to straighten the bent bits as they may snap off. Ask a metal conservator for advice. Very often lead soldiers are displayed in a case in regimental or battle formation. If a battle background is to be painted on to the case make sure the paint is on the outside of the glass as the paint may give off corrosive fumes.

HANDLING

As lead bends and dents so easily, be extra careful when handling lead objects. Always pick up a lead sculpture or object by the main part and not by the arms or other projections, even though these may appear to be convenient handles. The weight of the body may cause them to bend or tear off. It is also only too easy to squash or reshape an object. Do not stick self-adhesive tape or labels on to lead either because when they are removed they may pull off some of the protective patina.

Make sure your belt buckle does not scratch or damage an object as you lift it.

After handling lead objects make sure you wash your hands well.

CLEANING

Rare, old and precious objects should only be cleaned by a metal conservator.

Lead objects can be dusted and, if necessary, washed by wiping the surface with cotton wool swabs dampened with warm water containing a few drops of a non-ionic detergent (Synperonic N). Do not use other detergents. Rinse well with clean swabs dampened with clean water and dry with a soft, clean cloth.

Outside statues should be washed at least once a year to remove general grime and bird droppings. Use a soft bristle brush. Never use a nylon brush because it will score the surface. Lead can easily be damaged by over vigorous polishing or scrubbing with a hard brush, so treat it gently.

Once the object is completely dry, apply microcrystalline wax with a soft brush or cloth. Make sure the wax covers the whole surface and there are no patches left exposed. Buff gently with a soft, clean cloth. It is best to apply two coats of wax leaving an hour between each coat.

If the object has spots of severe corrosion seek advice from a metal conservator. It is important to check that the storage or display conditions are not causing the corrosion. Move the object if they are.

Always wash your hands well after cleaning a lead statue and never eat or drink while you are working on the object.

DISPLAY

Lead objects can be displayed almost anywhere, except they must not get too hot nor must they be near oak, cardboard, chipboard or vinegar. Do not put lead objects back into a room that has been newly decorated as the paint fumes can attack the surface. If the objects are displayed in a case it should be made of glass or perspex and metal and never of painted wood, oak, plywood or chipboard. These, including the paint, give off fumes which will corrode the lead. If lead objects are displayed on shelves, the shelves should be glass, perspex or metal for the same reasons.

Do not place large lead objects directly on to a stone or brick floor, put them on wooden slats or polythene.

Lead urns, particularly those which were intended to have plants in them, have a drainage hole in the bottom. Check that this is not blocked and that the water can run out freely. Urns that are going to be planted should always have fibreglass liners to prevent the earth from reacting with the lead and causing corrosion. The liners must have drainage holes. Check that the weight of the soil does not cause the urn to twist, buckle or split. A conservator specializing in lead will be needed for any repairs.

If using lead water cisterns for plants, make sure they are raised off the ground. Make a bed of flat stones, such as paving stones from a garden centre, ensuring that the gaps between the stones are small enough (max 2cms, ¾in) to prevent the lead from sagging into them. If the cistern is to be planted it must have good drainage holes so that the water does not collect in the bottom. Line the cistern with a fibreglass liner which is about 5 cms (two inches) smaller than the internal measurements of the cistern, this must also have good drainage holes.

Do not display outdoor statuary under trees because they will be scratched and become streaky as described in Bronze. Make sure the plinths are level so that the weight is evenly distributed and there will not be undue strain on weak areas. *See Bronze Display.*

STORAGE

Small objects should be wrapped in acid-free tissue and placed in a dry

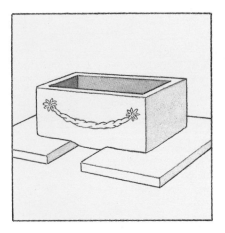

When a lead cistern is placed on a bed of flat stones make sure the gaps between the stones are small enough to prevent the lead from sagging

area. Never place objects in oak drawers or cupboards or boxes made of chipboard, cardboard, block board or plywood as they give off corrosive fumes. Store the objects in polythene boxes with perforated lids, to allow air circulation, or acid-free carboard boxes. Do not put too many objects in a box or pack the box so tightly that the objects get squashed. Use plenty of packing.

If outside lead objects are to be stored, say over winter, place them in as dry an area as possible, free from frost. Lead statues should not be laid down as the weight may squash an arm or knee. Do not stand lead objects directly on to stone, concrete or brick floors. Place them on wooden slats, cork or polythene sheeting.

If you wish to protect lead sculpture which is outside during the winter, cover it with polythene in which you have cut a number of holes to allow the air to circulate. Condensation will form inside sealed polythene which could cause more damage than leaving the object open to the elements.

IDEAL CONDITIONS

Household: Normal household conditions. Avoid hot areas.
Exhibition: Relative humidity 50–55 per cent. Temperature about 18°C (65°F)
  Light levels not critical. Do not use wooden showcases.
Storage: Relative humidity 45–50 per cent. Temperature about 18°C (65°F).
  Light levels not critical. Avoid wooden storage areas or cardboard boxes.

REPAIR

Do not attempt to repair lead. Adhesives can cause a lot of harmful corrosion and soldering should only be carried out by a metal conservator.

ORMOLU

Ormolu was used to make decorative objects and particularly mounts on furniture, ceramics, glass and clocks. The base metal is usually cast brass or bronze which is chased and covered with a thin layer of gold. Mounts of a similar appearance were made from bronze and dipped in acid, which made the surface gold coloured, and then lacquered, sometimes with a tinted lacquer. There are other inferior mounts which are made of gilded spelter which is an alloy of zinc and lead. These are much more brittle and will break easily. The gilding is also less well attached.

INSPECTION

If the gilding on true ormolu is worn through, the base metal will be the golden-brown colour of tarnished bronze or brass. If the ormolu is made of spelter the base metal will be grey. On spelter-based mounts there may be tiny pimples breaking through the gilding causing white or black discolouration. This never happens on true ormolu mounts. It is very difficult to differentiate between good quality lacquered bronze mounts and true ormolu.

Check that all fixing pins and screws are secure and not working loose.

HANDLING

Handle ormolu as you would brass and bronze but remember that the gilding is very thin and that the more you handle it the faster the gold will wear away.

CLEANING

The surface of ormolu is fragile as the gold is very thin. The coloured lacquer on bronze mounts is also thin and scratches easily. Ormolu should never get wet nor be rubbed or polished. To remove the dust from ormolu, brush with an artist's soft paint brush or a photographer's puffer brush. Ormolu should be dusted as lightly as possible and care should be taken not to snag any edges or fixings.

If there is a build up of old polish and dirt in the detail of true ormolu it can be removed by wrapping a few fibres of cotton wool around the end of a cocktail stick and moistening them with white spirit. Gently push along the crevice in one direction turning the stick as you go. Discard the swab when it is dirty. If it is a lacquered bronze mount you could try to pick out some of the build up with a dry cocktail stick. Do not scratch the lacquer or use white spirit which could dissolve the lacquer.

Do not allow candle wax to run down ormolu candlesticks. Protect them by placing plastic or glass wax-catchers on the candle holder. Any wax which does get on the ormolu is easier to remove when it is cold as it is more brittle, see Brass. Remove as much as you can with your fingernail and then wipe the surface with a swab of cotton wool dampened with white spirit to remove the rest. If the candlestick is not true ormolu removing the wax may also remove the lacquer. If the lacquer appears to be coming off leave well alone. Take care not to scratch the surface.

The gilding on ormolu will often have worn through on the raised areas of the mounts. This should never be retouched or regilded.

Other gold-plated objects should be cleaned in the same way as ormolu. *See also* Silver Gilt.

DISPLAY

Never place plants near ormolu as the dampness caused by watering can make the base metal corrode and discolour. Keep objects with ormolu away from heat or damp, but otherwise display it according to the other materials in the object.

STORAGE

Wrap the object in acid-free tissue and store it in a dry place. Do not allow ormolu to become damp. Make sure that the storage conditions are suitable for any other materials which make up the object.

IDEAL CONDITIONS

See Bronze, Brass and Zinc. Ideally ormolu should be kept dry (relative humidity about 50 per cent), however it is important to consider the other materials it is used with.

REPAIR

All repairs to ormolu should be carried out by a metal conservator or silversmith experienced in this kind of work. Never let anyone use lead solder on ormolu. Once on it is virtually impossible to remove.

PEWTER

Pewter is an alloy consisting mainly of tin with some lead. The Romans made pewter and it has been used extensively since the Middle Ages for domestic objects such as plates, tankards, bowls, spoons and candlesticks. The colour of the alloy varies according to the percentage of lead. Cheap, low quality pewter contained a high proportion of lead, was blackish-grey in colour and was dangerous to eat off. Better quality pewter contained copper but no lead and was nearly as bright as silver when polished. Pewter became popular for making Art Noveau objects when it was often used with other materials such as wood and ivory.

Pewter is very soft and is easily dented or scratched.

Old pewter mugs and plates should not be used for drinking out of or eating off because of the lead content.

Modern pewter bears very little resemblance to old pewter. It is a tarnish resistant alloy consisting mainly of tin and antimony. It is used for christening cups, napkin rings, tankards.

INSPECTION

Pewter, because it is alloyed with other metals is somewhat stronger than lead. *See* Lead.

HANDLING

Pewter bends, dents and scratches easily so be extra careful when handling it and putting it down. Do not bang pewter objects against a hard surface or stick self-adhesive tape or labels on to old pewter because when they are removed they can pull off some of the patina.

CLEANING

Do not clean any rare, old or precious pewter objects. These should be cleaned by a metal conservator.

Modern pewter should be dusted when necessary and occasionally washed in warm soapy water to remove any slight darkening or fingerprints. Rinse in clean water and dry with a soft, clean cloth.

Pewter in Art Deco and Art Nouveau objects is often used in conjunction with other materials such as ivory and should not therefore be immersed in water. The pewter on these objects can be cleaned with a cotton wool bud dipped in warm water containing a few drops of a non-ionic detergent (Synperonic N) or a mild household detergent (Fairy Liqid). Rinse with clean buds and water and dry thoroughly.

Old pewter should not be given a high polish but should have a dull gleam.

Normally, old pewter only needs dusting with a soft, dry cloth or chamois leather. If the surface is stained or dead you can improve the appearance by rubbing it with a mild abrasive. Use a rag impregnated with a light (3-in-1) oil and talc or some other very fine abrasive such as whiting. Polish gently over the surface

opposite Do not allow trees and bushes to grow too close to a lead sculpture

above Better quality pewter can be nearly as bright as silver when polished

of the pewter with a circular movement and wipe off with a clean soft cloth. Remove any remaining oil and talc with cotton wool swabs moistened with methylated spirits. Finally wash the pewter in warm, soapy water, rinse in clean water and dry with a soft clean cloth.

Some old pewter may have wart-like growths on the surface. If these spots have a hard skin and do not have any white powdery corrosion round them it is safest to leave them alone. Do not be tempted to grind them off. If a white powder should appear in small spots or the surface shows any sign of flaking consult a metal conservator.

DISPLAY

Do not put pewter back into a room immediately after it has been decorated as the paint fumes can attack the surface. The main problems for pewter are caused by its lead content, therefore for display conditions *see* Lead. Although oak is not good for lead, pewter can be displayed on oak furniture if there is a good circulation of air round it. Do not store pewter in oak furniture.

STORAGE

Wrap the pieces individually in acid-free tissue to protect them from physical damage. Do not put too many pewter objects in too small a box or container or else the pewter will dent. Avoid organic acid fumes. *See* Storage, Lead.

IDEAL CONDITIONS

Household: Normal household conditions

Exhibition: Relative humidity 50–55 per cent. Temperature about 18°C (65°F).

Light levels not critical. Do not use wooden show cases.

Storage: Relative humidity 45–50 per cent. Temperature about 18°C (65°F).

Light levels not critical. Avoid wooden storage areas or cardboard boxes.

REPAIR

Do not attempt to repair pewter. Adhesives can cause a lot of harmful corrosion and soldering should only be carried out by a metal conservator.

BIDRI WARE

Bidri ware is made mainly at Bidar near Hyderabad in India. The base metal is a type of pewter made of tin, zinc, copper, lead and occasionally iron, which is inlayed with silver and gold. The surface of the base metal is usually blackened so that the inlay shows up dramatically. Bidri ware can be very ornate and show a high degree of craftsmanship. It is usually used for hookah bases, trays, boxes.

Objects made from bidri should not be vigorously polished or the black surface will come off. Brush off the dust and wash the object in warm water containing a few drops of a non-ionic detergent (Synperonic N) or a mild household detergent (Fairy Liquid). If the object cannot be immersed in water, clean it using cotton wool swabs dipped in the soap solution. Rinse it with clean water and dry well with a soft cloth. Use a hair-dryer set on *Cool* to make sure it is

completely dry.

If the silver is tarnished it can be cleaned using a mild abrasive chrome cleaner (Solvol Autosol) applied on a few fibres of cotton wool wrapped around a cocktail stick. Do not get the polish on the other metal and wash it off well with water or white spirit. Most silver cleaners are more liquid than the chrome cleaner and so are more likely to get on to the other metal or to leave a powdery deposit in the depths.

Occasionally, rust spots can occur on the surface of a bidri object. This is most probably caused by the corrosion of iron casting pins that have been left in the object. If there are any spots of rust on the surface of the object carefully scrape them off with a sharp knife or blunt scalpel blade held nearly parallel to the surface. Take care not to scratch the metal. A little rust remove (Jenolite or Modolene) carefully applied on a few fibres of cotton wool wrapped around a cocktail stick and well washed off may help remove the rust (*see* Iron). Dry the object well.

Do not try to clean very corroded metal which has wart-like growths or green spots as if you remove them the corrosion may get worse. The object should be treated by a metal conservator.

Lightly wax the cleaned bidri object with microcrystalline wax to help protect the silver from tarnishing and to generally improve the appearance. Handle, display and store bidri ware as for Pewter.

SILVER

Silver is a soft, white, precious metal which has been used since about 3000 BC. It is too soft to use alone and so is alloyed with at least one other metal, usually copper. English Sterling Silver contains about 92.5 per cent silver.

Silver has been widely used over the centuries to make household and religious objects which can vary in size from thimbles and plates to large candelabra and even altar frontals and furniture. Silver may be decorated by engraving and embossing, precious stones can be set into it and enamels applied to the surface. Silver can also be used as a thin coat on a base metal and to decorate glass and ceramics. It can be beaten into silver leaf to decorate picture frames, statues,

leather and similar materials and is frequently used as an inlay to embellish wood or other metals or can itself be inlaid with other materials.

INSPECTION

Check the object for any joins that have come apart, loose pieces or similar physical damage. Check that pins securing the handles of teapots and jugs are not working loose. A good time to check the condition of silver objects is when you are getting ready to clean them. Any parts of an object which are have broken off can easily be lost. They should be kept in a safe place until the object can be restored.

Silver tarnishes very easily. The tanish is silver sulphide which appears first as a yellow film. The film soon becomes brown, eventually purple and then black when it is quite thick. The tarnish is caused by sulphur compounds such as hydrogen sulphide or sulphur dioxide in the atmosphere. These gases are in the air from industrial pollution, household coal and gas fires and other sources. Sulphur-containing compounds can also be found in some textiles, paints and rubber compounds, so surprising things such as household paints, vulcanised rubber flooring and draught excluders can make silver go black. Eggs, brussel sprouts, vinegar and salt also tarnish and corrode silver so they should be washed off cutlery as soon as possible.

Silver containing a large proportion of copper, either as an alloy or as a base metal for silver plate, may form green copper corrosion products, particularly if it is stored in damp conditions.

A silver object decorated with other materials such as gems, paint or inlay must be examined to make sure the gems are secure and the paint or inlay are not coming away from the metal.

If silver is used in conjunction with another material such as in figurines made of silver and ivory, check the condition of all the materials.

HANDLING

In the past, butlers used to wear cotton gloves when they were polishing and handling silver. There is a very good reason for this. The acids and oils in the skin are left on the surface of the silver when it is touched with bare hands. These acids and oils encourage tarnishing to begin and to accelerate. Once display silver has been cleaned and polished try to wear clean cotton gloves when handling it.

Silver is a soft metal that is easily scratched and dented by careless handling. Do not pick up silver objects by any protruding decoration. Always use two hands when carrying an object; place one under the base to take the weight and with the other support the object about two-thirds of the way up. Take care that your belt buckle or shirt buttons do not scratch the silver.

Carry candlesticks so that the weight is supported from underneath. Many candlesticks are not made of solid metal, but have a core of rosin or Plaster of Paris and they are not therefore very strong. Handle them very carefully. Do not set them down hard on the table as the core can crack and the silver may break at the waist. When putting candles into branched candlesticks support the sconce by placing your hand under it.

Do not leave tea, coffe, mustard pots or any other objects with hinged lids upside down on the draining board with the lid open after you have rinsed them out. This puts all the weight on the hinge and will eventually tear it out.

CLEANING

Rare, old or precious silver objects should only be cleaned by a metal conservator.

Before any cleaning is carried out the piece should be examined for delicate engraved or etched decoration, niello or other deliberate colouring.

Engraving and etching can be softened and worn away with polishing. To check if a heavily tarnished object is decorated in this manner hold it in the light and move it slowly around. Patterns can be seen against the reflection of the light.

Modern silver is sometimes deliberately coloured by the manufacturer, this could be an overall colour or colours, or a blackening in the depths to emphasize relief decoration. This is found particularly on modern jewellery. Modern coloured surfaces are not easy to detect but colour applied during manufacture is often harder to remove than ordinary tarnish. If you are cleaning a modern piece of silver

do not remove any stubborn marks unless you are certain that they are not part of the decoration.

Niello (*see* Niello) can easily be removed when cleaning a tarnished object, so examine the object carefully for niello first.

Before cleaning a silver object check it for tears, breaks and broken pieces as if they are caught by the polishing cloth further damage can be done.

Each time a silver object is cleaned and a layer of tarnish is removed, a small amount of silver is also removed. Eventually, the silver will wear away. If the object is too frequently or too harshly polished the silver will wear away faster. Careful handling and storage can help to reduce the amount of cleaning necessary. Modern silver cleaning materials also help slow the rate at which silver tarnishes. You should clean silver only when it actually needs it, not as a matter of course.

If the silver is combined with other materials, for instance wood in cigarette boxes, you must be careful that the cleaning substances you use on the silver do not harm the other materials.

Before cleaning silver, always cover the table, including the edge, with a soft towel or blanket so that the object is not dented or scratched by the table.

Remove any dust and grime before polishing a silver object as it can scratch the silver. Use a soft linen cloth, a Long Term Silver cloth, an artist's soft brush or photographer's puffer brush to flick off the dust. If the object is very dusty wash it in warm water with a few drops of a non-ionic detergent (Synperonic N) or a

When cleaning a silver object do not put undue pressure on any area. Support each area with your other hand

Materials used for cleaning silver

mild household detergent (Fairy Liquid). Rinse the object well in warm water and dry thoroughly with paper towels, a soft dust-free cloth or an *old* tea towel – new tea towels contain a dressing which make them stiff enough to scratch the silver.

Take care when you are cleaning and polishing a thin silver object that you do not put undue pressure on any area as the silver will gradually cave in. Support each area with your other hand as you clean.

LIGHTLY TARNISHED SILVER
If the silver needs a little more cleaning use Long Term Silver Foam which is a cleaning agent with a mild abrasive and is supplied with a sponge. Follow the manufacturer's directions carefully. Rinse off well in warm water. Dry and polish with a soft cloth.

If the silver is to be stored after cleaning it is a good idea to leave the object in a warm place for at least two hours to make sure it is completely dry before wrapping it for store.

TARNISHED SILVER
To clean very tanished silver use Silver Dip as it does not cause the silver to be worn away as fast as polishing with

an abrasive polish. Wear rubber gloves as it may cause skin irritation. It may also stain stainless steel surfaces if it is spilt. Silver Dip is supplied in a wide necked jar so that cutlery and jewellery and other small objects can be dipped directly into the jar. However, it is better not to do so because if the Dip is used too often it becomes stale and starts to deposit silver back on to the surface of the object. The deposited silver has a different texture and colour and looks unpleasant. It is *very* difficult to remove.

If you are cleaning one or two small silver objects it is not the end of the world if you dip them straight into the jar but when you are cleaning a number of pieces at once pour a small amount of Dip into another container and use the Dip in the second container. Throw the Dip away once you have finished cleaning your objects. Keeping Silver Dip for too long is a false economy.

Keep the objects in the Dip for as little time as possible, just as long as it takes for the tarnish to be removed. (It sometimes helps to move the objects about in the Dip). Take the objects out of the Dip and put them in a bowl of warm water containing some mild household detergent (Fairy Liquid). When you have finished dipping all the objects make sure you wash the Dip off thoroughly in the warm soapy water. Rinse the objects in clean warm water and dry them well. Polish them with a soft cloth. Do not use Silver Dip too frequently on plated cutlery as the silver layer will eventually disappear.

LARGER OBJECTS
Larger objects which will not fit into the jar should be cleaned by applying the Dip on cotton wool swabs or buds. Wear rubber gloves. Moisten the swabs with the Dip and work over the object with a circular movement to help the surface clean evenly. Do not allow the Silver Dip to stay on the surface for very long. Rinse it off with swabs of cotton wool dampened with clean water. Make sure you rinse the Dip off thoroughly and dry the object with paper towels or a soft linen cloth. If the piece is very large clean and rinse one small area before moving onto the next area.

DECORATED OBJECTS
Silver is frequently decorated with enamel or gem stones or other applied decoration. These objects should not get wet and should not be cleaned by immersing them in water or other solutions. However, the silver can be cleaned by using Silver Dip on a cotton wool bud and rinsing it off with a clean bud and water. Use the buds almost dry and make sure that neither the Dip nor the water gets under the decoration.

When the object has been cleaned, washed and dried, it can be lightly buffed up with a Long Term Silver Cloth.

FOR ADDED GLEAM
If you feel the silver has not enough gleam or if you prefer to polish silver, Long Term Silver Polish is preferable to a coarser metal polish. Apply the polish with a soft cloth and when it is dry polish it off with a clean, soft cloth. Wear rubber gloves. Make sure all the polish is removed, particularly from the crevices. A soft silver polishing bristle brush (plate brush) is very useful for finally polishing silver and removing any polish from the crevices.

ENGRAVED, EMBOSSED AND RAISED DECORATION
Silver objects with engraved, embossed or raised decoration should be cleaned with Long Term Silver Dip or Long Term Silver Foam. The foam can be applied using a soft bristle brush such as an artist's hogshair paint brush. Never use a nylon brush as the bristles have sharp edges. If you brush the raised decoration too harshly the top surface will gradually be worn away. Keep this brush for cleaning silver only, as any grit or debris left from other uses can be harmful.

If you prefer to use Silver Dip for cleaning these decorated silver objects, apply it using a cotton wool bud. If there is very stubborn dirt and tarnish in the depths of raised decoration it can be removed by using a wooden cocktail stick with a few fibres of cotton wool wrapped round the end dipped in Silver Dip to reach into the decoration. Rinse the Dip off the object well and dry with a clean, soft cloth. Provided the object will not be harmed by being immersed in water it is easier to rinse the Dip off by washing the object in a bowl of warm water.

Often highly decorated pieces have accumulated dirt and polish left in the decoration. You may want to leave it as it can be part of the attraction of the piece, but if it obscures the decoration it can be removed. Use a wooden cocktail stick with a few fibres of cotton wool wrapped around it and dampened with Silver Dip as described above. Make sure you rinse the Silver Dip off well.

Very stubborn deposits can be removed by using a mixture of methylated spirits and a few drops of ammonia (2–3 drops of ammonia in an egg cup of methylated spirits). Apply the solution using a wooden cocktail stick with a few fibres of cotton wool wrapped around it or on a cotton bud. Rinse the object well and dry it. As a last resort, carefully pick out thick deposits with a wooden cocktail stick, never use a metal point. Do not use this solution on silverplated objects as the ammonia can dissolve the copper.

Some books suggest cleaning silver electrochemically using an aluminium sheet of milk bottle tops. This is not a good method of cleaning silver as it removes more silver than is necessary and the process can be detrimental to the object. With modern cleaning materials there is no need to use this method.

LACQUERING
Silver can be protected from tarnishing by applying a coat of clear lacquer. The usual lacquer for silver is a cellulose nitrate based lacquer (Frigilene). Do not use polyurethane lacquers. The protection of lacquer does not last indefinitely but, if the surface is well prepared, the lacquer is well applied and the lacquer coating is not scratched or damaged, the silver should not tarnish for several years. Dust the object regularly to avoid a build up of dust and dirt.

Lacquer is particularly useful for protecting Sheffield plate, silver plate and silver plaques with light engraving which can be worn away by frequent polishing. However, lacquer does slightly reduce the shine and brilliance.

Do not use Long Term silver cleaning products before lacquering an object. They leave a tarnish inhibiting deposit on the surface of the silver which may stop the lacquer working effectively. Polish the silver with an ordinary silver polish (Silverglit or Silvo) or a mild abrasive chrome cleaner (Solvol Autosol).

After cleaning the object well, wash

off all traces of polish in warm soapy water, rinse it in clean water and dry. Leave the object in a warm area to dry thoroughly.

Degrease the surface by wiping it with cotton wool moistened with acetone or methylated spirits. Make sure all the fibres from the cotton wool are removed. Be sure that your bare hands do not touch the silver surface.

If you have an icing or pottery turntable available, it will make lacquering much easier as you can turn the table not the object. Make sure the turntable is clean.

For a lacquer to be effective it must be applied very carefully. Two thin coatings are much stronger than one thick one. The lacquer may be applied by brushing, dipping or spraying. Brushing is the most commonly used method as it is the most convenient.

APPLICATION OF LACQUER WITH A BRUSH

Use a soft, fairly thick, clean brush, preferably made of split bristles, camel or badger hair.

Ideally, the lacquer should be about the consistency of 3-in-1 oil. It should be thin enough to prevent it collecting in a thick film in the hollows as this catches the light and gives an unnatural shine. If necessary, thin the lacquer with a reducer supplied by the manufactuers of the lacquer. Do not make the lacquer too thin or the lacquer surface will have rainbow colours in it.

Work quickly in a warm, dust-free, well-ventilated room. For good coating the room should be 15°–20°C, (59°–68°F) and the relative humidity not higher than 70–75 per cent. Try not to paint the same area twice. Stipple the lacquer into the depths but do not let too much settle in them.

Allow the lacquer to dry completely before applying the next coat, ideally about twenty-four hours. Two coats should be applied.

APPLICATION OF LACQUER BY SPRAYING

If you have an air-brush you can spray on the lacquer. However, it is difficult to apply it well and evenly if you are not used to handling an air-brush. The solvents in the spray are likely to affect the first coat. Lacquers in aerosol cans are not good as the spray is uneven and not very fine.

APPLICATION OF LACQUER BY DIPPING

Small objects can be dipped into the lacquer and left to drain. The disadvantage of this method is that you often get a 'fat edge'. This is when the lower edges acquire a thick layer of lacquer during draining. Drops or tears also form. You can avoid this happening by lifting the object out of the lacquer more slowly than the rate at which the lacquer runs off. If you are dipping an object, one coat will probably be enough. Hold the object with polythene tweezers as they will not scratch the object nor dissolve in the lacquer or hang it by some cotton thread. Leave the object to dry on silicone or greaseproof paper so that it will not stick to the surface of the table.

If the lacquer coating is scratched or damaged the exposed areas of silver will tarnish rapidly and the silver cannot be cleaned without first removing all the lacquer.

TO REMOVE LACQUER

To take the lacquer off small silver objects dip them into acetone until all the lacquer is dissolved. Pour the acetone into a suitable sized glass or

metal container. It helps the lacquer to dissolve faster if you move the object around in the acetone. Do not put your fingers into the liquid. Acetone is flammable and is toxic in large quantities so it must be used in a well-ventilated room with no naked flames nearby. Remove the object from the acetone. Wipe the surface with clean swabs of cotton wool and clean acetone to remove the final traces of the lacquer.

Larger objects or those made of several materials should be cleaned by wiping the surface with swabs of cotton wool and acetone. Use each side of the swabs and discard them into a lidded container as soon as they become sticky. This prevents the acetone from continuing to evaporate into the room. When you have finished put the container outside with the lid off and allow all the acetone to evaporate. Finally put it in the dustbin. Wear rubber gloves.

Make sure all the lacquer is removed. Then clean, degrease and lacquer the object as described above.

DISPLAY

Place silver objects far enough back on tables and sideboards so that they cannot be knocked off on to a hard floor. Do not leave objects in view of the window where they will act as temptation for burglars. Coal and gas fires give off sulphurous fumes which tarnish silver, so if possible avoid rooms which have open fires. Objects on mantelpieces or above radiators can quickly be covered in a layer of soot or dust which is carried upwards by the heat. Heat and light can make silver tarnish faster so avoid placing silver in direct sunlight.

DISPLAY CASES

Some materials used in the construction of display cases can cause silver to tarnish quickly. This can continue to happen even after several years. If possible, check the cabinet before displaying a lot of silver in it. You can do this by cleaning two similar silver objects, such as two pieces of cutlery, in the same way. Then place one inside the cabinet and leave one in the room. If the one in the cabinet tarnishes faster you know that the cabinet is not suitable for displaying silver.

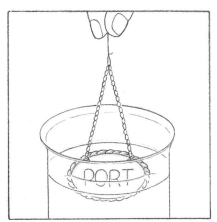

Applying lacquer with a brush

Applying lacquer by dipping

If you are making a new cabinet you can do a similar test to check the fabric with which you want to line it. In this case wrap the objects in the different fabrics and see which tarnishes first or last. Leave one unwrapped piece in the room as a standard.

A well sealed case made from pollution-free materials is the best way to display silver. It is possible to buy products which inhibit silver tarnishing by giving off a vapour. These are usually in capsule form and are placed inside the display case or storage area. However, they can cloud or craze the surface of perspex and may affect copper objects. If you use these always follow the manufacturer's instructions carefully.

STORAGE

If the silver is stored in conjunction with other materials such as wood or ivory, the storage conditions should suit the most sensitive material.

Silver objects should be stored in a clean, cool, dry, dark, well-ventilated, safe place, preferably not the airing cupboard, boiler room, attic or loft area. They should be wrapped in acid-free tissue to protect them from physical damage and tarnishing and then placed in perforated polythene bags. Either use ordinary polythene bags and make holes with a knitting needle or scissors, or use polythene food bags which are made with holes in them. Do not wrap silver in cling film or sealed polythene bags as condensation can form inside and may cause tarnishing or even the corrosion of other metals present, for instance the corrosion of copper in silver-plated objects.

Store silver wrapped in acid-free tissue inside a perforated polythene bag

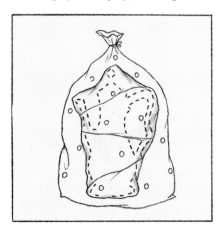

In the past, chamois leather, baize or felt were used to wrap silver. It is better not to use these materials as they give off sulphur compounds which tarnish the silver. It is now possible to buy cloth bags, wraps and roll ups (Tarnprufe) impregnated with a tarnish inhibitor. These not only protect silver from tarnishing but also against physical damage. They are most effective when totally surrounding the silver. The impregnated cloth becomes less effective as the chemicals are used up, but appears to have a life of at least ten years. This material should not be in direct contact with lead and pewter objects.

Silver can be stored in a box or trunk, but make sure that the weight of the objects does not squash those at the bottom. Put enough tissue as extra padding to prevent any dents or scratches.

IDEAL CONDITIONS

Household: Normal household conditions, avoid direct sunlight, open fires and other situations with tarnishing fumes.
Exhibition: Relative humidity 50–55 per cent. Temperature about 18°C (65°F). Avoid bright lights. Avoid tarnish inducing materials. Archaeological silver relative humidity 40–45 per cent).
Storage: Relative humidity 45–50 per cent. Temperature max. 15°C (59°F) Low light/dark. Avoid tarnish inducing materials. Archaeological silver relative humidity 40–45 per cent).

REPAIR

To repair silver well is a difficult and skilled job so unless you are very experienced at this sort of work do not attempt to solder pieces together yourself. *Never, ever* use lead solder on a piece of silver, use silver solder. Lead solder runs very easily over the surface and is virtually impossible to remove. It also makes future restoration particularly difficult. Silver objects should be restored by a qualified silversmith or a metal conservator.

Should you ever need to stick a loose piece back on to an object, wherever possible use an easily reversible adhesive (HMG or UHU All Purpose Clear Adhesive). These are often strong enough, they will not

harm the silver and are easy to remove when the object comes to be properly restored in the future. If you need extra strength use a quick setting epoxy resin adhesive (UHU Strong Bond or Super Epoxy). These are strong, set quite quickly (5–10 minutes), and are slightly easier to remove than a stronger epoxy resin (Araldite).

ARCHAEOLOGICAL SILVER

Silver that has been buried in the ground is frequently covered in a thick layer of a black, grey or purple waxy corrosion and possibly green copper corrosion products. Archaeological silver can be very fragile and brittle and should be handled with the utmost care. It must be cleaned by a conservator as the object can easily be ruined completely by an untrained person.

Store archaeological silver in a plastic box with a bed of acid-free tissue to protect it from physical damage.

NIELLO

Niello is a black mixture of silver, copper, lead and sulphur, fused with heat into incised decoration on the silver. It is frequently used to decorate silver objects such as jewellery and other decorative objects, particularly those made in India and the Far East.

Niello is difficult to detect on heavily tarnished silver as it is the same colour as the tarnish, but it does have a different surface texture. It is usually less reflective than tarnished silver and a denser colour.

CLEANING
Silver Dip should never be used on objects decorated with niello as the Dip will remove the niello in the same way as it removes the tarnish. If you think the object may be decorated with niello only use Long Term Silver Polish. The niello will begin to appear as you polish the surface as it cannot be removed as easily as tarnish. Take care not to polish any thin layers of niello away.

SILVER BASED ENAMEL

Cleaning the silver around enamel decoration is not easy as the enamel or the silver base can be damaged or stained by silver cleaning agents. If possible, polish the silver with a soft cloth, or even your finger, followed by a soft cloth. If polishing with a cloth does not clean the silver enough, use a few fibres of cotton wool wound round a wooden cocktail stick moistened with Silver Dip. Any excess solution can be absorbed on to a paper towel. Carefully clean the silver making sure you do not wet the surrounding surface. Wipe off the solution with a few clean fibres of cotton wool on a cocktail stick barely dampened with water. Dry the silver by rubbing over it with a cotton bud. It is essential that neither the Dip nor the water penetrate under the enamel.

SILVER INLAY

Silver is frequently used as an inlay to decorate wood, iron, brass, ivory, lacquer and other materials. Cleaning silver inlay is not easy as the surrounding material can be damaged or stained by silver cleaning agents. If possible, polish the silver with a soft cloth, or even your finger, followed by a soft cloth. Take care not to catch and lift any pieces of inlay which may be loose and proud of the surface. Where possible stick them down before cleaning (see Repair). If polishing the inlay with a cloth does not clean it enough use Silver Dip applied with a few fibres of cotton wool wound round a wooden cocktail stick as described in Silver Based Enamel.

Never use any metal polish as if this is allowed to get on to the surrounding material it will remain as a whitish powder and is virtually impossible to remove.

A thin coating of microcrystalline wax will help protect the silver from tarnishing.

REPAIRS
If the inlay is springing up from the ground material it can sometimes be replaced in position. Carefully clean out the old adhesive from the channel by using a wooden stick or needle but do not scratch the surround. Then degrease the underside of the inlay and, if possible, the channel. Moisten a few fibres of cotton wool wound round the end of a cocktail stick with acetone or methylated spirits. Take care not to get the solvent on the surrounding material.

Using a cocktail stick, place a very

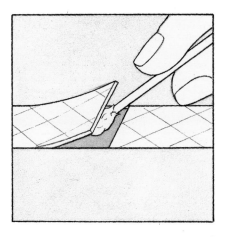

Degrease the underside of the inlay and the channel using a small swab

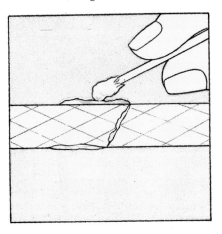

If any adhesive squeezes out wipe it off with a dry cotton wool bud

small amount of easily reversible adhesive (HMG or UHU All Purpose Clear Adhesive) in the channel. Too much adhesive will squelch all over the surface when you replace the inlay. If any is squeezed out, wipe it off with a dry cotton wool bud. The inlay then needs to be held in position until the adhesive dries. Lay some silicone paper over the inlay. Place an appropriate piece of thin board over the paper to protect the surface of the object and weigh the inlay down with a suitable size weight until the adhesive hardens completely, about twenty-four hours.

If, because of the shape of the object, it is not possible to use a weight, the inlay can be held in place by using some G-clamps or elastic bands to hold the board hard against the surface. Always use some board or cushioning under both ends of the G-clamp otherwise it will leave an impression on the object. The ends of the G-clamps can be cushioned by

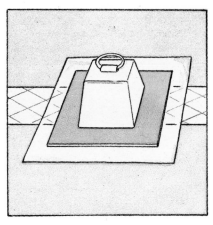

Cover the inlay with silicone paper and piece of thick board and weigh it down

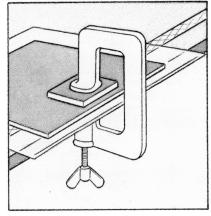

If it is not possible to use a weight, use a G-clamp

using double-sided adhesive pads. Stick one side of the pad to the G-clamp and leave the other with its protective cover on.

SHEFFIELD PLATE

Sheffield plate was produced from about 1740 until 1840. It was made by fusing silver on to a copper base and then rolling it into a thin sheet. When it was first used the copper base was silvered on both sides. It was used mainly for making candlesticks, coffee pots, biscuit barrels and other domestic items. Ribbons of solid silver wire were applied to the places most likely to wear through such as the rims and edges.

The coating of silver is very thin and will eventually wear away, exposing the copper underneath. Sheffield plate should therefore be polished as little as possible, or even better, not at all. Wash it in warm water containing a few drops of a non-ionic detergent

(Synperonic N) or a mild household detergent (Fairy Liquid), taking care not to allow the soapy water to soak into the inside of candlesticks and other hollow areas. If necessary, do not immerse the objects but use cotton wool swabs. Rinse thoroughly and dry with a soft cloth. They can then be buffed with a Long Term Silver Cloth. If Sheffield plate is very tarnished, clean it with Silver Dip on a cotton wool swab as described for Silver and wash well. Buff it with a Long Term Silver Cloth.

The solid silver wire applied to the rims and edges sometimes lifts and it is very easy to catch it with a cloth. This can tear the wire off which is extremely difficult to re-lay. You should therefore take very great care when drying and polishing the edges.

Sheffield plate benefits from being lacquered as it very much reduces the amount of polishing necessary. *See* Lacquering. Do not use Long Term Cleaning products if you intend to lacquer the object.

Worn Sheffield plate should not be replated. Nowadays, the silver is deposited on to the copper using an alternative technique which causes it to be a different colour.

SILVER GILT

Silver gilt is silver covered with a thin coating of gold. It is used to cover the inside of bowls, tumblers and salt cellars and to make wine labels, jewellery and other decorative items. It is also used to highlight decoration.

The gold itself does not tarnish and it will help protect the silver from tarnishing. Occasionally, the silver will tarnish through the gold. This tarnish has a petrol-like appearance rather than the black tarnish found on silver.

Ideally silver gilt should never be cleaned with any sort of metal polish or Silver Dip because these wear away the gold. Wash silver gilt objects in warm water containing a few drops of a non-ionic detergent (Synperonic N) or a mild household detergent (Fairy Liquid). Rinse thoroughly and dry with a soft cloth.

If you have a silver gilt object with silver tarnish on it which does not come off with washing and you are unable to take it to a conservator, clean it very carefully with Silver Dip on a cotton wool swab or bud as described in Silver. Do not rub the surface. Rinse the object very well in clean warm water and dry it with a soft, clean cloth.

Sometimes, the gilding will have worn off parts of the silver. Do not regild the object. The methods used now for depositing gold on the surface are different from the original mercury gilding which is now illegal unless the gilder has all the right equipment. The gold will be a different colour and texture.

SILVER LEAF

Silver leaf is used to decorate objects in the same way as gold leaf. It can be found on carved mirrors and picture frames, wooden furniture and leather hangings. Frequently it was coated with a layer of tinted varnish in order to make it look like gold.

Exposed silver leaf tarnishes extremely quickly and is difficult to clean because the leaf is so thin that it rubs through very easily. *See* Gold Leaf for cleaning.

Silver leaf on objects can be replaced where it is worn through, but this should be carried out by a gilder as it is not at all easy.

Sometimes, silver leaf is mistaken for aluminium leaf which has been used more recently in place of silver leaf as it takes longer to tarnish. This has a bluer colour and a more grainy texture.

For handling, cleaning, display and storage *see* Gold Leaf.

SILVER PLATE AND ELECTROPLATE

Silver plate or electroplate is made by depositing a thin layer of silver electrolytically on to a base metal such as brass, bronze, nickel silver or Britannia metal. Nickel silver is an alloy of copper, nickel and zinc and is almost silver in colour. Britannia metal is an alloy of tin and antimony. As the base metal is often silver coloured it is not always easy to tell when the silver is worn away. Electroplated silver has been produced since the 1840s. It is often stamped EPNS (Electroplated Nickel Silver) or EPBM (Electroplated Britannia Metal). It tarnishes more easily than Sterling Silver and should be stored and protected carefully.

The coating of silver is even thinner than that on Sheffield plate and is therefore easily worn away. For cleaning *see* Sheffield plate.

Like Sheffield plate, electroplate is a good candidate for lacquering.

Modern silver plate, particularly cutlery, can be replated when worn through. Replating early EPNS or other plated silver may affect its value, however.

SILVER ON PORCELAIN AND GLASS

Silver was occasionally used to decorate porcelain and glass in a similar way to gold by means of a very thin layer being fired into the glaze. Once the silver has tarnished it is not usually possible to bring back the silver appearance. If the layer has worn thin or completely away it is virtually impossible to restore it successfully. Silver or aluminium leaf can be applied but it never has the same sheen as the original silver and usually looks very tatty. The object is better left untouched.

TIN

Tin is a soft, white metal which is normally quite stable although it will react slowly with the atmosphere and the surface will become a dull grey. It has been known since prehistoric times both as the metal itself and as a constituent of alloys such as bronze, brass, pewter and Britannia metal. Plates, mugs, jugs, coins and buttons can all be made from tin and it has been used extensively for coating iron to preserve it from rust, this is known as tinplate (*see* Tinplate). Tin was also used for coating the inside of copper and bronze cooking and eating vessels to prevent the food from reacting with the copper and producing poisonous compounds. In antiquity tin was used as a coating for bronze to make jewellery.

INSPECTION

Tin is much lighter than lead but not as soft and it will not mark a piece of paper as lead will. Small pimples of corrosion can form on tin. Very little can be done about this.

Tin can also suffer from 'tin pest' which occurs at low temperatures. The metal changes its form, turns powdery and breaks up. It is very rare and there is nothing you can do about it at the moment.

HANDLING

Handle objects made from tin carefully so that the protective surface layer is not broken. Take care not to dent or squash them. *See* Pewter.

CLEANING

Rare, old and precious tin objects should only be cleaned by a metal conservator.

If tin jugs, plates or buttons have gone a dull grey colour it is best to leave them alone as the layer protects the tin from further corrosion. Tin objects should be dusted when necessary with a soft dry cloth. If the object looks very grimy it can be washed in warm water containing a few drops of a non-ionic detergent (Synperonic N) or a mild household detergent (Fairy Liquid). Rinse thoroughly in clean water and dry with a soft clean cloth. Never use wire wool or Scotchbrite.

Tinned copper vessels. The layer of tin on copper vessels should be polished with a Long Term Silver Cloth although frequent polishing of any kind will eventually wear away the tin. Do not use the cloth for polishing other metals.

For Display, Storage and Ideal Conditions *see* Pewter.

TINPLATE

Tin has been used extensively for coating iron to preserve it from rust, this is known as tinplate or tinned sheet. Tinplate is used to make toys, such as early cars and trains and money boxes, as well as manufacturers' containers for biscuits, cakes, polishes.

INSPECTION

Objects made from tinplate can have very sharp edges. The paint may chip or peal off or be worn off. If the surface of the tin has broken the iron below will rust, making rust lines and marks.

The layer of tin on the surface on tin sheet is very thin; if this is broken by scratching or denting, the iron base will very quickly rust. As the iron sheet is thin it will bend and dent very easily.

HANDLING

Handle toys and tin containers carefully, do not knock them against each other as this dents the metal and then breaks the seal of the tin or scratches the paint. Once the rust starts it will push through any painted decoration there may be on the surface. Handle tinplate objects as little as possible to prevent the decoration being worn away.

Take care not to cut yourself on the sharp edges.

CLEANING

To clean painted tinplate remove all dust and grit with a photographer's puffer brush or an artist's soft paint brush. Grit will scratch the surface of the paint and the tin layer.

Tins are often very dirty. Clean by washing them in warm water containing a few drops of a non-ionic detergent (Synperonic N) or a mild household detergent (Fairy Liquid). Do not leave the objects to soak in the water. Rinse them in clean warm water and dry them quickly and thoroughly with a paper or a soft clean cloth. Make sure the corners and turned over edges are dry by using a hair dryer set on *Cool*. It is important that the tins should not be wet for long otherwise the iron base will rust. Do not wash tin toys as they are very

The paint on tinplate objects may chip or peel off

hard to dry well and will rust and in addition the paint is likely to come off them. They should only be dusted with an artist's soft paint brush or a photographer's puffer brush.

Tins which are still dirty after washing can be cleaned by wiping the surface with a soft cloth or cotton bud moistened with white spirit. Take care that the white spirit does not remove the paint. Test the paint in a small inconspicuous area first to see that it is not affected by the white spirit. Dry the tin thoroughly with a clean soft cloth. Leave to dry completely.

Wax the object with microcrystalline wax applied with a soft brush or cloth and polish with a soft clean cloth. The wax helps protect the tinplate so make sure it covers the entire surface and no patches are left.

If the object is very rusty some of the rust can be removed by carefully scraping with a blunted scalpel blade held parallel to the surface. Make sure you do not scratch the metal or remove more paint. After removing the rust apply a little rust remover. (Jenolite or Modalene). Using a cocktail stick, wind a very small amount of cotton wool around the end, dip this in the rust remover, removing any excess liquid by dabbing the bud on a paper towel. Apply the remover very carefully to the rusty areas. Do not get liquid on the paint as it may damage it. Mop up any liquid from the surface with a paper towel. The exposed iron should turn a dark grey. Although not as pleasing to look at as the shiny metal colour of tin it will prevent more rust forming. Wax the surface with microcrystalline wax. If rust continues to form repeat the process. It may mean that some areas were left untreated the first time round.

Old, rare and precious toys and tins should not be repainted.

DISPLAY

Display tinplate objects in a dry room, away from places where they may become dirty quickly such as near fires and over radiators. Keep painted objects out of direct sunlight and do not place them where the temperature and humidity fluctuate a lot.

STORAGE

Wrap tinplate objects in acid-free tissue and store them in a cool, dry place. Damp will cause tinplate to rust. Do not put too many objects in one box as they can bend and squash under their own weight.

IDEAL CONDITIONS

Household: Normal household conditions. Keep painted tinplate out of direct sunlight. Tinplate should be kept dry.

Exhibition: Relative humidity 50–55 per cent. Temperature about 18°C (65°F). Avoid bright lights. Badly rusted tinplate should be kept at about 40 per cent relative humidity.

Storage: Relative humidity 45–50 per cent. Temperature max 15°C (59°F). Low light levels.

REPAIR

Tinplate can be repaired with lead solder using a soldering iron. Use a multi-core solder as used in the electronics industry and not a corrosive flux. Clean the edges of the join very carefully before soldering. Make sure the solder does not run over the surface of the object as it is difficult to remove. If the object is painted work from the back and use the minimum heat so as not to damage the painted surface. Do not repair a rare or precious object and do not try to repair any object in this way unless you are already experienced at soldering.

Small breaks can be repaired using an epoxy resin adhesive.

TOLEWARE OR TOLERWARE AND BARGEWARE

Toleware or tolerware is the American name for what in England is normally known as bargeware. The basic material is tinplate covered with a black or green varnish which is then baked on to produce a heat-resistant finish. Toleware is decorated with simple designs often of bunches of gaily coloured flowers, in gold and various colours. It has been produced from the mid-eighteenth century onwards, usually into trays, teapots, coal scuttles, candlesticks and mugs.

DISPLAY

It is particularly important that toleware objects should not be displayed over a fire, radiator or kitchen range as the heat could cause the paint to crack.

Handling, cleaning, storage and repair are as in Tinplate.

ZINC

Zinc has been smelted from about 1730. It is seldom used by itself but is alloyed with copper to make brass and lead to make spelter. Zinc is a hard, bluish-white metal which does not easily tarnish. It is used extensively for galvanising iron to protect it from rusting such as on modern sculpture, water tanks, buckets and liners for coal scuttles.

Zinc alloy is rolled into sheets to make, amongst other things, organ pipes. Zinc sheet, like spelter, forms tiny pimples of corrosion which break through any paint layer causing black or white discolouration.

Galvanised sheet corrodes when the zinc layer is broken and the iron is exposed to the atmosphere and rusts.

HANDLING

Treat galvanised objects carefully so that they are not scratched or dented. Do not scrape the surface or lean sharp objects against them.

Handle painted zinc objects such as organ pipes carefully so that the paint is not damaged, chipped or worn away.

CLEANING

Objects made from galvanised iron can be washed in warm water with a few drops of a mild household detergent (Fairy Liquid). Rinse the object in clean water and dry it well. Make sure the object is completely dry otherwise rust may start in the corners. If necessary, dry it with a fan heater.

Decorated organ pipes must be attended to by a conservator.

See Spelter for display, storage, ideal conditions and repair.

SPELTER

Spelter is the popular name for zinc. Spelter is an alloy of zinc and it usually contains about 3 per cent lead and other impurities. It was used to cast sculpture, clock cases, furniture mounts and other objects which were sold as cheap substitutes for those made of bronze. Spelter was mainly in use in the middle of the nineteenth century and the objects produced were ornate Victoriana. Often beautifully painted, the figures depicted Arab riders, St George and the dragon, nymphs in diaphanous gowns, Victorian interpretations of historical and romantic figures. Spelter is lighter in weight and is a much poor quality metal than bronze.

INSPECTION

People often mistake spelter for bronze. When you scrape the underneath of the base of an object made of spelter, however, the metal will be a greyish-silver colour rather than the golden colour of bronze.

Spelter statues are often poorly gilded and frequently decoratively painted, sometimes in very great detail, whereas bronze statues rarely are. On painted spelter objects tiny pimples of corrosion break through the paint layer causing black or white discolouration. If an unpainted spelter statue is left outside for any length of time it will develop a rough, cokey surface.

There is little that can be done to help spelter once it starts to corrode.

HANDLING

Spelter is a soft, brittle metal, and is usually thinly cast. Figures tend to break at the ankles, arms and similar weak areas. Therefore spelter objects should always be picked up by the most solid areas. Never pick them up by the arms or other protruding areas which could tear off. Carry objects so that the weight is supported from underneath. Make sure your belt buckle does not scratch or damage an object as you lift it.

Do not set spelter objects down very sharply on a hard surface or they may crack or dent.

CLEANING

Indoor sculpture Unpainted spelter sculpture can be cleaned and waxed in the same way as outdoor spelter sculpture, *see* below.

Painted spelter statues should be dusted with a soft, dry cloth. If the object is very dusty use an artist's soft paint brush or a photographer's puffer brush to remove the dust or grit which could damage the painted surface if rubbed into it with a duster.

If the sculpture is still dirty after dusting it may be possible to wash the paint but test the fastness of the paint first in an unobtrusive area. Clean a small area with a cotton wool bud dampened with warm water containing a few drops of a non-ionic detergent (Synperonic N). Do not use household detergent because the chemicals they contain could eventually affect the paint. Test each colour and if any colour at all comes off on to the bud do *not* continue with the washing.

If the paint does not come off during your tests wash the object with cotton wool swabs or buds moistened with the warm soapy water. Work lightly over the surface with circular movements. If the detail on the sculpture is very grimy, agitate the area with an artist's hogshair brush dipped in the cleaning solution. Do not scrub

so hard that you remove the paint. Rinse the sculpture well with clean swabs moistened with warm water and dry it with a soft clean cloth. Do not wax the surface as the wax could affect the paint. Take care that the soft cloth does not catch on any pieces as they could easily be torn off.

Do not attempt to clean painted spelter sculpture if the paint is lifting or to remove any tiny pimples of corrosion breaking through the paint layer. These must be dealt with by a metal conservator.

Gilded spelter objects can be cleaned in the same way but take extra care as the gliding is likely to come off easily. If it does come off, simply dust the sculpture with an artist's soft paint brush.

Outdoor sculpture Old, rare or precious spelter sculpture should only be cleaned by a metal conservator.

Spelter does not survive well in the open air but despite this a number of garden statues are made of it. Regularly remove leaves and debris from any crevices. Outdoor statues should be washed at least once a year to remove general grime and bird droppings. Choose a warm, dry sunny, summer's day. Wash the sculpture with warm water containing a few drops of a non-ionic detergent (Synperonic N) or a mild, household detergent (Fairy Liquid). Lightly scrub the surface using a soft bristle brush, never use a nylon brush as it will score the surface. Spelter can easily be damaged by over vigorous polishing or scrubbing with too hard a brush. Rinse the sculpture with several changes of clean water and dry it with a soft cloth. Allow the object to dry thoroughly.

When the sculpture is completely dry apply microcrystalline wax to protect it. Use a soft bristle stencil brush or toothbrush. Make sure the wax covers the whole surface and there are no patches left exposed, particularly on undersides. Polish the wax with a soft bristle brush or a soft dry cloth. Apply a second coat of wax an hour later.

The appearance of the sculpture can be maintained with regular care, *see* Bronze: Maintenance.

If the condition of a spelter statue

is deteriorating it should be brought indoors as soon as possible. There is very little that can be done to cure it.

DISPLAY

Indoor painted or gilded spelter sculpture should not be placed in direct sunlight, over radiators or close to a fire as the heat and light will affect the paint. Avoid displaying them in damp rooms and rooms where the temperature fluctuates greatly.

Unpainted statues can be displayed almost anywhere indoors, again avoiding damp.

It is better to keep spelter sculpture indoors but if you want to have them outside do not display them under trees, because they will be scratched and become streaky as described in Bronze. Make sure that plinths are level so that the weight is evenly distributed to prevent undue strain on weak areas. *See* Outdoor Bronze.

STORAGE

Spelter should always be stored in a dry, cool place. Wrap small objects in acid-free tissue and store them where they will not get squashed. Ensure that larger spelter objects are protected from being knocked as they break easily. Do not place them directly on to concrete, stone or brick floors as the damp will affect them. Place spelter sculpture on wooden slats, cork or polythene.

IDEAL CONDITIONS

Household: Normal household conditions. Away from direct sun for painted sculpture.

Exhibition: Relative humidity 50–55 per cent. Temperature about 18°C (65°F). Light levels 200 lux for painted sculpture otherwise not critical.

Storage: Relative humidity 45–50 per cent. Temperature about 15°C (59°F). Light levels as Exhibition. Avoid wooden storage areas or cardboard boxes.

REPAIR

Do not attempt to repair or solder spelter, it softens and melts very easily. Small breaks can be repaired using an epoxy resin adhesive (Araldite). Spelter should be repaired by a metal conservator.

COINS AND MEDALS

Coins are made of silver, gold, electrum, copper alloys, tin or tinned bronze, lead, platinum, zinc, iron, aluminium and cupro-nickel. Coins are quite robust and are not affected as much by the environment as are other objects made from the same metal. This is because the shape and the manufacture is very simple.

HANDLING

Always have clean, dry hands when you handle coins and medals and hold them by their edges as acid from your fingers can mark the surface. If you pick a coin up with tweezers use plastic rather than metal ones which will scratch the surface. Coins are often small and valuable and are easily stolen. Photograph your collection so that you have a good record of the coins. You do not have to photograph each coin individually.

CLEANING

Coin collectors are very fussy about the patina and the surface of the coin. The value of a coin or medal can be greatly reduced if it has been badly cleaned. Do not try to remove any corrosion and never polish or use abrasives. Remove the dust with a soft brush.

If you are fortunate enough to unearth a few coins in the garden do not attempt to clean off the corrosion. The coins may appear to be in good condition but they are probably made only of corrosion products, without any metal left. Once you start to clean them they may fall apart or the surface detail may be lost and the information can never be retrieved again. Some books recommend dipping coins in acid, lemon juice or vinegar. Do not do this, you could ruin or lose the whole coin.

Gold coins sometimes have a rich red patina. Unfortunately, it is rubbed off easily so handle them with care and do not clean them. Always handle gold coins by their edges.

DISPLAY

Coins can be kept in special cabinets or open-ended plastic envelopes or presentation cases. Make sure, however, that the materials used for a display case do not give off harmful vapours which could tarnish silver, copper or lead (see appropriate chapter).

If pinning the coins to a board for display make sure the fabric used for lining the board is not likely to tarnish or corrode the metal. Use stainless steel pins covered with plastic sleeves.

STORAGE

Store coins in a cool, dry, clean, well-ventilated area.

Do not store coins loose as they will damage each other.

A collection of coins must be easy to examine but it also must be thief-proof. Small collections can be stored with each coin in a small envelope about 7 cm (2.5in) square. Acid-free envelopes or good quality white paper ones are preferable but brown manilla envelopes will not do much harm; however do not use manilla envelopes for silver coins as they will cause the silver to tarnish. Information about the coin can be written on the envelope. The envelopes can then be filed in a cardboard or wooden box. Bendicks Bittermint Chocolate boxes

Photograph your collection so that you have a good record of the coins

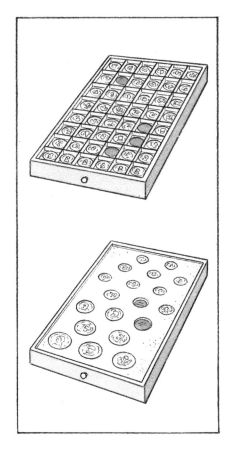

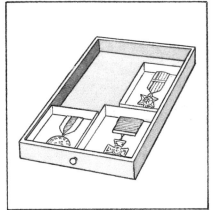

are very useful for storing the little envelopes.

Transparent plastic sheets made up of little pockets are slightly easier to use than paper envelopes. They can either fit into a loose leaf binder or be filed in a filing cabinet. Both sides of the coin can be seen easily through the plastic. It is easier to tell if one has gone missing but the disadvantage is where to put the information about the coin. Do not use these plastic pockets for coins made from iron, lead, zinc or aluminium as the plastic may affect the metal. Do not use sealed plastic envelopes.

Collections can be stored in shallow drawers. These are either purpose made or you can adapt shallow wood, steel or plastic drawers. If possible, avoid wood as most woods give off acidic fumes which are harmful to the coins. The drawers should have an inner base layer which contains different sized circular cut-outs or cells. The coins fit in the appropriate sized cell. The lining with the cut-outs can be made from wood or polystyrene. You may find it easier to divide the drawer up into square cells using strips of wood about 0.5cm (¼in) high. Metal or plastic drawers should be lined with a soft material which will help buffer the changes in humidity. White blotting paper is a good material for lining a metal or plastic drawer.

Coin collections can be stored in shallow drawers divided up with strips of wood to make square cells, or drawers with different sized circular cutouts

Medals can be stored using halves of small cardboard boxes

Brief information about the coin can be written on an acid-free card or paper disc and placed under the coin.

Medals are often very different sizes so it is not quite as easy to store them in this type of drawer. You can use a similar shallow drawer but make up the cells with strips of wood or with halves of small cardboard boxes of different sizes which will hold the medals. Line the boxes with acid-free tissue or paper.

Oak, sweet chestnut and most other woods give off organic acid fumes which make lead corrode very quickly. Do not use wood for making a case for lead seals or coins as it can cause lead to corrode. Keep lead coins in metal drawers lined with acid-free tissue or clean white blotting paper.

Equipment for displaying and storing coins can be bought from coin dealers.

IDEAL CONDITIONS

Household: Normal household conditions.
Exhibition: Relative humidity about 55 per cent. Temperature about 18°C (65°F). Avoid bright lights.
Storage: Relative humidity about 58 per cent or 40–45 per cent if there is active corrosion on the coins. Temperature about 15°C (59°F). Low light levels.

REPAIR

When a coin is made into jewellery the value of the coin is reduced. These coins can be polished with the appropriate metal cleaner.

SCIENTIFIC INSTRUMENTS

Microscopes, telescopes, theodolites, compasses and many other items are all scientific instruments. These objects are usually made from brass and other copper alloys, iron or steel, or silver or nickel alloys with other materials incorporated in them such as glass, shagreen, wood, leather, paper, textiles and plastics. Scientific instruments are often stored in purpose-made wooden or leather cases. They were, and in some cases still are, used for navigation, surveying, scientific examination, medicine and astronomy.

INSPECTION
The brass used in scientific instruments was frequently coated with a yellowish varnish. This should not be removed. If the instrument has been stored in bad conditions the brass may have corroded or tarnished. Check for the green spots of copper corrosion. The steel or iron may rust. Leather can crack, dry or have red rot. Lenses and leather may have mould on the surface. Wooden cases suffer from woodworm and other problems (see Wood). The lining of the case may be worn or rotted away (see Textiles or Paper).

HANDLING
Wear white cotton gloves before handling antique scientific instruments as sweat from fingers is very corrosive.

Before lifting or moving an instrument, any moving parts should be removed or tied down or carefully wedged into place with acid-free tissue. Do not pick these objects up by holding on to fragile projections. For instance, hold a microscope by the main arm not by the actual microscope piece. Support the weight from underneath with your other hand. Take care not to drop it as a sharp blow can dislodge lenses and upset springs, etc.

Use antique instruments as little as possible. The more they are used the more damage is caused from wear.

Do not open up a compass as it is filled with liquid. If the liquid has leaked and some air is in the reservoir it should be filled by a chandler or compass manufacturer as it is very difficult to expel the air completely.

CLEANING
Never clean rare, old or precious scientific instruments, this must be done by a metal conservator. Scientific instruments are delicate and a lot of damage can be caused by inexperienced handling.

The most important thing to remember when cleaning scientific instruments is that liquid should never be allowed to penetrate inside them.

It may be necessary to take the instrument apart so that each piece can be thoroughly cleaned. As you take it apart make a record as you go, either by drawing or taking photographs, to ensure you can put it back together again. It is very easy to forget how even the most simple things go together once they are in bits. Label each piece, including each screw, with letters or numbers. If any pieces are stiff or jammed do not force them.

Do not wash a scientific instrument or get it wet. Remove any dust with a soft brush or a photographer's puffer brush. Use a cotton wool swab or bud dampened with white spirit to remove dirt from the case and wood but take care not to get the white spirit on any plastic or rubber. Make sure you do not remove any of the original lacquer which might be left on the metal parts, particularly on the brass.

Unless the brass is in a very bad state, clean it with a cotton bud dampened with white spirit. Test the varnish by cleaning a small, inconspicuous spot first. If the varnish does not come off, continue to clean the object. If the brass is badly tarnished or has green corrosion spots, it may need to be stripped, cleaned and varnished or lacquered (see Brass). This should be done by a metal conservator.

Remove rust from iron or steel with a commercial rust remover (Jenolite or Modalene) applied with a cotton bud. Clean off the rust remover with a cotton bud dampened with white spirit. If the rust is thick scrape the bulk of it off carefully with a blunt scalpel blade, taking care not to scratch the surface or remove any surface colour such as blueing. Apply the rust remover to remove the last traces of the rust. When the metal is clean, apply a small drop of light oil, such as sewing machine oil, to the iron or steel for protection.

The leather can also be cleaned with white spirit but check that it does not take the colour off the leather. If the leather is very brittle use a little leather cream (see Leather) but do not use too much or the leather will become greasy. Grease will attract grit and dust which will damage the leather.

Remove dust off glass with a photographer's puffer brush or an artist's soft paint brush. Do not use proprietary glass cleaners as the chemicals they contain will damage the metal. A little spit on a cotton bud will help remove fly blow and any other marks from the glass. Polish the glass with a very soft cloth or chamois leather. Lenses scratch very easily. Keep your fingers off the lenses.

Washers and other parts made from rubber can be cleaned with a cotton bud dipped in water with a few drops of a non-ionic detergent (Synperonic N). Do not put organic solvents such as methylated spirits, acetone or white spirit on rubber. It is not often possible to find replacement gaskets for any that have perished. You may be able to make them from a bicycle or car tyre inner tube or from leather offcuts using the original as a pattern.

Check wooden cases for woodworm. Clean and treat them as you would furniture. If necessary, re-line the case using a suitable material such as velvet. If the instrument is made from silver, check that the new lining material does not contain anything that will make the silver tarnish (see Silver).

DISPLAY AND STORAGE
Display and store scientific instruments in a cool, clean, dry, dust-free area which is not so dry that the leather and wood will crack nor so damp that the metal will corrode. There should be good ventilation around the objects to prevent the metal from tarnishing and mould from growing on the organic materials. Do not store scientific instruments in an attic or loft where the temperature fluctuates greatly nor in a damp basement. Keep scientific instruments away from direct sunlight. Delicate instruments can be displayed under glass domes which are available from some clockmakers suppliers.

The best method of protecting scientific instruments from dust is to make fine linen or washed calico bags to cover them. Alternatively, you can lightly wrap them in acid-free tissue, but do not use too much paper as it will hold any damp from the atmosphere and encourage tarnishing. Do not use polythene bags to store scientific instruments, or leave instruments in cardboard boxes unless they are acid-free as normal cardboard is very acidic and will cause the metal to tarnish and the organic material to rot.

Any loose or broken pieces should be kept with the object. Do not attach them with self-adhesive tape or rubber bands, use good quality string or cotton tape. If the pieces are very small, place them in a good quality white envelope and label it clearly.

IDEAL CONDITIONS
Household: Normal household conditions.
Exhibition: Relative humidity 50–60 per cent, preferably 55 per cent. Temperature about 18°C (65°F) constant. Light levels and conditions to suit the most vulnerable material.
Storage: Relative humidity 50–60 per cent, preferably 55 per cent. Temperature about 15°C (59°F) constant. Low light levels. Conditions to suit the most vulnerable material.

REPAIR
Scientific instruments are very delicate and should only be repaired by someone qualified and knowledgeable in treating instruments.

CAMERAS

Cameras are similar to scientific instruments in that they are composed of a mixture of materials, including glass, leather, wood, brass, steel, textile, rubber and plastics.

Clean the camera as described above but never take it apart.

Cameras often contain a certain amount of varnished wood. Clean the wood as in Wood: Furniture, taking care not to remove any lacquer.

Protect the outside of the camera by applying a light coat of microcrystalline wax.

Do not attempt to clean or treat the inside of the camera.

Even early cameras were very sophisticated, so do not try to repair or restore the delicate mechanisms. This shold be done by a restorer of scientific instruments. If any part of the mechanism is stuck do not force it, seek expert help.

BAROMETERS

Barometers are instruments which measure changes in atmospheric pressure and are used to forecast the weather. Barometer cases are often decorated with ivory, mother of pearl, marquetery or metal inlay. The mechanism of most barometers is very delicate, it can include a long glass tube containing mercury and often a fine hair, thin piece of paper or chamois leather.

INSPECTION
Check the wood for the problems usually associated with wood (see Wood: Furniture) such as woodworm, missing or rising veneer, missing or loose inlay, and cracking. The hair-spring mechanism may be broken, in which case the needle will not move and may just fall to point downwards. The tube of mercury may break or the mercury break up within the tube. Inside the barometer there is a chamois leather membrane which may perish and affect the calibration.

HANDLING
Handle barometers with care, avoid sudden jolts and jars. Keep the barometer upright at all times, particularly if it is a mercury barometer as otherwise the mercury may separate into sections which are difficult to join together again.

If you are moving a mercury barometer any distance, remove the glass container with the mercury if it is possible. The mercury is a mobile heavy weight and it could smash the glass. If this should happen and mercury is spilled it should be cleared up at once as the vapour is poisonous. If you cannot remove the mercury, pack the barometer securely in an upright position in a sturdy box.

CLEANING
Clean the wood as for Wood: Furniture. Do not get cleaning materials into the mechanism.

Do not clean the glass with commercial glass cleaners as the chemicals they contain will harm the metal and the wood. See Cleaning a glass-fronted bookcase or Mirrors.

Take great care not to get the glass wet as water must not get behind the glass. Do not attempt to clean the dial.

DISPLAY
Barometers are usually designed to hang on a wall. Make sure that the fixing is strong enough and make sure the wall is solid and in good condition. If the barometer is to be hung on a partition wall, use the fixings which are specifically designed for hollow walls. This will prevent the barometer pulling itself off the wall. Avoid hanging a barometer on an outside wall as they are often damp.

Hang the barometer in a position where it will not get knocked and hit by people passing by. Do not display barometers in direct sunlight or near a direct source of heat.

STORAGE
Store barometers upright in a clean, dry room. Make sure they will not fall over. If possible, hang them on a dry wall out of harm's way.

Do not store barometers in an attic or loft where the temperature fluctuates wildly or in a damp basement.

To protect a barometer from dust, wrap it lightly in acid-free tissue or calico or an old, clean sheet. Do not leave it wrapped up tightly in a lot of padding as this will absorb damp which will affect the mechanism of the barometer. Do not wrap a barometer in sealed polythene. For long-term storage remove the glass containing the mercury and store it separately.

IDEAL CONDITIONS
Household: Normal household conditions.
Exhibition: Relative humidity 50–60 per cent constant. Temperature about 18°C (65°F), constant. Light levels according to the material of the case (light levels for Wood, 150 lux).
Storage: Relative humidity 50–60 per cent constant. Temperature about 15°C (59°F), constant. Low light levels. Take into account the materials of the case.

REPAIR
See Wood: Furniture for repairs to the case. Do not attempt to repair the mechanism yourself. There are specialist barometer restorers and some clock restorers also handle barometers.

117

MISCELLANEOUS

BICYCLES

Do not leave an old or antique bicycle resting on its tyres. If possible, hang it up by its frame from brackets fixed to the wall or a rope suspended from the ceiling. If you have nowhere to suspend it, turn it upside down on a sheet of polythene or wooden slates and rest it on its handlebars and seat.

If the tyres are rubber, try to keep them inflated. Dust them with talc and keep oil and petrol off them. If the wheels are wooden, check them regularly for woodworm (*see* Wood) and do not let them stand directly on a brick, concrete or stone floor. Insulate them with polythene, cork or wooden slats.

If the saddle is made of leather, clean it with saddle soap and then treat it with neatsfoot oil or leather dressing (*see* Leather).

Clean the chrome as described in Chrome and lightly wax with micro-crystalline wax. Do not get any wax on the rubber tyres.

Clean the paint work with a sponge or cloth wrung out in warm water with a few drops of a non-ionic detergent (Synperonic N) or a mild household detergent (Fairly Liquid). Dry the paintwork with a soft, clean cloth and lightly wax with microcrystalline wax.

Oil the mechanical parts, including the chain with light machine oil (3-in-1).

Cover the bicycle with a dustsheet or with a sheet of polythene perforated to allow air to circulate.

Try to keep old and antique bicycles in a dry area.

---

below *Napoleonic model ships made from bone*

right *A fine penny-farthing*

MODELS

Models can be made of many materials. The ones that immediately spring to mind are ivory, wood and bone but people have also used matchsticks or quills. The details of models can be extremely intricate and are very difficult to clean without causing damage. In addition, the thickness of the material of the individual pieces of the model is extremely thin and so it reacts very rapidly to any changes in the relative humidity or temperature. Most materials used to make models will warp, shrink, twist and distort if the conditions are not ideal. Any textiles or painted surfaces in a model will fade and deteriorate if they are displayed in too much light.

Models can also be made from glass, silver and other metals. These do not react as drastically to the environment but they are difficult to clean. (*See* appropriate chapter.)

Models must be kept in sealed glass or perspex cases to protect them from dust and insect attack. Take care not to use spotlights, have lamps nearby or to display the model where direct sunlight can fall on it, as all of these can make the temperature within the case rise.

Glass or metal models are not as vulnerable but should still be displayed in a case.

If for any reason it is necessary to clean a model, dust it very gently with a photographer's puffer brush or an artist's soft fine paint brush.

Store models in a cool, dark, dry area with a constant relative humidity and temperature. *See* relevant chapter for the different materials.

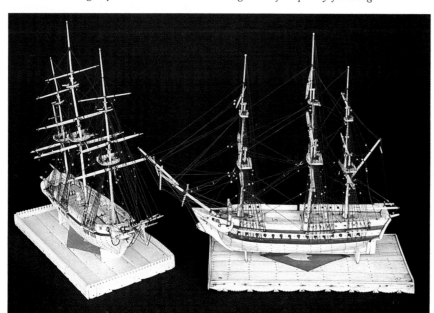

MUSICAL INSTRUMENTS

The care and maintenance of musical instruments is a huge and specialist field and it is beyond the scope of this book to give it sufficient coverage. Because of the complexity of the construction of musical instruments, the range of things that need to be known about the instruments is so great that people who own or collect musical instruments should not attempt to conserve or restore their collection themselves. The care and conservation of musical instruments should be left to a conservator specializing in this field. The damage that can be done in a very short time is great and irreparable and it is better to leave musical instruments alone than to have an inexperienced person deal with them. In particular, if your instruments are in the Stradivarius league you must discuss them with a musical instrument conservator.

That being said, many people have small collections of musical instruments that they have acquired over the years or brought back from their travels. These instruments need caring for as much as any others.

Musical instruments are made from a variety of materials such as silver, brass, ivory, felt, wood, gourds, leather, earthenware, shells, beads, iron, textile, skin and hair. Musical instruments are frequently made from a combination of different materials. A piano can have an iron framework, a wooden cover, ivory keys and felt-covered hammers. An African drum can have an earthenware body, a skin membrane and shell or bead decoration. A large number of instruments are made from organic materials such as wood or leather. These materials are very susceptible to changes in temperature and relative humidity as well as insect and mould attack.

The wood used for violins, guitars, lutes, harpsichords and other instruments can be very thin (about 2 mm $^1/_{10}$ in thick). Not only are these instruments delicate and likely to break if mishandled, they will split if exposed to low humidity and distort if they are too damp.

Different materials respond in varying ways to changes in the environment. This can make the materials distort, split or separate, for example the ivory on piano keys may curl up or inlay on a guitar may fall out. The fact that the different components require different conditions makes the caring for instruments very difficult.

Stringed instruments, particularly pianos, can be under a lot of tension from the tautness of the strings. Sometimes this tension causes or increases distortion.

INSPECTION

Check under the relevant chapters for further information on the materials used for the construction of musical instruments.

Ethnographical instruments should be checked for flaking or powdery paint, woodworm or other beetle infestation, fungi attack, dry and brittle leather and vegetable fibres. Often any rubber used in ethnographical instruments is made of natural rubber latex. This breaks down and becomes sticky. There is little to be done about it.

Examine musical instruments regularly for woodworm or moth infestation (*see* Wood and Textiles). If you have an instrument that has suffered woodworm attack seek professional advice as some woodworm treatments can change the tone of the instrument. Fumigation may be better than treatment with liquid woodworm killer.

HANDLING

Rare or valuable instruments should be played as little as possible to reduce the risk of damage and wear and tear, even though they were made to make music and it is a shame if they are not used for this. Therefore before playing an old musical instrument make sure that it is not already damaged and that it can stand up to the strain of being played.

Pianos and other instruments on legs should not be dragged across a floor but should be lifted and carried. If possible, use a dolly or trolley. The legs on pianos are not designed to take the moving weight of the instrument so they may well break or come loose. The castors were often added for effect rather than for use. Lift a piano by the main body and not by its cornice. Attach foam plastic or a clean blanket to the corners of a large instrument before moving it. Check that a piano or other instruments will go through doorways, corridors, stairs and round corners before you set off.

Grand pianos are very heavy because of the iron framework and should only be moved by professional piano mover.

When moving harpsicords, virginals and spinets two people will be needed to move the stand and two or three to carry the instrument itself. Take care not to scratch the surface of the wood with belt buckles.

Carry smaller instruments such as violins or flutes one at a time and do not carry a string instrument by its neck. Place your hands on the outside of an instrument when you carry it so that if you bump into a wall or doorframe your hand, and not the instrument will be squashed.

If the musical instrument has a carrying case check it occasionally to see that the handle and the closing fixings are still securely attached and that the internal padding is still doing its job.

Make sure that bits do not fall off instruments as you move them about. Protect drum skins from keys in doorways and other sharp objects. Some ethnographical instruments are flimsily constructed and the materials may be dry and brittle so examine them carefully before you move them.

Unless string instruments are being regularly used they should not be left with the strings at playing tension.

CLEANING

Instruments which have cases should be kept in the case and should not therefore need dusting or cleaning.

KEYBOARD INSTRUMENTS
Keyboard instruments can be dusted in the same way as furniture, *see* Wood. The interior of keyboard instruments should be cleaned by brushing with an artist's soft paint brush. Hold the nozzle of a vacuum cleaner in the other hand to catch the dust but make sure that it does not hit the instrument. If the soundboard of an instrument is decorated take care that the paint does not come off when cleaning.

Piano and organ keys are usually faced with ivory, bone or celluloid and can be cleaned by wiping the surface with a swab of cotton wool barely moistened with warm water containing a few drops of a non-ionic detergent (Synperonic N) or a mild household detergent (Fairy Liquid). Pianos and organs made after 1880 usually have celluloid faced keys. If these keys are still dirty after washing, polish them lightly with a mildly abrasive chrome cleaner (Solvol Autosol) on a cotton wool bud. Clean one key at a time. To avoid getting cleaner between the keys, lift each key between your thumb and forefinger using them to depress the keys on either side. Polish off the cleaner with a soft, clean cloth. Do not try to bleach piano or organ keys of any type.

STRING INSTRUMENTS

Remove the dust with an artist's soft paint brush or photographer's puffer brush. Take care not to damage the rose of guitars and lutes.

WOODWIND INSTRUMENTS

Carefully dust the surface of woodwind instruments with a soft, lint-free cloth. If you need to clean under the key levers use a strip of the same cloth or an artist's soft paint brush. Do not lubricate the mechanical parts of woodwind instruments if they are only used for display.

BRASS INSTRUMENTS

Brass and other metal instruments that are regularly played can be polished using impregnated wadding (Duraglit or Silverglit), *see* Brass. Brass instruments on display can be cleaned in the same way. However, they should be cleaned as little as possible because polishing removes a thin layer of metal and eventually the metal can become extremely thin and the maker's name, engraving and decorative designs can be worn off. The silver plate will also wear off silver-plated instruments if they are polished too often.

Silver instruments can be buffed up with a Long Term Silver Cloth. Gilded metal instruments should not be polished.

Brass and other metal instruments that are purely on display can be protected from further tarnishing by lacquering, *see* Silver. Otherwise apply a thin coat of microcrystalline wax with a bristle brush all over the surface and polish it off with a soft cloth.

Do not take woodwind or brass instruments apart unless you know exactly what you are doing.

DRUM HEADS

Clean drum heads with gum eraser granules (Draft Clean) as described in Leather. Do not clean painted drum heads in this way as the paint may come off. Lightly dust them with an artist's soft paint brush.

DISPLAY

Display instruments away from direct sunlight in a clean, dust-free room. Do not place them near radiators or open fires. Make sure that instruments are not placed where they might be physically damaged, whether by handling or accidental kicking.

Do not allow musical instruments to get too damp or too dry. It is important that the relative humidity should remain as constant as possible. In winter remember that the relative humidity is often very low in cold weather and the problem can be made worse by central heating going on and off. Do not display musical instruments in hallways or near doors or hot water pipes as the temperature and relative humidity will fluctuate. The ventilation around the instrument must be adequate to prevent mould growth.

Take care when watering plants on a piano that the water does not get on to the polished surface or into the mechanism, *see* Furniture.

STORAGE

Store musical instruments in a cool, dry, well-ventilated room away from direct sunlight with as constant a temperature and relative humidity as possible. Keep musical instruments away from outside walls or windows as there may be damp or condensation.

Slacken the tension of the strings on stringed instruments. The various mechanisms of harpsichords and early pianos should not be left engaged.

Do not hang a stringed instrument only by its neck. The weight should be supported from underneath the main body of the instrument.

Do not stand musical instruments directly on to a stone, brick or concrete floor. Place them on wooden slats, cork or polythene sheeting.

Moths will attack felt and baize used in instruments unless they are clean and stored with naphthalene (mothballs) or paradichlorobenzene (PDB) crystals. Do not let the crystals come into direct contact with varnished surfaces or paint as they can damage the surface. Hang dichlorvos strips (Vapona) in the storage areas to protect against woodworm and other insects.

IDEAL CONDITIONS

Household: Normal household conditions.
Exhibition: *See* relevant material.
Storage: *See* relevant material.

REPAIR

Do not attempt to repair instruments yourself. They should be repaired by a musical instrument conservator. Remember that not all instrument makers are good or experienced restorers.

Do not try to play a damaged instrument, it could cause further damage.

OFFICE EQUIPMENT

Office equipment includes typewriters, telephones, die-stamps and punches. They are usually made from a mixture of materials such as metal, plastic, textiles and rubber.

Remove any dust from the object with a soft brush or a photographer's puffer brush. If the object is very dusty and particularly if it is greasy, loosen the dust with a hogshair brush and catch it with a vacuum cleaner held in the other hand.

Most materials apart from plastic and rubber can be cleaned with a cotton wool swab or bud dampened with white spirit. This is preferable to getting the object wet. Before cleaning, test clean an inconspicuous spot to make sure that the paint or varnish is not affected by the white spirit. If it is, clean the object with cotton wool swabs dampened with water containing a few drops of a non-ionic detergent (Synperonic N) or a mild household detergent (Fairy Liquid). Do not get the object very wet. Rinse with clean swabs dampened with water. Make sure the object is thoroughly dried by wiping it with a soft cloth followed by drying with a hairdryer set on *Cool* or leaving the object for a few hours in a warm place.

Do not use solvents such as alcohol, white spirit or acetone on rubber or plastic. Clean them with the soapy water solution.

Old gungy oil from machines such as typewriters can be removed with paraffin but take care not to get the paraffin on plastic or rubber. Relubricate the mechanism with a light oil such as sewing machine oil. Apply the oil very sparingly and do not leave it on painted, plastic or rubber surfaces.

If the paint is damaged it is not usually recommended that you repaint the object as the pieces are of more historic interest with their original paint work.

A thin layer of microcrystalline wax applied with a soft brush helps protect the metal and other materials and improves the appearance. Do not let wax get on to rubber, however.

See under the individual materials for more information on handling, cleaning, display and storage.

PLASTICS

When plastics were originally developed they were used for making moulded objects such as picture frames, jewellery and imitation jet. They were made of an organic binder such as blood or casein mixed with a filler to make them rigid and give them bulk. Some plastics are much more stable than others. Usually they begin to flake or crack up because the organic binder breaks down and any oils contained in the plastic gradually evaporate.

The first man-made plastic to be developed was cellulose nitrate or celluloid which was first made in the mid-nineteenth century. For a long time it was the only synthetic plastic and it is still used for ping-pong balls and spectacle frames. When celluloid was first developed it was used to imitate bone, ivory and tortoiseshell as well as to make photographic nega-

tives and film. Celluloid was also used for dolls' heads, cutlery handles, dental plates, buttons, toothbrushes, dice, fountain pens, bicycle pumps, piano keys and floating toys. It can range in colour from transluscent, almost water-white to pastel shades or darker shades and can be mottled or have a pearl-like appearance. Celluloid can be identified by its characteristic smell of camphor. If the smell is not immediately obvious you will be able to smell it if you scrape an unobtrusive area very slightly. Celluloid can decompose in sunlight and room temperature giving off acidic fumes which will harm other objects. It is also a fire hazard as it is flammable and can spontaneously ignite although this rarely happens.

At the turn of the century cellulose acetate was patented, one of its main advantages over cellulose nitrate was

that it was not flammable. It is used now as a base for films, and for cutlery handles and fountain pens.

Casein was developed a few years later and was used mainly for buttons and knitting needles. Casein has a characteristic taste which you would recognise if you had ever sucked casein buttons as a child but this would not be considered good conservation or analytical procedure!

An imitation ivory known as 'French ivory' was made of a mixture of cellulose nitrate, casein and pigments. It looks very like genuine ivory and even had the characteristic fine lines of ivory. These lines are produced during the manufacturing process and are likely to be more even than those on genuine ivory.

These first plastics were based on natural materials. The first completely synthetic resin was Bakelite (phenol formaldehyde). Bakelite was used for electrical insulation and plugs and light fittings were made from it, so too were wireless cabinets, egg cups,

left and right *Musical instruments are usually made from a mixture of materials*

above *A thin layer of microcrystalline wax will help protect the metal and other materials in an old typewriter but take care not to get the wax onto any rubber parts such as the roller*

tobacco jars, electric clock cases and many other items.

Another similar totally synthetic material made from urea-formaldehyde was developed. It was white and could be moulded which meant that objects could be manufactured in pale and marbled colours. Melamine was developed from these early urea-formaldehyde plastics. It is difficult to

differentiate Bakelite from early Melamine although Bakelite is usually brown or mottled. Objects made from ureas are usually a pale colour and mottled.

By the mid 1930s Melamine (melamine formaldehyde) had been developed which was and still is used for making moulded tableware and picnic-ware as well as Formica and other laminates.

After the 1930s the plastics industry really developed. Polyvinyl chloride (pvc), polystyrene, polythene, epoxies, nylon and acrylics were all made in large quantities. Many are thermoplastic which means that they can be heated until they soften, then they can be worked and will return

to their original characteristics when cool. The advantage of this is that they can be made into fibres, rod, sheet, or moulded and used to make a vast range of objects. New plastics are being developed all the time.

A great deal of modern jewellery is made from polyester, acrylic, and epoxy resins. These resins are fairly stable but like other plastics they may discolour with light and time and can be affected by organic solvents or vapour.

INSPECTION

Most early plastics are affected by moisture in the air as well as by light, both of which can cause the material to break down. As the earlier plastics become older they will become more fragile and brittle and harder to fix.

HANDLING

Handle plastics with care as the early plastics can be very brittle. The surfaces can scratch easily. Some plastics are quite brittle so do not put them down sharply on a hard surface. Do not knock plastic objects against other objects (*see* Ceramics).

CLEANING

Brush off any dust with an artist's hogshair brush or a photographer's puffer brush. Do not immerse early plastic objects in water. Wipe the surface with a cotton wool swab or cotton bud dipped in warm water containing a few drops of a non-ionic detergent (Synperonic N) or a mild household detergent. If the object is very dirty a few drops of ammonia in the solution may help remove grease. Rinse the object with a clean cotton wool swab or bud moistened with clean water and dry with a soft cloth. Do not use any heat to dry the object.

Solvents such as acetone, white spirit or alcohol affect most plastics so do not use them to clean objects.

If the surface is very scratched it may be possible to improve it by rubbing lightly with a little mildly abrasive chrome cleaner (Solvol Autosol) on a cotton wool swab or bud. Wipe the polish off with a moist swab of cotton wool and pat the object dry because if you try to polish the abrasive off, the surface of the plastic may become charged with static electricity and pick up dust and fluff. Do not use any other abrasive polish (Brasso) as the solvents can harm the plastic, particularly celluloid.

If you have objects made from acrylic sheet (Perspex, Plexiglas) flick or brush the dust off rather than wiping it off as if you rub the plastic it will become charged with static electricity and pick up more dust.

DISPLAY

Display plastic objects out of direct sunlight and do not place them near a radiator or fire. Most plastics, particularly celluloid, discolour if placed in direct sunlight or exposed to warm temperatures. Never allow celluloid to get too warm. Keep objects in a steady relative humidity and do not use spotlights and other bright lights.

Most plastics will fade and if you place objects on or against them they will fade unevenly. Celluloid should never touch any other object. If a celluloid object is displayed on polished furniture stand it on a cork mat to prevent it harming the surface.

Celluloid was sometimes used to make imitation amber or other beads which were strung into necklaces or bracelets with metal beads. The gases given off by the slowly deteriorating celluloid can make the metal corrode. The copper in a silver alloy, for instance, will form green corrosion products. Not a great deal can be done about this apart from keeping the necklace where there is good ventilation and checking it from time to time. Wrap it in acid-free tissue.

STORAGE

Store celluloid away from other objects, particularly metal which will be corroded by the fumes given off by the celluloid. Keep plastic objects, particularly celluloid, in a cool, dark, dry place with a steady temperature and relative humidity.

Celluloid and early plastics must be stored where the ventilation is good so that the harmful gases given off slowly are wafted away. Never store these objects in plastic bags or sealed containers. Wrap in acid-free tissue to keep them free from dust.

Celluloid should be stored at a low temperature, *see* Photographs.

IDEAL CONDITIONS

Household: Normal household conditions. Constant. Avoid direct sunlight.
Exhibition: Relative humidity about 50 per cent, constant. Temperature 13°–18°C (56°–65°F), constant light levels low about 150 lux.
Storage: Relative humidity about 50 per cent constant. Temperature 13°–15°C (56°–65°F), constant. Dark. Well-ventilated.

REPAIR

The deterioration of plastics is still not well understood so how to treat a plastic object which is cracking up or flaking is not yet very clear. If you have an object which is decomposing, seal it in a glass jar and keep it away from other objects. Loosen the lid of the jar periodically to allow the fumes to escape. Consult a conservator who has had experience of working with plastics.

Broken plastic objects are often difficult to repair because most modern adhesives will not stick pieces together for long. Whether or not an adhesive will work on a plastic object very much depends on what the adhesive and the object is made from.

Easily reversible adhesives (HMG or UHU All Purpose Clear Adhesive) contain solvents which can soften some plastics. Epoxy resin adhesives (Araldite) do not stick most plastics. The cyanoacrylate instant adhesives do stick some. If you have a valuable piece it would be sensible to leave it alone until more is understood about plastics.

It is sometimes recommended that you should try to weld plastics together. Do not attempt to do this. They are flammable and would soon be ruined by welding.

RECORD/DISCS

Flat discs or records took over from cylinders as a method of reproducing music at the end of the last century. The early records were made from shellac. They were black and brittle and are often referred to as 78s as they turned at 78 revolutions per minute on the turntable. Later they were replaced by records made from much tougher and more flexible plastics.

HANDLING

78s are very brittle so they should be handled with great care. They also scratch easily so always keep them free of dust and keep the card sleeve on when the record is not being used. If the sleeve is missing make one up from acid-free card. Avoid touching the playing part of the record as the oil left from fingers collects dust.

Do not hold the record at the edge with one hand as a piece can snap out of the edge. Hold the record with two hands and, where possible, support the weight of the record on the palm of you hand and hold it secure with the other. Do not carry many records at the same time.

If you are looking through records

that are stored like index cards (i.e. on their edges in a box) take care that the edge does not snap off the lower half of the record as you flip through them. When removing or replacing a record into a shelf take care not to chip the outside edge.

Keep records cool as the shellac warps very easily at fairly low temperatures. When these records were in production they were often turned into flower pots by dipping them in hot water and moulding them around a pot.

The more records are played the faster they will wear out, particularly if they are dirty and the needle is blunt. Always clean a record before you begin playing it. You should make recordings on tape or cassette of your early records and listen to these.

CLEANING

Brush dust off with a soft brush or a photographer's puffer brush. Wipe the record over with a soft sponge dipped in warm water containing a few drops of a non-ionic detergent (Synperonic N) or a mild household detergent (Fairy Liquid). Wipe the sponge around the record in the direction of the groves. Do not scrub the surface. Rinse with the sponge well rinsed out in clean water. Pat the record dry with a paper towel. Allow the record to dry naturally. Do not attempt to dry a record with any form of artificial heat. Remember records break very easily.

45s and Long Playing records can be cleaned in the same way. More modern records should be cleaned according to manufacturers' instructions.

DISPLAY AND STORAGE

Keep records out of direct sunlight and away from radiators or fires as the shellac will warp easily. Ideally, records should be kept in their dust sleeves and stacked vertically like books. It is important that they should not be squashed too close together nor be too loose. Divide the shelf up with vertical dividers like pigeon holes so that each section holds about ten records. This will prevent too much pressure or weight being on one record. The records should not be allowed to lean, they must be kept vertical or they may crack. Use a block of wood or bookend to keep the records upright. The shelf must be as wide or wider than the records. If you keep your records in boxes, again divide it into sections so that not more than about ten records are in each section. The dividers must be fixed vertically into the box so that they do not lean over with the records.

Keep records in a cool, dry, clean area. Do not store in the attic which can be very hot or cold, nor in a damp basement. Keep the temperature and relative humidity as steady as possible.

IDEAL CONDITIONS

See Plastics.

REPAIR

Do not attempt to repair broken records. It may be possible to have a recording made from a broken record, however.

CYLINDERS

The first phonographs used cylinders for reproducing sounds and music. They were originally made from wax and then from an early synthetic thermosetting material (*see* Plastics). *See* Wax for wax cylinders. Keep cylinders in their protective sleeves. If the sleeve is missing, make a new one from acid-free card or wrap in acid-free tissue. The cylinders can be stacked on their side but do not pile them up or the bottom ones will be crushed. They are very brittle and break easily.

Clean and store plastic cylinders as for Records and Plastics.

TAXIDERMY

Taxidermy includes preserved small and large animals, birds, butterflies, moths and insects, eggs, shells and fish, reptiles and amphibia. During the nineteenth and early twentieth centuries it was popular to bring home trophies from hunting expeditions at home or abroad, so the walls of large houses could be adorned with heads of deer and foxes as well as giraffes and tigers. At the same time people studied and collected small mammals, birds and insects.

For a stuffed animal or bird to survive for a long time the preparation and preservation process must be carried out well and carefully. If you want to have an animal or bird stuffed make sure that the taxidermist has a good reputation, *see* Introduction: Finding a conservator. It is also important to remember that today there are many laws about killing wildlife so if you are hoping to build up your own collection check that you are not doing anything illegal.

INSPECTION

The colour of most animals, birds and insects fades very rapidly but under the right conditions the colour may last from five to fifty years depending on the intensity of light and other circumstances. Light also causes the skin, feathers and fur to break down.

If specimens are kept where the humidity is too high mould will grow and internal wire supports which give the animal its shape will rust causing the animal or bird to collapse. If the humidity is too low the skin becomes too tight and brittle, it will crack and any sewn seams will split.

Insect attack is one of the greatest problems for collections. The main enemies are moths, carpet beetle, booklice and mites which all eat fur, feathers or flesh.

Many animals, insects and birds are kept in glass cases. Check that these are properly sealed so that insects and dirt are kept out. Any stored cases should be examined at least once a year for insect attack and any new specimens inspected for insects. The signs to look for are:

1. falling hair or feathers – you can check for moulting by gently brushing the hair while placing a piece of paper underneath the animal. If the hair comes off in any quantity it will show up on the paper.
2. Bald patches – check the pads of animals and around the head and under the wings of birds.
3. larval cases may be found on the base or in the fur or feathers.
4. small holes in the legs, feet, bill, between the rays of fins.
5. frass on the base or in the store (frass is insect dropping which can range in texture from fine powder to pellets, it is usually brownish).

If the animal or bird is moulting but there is no sign of insect attack, it could be that the sample has been badly cured. If this is the case the specimen will become bald extremely quickly, so consult a taxidermist. It could also mean that the specimen is very old, in which case not a lot can be done.

TREATMENT OF INSECT ATTACK

If insects appear to be attacking the specimens very seriously you will need to get some help from a taxidermist as your collection can be destroyed in a very short time.

If the infestation is not too great you can sometimes kill it with nepthalene or paradichlorobenzene (PDB). If the animal is in a case, place a small pile of flakes of PDB or moth balls in an unobstrusive spot. Renew the PDB every six months.

If the animal is not in a case put it into a sealed polythene bag or sealed container with dichlorvos strips (Vapona). The number of strips needed varies according to the size of the animal or bird. An animal about the size of a small dog will need about six strips. Leave the animal in the sealed bag for about four to six weeks, Unseal the bag in the open air and leave the animal in the open for a few hours as the concentrated vapours are toxic to humans.

Recently inhabited birds' nests are a breeding ground for the sort of insects that attack stuffed animals and fleas so if you are making up a new case with birds and animals do not use birds' nests unless they have been treated with a dichlorvos strip.

HANDLING

All specimens and cases should be handled as little as possible and with great care. The specimens can break very easily. Never pick an animal or bird up by its head, neck, limbs or tail. Carry the animal with two hands, supporting the weight from the main part of the body. If the animal is mounted pick it up and carry it by the base but, where necessary, prevent the animal from swaying and breaking at the ankles by holding it steady with one hand. Never carry more than one small specimen in each hand. Do not try to move a large animal on your own. Ears, limbs and tails are very fragile and break easily with careless handling. Eggs should always be handled with the utmost care.

One process of preserving animals and birds used to involve arsenic or DDT. If you are handling old specimens take health precautions such as wearing gloves, a particle filter mask

and an overall as the dust that comes off these specimens will be toxic.

CLEANING

Prevent stuffed animals and birds from getting dirty as the wear and tear and physical damage from cleaning can cause harm. Specimens in cases should need very little cleaning and this can usually be carried out while checking for insect attack. Free-standing specimens may need more cleaning, at least twice a year. Very dirty animals or birds should be cleaned by a taxidermist or conservator.

Cleaning should be carried out away from other specimens to prevent spreading insects from one specimen to another. If possible, clean specimens outside on a warm, still, dry day.

Before cleaning, check that a specimen is not moulting. If it is not, blow the dust off with a photographer's puffer brush or a hairdryer set on *Cool*. Alternatively, brush the specimen with an artist's soft paint brush in the direction of the growth of the hair. If there is a lot of dust, catch it by holding the nozzle of a vacuum cleaner on a low setting in your other hand. Cover the end of the nozzle with a piece of nylon net (*see* Textiles). Do not directly suck the dust off or you will take the fur and feathers with it. Rearrange the fur with a wide-toothed comb. Gentle stroking with your hand or finger may produce a lustre but do not add oil.

The eyes, teeth and hooves can be cleaned with a cotton wool bud dampened with isopropyl alcohol. Take care not to get any alcohol on the skin. Clean the fragile ears very carefully.

Dust noses and antlers with an artist's hogshair brush. *See* Antlers.

Elephants, rhinos, giraffes and other large animals should be cleaned by brushing off the dust with a 5 cm (2 in) paint brush while holding the nozzle of a vacuum cleaner in the other hand to catch the dust. Take care not to touch the animal with the vacuum cleaner.

Brush a lion's mane with a soft brush but watch out for the ears.

BIRDS
Remove the dust from feathers by brushing them with a clean feather or by blowing gently with a hairdryer set on *Cool* in the direction of the growth of the feathers. Make sure that the

opposite *Celluloid and other early plastics were used to imitate bone, ivory and tortoiseshell*

above *Specimens in cases should need very little cleaning*

hairdryer does not cause any damage. Use a needle to relay the feathers.

Do not try to clean very dirty birds, this should be done by a taxidermist.

Sometimes grease marks appear on the bird's feathers, this may mean that the bird has been prepared badly, in which case it should be isolated as it will attract insects. A taxidermist may be able to correct the situation.

Dust birds' eggs with an artist's soft brush. Do not try to wash them.

SHELLS
Remove any dust with a soft clean duster or a hogshair brush. Most shells can be washed but it is safer not to wash spiral shells as they often contain dried remains which will decompose if they get wet and will smell disgusting. Other shells can be washed in warm water containing a few drops of a non-ionic detergent (Synperonic N). Rinse them in clean water and dry carefully with a paper towel or soft cloth and finally with a hairdryer set on *Cool*.

OSTEOLOGY MATERIAL
Osteology material includes loose bones and teeth as well as skeletons. If these are very dirty or greasy they should be dealt with by a taxidermist. Otherwise brush off the dust and, if necessary, wash them with warm water containing a few drops of a non-ionic detergent (Synperonic N). Rinse and dry with a paper towel or soft cloth. Allow to dry naturally.

BUTTERFLIES, MOTHS AND INSECTS

Do not touch the specimens. If the base of the drawer or case in which the collection is kept is dirty, very carefully dust it with an artist's soft paint brush or a hogshair brush, taking care not to touch the specimens. When you clean the glass make sure that no water gets into the case.

GLASS CASES

Many specimens are displayed in glass cases. Glass domes can be washed in a plastic bowl in warm water and mild detergent. Rinse in clean water and dry with a soft cloth or paper towel. Make sure that the dome is well sealed when replaced. Glass domes which are not very dirty need only be wiped with a dry chamois leather. *See* glass.

The glass of boxes or frames should not be cleaned with commercial glass cleaners as they contain chemicals which could harm the case or specimens. Wipe the glass with a damp cloth or chamois leather. If it is very dirty, add a little isopropyl alcohol to the water. Rinse using a clean cloth and clean water. Polish with a soft clean cloth.

Make sure all cases, frames and boxes are well sealed so that insects and dust cannot penetrate. Rubber and leather seals are used in some boxes but others are often sealed with tape. Do not use self-adhesive tape, use brown paper tape with a water-soluble adhesive.

DISPLAY

Small animals, birds, insects and even fish should be displayed in glass cases. This makes handling easier and reduces the need for cleaning. Larger animals are usually free standing.

All specimens should be displayed away from direct sunlight and in as low a light level as possible. If you have a large collection ultra-violet absorbing filters on the lights and cases would be a good idea. Specimens should also be displayed in a room where the relative humidity is constant and is not too high or low.

Free-standing animals and mounted heads should not be placed near or over an open fire, radiators or other heat sources as they will get very dirty and the change in temperature and humidity will destroy them. Place them where they will not be easily touched. Fur wears off very quickly.

Use as much acid-free material as possible to make up the cases and supports, particularly when displaying eggs and shells which are attacked by acids. Avoid using materials such as cardboard, oak, blockboard or chipboard which give off acid fumes.

Use PDB or moth balls in cases of animals and birds to help prevent insect attack.

Insects should be displayed with a little insect repellent in the case. Use stainless steel pins and acid-free material or cork for the display.

STORAGE

Store specimens in a cool, dry, dark, dust-free area. The store should be kept clean to discourage insects.

Make sure the specimens are carefully stored and not overcrowded, otherwise necks, legs, limbs and tails may be broken. Make sure that the specimens do not touch each other and cover them with a clean dustsheet or a cotton sheet. If you use polythene make sure you tent it over the specimen so that it does not touch it. Do not stand specimens directly on a stone, brick or concrete floor, place them on wooden slats, cork or polythene sheeting.

Insects or small creatures should be stored in drawers with a little napthalene or PDB which should be renewed every six months. Make sure the insects do not touch each other or the insecticide.

Store other animals lightly wrapped in acid-free tissue. Place some insect repellent in the cupboard. If the animals are not mounted but need support make some pads from acid-free tissue for them to sit on.

Check the store at least once a year for insect damage and other problems.

Do not use cotton wool as padding for eggs, shells or small creatures as the fibres cling and cotton wool attracts damp and mould. Use crumpled acid-free tissue.

IDEAL CONDITIONS

Household: Normal household conditions. Avoid direct sunlight.
Exhibition: Relative humidity 50–55 per cent. Temperature 15°C-18°C (59°–65°F). Low light level 50 lux.
Storage: Relative humidity 50–55 per cent. Temperature 15°C (59°F). Low light level, dark. Keep dust- and vermin-free.

REPAIR

Apart from very minor repairs any damage should be dealt with by a taxidermist. Any loose teeth can be stuck back in place using an easily reversible adhesive (HMG or UHU All Purpose Clear Adhesive). If the skin splits from being too dry or grease appears from bad preparation get help from a taxidermist. Not all taxidermists are trained or experienced in looking after old specimens. Check their training.

The material used for modelling lips and gums sometimes shrinks, cracks and detaches itself from the skin and bone. Hairline cracks can be filled with wax and painted; anything larger should be repaired by a taxidermist.

FISH, REPTILES AND AMPHIBIA

The old method of skinning and mounting fish and reptiles is hardly ever used now as these days the fish or reptile is moulded and then cast in resin and painted. If this is expertly done the results are excellent and often more accurate then the traditional techniques. In the past the heads of fish often had to be remodelled completely because they changed shape so much; they also changed colour. Amphibia and reptiles were slightly less difficult.

Traditional specimens are easily damaged by careless handling. Feet and claws in particular break off. Sometimes the fat left inside fish, reptiles or amphibia oozes out and encourages the bacon beetle. The specimen will need degreasing and repainting by a taxidermist. Insects go for the head and fins in particular. *See* Taxidermy for information on handling, display, and storage.

Early casts of these specimens were made in plaster. These can chip easily if handled roughly. Do not get a plaster cast wet. Modern casts are usually quite robust but thin or delicate areas may break if handled carelessly.

BOTANICAL COLLECTIONS

If you collect plants remember that there are laws about which plants you can pick and that it is illegal to uproot plants without the owner's permission.

Dried plants are very brittle and should be handled with care. Check for insect attack and store them with an insecticide (Paradichlorobenzene).

FOSSILS, ROCKS AND MINERALS

Many people collect minerals, rocks and fossils for their decorative appearance as well as for scientific study.

INSPECTION

Some semi-precious stones such as topaz, sodalite, fluorite and barytes change colour if exposed to strong sunlight. Some revert back to their original colour in the dark. Some silver salts disintegrate with air and light and must be stored in light-proof boxes made from acid-free materials.

Minerals and fossils are particularly prone to changes in temperature and relative humidity. Opals, amber and shale are particularly affected. Pyritic samples will oxidise if the relative humidity is too high (keep below 55 per cent RH). Marcasite which is used in inlays can form a white feathery encrustation if it is kept in damp conditions. If the relative humidity is not controlled other problems such as deliquescence, hydrolysis, efflorescence, hydration, shrinkage and distortion may occur.

HANDLING

The physical strength of samples varies enormously. Some minerals are very brittle and should not be exposed to sudden jarring or vibrations. Carry the specimens carefully. If you are carrying more than one at a time use a tray or box and make sure they do not jostle each other. If you are trans-

...make ...ing to ...e car. ...p with ...hed by ...m the ...ens to ...e.

...oft brush ...nerals can ... do not ...g.

DISPLAY

Collections are best displayed in glass cases or glass-fronted cabinets as this protects them from dust and from being lost. Keep them out of direct sunlight. Do not display samples over a fire, radiator or other heat source. Do not use cotton wool as padding because it absorbs moisture and the fibres can catch on the specimen. Make sure that the samples are displayed on enough shock-absorbing material such as pads of acid-free tissue or expanded polystyrene. Wood used to make cases helps absorb vibrations but do not use oak or other materials which give off acidic fumes. Do not display specimens near continuous noise or vibrations, for instance from air-conditioning, roads or railways and building works.

STORAGE

Store minerals and fossils in a clean, dry, dark area, free from vibrations and changes in the relative humidity. Minerals and fossils should be stored in wood, although not oak or chipboard, rather than metal cupboards or cabinets, to help reduce vibrations and buffer changes in the relative humidity. Specimens that are likely to be damaged by vibrations should be placed on some foam plastic or expanded polystyrene. Cover the foam with acid-free tissue. Do not use cotton wool as padding.

IDEAL CONDITIONS

Household: Normal household conditions. Avoid direct sunlight.
Exhibition: Relative humidity 50–55 per cent constant. Temperature 10°–20°C (50°–68°F), constant. Light levels critical for some samples, 50 lux. Protect from vibrations.
Storage: Relative humidity 50–55 per cent constant. Temperature 10°-15°C (50°–59°F), constant. Low light levels, dark. Protect from vibrations.

REPAIR

In the past fragile minerals or fossils were consolidated with wax or resin or coated with lacquer. This has been found to be harmful to the specimens. If you have any specimens which are disintegrating or in need of consolidation consult a geological conservator for help and advice. Minor repairs can be carried out using an easily reversible adhesive (HMG or UHU All Purpose Clear Adhesive).

TOOLS

Craftsmen's tools are much sought after nowadays as collectors' items. Carpenters' planes, gardeners' scythes, butter moulds and silversmiths' tools in particular are all worth saving. Check any wood for woodworm. This can be treated with a woodworm killer (Cuprinol Low Odour) but make sure the area you are working in is well-ventilated and be sure to wear protective clothing, see Wood: Woodworm. Once the liquid has dried treat the wood with a little teak oil and lightly buff it with a soft cloth.

The brass components of the tools can be polished in the same way as furniture fittings (see Brass) and any rust can be removed from the iron or steel (see Iron). The iron should be protected with a thin film of microcrystalline wax.

If the tools are stored in an outhouse make sure it is dry and inspect the tools regularly for woodworm and rust. Old, precious or rare tools should not be stored in an outhouse.

PAINTINGS

OIL PAINTINGS

Oil paint was developed during the Renaissance and has been used by artists since then in many different ways. The paint is made up of pigment mixed with a binding medium and it can be applied in a thin layer or so thickly that the picture is textured. The base used for the oil painting is normally stretched canvas although wooden panels are often used. However, hardboard, glass, leather, vellum, silk, stone and copper have all been used as a support.

The canvas is generally tacked to a wooden frame known as a stretcher which has wooden wedges knocked into the corners to pull the canvas tight. Some canvases are on strainers instead of stretchers. Strainers are rigid frames that cannot be expanded. The stretcher or strainer is usually placed in a deep rebate in a frame. Frames for oil paintings do not usually have glass in front of the picture.

INSPECTION

Canvases easily split, dent or bruise. The outline of patches or labels stuck on the back of the canvas can show on the front. Anything resting on the front or the back of the canvas can leave an impression.

The environmental conditions can affect a canvas a great deal. Changes in relative humidity cause it to stretch and contract and this movement may make the paint crack, lift and flake. If you notice that the paint is lifting, take the picture for restoration as soon as possible. It is far easier for a restorer to fix back lifting paint than to reposition and attach a flake that has fallen off. This is very much a case of a stitch in time.

Look for cracked, flaking or blistering paint. A bloom on the surface may indicate that the air is too damp. Check for holes and tears in the canvas. The tacks holding the canvas to the stretcher sometimes rust and weaken the canvas around them.

Check that the chains, wires or cords used to hang the picture are strong and are not frayed or corroded near the fixings. Check also that the fixings in the wall and on the frame are strong and robust.

Inspect paintings regularly so that if there are any problems occurring they can be dealt with before they become too severe.

HANDLING

Do not touch the surface of a canvas and, if you have a lot of visitors, make it difficult for them to do so by placing a table or some other piece of furniture under the picture so that they cannot easily reach it.

Make sure you do not damage paintings while moving large furniture, sculpture or ladders.

If paintings are displayed in rows on a wall always remove the lower ones before the upper ones. In the same way if you have to do any work such as rewiring or decorating to the wall or ceiling above a painting remember to remove the painting or protect it before you start working.

If you are taking down a painting make sure that anything it could damage, or that could damage it, is out of the way. Framed pictures are heavy so you usually need two people for this job. If chain is used for hanging a picture, mark the links which hooked on to the fixings in the wall with a piece of cotton or string before you take the chain off. This will make rehanging the picture a lot easier. Make sure that a hook or chain or part of an alarm system does not fall on to the painting and bruise the surface. This sort of mark is very difficult to get out. Keep the painting upright as you lower it to the floor. If you rest the frame on the floor, tip it back very slightly so that the edge behind the carved moulding of the frame is resting on the floor. If the frame is fragile make sure that the floor is well padded with pillows, pieces of carpet or a mattress.

At least two people should carry a large oil painting. Carry the painting vertically, holding it so that the longest sides are horizontal. Lift it by the frame only, never hold on to the stretcher and do not touch the canvas. Watch out for the tops of doors and ceilings, particularly when going up or down stairs, also look out for door knobs and keys. Decide where you are going to take the painting before you set off and make sure the route is free of all obstructions such as electric leads and rollerskates. Check that you have somewhere suitable to put the painting down once you have reached your destination. If one person watches the front of the painting and the other the back you are less likely to damage it by not noticing a door knob or similar hazard.

If you are moving a number of objects at the same time do not carry a sculpture and a painting on the same trolley. If you lurch at all, the sculpture is likely to go through the painting.

Do not use aerosols or other sprays near pictures and never use insecticides or oil-based pesticides (Cuprinol or Rentokil) on the frame or the wood of the stretcher. The constituents of the insecticide can cause a lot of damage to the painting. *See below* for treating woodworm.

If you notice that the surface of the paint is beginning to lift or flake and you cannot get a restorer to come and look at it quickly, take the painting down and lay it face up so that the paint will not fall off. If you have to move the painting to another room make sure that the conditions in the new room are similar to those in the original room otherwise the flaking may become worse.

If you have to take a picture to a restorer or are moving it any distance, lay it flat, face up, on a duvet or eiderdown in the back of the car. The duvet will cushion the painting from bumps and jars and reduce vibration. If the picture is glazed, stick self-adhesive tape in a star shape over the glass so that, should the glass break, the damage that the fragments could cause will be minimized.

If a painting is damaged, save any pieces of paint or frame which may have been knocked off. Avoid fiddling with the damaged area but get the painting restored by a painting restorer as soon as possible.

If the painting has been damaged by water from a burst pipe or flood, leave it hanging in position until a restorer can come and check it. If the frame is no longer strong or the picture is still in danger from the water then you must remove it from the wall. If it has to come down, lie it flat, face up. Raise the frame up on wooden blocks so that air can circulate under the painting to dry it out. Do not touch the back of the painting or let the blocks touch the back. Allow it to dry naturally in a well-ventilated room, do not use any heat. The surface of the painting may develop a white bloom. This should be checked.

RETENSIONING THE CANVAS
For many reasons a canvas may become loose. You should never attempt to retension an old, precious, or rare painting, but you may wish to retension one found in the local junk shop. It is very easy, however, to split a canvas while retensioning it.

Do not attempt to take any picture which may be of importance out of its frame. This should only be done by a painting restorer.

To retension a canvas, take the stretcher out of the frame. Sometimes the stretcher is held in place in the frame with iron nails. These may either be driven through the stretcher to the frame or bent over the stretcher to hold it in place. The nails can be pulled out using pliers. Pull them out at the same angle that they were knocked in so that the stretcher or the frame does not split.

Canvases on strainers rather than stretchers may also need retensioning if the canvas has sagged or distorted. In this case the strainer will need to be replaced and this should only be done by a painting restorer.

Before retensioning, check that the canvas has not weakened. The front edge of the stretcher takes most of the strain so look along it to check that the canvas is not worn through. If the tacks at the side or back are rusty the canvas may have rotted around them. Provided the canvas is strong enough you can hammer copper or rust-proof tacks between the old ones. If the canvas is so weak you cannot do this, the picture will have to be 'lined'.

Before retensioning, remove any dust and debris from between the canvas and the stretcher. *See* Cleaning.

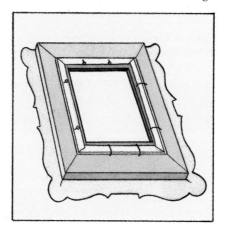

Sometimes the stretcher is held in place with iron nails

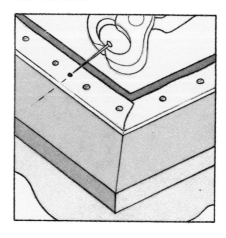

The nails should be pulled out at the same angle that they were put in

Use a small hammer to lightly tap in the corner wedges. Work around the picture from corner to corner so that the tension is equal. Do not hammer too strongly in one corner at a time. If any of the wedges are missing they should be replaced. Take great care not to mark the canvas with the hammer and do not retension so much that the canvas splits.

If you are unable to retension the canvas because it is weak it will need to be lined. Lining must be carried out by a painting restorer. The canvas is taken off the stretcher, another piece of canvas is adhered to the back and the newly backed picture is replaced on the stretcher.

CLEANING

Do not attempt to clean an old, rare or precious picture. A great deal of irreparable damage can be caused by unskilled people attempting to clean or treat pictures.

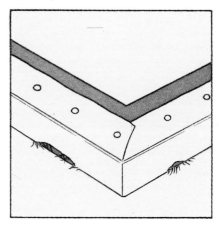

The canvas may be worn through on the front edge of the stretcher

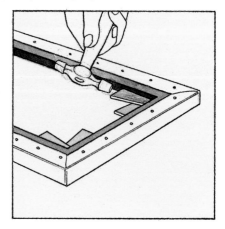

Gently tap the corner wedges with a small hammer

Do not attempt to clean in any way any painting with cracked, flaking or blistering paint as it will only make the problem worse. Take it to a restorer.

However, if you pick up a painting at the local jumble sale or junk shop you will probably wish to clean off the surface dirt in order to see what you have got.

Using a vacuum cleaner on a low setting, vacuum up all the dirt on the back of the frame and then go all over the back of the canvas. Do not let the vacuum cleaner touch the canvas. Do not vacuum a very weak canvas.

Most oil paintings were protected with a coat of varnish. With time, the colour of the varnish changes, becomes yellow and may even turn brown. The varnish also absorbs and collects dirt and grime. This is particularly true of many pictures which were hung over fireplaces. Many paintings look much more sombre than they were originally intended to be. Removing the varnish is a skilled job and should be carried out by a restorer.

A great improvement can often be made to a painting by removing the surface dirt. Before cleaning an oil painting, tuck folded acid-free tissue or card between the stretcher and the back of the canvas. This prevents the stretcher marking the canvas while you are working on the surface. Remember to remove the padding once the cleaning is complete.

Either place the painting on a secure easel or lay it flat on a clean table.

One of the safest ways of removing surface dirt is with spit, although you should test a discreet corner of the painting first. Using a cotton wool

Before cleaning a painting tuck folded acid-free tissue between the stretcher and the back of the canvas

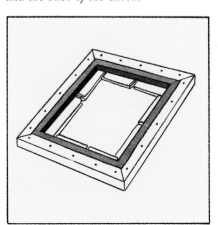

bud, dampen the end with your spit and clean the surface using a light circular motion, turning the bud as you go. Examine the bud. If it appears to be picking up paint or varnish and not just dirt do not continue. Discard the bud when it becomes dirty, only clean a small area at a time and do not press on the canvas.

If spit does not remove the dirt you could try using a bud barely moistened with white spirit. Do not use white spirit on recent paintings, however, as this will take off the varnish. If the picture has been varnished with a wax-based varnish this will also be removed by the white spirit. It is important to test a small corner of the painting before cleaning it with white spirit.

If either of these methods have removed the surface dirt, and the cleaned picture looks dull, very lightly wax it with microcrystalline wax. Apply the wax with a soft lint-free cloth and polish it very lightly taking care not to press on the canvas.

If a painting has become mouldy from bad storage, take it into a drier room to dry out. Do not heat it. As soon as you get a dry day take the picture outside and gently brush the mould off the back and the front with an artist's soft paint brush. Make sure you do not spread the mould spores by brushing the mould off indoors. If necessary, clean the front with spit on a cotton wool bud as described above.

Sometimes the varnish develops a bloom. This can be caused by a variety of conditions, particularly by high relative humidity. It may be possible to remove the bloom with spit as above and a little microcrystalline wax may prevent further bloom forming.

Occasionally birds get into a room and leave droppings on a picture. If the painting is valuable it should be cleaned off by a restorer but if not, allow the droppings to dry out. Then gently scrape off the bulk of the droppings and then brush off as much as you can of the rest with a soft brush. Once you have got rid of most of the droppings remove the rest by wiping the area with a cotton wool bud dampened with spit. Work towards the centre of the dropping so as not to spread it any further out. Do not try to remove the dropping when it is still wet as you will rub it into the picture and smear it over the surface.

DISPLAY

Do not hang paintings near or over radiators, heating vents, pipes carrying hot water or on walls with internal flues or hot pipes running through them, all of these warm up the wall considerably. Do not hang a picture over a fireplace which is in use. In particular, paintings on wooden panels should never be placed near an open fire or any other heat source. Heat will harm the canvas, wood, paint and varnish and will cause dust to rise and be deposited on the surface.

Do not hang pictures in a draught. It is very important that the temperature and relative humidity should be as constant as possible for paintings to survive. Do not hang in direct sunlight.

Pictures must be hung so that air can circulate around them. Often they lean forward off the wall which allows the air to circulate. If you hang pictures on an outside wall put corks on the lower corners of the frame to insulate the frame from the wall.

Do not hang pictures where they might be knocked by passing people such as in narrow passageways or on the stairs. If they have to be hung in these positions they should be glazed for protection.

Insulate pictures from an outside wall by putting corks on the lower corners of the frame

Do not hang paintings in dining rooms over a sideboard where steam and splashes of grease can affect them.

Oil paintings are not as sensitive to light as watercolours or textiles. However, lights generate heat which can be harmful, so avoid using spotlights or hanging the painting over a table lamp. Picture lights also give off heat and can heat up a small area of canvas quite considerably, so never leave picture lights on for a long time. Never use picture lights on panel paintings or paintings on vellum.

You can hang pictures by a cord or chain from a picture rail. If you do not want the cord or chain to show, the picture can be hung by fixing two strong hooks to the back of the frame and using short lengths of picture chain to suspend the picture from two screws Rawl-plugged into the wall. How much the painting leans forward depends on how low or high the hooks are on the frame and the length of the chain. Paintings which are quite high up a wall may need to lean forwards more than usual. This can be done by fixing the hooks by which they hang towards the centre of the frame.

Heavy frames also need to be supported from underneath to prevent too much strain on the joints of the frame and to minimize the risk of the chain breaking or the fixings coming out of the wall. This can be done by fixing two or three brackets to the wall on which the base of the frame can rest. When the lower edge of a frame is supported make sure that the picture wire or chain is held taut. If it is not it may come off the wall fixing. To prevent this, tie the wire to the fixing.

Do not hang paintings on freshly plastered walls for several months until the plaster has dried out or on freshly painted walls until the smell of

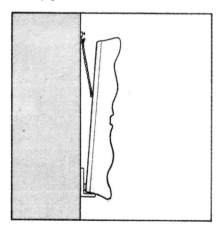

the paint has completely gone.

Some paintings are fixed in architectural frames. These are part of the building. The area behind the painting is usually not plastered in order to leave a gap for air to circulate. Never paint the wall surrounding the frame with modern plastic-based paint, use old fashioned limewash. Plastic-based paints do not allow water to pass

through them so that if there is any damp in the wall it will come out through the unplastered and unpainted wall behind the picture rather than through the rest of the wall. Do not plaster or paint the wall behind a painting in a fixed architectural frame.

FRAMING

Oil paintings are usually displayed in frames which are not glazed. Sometimes glass or acrylic sheet (Perspex or Plexiglas) is used for protection against dust and physical damage. Acrylic sheet has the advantage over glass in that it is lighter and does not shatter but it does scratch and attracts dust more easily.

The frame must have a rebate deep enough to take the stretcher. Line the rebate with a soft velvet ribbon to prevent the varnish and paint being scraped off the canvas. The stretcher can be held in place with brass plates or mirror plates which are screwed into the frame and overlap the stretcher. These plates are a more efficient method than the bent nails used in the past. Cork pads placed between the plates and the picture will hold the picture in place firmly but will allow

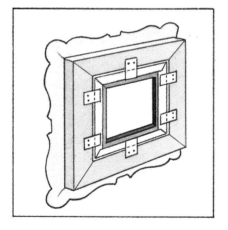

for any slight movement of the picture. The pads can be cut from cork tiles. If the rebate is too large for the picture, pack it out with balsa wood or cork.

STORAGE

Store paintings in a cool, dark, clean, dry place. Avoid cellars which are often damp and attics as they get very hot or cold. Keep paintings away from boilers, hot pipes and draughty areas. If the storage area has been recently redecorated make sure that the plaster is completely dry and that the smell of the paint has completely gone. If you do not have a suitably dark room, keep the curtains drawn or the blinds closed as much as possible as this helps reduce the light levels and stops the temperature and humidity fluctuating.

Where possible, hang pictures to keep them out of harm's way. Avoid hanging them on an outside wall but, if you have to, use corks to insulate them. If you cannot hang them, but need to store pictures for some time, you can make a wooden construction like an extra large plate rack that they can slot into.

Unfortunately, because of lack of space, pictures often have to be stacked against the wall. This is potentially harmful as the pictures can be damaged by human feet, corners of other frames or vacuum cleaners. If you stack pictures this way make sure you do not place them against a radiator or heating pipes or under a window. If they are on a stone floor put some wooden battens, cork or a piece of carpet with some polythene under it to protect them from damp.

Remove picture lights, brackets, wires and other projections that may harm the frame or the picture. Make sure nothing touches either side of the canvas, particularly not another frame or the hanging chain or wire. Always stack the pictures in order of decreasing size and do not put too many pictures in one pile. Place a sheet of hardboard between every second one to prevent too much

Use metal brackets underneath the frame to help support the weight

Brass plates will hold the stretcher in place. Place cork pads between the plates and the pictures. Use balsa wood to pack out the frame if the rebate is too big

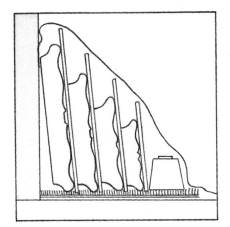

When stacking framed pictures against a wall place pieces of hardboard in between

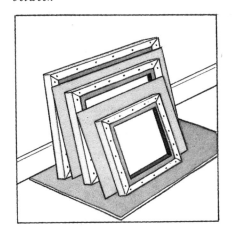

Stack unframed pictures separately

above *Miniatures can be painted in watercolour or oils*

weight resting on the first picture and to protect the frames. Make sure that the pictures will not slip down on the floor by placing a weight against the base of the outer one. If the frames are very plain you can place the pictures facing each other which will protect them from dust. Do not stack paintings with very ornate frames. Cover the stack with a clean sheet or blanket. Do not cover it with polythene sheet as condensation may form.

Stack unframed paintings separately from framed ones. Stack them so that the canvas is facing the wall. Only the top, front edge of the canvas should touch the back of the one in front. Make sure that the main area of canvas is not touching anything. Try to keep paintings of the same size together.

IDEAL CONDITIONS

Household: Normal household conditions. Avoid direct sunlight and keep temperature and relative humidity constant.

Exhibition: Relative humidity 50–60 per cent constant. Temperature about 20°C (68°F), constant. Light levels 200 lux.

Storage: Relative humidity 50–60 per cent, constant. Temperature about 15°C (59°F), constant. Light levels as low as possible.

REPAIR

If a painting is damaged, avoid fiddling with the tear or hole but get it restored by a painting restorer as soon as possible. If a painting falls off a wall it is as well to get the frame checked, even if it appears to be undamaged.

Any major repairs should be carried out by a painting restorer. If the paint is cracked, flaking or blistered take the painting to a painting restorer for treatment.

If you are repainting or repairing the frame of a picture you should take the painting out of the frame but if this is impossible, protect the painting by covering it with a piece of clean cloth or tissue paper. (See Frames.)

PANEL PAINTINGS

Wooden panels have often been used as the support for paintings. Many different types of wood have been used and the panel can either be a single piece of wood or made up of many pieces. The pieces of wood are usually held together with battens or cradles. Sometimes the pieces of wood making up a panel may have their grain running in different directions and this can cause problems.

Paintings on wooden panels should be treated in the same way as canvas paintings but they are particularly sensitive to changes in temperature and relative humidity and can easily split and crack. Make sure that panel paintings are not in a room where the heating goes on and off in winter or where they are exposed to fluctuating conditions. It is better to leave the heating on low all the time than to have the room hot by day and cold by night. It is important that panel paintings be displayed and stored in controlled conditions.

The panels are usually slightly warped, so check them regularly to make sure that the amount or the direction of the warp has not altered and that no new cracks have appeared. Check also that the paint is not cracking or flaking. The panel usually has a convex curve, and provided that the degree of the curve remains the same this is quite acceptable. Do not try to straighten a panel painting.

However, if the curve of the panel changes at all, particularly if it begins to curve in the opposite direction, all is not well and you should consult a painting restorer as soon as possible. Do not remove the painting from the room in which it is hanging as a sudden change of conditions could make the situation worse. A restorer should be able to advise you on the best way to look after a panel painting.

Never attempt to clean or restore a panel painting yourself.

If a panel painting is to be framed this must be carried out by a framer specializing in panel paintings as it is important that the frame is not too tight. It is advisable to use a backing board behind a panel painting as this helps buffer it from changes in relative humidity as well as keeping it clean.

Never use a picture light on a panel painting or have table lights or spot-lights shining on it.

Wooden panels may suffer from woodworm or other wood boring insects and dry rot. Never attempt to treat them yourself. They can be treated, but only by a restorer as the solvents used in insecticides can soften or change the colour of the paint.

ICONS

Icons are similar in structure to panel paintings. They often have metal and enamel decoration. Icons are a very specialized area of painting and should only be dealt with by a conservator specializing in the conservation of icons. They should be handled, displayed and stored as for Panel Paintings.

PAINTINGS ON METAL

Thin copper sheets have sometimes been used as a base for paintings. These sheets are fragile as they can be bent and dented very easily. Paintings on metal should be framed and handled with care. If they are bent it is virtually impossible to straighten the metal without damaging the paint.

Keep paintings on metal in dry conditions to prevent the metal corroding (*see* Copper) and keep them in a steady temperature because if the metal expands and contracts with changes of temperature the paint will crack and flake off. Paintings on metal should be kept in a room where the heating does not go on and off causing fluctuations in temperature.

MINIATURES

Miniatures can be painted in water-colour or oil paint and many different supports are used. Miniatures in watercolour are painted on ivory, vellum or paper, oil paint is used on metal such as silver or copper. Many miniatures are made in enamel.

Miniatures are all very delicate and should be handled and treated with care. For more information on the different materials used for the base see the appropriate chapter. *See also* Watercolours and Oil Paintings.

The ivory base used for miniatures was often very thin and even more susceptible to changes of temperature and relative humidity than larger pieces of ivory. If the air is too dry the ivory will warp and crack causing the paint to flake off.

Vellum is less sensitive than ivory but if the conditions become too damp mould will readily grow on it. After the end of the eighteenth century, the watercolour used for painting minia-tures was mixed with a lot of gum to give the paint a shiny, almost varnished appearance. The gum can become sticky and mould will grow on it if the air is too damp.

INSPECTION

Examine miniatures to make sure that they are not warping or cracking, that the paint is not flaking off and that mould is not growing on the surface. Sometimes there may be condensation behind the glass in the frame. If this happens the miniature will have to be reframed and the miniature should be displayed in a room with a more constant temperature and relative humidity. For more information see the appropriate section for the base material. Do not remove miniatures from their frames to inspect them as they are very vulnerable when unframed.

CLEANING

Do not attempt to clean or restore miniatures. This should be done by a conservator or painting restorer. Dust the outside of the glass with a soft clean cloth or chamois leather. A little spit on a cotton wool bud will help to remove fly blow and other marks. Do not use commercial glass cleaners. *See* Frames.

DISPLAY

Watercolour miniatures are even more sensitive to light than watercolour pictures. Display them in low light and, if possible, keep them in drawers of cabinets which can be closed when the miniatures are not being looked at.

If you hang miniatures, keep them away from radiators, fires, lights and draughts. Do not hang them where direct sunlight will fall on them and do not hang them on an outside wall or near an outside door. For further information *see* Watercolours.

STORAGE

Wrap miniatures in acid-free tissue and store them in a cool, dry, clean, dark area. You should not wrap them in sealed polythene as condensation could form inside, nor wrap in cotton wool as it will absorb moisture and the fibres will stick to the object.

IDEAL CONDITIONS

Household: Normal household conditions. Keep out of direct sunlight and in constant conditions.
Exhibition: Relative humidity 55 per cent. Temperature 13°–15°C max,

(55°–60°F), constant. Light levels 50 lux.

Storage: Relative humidity 55 per cent. Temperature 13°–15°C max, (55°–60°F), constant. Light levels 50 lux or lower.

REPAIR

Do not attempt to repair or repaint a miniature. This should be carried out by a painting restorer experienced in this type of work.

WALL-PAINTINGS

Wallpaintings are paintings which are painted directly on to wall plaster. The most famous example is probably the Cistine Chapel in Rome, but there are many other less well-known ones. The term 'fresco' is often inaccurately used to refer to all types of wallpainting. If the painting is a true fresco it is painted while the wall plaster is still wet. The pigment soaks into the plaster and reacts with it so that when the plaster is dry the pigment is securely held in place. Unless the wall or plaster is damaged, frescoes are fairly resilient. Other types of wallpaintings are made by painting directly on to the dry plaster. The medium used to bind the pigment and fix it to the plaster can be egg, honey, drying oils, acrylic or many other materials. How long a wallpainting lasts very much depends on how well it was made, what the paint medium was, how damp the wall is and what the room is used for.

INSPECTION

It is not always easy to differentiate between a true fresco and a wallpainting, particularly if it has been restored. However, if you look closely, the colouring of a fresco appears to sink into the plaster and become part of the plaster and the colour is not built up on the surface.

Check that the wall or plaster that the wallpainting or fresco is painted on is in good condition and that the plaster is not loose. The paint may be peeling and flaking off, this is often caused by damp in the wall. Most walls are naturally damp but this will not necessarily harm the painting so long as the amount of dampness in the

wall remains constant.

If the wall is very damp or the amount of dampness fluctuates, white crystals may appear on the surface and they can push the paint off. Often walls are damp and dry in cycles according to changes in the weather and the seasons and it is this changing which will most likely cause the paint to flake off. If the wall appears unusually damp try to find the reason for it and when you do, get it put right as soon as possible. The damp could be caused by a leaking roof, poor guttering, no damp course, a bridged damp course, leaking pipes and things stacked against the outside of the wall, such as a pile of logs.

The wallpainting may have to be removed if the wall is in bad condition. This should be done by a wallpainting conservator. If the wall can be repaired it may be possible to replace the painting.

If you own a wallpainting which is deteriorating, even very slowly, you should get advice from a conservator as soon as possible. The sooner the problem is solved the better.

CLEANING

Do not attempt to clean a rare, precious or ancient fresco or wallpainting, particularly those in churches and historic houses. This must be done by a specialist wallpainting conservator. Never clean a wallpainting with flaking paint or a deteriorated surface.

You can clean a modern oil or acrylic painting which is in a sound condition by removing any dust with a clean, dry, soft brush such as a ponyhair fitch or a fat make-up brush. Catch the dust with a vacuum cleaner held in your other hand. Take care not to let the nozzle of the vacuum cleaner touch the paint.

Some wallpaintings in a good condition may be further cleaned by using a cotton wool swab dampened with warm water containing a few drops of a non-ionic detergent (Synperonic N). Do not use household detergents as the additional chemicals they contain can cause long-term problems. Before cleaning the wallpainting, test a tiny area of each colour in an inconspicuous spot to make sure that the paint will not come off with the water. Provided only dirt comes off, work over a small area using a circular motion, working from the bottom upwards. Do not rub hard

or the paint will come off. Change the swab as soon as it becomes dirty. Rinse the area with a clean swab barely moistened with clean warm water. Move on to the next area. Allow the painting to dry naturally.

The wallpainting may not clean up evenly all over. To avoid it looking patchy do not overclean any one area. It is better to evenly and lightly clean the whole wallpainting twice than to overclean some areas the first time.

If the wallpainting cannot be cleaned with soapy water you could try using spit on cotton wool buds. *See* Oil Paintings.

DISPLAY

A wallpainting must be protected from physical damage caused by passing people, the backs of chairs and vacuum cleaners. If necessary, rope off the area or attach a sheet of acrylic sheet (Perspex or Plexiglas) in front of the painting. Fix the sheet to an unpainted part of the wall. Make sure that there is plenty of space, at least 2.5cm (1in) between the wall and the acrylic sheet.

Avoid shining bright lights on to a wallpainting.

Do not paint around wallpaintings with modern plastic-based paints. They do not permit the wall to breathe therefore any damp in the wall will be forced to come through the wallpainting.

If you are worried about the state of a wallpainting, discuss its care with a wallpainting conservator. Do not attempt any kind of restoration yourself.

IDEAL CONDITIONS

Constant relative humidity and temperature, low light levels.

REPAIR

Wallpaintings should only be repaired by a wallpainting conservator.

WATER-COLOURS

See page 147.

PAPER, PRINTS, DRAWINGS AND MANUSCRIPTS

Paper was being made in China by the beginning of the second century AD and it was introduced into England by 1500 but it was not until the seventeenth century that it was widely used.

Paper can be made from a wide range of materials: from rags, hemp, wood bark and maize as well as wood pulp. The surface of paper has to be treated or sized so that it can be written or drawn on. Many materials have been used as size but the most common is gelatin.

Paper is used as a support for many things, including manuscripts and documents, watercolours, gouache, drawings, prints and maps. It is used for Valentine cards, fans, models, posters, screens, lampshades and 1960s throwaway clothes.

INSPECTION

Light, temperature, relative humidity, insects, mould, acidity and people can all harm paper. Light will fade colours and make the fibres brittle, and the higher the temperature the faster the deterioration. The gradual but irrevocable effects of light are rarely noticed until the damage has been done. All light fades prints and drawings and bright light makes them fade much faster than low light.

If the atmosphere is too damp mould and mildew will grow. The most familiar type of fungal attack is known as 'foxing', which stains the paper with orangey-brown spots. The familiar, friendly, musty smell of old paper is a sign of danger. Mould spores can lie dormant for years but can spring into action when the relative humidity is high or the ventilation inadequate. If the atmosphere is too dry the paper will become brittle and buckle and any paint on the surface may flake off. If the atmosphere fluctuates greatly the paper will disintegrate.

Paper is also affected by acids which can be in the ingredients from which it was made or in the ink which was used on it or in the atmosphere. The paper will first turn yellow, then eventually dark brown and become very brittle. Paper made before 1760 is more stable than later paper because the ingredients were purer and less acidic. However, some paper made now is acid-free and is therefore very durable.

The paints used on the paper can also be affected by the environment. Not only can they start to flake off if the relative humidity fluctuates but they can even change colour. For instance, white and red pigments made from lead compounds may turn black in polluted air as may the silver used in Persian miniatures to represent water.

Check all paper, be it watercolours, books or documents, for yellowing, buckling, brittleness, mould and foxing, fading and evidence of insects. Check also that any paint or decoration is not flaking off or very powdery.

Check for gnawed surfaces or holes made by silver fish or woodworm on their way to a better diet. If picture frames are badly sealed, thunder bugs or thrips will get behind the glass, die, and stain the paper.

Paper screens and other paper objects suffer just as badly from too much light, damp and heat. All conditions which may appear to apply only to prints and drawings apply to any object made from paper.

HANDLING

Handle all paper, particularly unframed paper, as little as possible. Paper is much safer to handle if it is mounted correctly. Always make sure you have clean hands. If you are unpacking watercolours or documents, make sure that the table or

left *It helps to protect watercolours from daylight if you hang them on a window wall*

desk is clean and that there is enough flat clear space to put them on. Remove pens, ink, tea, coffee, flower vases and small children with sticky fingers as far away as possible.

Rough handling will tear paper. A lot of damage is also caused by cleaning and restoration carried out by amateurs and by the use of poor quality materials for mounting and framing.

Do not pick up a sheet of paper by one edge, always slide your hand underneath it to support the weight.

If the paper has a surface decoration of paint, chalk, crayon or charcoal do not touch the surface and handle it with great care, particularly if the decoration is powdery. Chalk, pastels, crayon and charcoal come off very easily. (*See* page 147).

Large, framed watercolours, engravings, prints and documents are surprisingly heavy. Put them down gently or the glass may shatter and could damage the paper.

When framed pictures are to be transported any distance make a star of self-adhesive tape on the glass in case it breaks. Remove any hanging chains which can cause damage.

Damaged or 'tired' frames or mounts no longer protect the paper. When remounting and framing, always use good quality materials and acid-free card. Old, rare, precious or fragile works on paper should be mounted and framed by an experienced paper conservator or framer.

Sometimes the paint or pigments stick to the glass in the frame. Do not try to take the picture out. This should be done by a professional conservator.

UNFRAMING A PRINT OR DRAWING

To take a print or drawing out of a frame, first vacuum away any dust or dirt from around the picture. Remove wires and fixings. Place the frame face down on a table covered with a clean sheet or blanket. Carefully cut and remove the tape from the back of the frame with a knife. There may be labels on the back of the picture which you want to keep. These can be removed from the backing board later.

The pins securing the backing board to the moulding can be removed by pulling them out with pliers. Hold the frame firmly. If you are right-handed, start by removing the pins in the left side of the frame. Hold the top of the

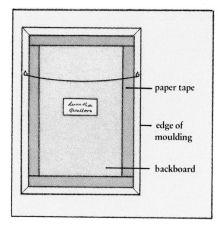

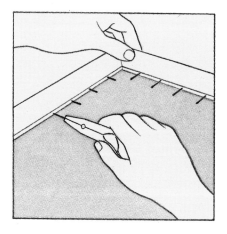

Carefully cut the paper tape on the back of the frame with a knife

Pull the pins from the frame with pliers, pulling across your body

pin firmly with blunt-nosed pliers or pincers and pull them out gently. Pull parallel to your body and the table top. Loosen any rusty pins by gently moving them backwards and forwards before pulling them out. Remove all the pins from one side of the frame and then turn the frame clockwise to remove the pins from the next side.

Make sure you are always pulling parallel to and across your body. Recent frames may have diamond or U-shaped pins. These should be gently eased out with a screwdriver.

Carefully vacuum away any loose dirt you may have made when removing the pins, taking care not to suck up the paper.

Gently lift the drawing out of the frame. It may be easier to tilt the frame and let the drawing fall on to the palm of your hand. If the picture is taped to the glass, carefully cut the tape with a sharp knife. If you are going to keep the frame, replace the backing board into it, even if you intend to replace the board eventually. It is safer for the glass and the frame.

DEMOUNTING

If a paper object is on a mount which is damaged or discoloured, particularly if the mount has turned orange or brown, you should replace it. The paper is usually attached to the mount with hinges or guards (*see* Mounting). Using a sharp knife, carefully slit the hinges taking care not to cut the paper. Then lie the paper face down on a clean surface. Gently remove the hinges from the back of the paper using metal tweezers. If they do not come off easily leave them alone. It is unlikely they will do any harm.

If the paper has been stuck on to the board with adhesive it is best to get professional advice from a paper conservator. However, should you attempt to remove it yourself, remember that you must remove the card from the picture and not the picture from the card. Sometimes a work on paper is directly stuck around its edges on to the back of the mounting board. This is particularly difficult to remove and you should get help from a paper conservator.

Since the 1930s many works of art on paper have been dry mounted on card. This is done by sandwiching a layer of tissue impregnated with shellac between the work and the mount and then hot pressing it. You can usually tell what has been dry mounted as there will be a shiny margin around the print or drawing. It is very difficult to separate the paper from the mount as the adhesive is usually insoluble but if the card is not acid-free it ought to be removed. This will have to be done by a paper conservator.

MOUNTING

A lot of damage can be caused to paper by using poor quality mounting board, self-adhesive tapes, dry mounting tissues and mounting sprays, as well as using the wrong adhesive for attaching the mounting hinges to the picture; these include rubber-based adhesives like Copydex and Evostik Impact or HMG and other clear adhesives.

Always mount works of art on paper on to acid-free board. This does not only apply to valuable works. Cheaper prints are more likely to be on unstable paper and the acid free board will help preserve them. A four-ply thickness of board should be used as the mount behind the print or drawing. The overmount should be thick enough to hold the print or drawing well away from the glass. If you do not want to use an overmount, a fillet of acid-free board can be used.

If you cannot find board thick enough for what you want, stick a number of layers of thinner board together using starch paste or wallpaper paste and press them together. Weight them flat.

Never paste a print or drawing directly on to the mount. It should be secured to the mount by hinges or guards. These are made from strips of Japanese tissue paper or thin acid-free paper. Use starch paste as the adhesive (*see* Repair). Never use self-adhesive tape or 'conservation' tape.

For small prints, put a simple L hinge at both top corners.

If you have a larger print you can use drop hinges which are held in place by a second strip of paper going across them. However, in order that the hinges do not show, the edge of the paper will have to be covered by the front mount. If there is no margin around the picture it will mean that some of the painting will be covered.

If the corners of the print are not going to be seen you can make small triangular envelopes to go over them from Japanese tissue or acid-free paper. If the corners will show but you want to use this type of mount, you can make the envelopes from polyethylene terephthalate sheet (Melinex or Mylar) and stick them down with an easily reversible adhesive (HMG or UHU All Purpose Clear Adhesive). Make sure that the adhesive is dry before you insert the print.

Instead of using envelopes of poly-

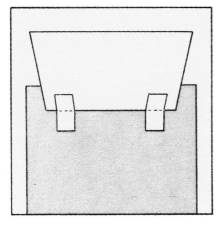

Mounting a picture using a simple L-hinge made from Japanese tissue paper

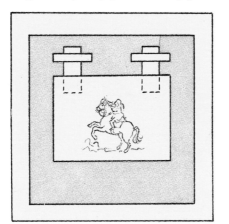

Drop hinges

Triangular envelopes

Strips of polyethelene terephthalate

The back board and overmount can be hinged together

ethylene terephthalate sheet, the print or drawing can be secured on to the back mount with strips of the sheet. Cut the strips about 2cm (½in) wide and secure the end to the back mount with the same adhesive.

Once the print or drawing has been hinged on to a back mount it will need a frame or overmount with the appro-

priate sized opening to protect the surface. This is also made from acid-free board and should be the same size as the backboard. The backboard and the overmount can be hinged together on the left-hand side with a strip of paper or fine fabric such as lawn or linen stuck down with starch paste or wallpaper paste. Do not use self-adhesive tape. Do not stick the overmount directly to the back mount. The overmount for pastel and chalk drawings needs to be made from thicker board than is necessary for watercolours. This is to protect the powdery surface and to improve air circulation.

If the print or drawing is not going to be permanently framed it can be protected further by using a piece of acid-free board the same size as the back mount and hinged on to the left-hand side with linen or paper tape. This extra piece of board can then be turned to the back when you want to display the picture.

To make storage and display easier,

Further protection can be given by hinging a piece of acid-free board onto the front

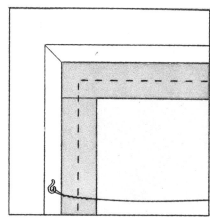

Seal round the back of the frame with gummed brown paper tape

Gummed brown paper tape can also be used to seal round the inside of the glass and the moulding

it is better not to have too many different sizes of mount.

FRAMING
If you are doing the framing yourself make sure you have plenty of clean, clear, table space.

The frame must be deep enough to hold the backing board, mount boards and the glass. It also must be strong enough to support the weight, particularly of the glass. Make sure that the moulding is well secured at the corners.

Use good quality, and; wherever possible, acid-free materials.

The backing board should be made from hardboard or marine ply and coated with polyurethane varnish. This helps stop harmful chemicals from the wood penetrating the paper. The hardboard should be slightly smaller than the moulding to allow air circulation.

Glass or polymethyl methacrylate sheet (Perspex or Plexiglass) or polycarbonate sheet can be used. Glass scratches less but breaks more easily and lets through more ultra-violet radiation than the other two, also water may condense on glass. Polymethyl methacrylate and polycarbonate sheet are lighter, less reflective and can be ultraviolet filtering. However, they should *never* be used on pastel, chalk and charcoal drawings as the static electricity from the sheet pulls the powder off the paper. Polycarbonate has a slightly better ultraviolet barrier than polymethyl methacrylate. Use anti-static cleaners for cleaning the plastic sheet.

Dust and insects are kept out of the frame by sealing the back round the edge of the frame and the backing board. Use gummed brown paper tape and not self-adhesive tape as this does not last as long. In some areas, particularly dirty cities, it is sensible to seal around the inside edge of the glass and the moulding as well. This prevents dirt, dust and thunder bugs getting in. Again use gummed brown paper tape.

There are ready-made frames available which have no moulding, the glass and the hardboard are clipped together. These should not be used for long-term framing as they are open to dust, insects and air pollution.

DOCUMENTS WITH SEALS ATTACHED
Documents which have seals attached to them should be mounted and framed by a paper conservator or experienced framer. The seal needs to be supported so that it does not put a strain on the paper. The moulding of the frame will need to be deep enough to accommodate the thickness of the seal. Wax seals are usually brittle and easily broken. *See* Wax. They are difficult to restore so they should be taken to a conservator if necessary.

See Lead for the care of lead seals, but remember that lead is attacked by organic acids found in wood and wood-based boards, cardboard and some paper.

CLEANING
Cleaning paper or works of art on paper is a tricky process and should be carried out by a paper conservator. If you don't know what you are doing and you clean watercolours, drawings and some prints you may loosen all or part of the picture, so don't do it. Never attempt to clean old, rare, precious or fragile works of art on paper. *Never* touch drawings where the medium is powdery, such as pastel, chalk and charcoal.

Dry cleaning using an eraser can be carried out on some prints or drawings but should only be done where the paper is in good condition and where the ink will not be rubbed off. Do not attempt to clean pencil drawings, watercolours, hand-coloured prints, or chalk, pastel and charcoal pictures in this way nor a picture of any value or historic importance. Also do not clean brittle paper or long fibred paper such as oriental or Chinese papers or any other soft or fibrous papers.

Before you attempt any cleaning, brush the surface with a soft sable brush to remove the dust. If the paper has mould on it brush the mould off outside so that the spores do not spread. You may need to pick off any fluffy mildew growths.

You can dry clean some black and white prints and ink drawings using an eraser. Do not think that you can just clean off small areas of dirt. Unless you clean the whole surface of the picture it will appear patchy.

If you use an eraser for cleaning prints and ink drawings work with great care and test the paper in the margin first. Put a sheet of clean white blotting paper on a flat, clean surface and place the picture on top. You will need to weight one end to stop the paper slipping. Use a fairly heavy book or any other suitable object. Place a sheet of clean white blotting paper under the weight to protect the paper from it. The best erasers are the plastic dough-like ones (Staedler–Mars–Plastic No. 526 50 or Rowney putty rubber). Use the eraser in one direction, in straight lines only. Do not rub in circles. Turn the eraser over as soon as it gets dirty. If the fibres of the surface of the paper start to lift, stop.

Dirt that is more ingrained can sometimes be removed by using an erasing powder (Draft Clean). This is grains of gum eraser which you can lightly rub over the surface of the paper. Use your fingers to rub the powder in straight lines working in one direction only. You may find it easier to put a small amount of grains into the middle of a square of muslin and make a bag. Again, use it in only one direction. Brush off the loose erasing powder when you have finished with an artist's sable hair brush.

Mounts can also be cleaned using an eraser or powdered gum eraser.

Do not try to remove wax or grease marks from paper. Do not use any solvents, particularly not petrol, paraffin, lighter fuel or white spirit. Not only are they more than likely to damage the picture, they are also highly flammable, toxic and dangerous to have around.

WASHING PRINTS
Ideally, no one except a paper conservator should wash prints, drawings and other works on paper as a great deal of irreparable damage can be done very quickly. However, if you feel you really have to wash your print the following washing technique is the least harmful method. On no account attempt to wash watercolours, pastel, charcoal, gouache, ink drawings, hand-coloured prints or brittle or soft fibrous paper or any picture or print of any value or historic importance. It is better to live with a dirty picture than no picture at all.

First, brush off any dust with a soft sable brush and try dry cleaning the print as described above. If the paper needs further cleaning and you are absolutely sure that the ink is not water soluble and that the paper is strong and good quality and in good condition, it can be carefully washed.

Shallow trays such as those used by photographers are useful for washing prints, but if these are not large enough use a flat bottomed sink. Do not try to clean paper in a curved basin. The paper must be supported at

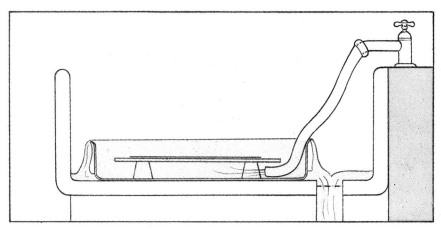

Washing a print. Take care that the water does not run directly onto the paper

all times because when it is wet it will disintegrate when you handle it. Use a sheet of glass, acrylic sheet (Perspex, Plexiglas), polyethylene terephthalate (Melinex, Mylar) or Formica as the support. The sheet must be larger than the print because once the print is wet you must only handle the support never the print itself.

Put some cold water into a shallow tray. Slowly slide the support and the print into the water at an angle allowing the paper to absorb the water as you lower it in. If you do this too quickly the paper will float off the support. Leave it in the water for about an hour. Slowly lift the support out of the water at a slight angle to allow the water to run off. The print will adhere to the support. If the print is not much cleaner repeat the process using warm, not hot, water. This should remove most of the dirt.

If further cleaning is still necessary, add a few drops of a non-ionic detergent (Synperonic N) to some warm water; do not use any household detergent. Lower the print and support into the soapy water as above and leave it to soak for about half an hour.

The print must then be thoroughly rinsed in clean water so that all the non-ionic detergent is removed. If detergent is left in the paper, it may eventually discolour.

Rinse by leaving the print to soak in changes of distilled or de-ionised water for about an hour, changing the water every ten to fifteen minutes. To change the water, lift out the print on its support, throw the water away, refill the tray and replace the print. Do not try to tip the water out and refill the tray with the print still in it.

Another way of rinsing the print is to run cold tap water slowly but continuously into the bottom of the

tray using a piece of hose. The end of the hose must be below the print so if necessary raise the support on four similarly sized egg cups. Make sure the water does not run directly on to the print or it will force a hole through the delicate wet paper. Leave the water running for about half an hour and then give a final rinse using distilled or de-ionised water.

Lift the support and the print out of the water, place on a flat surface and mop up the excess water around the print with pads of white blotting paper. Do *not* touch the paper or it could disintegrate.

Leave the paper to dry naturally where there is good air circulation. The print will dry flat and crease-free against the support. When it is completely dry the paper will lift off the support. Handle the paper with extra care as the washing may have removed the size and weakened it.

Never use any form of bleach. Some books recommend domestic bleach or sodium hypochlorite for cleaning paper; **never** use these as they will damage the paper in the long term if not in the short term.

If stains cannot be removed with washing, take the print to a paper conservator.

CLEANING FRAMES
See Frames.

Rubbing the glass in a frame causes static electricity. Do not polish the glass of pastel, chalk or charcoal drawings as the loose pigment will be lifted by the static electricity.

DISASTERS
Paper, more than any other material

is harmed by water. If it does get wet it should be dried out as quickly as possible without using heat.

Lay it face up on a sheet of clean white blotting paper or a white paper towel and allow it to dry naturally.

If the disaster is still out of control and you have not got time to find sheets of blotting paper, put the wet prints and drawings in the freezer. Keep them flat on a tray; if you have to use a baking tray cover it first with aluminium foil or clean silicone paper. If you have a number of pictures which you need to freeze, interleave them with clean silicone paper, cling film or aluminium foil. Leave the paper objects in the freezer until you do have the time to look after them properly. When you take them out of the freezer take care not to snap them. Let them thaw out, face upwards, on a sheet of white blotting paper or paper towel. If they are in a block allow the block to defrost, then carefully separate each piece of paper and dry them individually.

If water gets behind the glass of the frame remove the picture from the frame and dry it out in the same way. Do not try to remove the mount or handle the paper more than is absolutely necessary when it is wet as wet paper is extremely fragile.

If rare, precious or old paper is damaged by water, put it in the freezer and consult a paper conservator.

DISPLAY

The ideal conditions in which works of art on paper should be kept, are not, unfortunately, ideal for us. Works of art on paper ought to be kept in the dark, at an uncomfortably low temperature, in very clean air and with a constant relative humidity. The best you can aim for is as low a light level as possible and as cool and steady a temperature as you can manage. Beware of the relative humidity changing as the central heating goes on and off. If you have valuable paper objects either keep the heating on to try to keep the relative humidity constant or use a humidifier and dehumidifier. (See Relative humidity p 10). Any work of art on paper which is extremely valuable or fragile probably should be kept in the dark and a facsimile used instead.

All pictures and documents on paper should be displayed in a frame (*see* Framing above) or, in the case of three-dimensional objects, in a box or a glass-fronted case.

Do not hang prints or drawings over direct heat sources such as fires, radiators or lamps and do not put them near external doors or in a room where the temperature fluctuates. Swop your pictures round from time to time, particularly if some are in lighter or warmer rooms than others. Do not hang them in rooms which may get very steamy, such as in bathrooms or kitchens.

Position prints and drawings so that they receive minimum light and where direct sunlight cannot fall on them. Corridors and halls often have poor lighting so are better than living rooms. Often the darkest, most appropriate place to hang them is on a window wall but take care that it is not damp. You can insulate the frame from the wall and improve the ventilation behind the picture by fixing some cork on to the bottom of the frame. Slices off a clean wine bottle cork are ideal. Cut them about 1cm (½in) thick and stick them on to the lower corners of the frame with PVA emulsion (Evostick Resin 'W') or an easily reversible adhesive (HMG or UHU All Purpose Clear Adhesive).

In order to reduce the amount of light a picture is exposed to, close shutters or draw curtains when rooms are not in use. Blinds are very useful for cutting out the light. Roller blinds made from plain calico can reduce the light level effectively without plunging the room into total darkness. Sometimes it is not necessary to pull the blinds down completely. They can be effective if only pulled down far enough to cut out direct sunlight.

Ultra-violet screening films can be applied to windows, picture glass and fluorescent tubes. Their effectiveness varies and probably leads to a false sense of security but if you must hang your pictures in unsuitable places ultra-violet screening will help. Ultra-violet screening acrylic sheet (Perspex, Plexiglass) is available and can be used for framing pictures or for double glazing.

Do not apply ultra-violet filters directly on to stained or painted glass or early leaded glass. For advice on the most effective ultra-violet screening consult a conservator rather than the retailer or manufacturer.

If you have any choice, paint the walls of the rooms in which you wish to hang prints or drawings a pale colour. If you put them on dark walls you will need extra light to see them, pale walls, however, will reflect light and reflected light is less harmful than direct light.

If you use spotlights in a room make sure that the light is not too bright and is not directly shining on to the picture. In addition, spotlights can generate a lot of heat. The heat from lights, particularly in cabinets, can sometimes be more damaging than the light itself. *See also* Introduction.

Do not use string for hanging pictures as it is not strong enough and rots very quickly. Use good quality picture wire or, for heavy pictures, brass chains. Nylon or terylene cord is quite strong but it may stretch. One hook or nail in the wall is not strong enough for anything other than small pictures. Plug two screws or hooks into the wall and hang the picture from them. If theft is likely to be a problem, pictures screwed to the wall rather than hung from a hook are harder to steal, but make sure there is adequate ventilation behind the picture by sticking a spacer between the wall and the frame. Avoid screwing a picture to an outside wall.

STORAGE

The ideal storage conditions for paper are a clean, dry, cool, dark, well-ventilated, dust-free room, free of pests and with a steady temperature and relative humidity. So store paper in the dark away from heat and moisture. Never store paper in attics as the temperature fluctuates too much, nor in basements as they are usually too damp. If you are storing paper in cupboards or drawers make sure that there is adequate ventilation to prevent mould growth. The cupboard should not be flat against a wall, particularly an outside wall. Leave at least 7cm (3in) all round for air circulation.

Line cupboard shelves or drawers with acid-free tissues to help absorb any acid in the air and keep the relative humidity constant.

Check the drawers or storage areas regularly so that any damage can be seen before it becomes serious. Foxing, for instance, when it first appears, can be brushed off and, if caught in time, will not stain the paper.

A small pile of paradichlorobenzene crystals on a saucer in the cupboard or drawer will help protect the paper against insect and mould attack. Do not let it touch the paper. Clean storage area regularly and, if there are mice in the house, put mouse poison down.

If you have a lot of documents, prints or drawings you should ideally keep them on steel shelving rather than wood as, although wood helps buffer the relative humidity and is cheaper, steel cannot rot, does not encourage insects and does not contain impurities which could filter into the paper. Use plenty of acid-free card or paper in the packing.

UNFRAMED PAPER

Carefully remove any paper clips, rubber bands, pins and self-adhesive tape as well as mouldy or damaged mounts before storing unframed paper. However, paper on mounts is less vulnerable than unmounted paper so correctly mount as many pictures as possible, even for storage.

Unmounted prints and drawings should be interleaved with acid-free tissue and stored separately from mounted ones.

Solander boxes made from acid-free materials are the best things to use for storing unframed paper. They can be bought in various sizes or they can be made to measure for specific objects.

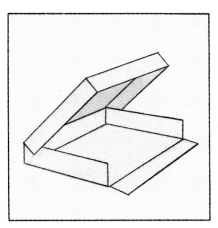

A Solander box

The lid lifts off the box and one side opens so that the paper can be withdrawn easily.

Store the Solander boxes horizontally, if they are stored vertically the paper will buckle. Try to keep damaged and undamaged paper separately. Do not store foxed or stained paper or paper suffering insect attack with paper in good condition. Do not put paper which is in good condition

into a folder or box which has been used for foxed or damaged paper.

Artists' portfolios are not very good for storage as the paper tends to buckle and they do not keep the insects and dust out. However, they are better than nothing. Place acid-free tissue between each document and store the folder horizontally.

If you only have a few prints or drawings you may prefer to make a simple folder out of strong acid-free card. Make one folder for each print or drawing. Cut the card to the correct size and score it with a blunt knife along the lines where you want it to bend. If you want to tie the folder closed use white cotton tape.

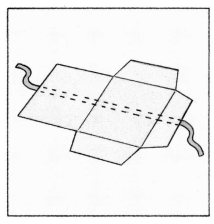

A simple folder of acid-free card

FRAMED PRINTS OR DRAWINGS
See Frames.

LARGE DRAWINGS, MAPS AND CHARTS

Very large prints, drawings, maps and charts can be a problem to store. They are safest if framed. If this is not possible store them flat in a plan chest, but make sure there is some ventilation in the chest. If the drawers are very tight fitting and the ventilation is poor do not use the chest unless it is of no value, in which case you could drill some holes in the back of the drawers to improve the air circulation. Place acid-free tissue between each work and try to keep works of roughly the same size in each drawer. A sheet of acid-free card on the top of the prints and drawings in each drawer will help prevent the top picture becoming caught when the drawer is opened. Write a list of the contents and their order on the outside of each drawer.

IDEAL CONDITIONS

Household: Normal household conditions. Avoid sunlight, high or fluctuating temperature or relative humidity. As low light levels as possible.

Exhibition: Relative humidity 50–60 per cent, constant. Temperature 15°C (60°F). Light levels 50 lux.

Storage: Relative humidity 50–60 per cent not below 40 per cent or above 65 per cent, constant. Temperature 13°–15°C (56°–60°F), constant. Light levels as low as possible. Keep clean and vermin-free.

REPAIR

Repairing paper requires expert knowledge. Do not attempt to repair old, rare or precious works on paper, paper with historic interest, very weak or brittle paper or drawings with loose pigments such as pastel, chalk and charcoal. Take these to a paper conservator. However, on less valuable prints and drawings it is sensible to repair a tear at once.

TO MEND A SMALL TEAR

Never use self-adhesive tape for repairing paper. Japanese tissue paper or acid-free tissue should be used with starch paste. *See below* for instructions on how to make the starch paste. If you cannot make starch paste use light wallpaper paste (methylcellulose). This is not as good as starch paste as it is too wet but it is preferable to other commercially available alternatives.

Before repairing the paper, remove any dust from around the tear with an artist's soft paint brush. Lay the print or drawing face down on a clean smooth surface such as glass or Formica. Adjust the tear so that it fits closely together. Usually paper tears so that one side fits over or under the other, so make sure that the overlap is on the correct side.

Tear a piece of Japanese tissue paper slightly longer than the tear and about 2 mm (⅛ in) wider on each side. The Japanese tissue paper should be torn and not cut as the frayed edges of torn paper lie flatter and do not cause a hard line. It may be easier to tear the paper by first painting an outline of the shape you want with water and a fine paint brush. This softens the

Paint an outline of the shape of the patch you need onto the Japanese tissue using water on a paint brush

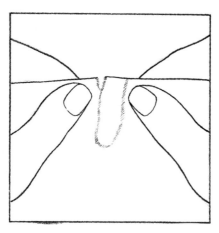

Gently pull the excess tissue away from the patch

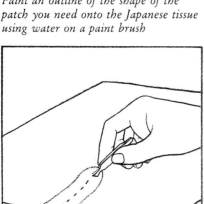

Place the patch over the tear using tweezers

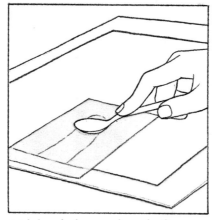

Lightly rub the tear through silicone release paper using the back of a spoon

paper and you can then pull the excess tissue away from the piece you want. Lay the patch of Japanese tissue paper on a piece of glass or Formica and paint on the starch paste. The paste should not be too wet otherwise the water will be absorbed by the print or drawing and stain it.

Use tweezers to pick up the patch and lay it gently over the tear making sure the edges are still close together. If you hold the patch with your right hand, keep the paper and tear steady with your left. Gently pat the patch into place with your finger. Place a piece of clean white blotting paper under the tear and cover the tear with a piece of silicone release paper. Lightly rub the tear through the silicone release paper with the back of a spoon or your finger tips to burnish it down. Remove the silicone paper and put some clean white blotting paper over the tear. Place a sheet of glass over this and a light weight on top.

Leave for at least ten minutes.

Long tears can be repaired in the same way but they are difficult to manage in one go so repair them in stages starting from the inner edge. The repairing tissue paper patches should butt up to each other rather than overlap but there should not be a gap between them.

REMOVING CREASES

Creases from folds can sometimes be pressed out of paper. Lay the paper on some white blotting paper on a smooth, hard, flat surface and cover it with another sheet of white blotting paper. Put a sheet of glass or a flat sheet of board over the picture. Place some weights on top of the board and leave for at least twenty-four hours or longer.

An iron can also be used on prints in a good condition. Lay the print face down on clean white blotting paper and cover it with another sheet of blotting paper. Use the iron set on *Cool* and press lightly.

If the print or drawing can be washed (*see* Cleaning) and you have been unable to remove the crease by dry pressing the paper it may be possible to remove the crease by damp pressing. Lay the print face down on a piece of clean white blotting paper on a smooth, hard, flat surface. Lightly and evenly dampen the complete back of the picture by spraying it with distilled or de-ionised water using a hand-held plant spray. Cover the paper with a sheet of clean, white blotting paper and a sheet of glass or Formica and leave it to dry for about twenty-four hours.

STARCH PASTE RECIPE

100g pure starch (arrowroot, wheat or rice flour)
800 ml distilled or de-ionised water.
Mix the flour to a smooth cream with a little of the water in a bowl. Do not use a steel or copper container. Boil the rest of the water and then pour it into the cream, stirring continuously. Heat the cream in the bowl by placing the bowl in a pan of boiling water. Do not heat the cream directly. Stir the cream until it thickens. Continue to heat it for a further ten minutes. Remove it from the heat and pour it into a suitable storage jar. Cover the top of the paste with a sheet of paper to prevent a skin from forming. The waxed paper discs used to seal home-made jam are ideal.

The paste should keep for a few days in the refrigerator. If it starts to go sour or mouldy do not use it.

If the paste is too thick to use, decant enough for your immediate use and thin it with a little water. Do not make it too wet.

TYPES OF PRINTS AND DRAWINGS

WATERCOLOURS, GOUACHE

Watercolours and gouache paintings have been very popular since the eighteenth century. If the conditions in which they are kept are too dry the paint flakes off. If they are too wet mould grows on the paper, on some pigments and on the binding medium, particularly if honey was the medium. Gouache is slightly chalkier and flakes even more easily than watercolour. Neither should be touched on the surface as grease and dirt from the fingers leave a stain.

Light is the greatest enemy of watercolours. Many pigments fade but not all to the same degree. Some pigments darken with light and atmospheric pollution. This means that the balance of the composition can change.

Keep the light levels as low as possible. Do not use picture lights on watercolours and do not hang watercolours near table lights. If the room is not being used, hang a cloth over the picture or place it face down on a covered table.

Never attempt to wash watercolours or gouache.

INK DRAWINGS

Inks fade very quickly so keep ink drawings in low light. Do not touch the surface as ink easily smudges.

There are four main types of ink which have been used in the past:

1. Carbon black used by the Egyptians and Chinese.
2. Iron gall which is made from mixing galls from oak trees with ferrous sulphate and gum arabic. They are very acid and sometimes the ink eats away the paper leaving it looking like lace. Sometimes these drawings can be de-acidified by a paper conservator.
3. Bistre is a brown ink made from tar extracts from wood and soot.
4. Sepia is made from the ink sacks of squid, octopus and cuttle fish. It was used widely in the nineteenth century.

Never attempt to wash ink drawings.

below *Repeated folding and handling has weakened the paper causing the creases to crack. Self-adhesive tape soon becomes brittle and ineffective and stains the paper*

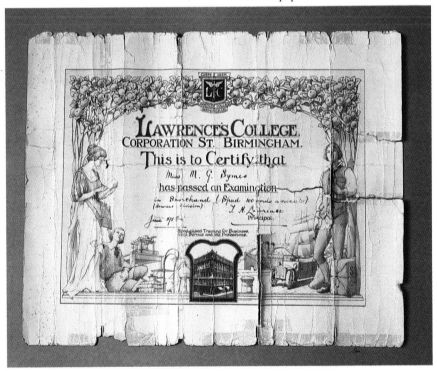

CHALK AND PASTEL PICTURES

Chalks and pastels have been used for drawing since the fifteenth century. Earth colours were the first colours to be used. Pastel painting became popular in the eighteenth century. Chalks and pastels are alkaline and so help preserve the paper. There were a very wide range of colours available and the pigments were bound with a variety of materials including gum arabic, beer, sugar candy and milk. These binding media encourage mould so it is particularly important to try to keep chalk and pastel pictures dry.

Large chalk and pastel pictures were sometimes made up of several pieces of paper attached to canvas or board. Occasionally, chalk and pastel drawings were stuck on to vellum or taffeta. This mixture of materials can cause severe problems (*see below*).

The chalk and pastel is usually very loose on the paper surface so handle the drawing with the utmost care. Do not touch the surface with your fingers as the chalk or pastel will smudge. Do not try to fix the pigment with modern fixatives as they can change the colour, seal in the dirt and cause more harm than good.

Chalk and pastel drawings are far safer if mounted and framed. The overlay mount should be deeper than is necessary for watercolours to stop smudging and to help air circulation. Use glass in the frame not polymethylmethacrylate (Perspex, Plexiglas) sheet and do not polish the glass, otherwise the chalk will be lifted off the surface by the static electricity.

Do not hang a chalk and pastel drawing on a wall which receives any vibrations such as one with a door or one near a boiler as the pigment will be gradually shaken off the paper.

These drawings fade very easily so display them where the light levels are as low as possible.

In some old frames the glass touches the pigment. These drawings should be reframed by a conservator or experienced chalk and pastel drawing framer only.

If a chalk or pastel drawing is unframed, store it in a box with a gap between the surface and the lid. Each

147

drawing should have a separate box. The picture will be safer it if is mounted on acid-free card but it must have a cover mount.

Never try to clean chalk or pastel drawings.

CRAYONS

Crayons are made from pigments bound in a fatty material. They have been used widely since the nineteenth century. They are more robust than pastels but they still smudge and are affected by light. *See* Pastels.

GRAPHITE AND CHARCOAL

These drawings also smudge and the graphite and charcoal can be wiped off by careless handling. Do not attempt to clean them or use modern fixatives. Keep graphite and charcoal drawings mounted and framed in the same way as chalks and pastels. They are not as sensitive to light as chalks and pastels but the paper itself will still be damaged by light so control the light levels in the normal way for paper.

PRINTS

Prints are often in bad condition as they have been treated with less care than paintings. Until recently, most prints were monochrome as coloured printing was not widespread until the nineteenth century. Early coloured prints were coloured by hand and behave in a similar way to watercolours.

Prints are produced by transferring a design from a piece of metal, lino, stone, wood or other material on to paper. A print that is made from a metal plate usually has a 'plate mark', i.e. an impression of the metal plate. The 'plate mark' should never be removed.

Prints often have an undulating surface because of the method of printing used. Do not try to flatten them. Do not press them on to a backing. If they need to be backed for strength this should be done by a paper conservator.

JAPANESE PRINTS

Japanese prints are fragile; the vegetable pigments fade extremely quickly and the paper is very delicate.

Do not expose to them light for any length of time. Handle them carefully as they are easily damaged. Do not allow them to become wet.

PRINTS OR DRAWINGS ON TEXTILES OR PANELS

Prints or drawings are sometimes stuck on to stretched linen or cotton, wooden panels or vellum using starch or animal glue. This mainly occurred in the eighteenth and nineteenth centuries.

When the paper is stuck to a textile it eventually breaks up because the paper and textile expand and contract different amounts with changes of temperature and humidity. Dust also gets into the paper and it is more prone to mould attack so it is often very deteriorated and brittle. Do not attempt to separate the paper from the textile. Do not attempt to clean these. They should only be dealt with by a paper conservator. Display and store prints and drawing on textiles in a temperature and relative humidity which is as constant as possible (about 50 per cent).

Paper stuck on to a wooden panel can suffer even more damage than when it is on a textile. The acids in the wood make the paper turn brittle and discolour. In addition, the movement of the wood makes the paper crack. Sometimes slightly alkaline gouache or pastels last longer than other paper on panels. The panel may be attacked by woodworm which do not discriminate between paper and wood and will bore through both.

Do not try to take the paper off a wooden panel yourself, this should only be done by a paper conservator. Display and store paper on wood in a very constant temperature and relative humidity (about 55 per cent).

Oriental paintings on paper and textiles, including Tangkhas, also come into this group. Their maintenance and cleaning is so specialized that they should only be dealt with by a conservator experienced in this type of work.

OLD MASTER DRAWINGS

Old master drawings were often drawn in iron-gall ink which causes problems to the paper. The ink would originally have been black but is now brown. Sometimes the ink 'eats' its way through the paper. These draw-

ings should be displayed and stored in Exhibition conditions (*see* page 145).

MAPS AND PLANS

Where possible, maps and plans should be stored flat and not rolled or folded. They are best stored in shallow drawers such as in a plan chest. Make sure there is sufficient air circulation within the chest (*see* Storage, page 144). If the maps or plans are referred to frequently it is probably better to store them by hanging them vertically from purpose-made racks.

Very large maps and plans may have to be rolled. Use a large diameter acid-free cylinder which is a few inches longer than the width of the map. Most maps can be rolled on a tube with a diameter of between 10 and 12 cm (4–5 in). Smaller maps may be rolled on a smaller tube but never less than 5 cm (2 in) diameter. Roll the map around this, interleaving it with acid-free tissue. Wrap the roll in acid-free tissue or thin card and then put it in a washed calico case or one made from an old sheet. Do not stand the roll on its end but keep it horizontal. If possible, hang the roll from brackets in the same way as rolled textiles (page 181) so that the weight is not pressing down on the map.

WALLPAPER

If you have early wallpaper or hand-printed paper which you wish to preserve, it should be protected from light as much as possible. Use blinds and ultra-violet filters where possible. Do not let the paper get damp and do not use wood preservative, fungicide or metal cleaners in the room nor any other materials such as floor cleaners which may give off chemicals potentially harmful to the pigments. Metal fixings which have to be screwed on to the wall through the paper such as light switches should have a piece of acid-free paper between the fixing and the paper as the metal can affect the colour of the pigments.

PAPYRUS

Papyrus (Cyperus papyrus) was grown in the Nile delta and used since very early times to make ropes, sails, matting, cloth and, later, a paper-like material used for writing on. Papyrus was used in Egypt from about 9000 BC to the ninth century AD when paper took over. It is thought to have been made by beating strips of the stem of the plant so that they stuck together. The sap acted as an adhesive and as a size. Long rolls were made by joining small strips with starch paste. Not only was papyrus used for documents but old papyrus manuscripts were used as one of the layers of mummy wrappings and is known as cartonage. In recent years papyrus has been produced for tourists.

Papyrus should be cared for in a similar manner to paper. It will become brittle if it is kept too dry. Keep it at a relative humidity of about 55 per cent to prevent mould growing and to stop the papyrus becoming too brittle.

Should you possess some papyrus cylinders do not try to unroll them yourself. It is a highly skilled job and should only be carried out by a conservator experienced in this kind of work. Similarly, papyrus should be cleaned, mounted and repaired by a conservator.

Modern day papyrus can be mounted on acid-free board and framed in a similiar manner to paper.

POSTERS

Posters are usually made from cheap paper and because they are frequently roughly handled, they are often brown, brittle and torn. They should be handled and cared for in the same way as paper.

Do not 'lay down' posters, i.e. stick them down on to a support or on to a board. Do not use Blu-tac, drawing pins or self-adhesive tape to display them as they will stain or tear the paper. Posters will last much longer if they are framed.

Repair tears in posters before framing them as described in Paper, do not use self-adhesive tape.

Use good quality acid-free materials for mounting and framing as these help absorb the acid in the poster itself and so prolong its life. If possible, mount posters on a backing board and use an overlay mount in the same way as mounting a print or drawing. The overlay mount increases the air circulation which is better than having the poster pressed directly against the glass. Inexpensive frames of hardboard and glass clipped together are useful for framing posters but they do not keep out dust or insects. Old, valuable or treasured posters should

therefore be in frames with a moulding.

If possible, store posters flat in a plan chest or box of the right size. Interleave them with acid-free tissue and cover them with acid-free card. This should help buffer the acid in the poster. If this is not possible roll them around an acid-free cardboard tube as described in Maps and Plans.

Because posters were not designed to last they were made from and printed with poor quality materials which are easily damaged by water. Many posters today are printed on good quality paper but these cannot be washed either as the 'glaze' or finish will be ruined. Some posters can be de-acidified to help preserve the paper but this should be done by a paper conservator.

PARCHMENT AND VELLUM

Parchment and vellum have been used for drawings, prints and miniatures. *See* Leather for handling, display and storage.

EPHEMERA

Ephemera includes anything which is not meant to last but which we keep or collect. It is the sort of thing that might be put in a scrapbook, such as postcards, cigarette cards, beer mats, book matches, comics, tickets, magazines, newspapers and cuttings, programmes, instruction manuals, pamphlets, advertisements and invitations. The fact that these things were not designed to be kept means that they are usually made from paper, and cheap paper at that. They are likely therefore to go brown and become brittle very quickly and the printing will fade and discolour.

Handle ephemera as little as possible and do not unfold them repeatedly.

If you want to display your collection it will survive better if it is correctly mounted and framed (*see* Paper).

If you prefer to stick smaller items on to a backing card, stick them down with starch paste on to acid-free card. Do not use spirit gums or rubber-based adhesives. If you cannot make starch paste use wallpaper paste. Once they have been stuck on to the card they can then be framed.

Very small objects such as cigarette

cards and bus tickets are better displayed and kept in an album. Stick them in with stamp hinges or corner photograph hinges. Where possible, use acid-free materials.

Store ephemera in a clean, dry, dark, cool place with adequate ventilation. Keep the area clean to reduce attack by insects and mice. *See* Paper for storage.

Larger objects such as comics and programmes are better stored horizontally and, if possible, unfolded. Avoid storing ephemera directly on a floor.

If you take your collection seriously, store it in acid-free Solander boxes and interleave the objects with acid-free tissue (*see* Paper).

Do not tie bundles together with string or rubber bands but use white cotton tape. If Solander boxes are not available keep out the dust and dirt by wrapping the bundles in acid-free tissue. Never wrap them in polythene or store them in sealed plastic boxes unless the lids are pierced to allow the air to circulate to prevent condensation. Most cardboard boxes give off acid vapour so, where possible, avoid using them for storage, although a shoebox will protect your collection better than leaving it loose.

The conservation and restoration of these items is difficult because of the poor quality paper. If your collection needs conservation consult a paper conservator. If you have a large collection it is sensible to ask a paper conservator for advice on display and storage.

STAMPS

Stamps are a very specialist area of ephemera. Beginners should use commercially available stamp albums and stamp hinges. If the collection is rare or valuable use acid-free materials and consult a specialist stamp dealer.

BOOKS

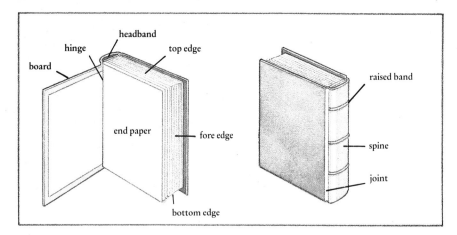

Books are made of a cover and pages. The pages are usually made from paper, although vellum, parchment and cloth are also used. The cover can be made from a variety of materials, including leather, paper, wood, ivory, papier mâché, cloth and vellum. Some covers can be highly decorated with gold leaf or others can have carved ivory or wood decoration or metal studding and hinges fixed on the binding. The type of binding does not necessarily indicate the value of the book, for instance some paperback books are more collectable than some leather bound books. All books should be treated with the same care.

Some books have a dust jacket or dust wrapper which is an extra paper cover on the outside to keep the cover clean. This should be kept with the book. Some dust covers are made of card and are more like boxes that the book slides into for protection.

INSPECTION

Books can suffer from physical damage caused by rough or careless handling as well as the normal deterioration attached to the individual materials that go to make up a book. For example, the paper can become foxed or go brown and brittle, the textile used in some covers can fade or become very fragile, the leather can go mouldy or become dry and brittle, the animal glue can attract mould. Insects will eat leather, cardboard, paper, vellum and almost anything used to make up a book and they are encouraged by household dirt.

When examining a book, look for signs of insect attack, such as silver fish and woodworm, and for mould, mildew and foxing. Woodworm make small holes and silver fish nibble away at the surface of the leather or paper making it look lacey and frayed. Mice and dogs like the adhesives used in bookbindings, as well as the leather and mice particularly enjoy the paper for making nests.

Look for loose or detached plates, illustrations and sections or pages and make sure they stay with the right book in the correct place. Check also for dusty top edges, broken hinges and a torn spine. If the binding is leather, look for dry or crumbling leather which may only be patches from wear or could be red rot.

HANDLING

Handle books carefully as they are easily damaged. If a book is in bad condition it should be handled as little as possible.

REMOVING A BOOK FROM A SHELF
Do not pull a book out from a shelf by grabbing the top of the spine or the sides of the spine as it will eventually break. If your hand will fit between the top of the book and the shelf above, reach to the fore edge of the book and gently push the book out towards you. If there is no space for your hand push the books on either side of the book you want further back into the shelf. This will allow you to get a better grip on the sides of the book you want. Shelves should never be packed so tightly that it is hard to get the books out. When removing large books, make sure you support the weight underneath before

Removing a book from a shelf correctly

you pull them off the shelf.

Do not open a dirty book until the dust and grime have been removed. *See* Cleaning.

OPENING A NEW BOOK
It is easy to break the spine of a new book when opening it; this eventually causes the sections to come loose. Breaking the spine can be avoided by opening the book a section at a time. Hold the unopened book firmly with the spine resting on the table. Open the front board and allow it to lie flat, then open the back board. Open a small section of the front of the book and place this gently on the front board, take a similar sized section of the pages at the back of the book and repeat. Then another section from the front and then the back. Repeat this until the book is open at the centre.

CARRYING BOOKS
Do not carry too many books at once. In particular, do not carry a pile held

steady by your chin as some are likely to fall out from the middle. It is easier and safer to use a tray. Try to carry books of the same size together. If you are moving books some distance or upstairs, put them in a box. Lie the books down on their side rather than on an edge and do not jam too many in at once. Put wedges of acid-free tissue paper in to stop any books sliding about. If you fill a box up, make sure that you can lift it and that the bottom of the box will not fall out. Do not put books loose in a car as a sudden jolt will send them flying.

STACKING BOOKS
If you have to stack books temporarily or you do not have enough space in your bookshelves keep the books on their sides, do not stack them on their fore edge as this will damage the spine and the sideboards and possibly the paper. Keep the piles small and try to keep the same sized books in each pile. If this is not possible, put the smaller books on top of the larger ones. Do not stack books with three-dimen-

sional covers such as those with studs or metal fixings.

Silk and paper bindings are particularly fragile and will split and stain very easily, so handle them with particular care and always have clean hands.

Books which have maps and documents attached to them need to be handled carefully as the maps tear very easily. Open the map or document as little as possible.

Books often have postcards or bookmarks or even pressed flowers in them. These may be part of the book's history and, if so, should be kept with it. If they are making the book too fat and putting extra strain on the binding put the pieces in a well marked, good quality, white envelope and keep it safe. Keep a piece of paper in the book that says where you have put the bits. Any loose pieces of binding should also be kept in a labelled envelope until the book goes for restoration.

If the spine and boards of a book are loose but you do not want to have it restored for the moment, tie the

Book spines will be damaged by incorrect handling

book up with white cotton tape. Tie the tape in a bow so that it is easy to undo. Do not hold the book together with rubber bands or string as they can cause damage. If the book is fragile or precious, make a simple wrapper out of acid-free card and tie it closed with tape.

DOG EARS
Corners of pages are often turned down to mark the page. This harms the paper and lets in dirt. Gently undo the corner and leave the book closed with a small weight on top of it such as another book – telephone directories are very useful for this. Do not straighten the corner if the paper is very brittle as the corner could break off; this often applies to books made after the nineteenth century.

Sometimes a dog-eared corner is of historical interest as it shows something about a particular owner. In this case do not undo the corner.

Occasionally, you find corners which were turned in before the pages were guillotined. Do not trim these as they are evidence of the manufacturing process.

CLEANING

Old, rare, precious and fragile books should be cleaned by a book conservator, but there is a great deal you can do to keep your books clean and in good condition.

Try to clean books and the bookshelf regularly, about every six months. Take the books off the shelf one at a time and dust it. Look for silver fish, mould, woodworm, earwigs and mouse droppings. Keep the books firmly closed as you take them off the shelf so that the dust does not get between the pages. Then dust the top edge and the other edges of the book by holding it under your arm so that your hand is holding together the fore edge.

If the book is not very dusty gently brush the dust off the top edge with a soft brush such as a shaving brush. Use an artist's hogshair brush to remove the dust and dirt from near the headband. If the edges of the pages are still dirty and they are not gilded or decorated, rub over them gently with a soft eraser such as the putty type eraser used for cleaning paper. Use the eraser in one direction only, working with short strokes from the spine to the front. Some early and valuable books had scenes painted on the fore edge which do not show unless the book is slightly fanned out. Make sure you do not remove this by accident when cleaning the edges.

If the book is very dusty you may need to vacuum the top edge using a soft brush attachment. If the cover is not in very good condition it is safer to hold the book closed between your knees and gently brush off the dust with an artist's hogshair brush. Hold the nozzle of the vacuum cleaner in your other hand to catch the dust. Cover the nozzle with a piece of fine net (*see* Textiles) to prevent loose pieces of the cover from being sucked up into the cleaner.

If the pages are slightly cockled, some dust will have penetrated between them. Dust this off with a soft brush page by page. Never bang books together to remove the dust.

Clean the sides of the cover and the spine with a duster, taking care not to catch the edges or pull off bits of the binding. If any pieces do come off keep them safe in a clearly marked envelope until you can get the book repaired.

If, after dusting, an old or rare book or a book that you treasure needs further cleaning do not attempt to do it yourself. It should be cleaned and treated by a book conservator.

Do not try to clean a book cover with an eraser as you will get a stripey effect. Do not wash a book cover.

If the binding of the book is made of leather and it is very dry, do not polish it with wax but rub in a little leather cream dressing which is a water-based emulsion (Connolly's Hide Food, Bavon or Pliancreme). Apply the cream very sparingly on a lint-free cloth or with your fingers. Before applying the cream, check that it does not remove any colour by testing it on a small inconspicuous area. Leave the book standing open with the pages slightly fanned and allow the cream to dry for twenty-four hours. Then lightly buff up the surface. If the book is very dry several applications may be required but the cream should be given at least twenty-four hours to dry between each application. Make sure you use only a little cream as it is very sticky and can attract harmful dust and grit as well as insects. If the surface feels very waxy or greasy after twenty-four hours remove the excess wax with a sponge or lint-free cloth barely moistened with white spirit.

Do not use any creams or leather preparations on vellum or parchment bindings. Books made from vellum or parchment should be cleaned and treated by a book conservator.

Price tickets can be very difficult to remove from book covers. They sometimes peel off more easily when warmed with a hair dryer. Do not get them too hot or you will damage the paper or the binding. Take particular care if peeling a ticket off leather as the top surface is often pulled away with the ticket. If possible, get a book binder to remove the ticket for you. A little white spirit on a cloth may remove the adhesive left behind by a ticket.

STAINS

Coffee, tea, ink, grease, oil and other stains are difficult to remove. You could make a stain much worse by attempting to clean it yourself and you will also weaken the paper or the binding. If the stain really bothers you take the book to a book conservator.

PENCIL MARKS

Pencil marks on the pages and the endpapers inside a book usually add interest and should not necessarily be removed. However, if you want to get rid of them it is possible provided that the paper is not coloured and is in good condition.

Make sure that you have a clean working area and clean hands. If you are going to clean the inside of the front cover or a page near the front of the book open it and place a book of a similar size under the front cover to stop any strain on the hinge. Use a soft eraser of the plastic putty-like type. Use the eraser in one direction only working in straight lines from the spine to the fore edge of the book. Do not rub in circles. Turn the eraser over as soon as it gets dirty. If the fibres of the surface of the paper start to lift, stop.

Pencil underlining can sometimes be taken off by using the putty-type rubber and moulding it into a small point. Again, work in one direction only and use short light strokes and work from the hinge towards the edge of the book. Stop cleaning if the print starts to come off. *See also* Paper.

FOXING

Brown spots on the paper from 'foxing' (*see* Paper) are difficult to remove and should only be done by a book conservator. This is because to clean the paper properly the book has to be dismantled, the paper cleaned and the whole thing reassembled. On no account use domestic bleach to remove foxing as it suggested in some books.

MILDEW AND INSECTS

If a book has got very damp it will cockle, stain and warp, and mildew and mould are likely to develop. To dry the book or if it has some mildew on it, stand it on one end and open it out so that the papers are fanned out and all separate. Allow the book to dry in a warm, well-ventilated area but do not use direct heat as it will cause even worse damage. Once the book is dry take it outside and brush off any powdery mildew with a clean hogshair brush or shaving brush. Take care not to spread the mould spores on to other books or objects. Wash and dry the brush after use. Examine all the books which may have been affected. Check why the damp has occurred and take steps to correct it.

If you find insects or evidence of insects, take the books outside and carefully brush them out. Clean the shelves well before putting the books back. If the shelves themselves have woodworm remove the books and treat the shelves as in Wood. Do not replace the books for at least three weeks.

FLOODING

Should your books become flooded from burst pipes or similar disasters, you need to act quickly. You will not have the time or the space to dry out all the books correctly at once as you will have other things to worry about. So put them in the deep freeze until you can deal with them.

While the books are being frozen make sure that they do not touch each other. Once they are frozen they can be carefully stacked in the freezer. When you are in a position to dry the books, take them out of the freezer, a few at a time, and allow them to defrost. Lie each book on its side on a sheet of clean white blotting paper and take up the excess water by putting clean white blotting paper between the pages. Make sure you do not force the spine. When the book is no longer dripping wet, stand it on its bottom edge and fan the pages out so that they are all separate. Allow the book to dry at room temperature and make sure there is good ventilation in the room. Do not be tempted to speed up the drying by using heaters. Do not dry more books than you can cope with at one time, leave the rest in the

freezer until you have more time and space.

If your books are very valuable it is worth paying to have them freeze dried. This is a more efficient way of drying them out. The cost is based on the weight of the books. Seek advice from the National Preservation Office at the British Library.

DISPLAY

Books on exhibition should be displayed under the same conditions as Paper and Leather. The display area should be clean and dry with a steady temperature and relative humidity and as low light level as possible. *See* Paper and Leather.

If an open book is put on display, do not leave it open on one page for long. If it is open near the front of the book, support the front board by placing a smooth piece of wood or acrylic sheet (Perspex, Plexiglas) or some other support underneath it. The same applies if the book is open near the back. Where a book has a tight spine it should be displayed on two wedges which will support both the front and the back board evenly. Open books should be displayed under glass to protect them from dust.

Ultra-violet filters should be used to protect the book and the light levels should be as low as possible.

Books in shelves should be kept in as dark a room as possible. Use blinds to cut out the light (*see* Textiles). Libraries with good quality books should have ultra-violet filters on the windows and lights. The temperature should be as low as possible but it should also be constant. It is better to have a higher constant temperature

than a lower fluctuating one. Keep fan heaters, radiators, and electric fires away from books.

If you keep books in a glass-fronted cabinet make sure that there is adequate ventilation and put a saucer of paradichlorobenzene crystals in the case to discourage mould and insects.

BOOKSHELVES

Bookshelves should be clean and strongly constructed. The shelves should be made from wood, preferably hardwood. The surface should be smooth but it does not have to be polished. If the shelves are movable you can alter the height to suit the books and so use the space more effectively.

The shelves should be at least 2cm (¾in) thick and 23cm (9in) deep. They must be deep enough so that books do not stick out beyond the front edge of the shelf. No shelf should be longer than 76cm (30in) without being supported, otherwise it will sag with the weight. The distance between the shelves depends on the size of the books. Leave a gap of 2.5cm (1in) between the back of the shelf and the wall to allow air to circulate. If the shelf is on an outside wall this 2.5cm (1in) gap is extremely important. Some permanent shelves are built directly against a wall with no space between them and the wall. In this case drill holes of 2.5cm (1in) diameter at 10cm (4in) intervals along the back of the shelves themselves. Fix a thin strip of wood along the shelf in front of the holes to prevent the books being pushed back and covering the holes.

Built-in shelves often have a backboard; it is important that air can circulate between the wall and the board, particularly if it is an outside wall which ideally should be damp-proofed. There should be an unobstructed gap between the wall and the backboard. The case should have adequate ventilation holes through the top and bottom of the backboard. The size of the holes depends on factors such as the size of the gap between the bookcase and the wall but a rough guide is make holes of about a 2.5cm (1in) diameter at 15–25cm (6–10 inch) intervals. These holes should be covered with a fine metal gauze to keep out insects and dirt.

Make sure you have enough shelf space so that the books are not too tightly squashed together and difficult

Drying a book correctly

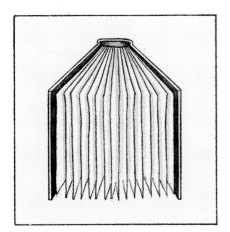

If a book is displayed open support the front and back boards on wedges

to remove. However, the books should not be so loose that they lean over and are not supported, as this coould break the spines. You can always fill any spare space at the end of the shelf with hardwood blocks which are more supportive than most bookends.

Where possible, keep books of the same size together on a shelf. Very large books often have to be laid on their side as they cannot support their own weight and shelves are often not large enough. Make sure that the whole of the side of the book is supported by the shelf otherwise the book will bend and distort.

If the shelving system has metal strips up the sides of the uprights put a piece of acid-free card between the metal and the book so that the book is not marked or harmed by the metal.

Books with metal clasps or bosses must be kept separate from other books as they will damage them. You can protect these books a little by making a simple folder of acid-free card.

If you wish to write any identifying name or number inside a book use pencil not ink or ball-point pen.

Small children can cause a lot of

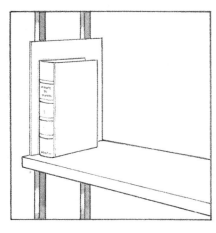

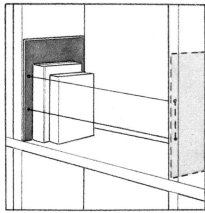

damage to books by pulling them out of shelves. A simple way of protecting the books is to string some nylon fishing line or cotton tape across the front of the shelf. Make sure that the line does not touch the back of the books. Cut two pieces of hardboard to fit either end of the shelf, these should be the same height as the shelf and should project slightly beyond the spines of the books. Paint the smooth side of the hardboard with polyurethane varnish. Make two holes in each piece of hardboard the same distance apart. Place the hardboard sheets at either end of the shelf with the smooth side against the books and the edge with the holes sticking out. Thread the line or tape through the top hole, across the books, and then through, down and back through the other holes.

STORAGE

Store books in a clean, dry, well-ventilated, dark area. Do not store books in basements, cellars and outhouses which are damp, or in lofts or attics where the temperature can fluctuate greatly. Hang an insect repellent strip in the storage area and place a saucer of paradichlorobenzene crystals in any closed cupboard or chest.

Stored books should be inspected regularly for mould and mildew, mice and insects.

Books survive better in book cases or on shelves rather than in chests, drawers or boxes. If you have a lot of books to be stored long term it is worth investing in good shelving.

IDEAL CONDITIONS

Household: Normal household conditions. Avoid direct sunlight and damp rooms.
Exhibition: Relative humidity 50–60 per cent, constant. Temperature 15°C (59°F). Light levels 50 lux.
Storage: Relative humidity 50–60 per cent, constant, not below 45 per cent nor above 65 per cent. Temperature 13°–18°C (56°–65°F), constant. Light levels as low as possible. Keep clean and

above Separate books from metal shelving with acid-free card

left A simple method of protecting books using nylon line

vermin-free. Good ventilation essential.

REPAIR

Book restoration is a highly skilled job, so rare, old or precious books should be restored by a book conservator or binder.

If you do any minor repairs yourself *never* use self-adhesive tapes or document repair tape for repairing either the binding or the paper. To repair tears in pages use Japanese tissue paper or acid-free tissue and starch paste as described in Paper. If you need a stronger support use muslin with the same paste. It is important to remember that any repairs carried out to a book should be able to be easily undone without causing damage to the book.

TEAR IN A PAGE
To repair a tear in a page *see* Paper, but place some waxed paper or silicone paper underneath the page and on top of the repair to separate it from the other pages. If the book is used a lot repair both sides of the page. Close the book and put another book on top and leave it overnight. When the repair is dry, very carefully peel off the waxed or silicone paper, the print should be visible through the tissue.

HOLE IN THE PAGE
Repairing a hole in a page is similar to a tear. Use a piece of Japanese tissue slightly larger than the hole. Protect the other pages with waxed or silicone paper as before. Apply the paste to the Japanese tissue and place over the hole, put waxed paper over this, turn the page over and repeat.

HINGES
The hinge where the cover board is joined to the book itself frequently becomes slack, loose or broken. The endpapers cover over the hinge and often hold the book together if the hinge is broken. If the endpapers are damaged it is perhaps a sign that the hinge is damaged. If the hinge is loose or completely broken the book should really be rebound for a proper repair. However, it is possible to do some minor or temporary repairs yourself on books that are not rare or valuable.

CRACKED HINGE
Do not use self-adhesive tape to repair a cracked hinge. It may damage the

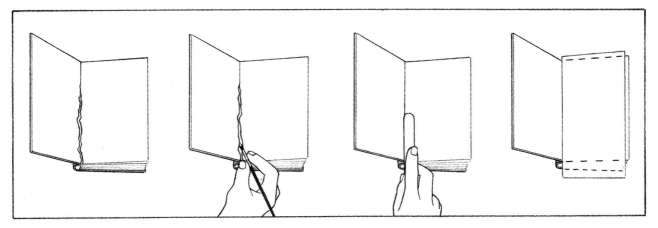

Repairing a book's cracked hinge

paper and will very quickly become brittle and ineffective. Usually the hinge is cracked at the front or back of the book. If necessary, clean any debris or dirt from the crack. Open up the crack a tiny amount but do not cause any further damage. With an artist's small paint brush place a small amount of starch paste or PVA emulsion adhesive (Evostik Resin 'W') or light wallpaper paste along the crack. Using a flat knife, replace the torn pieces of paper to their original position. Gently remove any excess adhesive with a barely damp cloth. Put some waxed paper along the hinge to prevent the adhesive spreading on to the paper. Close the book and press down all along the hinge on the outside. Press the book for twenty-four hours.

If the hinge is cracked in other places in the book use the same process but use very little adhesive to make sure it does not get on to the paper.

DETACHED COVER

If the cover or spine is detached the book should be rebound. There are temporary measures that you can take but they seldom hold up for long as they put extra strain on the fly leaf.

LOOSE PLATES, ILLUSTRATIONS AND PAGES

Sometimes full-page illustrations become loose. They can be replaced in position using a narrow strip of Japanese tissue paper. Tear a narrow strip about 1cm (½in) wide of tissue and cut it to the same length as the height of the book, i.e. the length of the spine. Fold the strip in half lengthways and put some starch paste or light wallpaper paste on one half of

the strip. Lay this half along the edge of the plate with the fold along the cut or torn edge and press down so that it is smooth. Put the plate in position with the inside edge up against the hinge. Apply starch paste to the other half of the tissue and press this on to the adjacent page. Place some folded wax paper the full length of the hinge, close the book and press for twenty-four hours.

Often the plate will stick out slightly further than the other pages. Some books advise you to cut the inside edge of the hinge to make it the right size. If you do this and then in later years come to have the book rebound, the plate will be too small to be sewn into the book correctly. It will then have to have a piece added. Unless the plate will be damaged by sticking out slightly it is better not to cut the plate.

Sometimes it is possible to replace a page or plate by using a small amount of adhesive along the hinge and aligning the page in place. Wax paper must be placed on both sides of the page just short of the hinge. Close the book and press for twenty-four hours.

GILDING

If any gold lettering or tooling is missing it should not be replaced with gold paints as they tarnish very quickly. Gold leaf should be used and this is a job best carried out by a bookbinder.

VELLUM AND PARCHMENT

Vellum and parchment were used to cover some special books and were also used for pages in some early books. Vellum and parchment are particularly vulnerable and should be displayed and stored in good

conditions. Do not try to clean, treat or repair them yourself. Dust can be removed with a soft brush but further treatment should be carried out by a conservator. *See* Parchment and Vellum.

PAPERBACK BOOKS

The first paperbacks, early Penguins, were produced in order to make books accessible to everyone. They were very cheap to buy and were not expected to last. They were made from poor paper which quickly yellowed and became brittle and the binding was usually weak. Many paperbacks made over the last few years are of better quality materials and are more durable.

Paperbacks books should be cared for in the same way as other books. Handle them with particular care as they are very likely to fall apart. Very fragile or valuable paperbacks should be kept in acid-free Solander boxes. If there is more than one book in a box, wrap each one in acid-free tissue. The acid-free board and paper help to reduce the harmful action of the acid in the paper of the book. If you cannot keep your books in boxes, a simple folder can be made from acid-free card which can be wrapped around the book and tied up with tape. Ready-made folders can be bought from specialist suppliers.

LOOSE SPINE

A loose spine can be stuck back in place using a small amount of starch paste. Starch paste should be used in preference to PVA emulsion or other adhesives which are often recommended.

LOOSE SECTION

Sections of a paperback frequently

become loose. If the section is completely loose, paint a small amount of starch paste along the back of the section. Carefully place the section in place, making sure it is in contact with the spine. Remove any excess adhesive with a barely damp cloth. Place a strip of silicone paper between the pages on either side of the section well back towards the spine but not so close that it too becomes stuck in place. Press the book for twenty-four hours.

If the section is broken up so there are some loose pages, line up all the pages carefully so that the section is complete and paste a strip of Japanese tissue paper along the back and about 1 cm (½ in) into the front and back pages of the section. Once this has dried replace the section in the book as described above.

If the section is loose but not completely separate carefully paint adhesive where it is loose and press as above.

PHOTOGRAPHS

Photographic prints, negatives and cinematographic film are all made from a light-sensitive material which is stuck on to a base. The base for prints is usually made from paper and for negatives and cine film it is usually a transparent plastic. The light-sensitive material consists of silver salts suspended in gelatin. The silver salts change colour when exposed to light. There is also an adhesive which attaches the gelatin layer to the paper or plastic.

After the film is exposed to light it is processed with chemicals so that the image is fixed into the gelatin layer. This prevents the image fading and stops the silver salts continuing to react to light. Unfortunately, despite this processing the image will eventually fade or change colour in light and will be affected by atmospheric pollution. The base itself also deteriorates in time, for instance, the paper may be acidic and much of the early transparent material was made from cellulose nitrate which deteriorates slowly and when in adverse circumstances can explode. If the chemicals from the processing are not completely washed off they too will eventually affect the image.

The positive and negative images are both made in the same way. The difference between them is that in the positive image (e.g. the print) the light and dark correspond to light and dark as we see them and in the negative they are in reverse. The negative is usually transparent and the positive (the print) is not.

Both the positive and negative deteriorate in the same way and therefore require similar conditions for care and handling.

See below for Nitrate film, Daguerrotypes, etc.

INSPECTION

Light, humidity, temperature, acids and pollution can all cause photographs to deteriorate.

Light deteriorates the paper and makes the image fade. If the humidity is too high mould may grow and the gelatin will become sticky and spread out, it also provides food for fungi and if the humidity is too low the paper will become brittle. If the humidity fluctuates from damp to dry the emulsion will crack and flake.

Fingerprints leave a residue of grease and acid on the surface of the negative or photograph which eventually harms the image. Harmful acids which cause the image to deteriorate can also be in the paper used as a base as well as in the card and board used for mounting a photograph.

The silver in the emulsion is easily affected by chemicals in the air. Dark spots first appear on the image and eventually it becomes yellow or it fades completely. The main hazards to the silver are from chemicals in wood, cardboard, paper, bleaches, some plastics, fresh paint, photocopiers, car exhaust fumes, air pollution and sea air. It can also be affected by ammonia from cleaning materials, sulphur given off by deteriorating rubber such as rubber seals, bands, floors and rubber-based adhesives. All these, as well as handling and use, work towards destroying the film or print. It is surprising that any photographs survive at all.

HANDLING

Never touch the surface of the image on the print or the negative. If the photograph is to be handled a lot, mount it on acid-free card or put it in a transparent polyester envelope.

Handle negatives, including modern ones, by their edge and by the shiny, non-emulsion side. Keep the matt emulsion side towards you to ensure that it is not damaged. It is safer to keep negatives in transparent polyester envelopes and handle the envelopes.

Avoid storing and handling photographs in the dark room as the chemicals and water in a dark room can cause a great deal of damage. Do not write on the back of prints with a sharp pencil or ball-point pen.

In many cases it is not possible to preserve an old photograph or negative so you may have to have a copy made which will outlive the original. If you find an old negative and wish to have a lot of prints made from it it is better to have the old negative copied and make the prints from the new negative. Most professional photographers will be able to do this for you.

If a photograph is to be a permanent record do not use resin-coated paper and tell the photographer to treat and wash the print thoroughly.

Never use self-adhesive tape on photographs. *See* Repair.

See Paper for more information on handling.

CLEANING

Do not attempt to wash or clean a print or negative yourself. Remove any dust with a soft camel-hair brush or a photographer's puffer brush.

DISPLAY

Photographs should be displayed under the same conditions as prints and drawings. They should also be protected from light, so keep the light levels as low as possible.

Hang photographs away from areas where there might be changes in temperature or humidity, such as near a door or hot water and heating pipes.

Do not dry-mount photographs. Use acid-free card and good quality products for framing. Always use a fillet or overmount to keep the photograph from touching the glass. There are ready-made frames available which have no moulding – the glass and the backboard are clipped together. These should not be used for long-term framing as they are open to dust, insects and air pollution.

Photograph albums are a good way of keeping photographs safe and of displaying them. The pages should be made from acid-free card. Corner mounts or stamp hinges are the safest way of fixing the photograph. Do not stick the photograph on to the paper. Do not use self-adhesive albums. *See* Photograph Albums.

See Paper for more information on display.

STORAGE

Prints, negatives and cinematographic film all need the same conditions for storage. However, you should store negatives and prints separately to avoid contaminating the negative with impurities in the paper of the print.

Photographs should be stored in a cool, dark, clean, well-ventilated area with a constant relative humidity. Do not store photographs and film in or near wood furniture, newly painted or varnished furniture or near a photocopying machine and try to avoid using cardboard boxes. These all give off chemicals which will damage the image on the photograph. Ideally, photographs should be kept in a metal cabinet which has an enamel finish. The cabinet should have holes for ventilation with some fine muslin or dust filters over them to keep out the dust. Try to keep photographs away from harmful atmospheric pollution. It is not easy to meet all these conditions in an ordinary household but you should aim to get as near as possible.

Photographs can be kept in acid-free Solander boxes on open shelves as described in Paper. Interleave the photographs with acid-free tissue to help buffer the effect of the environment and the paper. Store the box horizontally. If it is placed vertically the photographs will buckle unless the box is full. As with prints and drawings, photographs should be mounted, where possible, on acid-free card and stored on their mount in Solander boxes. The mount helps protect them.

Although a shoebox is made from cardboard which may give off harmful chemicals it is better to use one than to have the photographs loose in a drawer. Line the box with acid-free tissue and interleave the photographs with more tissue paper. This helps buffer the harmful effects of the cardboard.

Photographs are protected if they are stored in envelopes made from paper or transparent plastic. Paper envelopes should be good quality and, if possible, acid-free. Do not store more than one photograph in an envelope. If you write any form of identification on the envelope do it without the negative or print inside.

The best method of storing photographs, particularly very fragile or much handled prints and negatives is in transparent polyethylene terephthalate sleeves (Melinex, Mylar). Make sure that the relative humidity does not get too high or the gelatin will swell and leave the image stuck on to the smooth polyester surface.

Make sure that any plastic envelopes used for storing negatives, film or prints are not made from polyvinyl chloride. If the plastic is referred to as 'vinyl' it may be polyvinyl chloride (PVC) which is harmful to the film. If in doubt, avoid soft, flexible plastic envelopes. Polyethylene or polypropylene or polyester envelopes can all be used.

Do not store prints or films in a basement which may be damp or an attic where the temperature fluctuates a lot.

Store nitrate based film (*see below*) separately from other film.

Photographs are very badly affected by water as it dissolves the gelatin. If they become wet do not touch the image. If possible, leave the photograph to dry, face up, in a well-ventilated room. Do not dry the photograph with artificial heat. If several photographs are stuck together or are thought to be stuck together do not try to separate them. Take them to a photographic conservator for treatment. Like paper, if you cannot deal with wet photographs immediately put them in the freezer until you can dry them out. They may be brittle when frozen so take care not to crack them. Thaw them out very slowly.

IDEAL CONDITIONS

Household: Normal household conditions. Avoid direct sunlight and very damp, dry or fluctuating conditions.

Exhibition: Relative humidity 40–50 per cent constant. Never higher than 60 per cent. Prints ideally 40 per cent. Temperature about 18°C (65°F). Light levels 50 lux.

Storage: Relative humidity 40–45 per cent, constant. Temperature 10°-15°C (50°–60°F). Relative humidity is the most important to keep constant. Low light levels or dark.

Nitrate and colour cine film must be kept at much lower temperature. Colour photographs and film are very sensitive to light. *See below*.

REPAIR

Tears can be repaired on the reverse side of prints by using Japanese tissue and starch paste as described in Paper. Take care not to get any paste or water on the print itself. Negatives, cinematographic film and old, rare or precious prints should be taken to a photographic conservator for advice.

Some prints curl up, particularly if they have been stored unmounted in a dry environment. These can usually be flattened by placing them between two sheets of clean, dry, white blotting paper or polyester sheet. Lay a sheet of glass or flat board over this and then put some weights on the sheet. Leave for several days. Do not try to flatten very early or brittle photographs. The emulsion may crack and flake. This should only be done by a photographic conservator.

AMBROTYPE

The ambrotype was produced from about 1854. The image was produced on glass. It appears as a positive image, although it can be seen as a negative image if the light strikes it from a certain angle. It was produced in the same sizes as the daguerreotype and the same type of glass and leather case was used. A black surface is placed behind the negative so that the positive image shows up.

Handle very carefully so that the glass does not break. Clean off the dust with an artist's soft paint brush or a photographer's puffer brush. Do not touch the image. If in need of further cleaning or repair an ambrotype should be taken to a photographic conservator.

CINEMATOGRAPHIC FILM

8 mm and 16 mm film have always been made of safety film or, more recently, polyester based film, so they are fairly stable but they should be stored carefully. However, 35 mm film was made from nitro-cellulose until 1951. It is very unstable. *See* Nitrate Film.

Acetate film was used as a base for 16 mm film from 1922 but it was not until 1948 that it was used for 35 mm cinema films. If it is stored well it is fairly stable. *See* Safety Film.

Colour cine film is particularly sensitive to everything. Keep colour cine film in sealed containers at a very low temperature or even in a refrigerator. *See* Colour Film.

COLOUR PHOTOGRAPHS AND FILM

The first colour was added to black and white films by hand, this was even done on daguerreotypes and lantern slides. Some colour processing was carried out as early as 1907 but it was not until the 1950s that it was widely available. At the moment not a lot is known about how and why colour film deteriorates, only that it is even more sensitive to light and fluctuations

in the relative humidity and pollution levels than black and white film so it must be displayed and stored even more carefully. The discolouration of the film is uneven so that the balance of the colour changes. Colour film is so vulnerable that it is better to display a copy rather than the original. It appears that the colour image is more permanent on a slow speed film.

Some colour transparencies or slides can survive very well without too much colour change while others discolour completely. Where possible, do not view old slides through a projector but use a hand viewer as the heat of the projector can greatly speed up the deterioration. If you must use a projector use one with a fan and heat-absorbing glass and only leave the slide in for ten seconds or less. Even better, have a copy made of the transparency and use that.

STORAGE

Ideally, colour film should be stored at -5°C (21°F) at a relative humidity of 20–30 per cent. This is not always possible and, in addition, can cause condensation problems and makes handling difficult. Keep colour film at as low a temperature as possible and a relative humidity of about 40 per cent, which is quite dry. Keep both colour film and prints dust-free and store them in plastic envelopes (*see* Photographs: Storage).

DAGUERREOTYPE

The daguerreotype was invented in 1839. It was made up of a sheet of highly polished, silver-plated copper. The image was made directly on to the metal without the intermediate negative stage. The image on the metal can appear to be either negative or positive depending on the angle that the plate is held and at which the light strikes the surface. The image cannot be reproduced from a daguerreotype apart from by re-photographing and printing. The daguerreotype was usually produced in standard sizes and in a glass and leather case. Daguerreotypes are rare but are the sort of thing you might find in the attic of an old family house. If you find one, treat it with care and ask for professional help sooner rather than later.

Daguerreotypes are quite robust but the metal will corrode if they are kept in damp conditions. They should be handled with care to ensure that the

glass covering does not crack. If this happens the image will tarnish. Never touch the metal surface. Carefully remove any dust with an artist's soft paint brush or a photographer's puffer brush. If any further cleaning is required it should be carried out by a photographic conservator. If the binding of the daguerreotype has to be replaced use only acid-free paper and an easily reversible adhesive.

GLASS NEGATIVES

Glass negatives are not the same as glass lantern slides because the image on them is a negative while the image on a slide is a positive. Usually the image of the glass negative is on the surface of the glass, so make sure you do not touch the image. Sometimes they are double glazed like lantern slides.

Handle and store glass negatives in the same way as lantern slides.

LANTERN SLIDES

Lantern slides are a positive image on a transparent base. They are usually 3¼ in by 4 in in size and can be both black and white or coloured. The image is sandwiched between two plates of clear glass with the edges bound together with black tape. They should not be confused with glass negatives which vary in size and have a negative image.

Lantern slides are usually quite stable so if handled carefully they are quite durable. They break very easily. It is safest to keep them in individual polyester envelopes. If you cannot get these, interleave the slides with acid-free paper or a double thickness of acid-free tissue paper. If you have the original box store them in that. Keep them at a temperature of 10°-12°C (50°-54°C) and at a relative humidity of 40–50 per cent constant. Do not mend broken slides. This should only be done by a conservator experienced in this sort of work.

NITRATE FILM

Nitrate film was used for film and cinematographic film from 1899 to 1939 but any 35 mm film made before 1951 could be nitrate film. Cellulose acetate or 'safety' film was used from about 1930 onwards but for some years both were used. Nitrate film has recently come to the attention of the public because of the dilemma of national film archives in many countries whose early films are deteriorating before the eyes of the custodians.

The nitro-cellulose base deteriorates giving off acid which accelerates the decomposition of the film. Nitro-cellulose film is a fire risk as it can spontaneously combust. The signs of deterioration are a faded image with brownish or yellow discolouration. The emulsion becomes sticky and then softens, the negatives weld together and eventually they disintegrate into a brownish powder which has an acrid smell.

If you think you might own some nitrate film a photographer ought to be able to tell you whether it is or isn't. If he cannot, try to find a photographic conservator who can tell you, as it is better to be safe than sorry.

IDENTIFICATION

Early negatives usually have 'nitrate' or 'safety' printed on the side. If they do not or you are unsure, there is a test which may help you identify the film.

Cut off a tiny piece of negative and place it on a non-flammable surface away from the rest of the film and any other flammable material. Hold a lighted match to it. If it burns easily it is nitrate film, if it does not it is safety film.

If you have nitrate films and you wish to keep them, store them away from other photographs. Keep at a temperature of about 2°-5°C (35°-40°F) and a constant relative humidity of 50 per cent. Keep them well ventilated and open the envelopes of large negatives or the tins of film regularly to allow the gases to escape.

POLYESTER BASED FILM

Polyester based film replaced acetate based film for 8 mm and 16 mm cinematographic film and still negatives. Sound track is also made from polyester. It is long lasting but not yet suitable for archives because the emulsion does not bind firmly onto the polyester base. It should be treated in the same way as other photographs.

RESIN-COATED PAPER

Resin-coated paper is now very widely used for colour and black and white prints. Under normal conditions the image fades and deteriorates faster than on conventional paper. For this reason if you take any photographs for permanent records make sure they are not printed on to resin-coated paper.

SAFETY-BASE FILM

Safety-base film, which was first made from cellulose acetate, began to replace cellulose nitrate film from the early 1930s. It is a great deal more stable than nitrate film.

Cellose acetate film requires a relative humidity of 40–50 per cent and temperature 10°-12°C (50°-54°F). If the relative humidity is kept constant at the right level it does not matter if the temperature is higher. Do not let acetate based film get too dry or the gelantin and acetate will crack, shrink and flake. If the relative humidity is too high fungi will grow, the plasticiser will crystallize and the image will be distorted. If the temperature fluctuates the emulsion will become detached from the base. Cellulose acetate film can discolour.

TINTYPE

The tintype or ferrotype was used a little later than the ambrotype but was produced up until the twentieth century. It is a direct positive image on a thin, sensitized iron plate. The image is dull grey and often varnished. The reverse is painted black or dark brown. Tintypes were produced in many sizes and are sometimes found in daguerreotype or ambrotype cases.

Keep tintypes dry to prevent rust forming. Do not touch the image, carefully remove any dust with an artist's soft brush or photographer's puffer brush. If you think you might own one seek help from a photographic conservator.

PHOTOGRAPH ALBUMS

Old photograph albums should be stored in an acid-free box, such as the Solander boxes made for books. If this is not possible, wrap them in strong-acid-free paper and tie them with white cloth tape. Do not use rubber bands. If the paper of the album is not good quality place acid-free tissue between the pages, this will help buffer the acid and protect the photographs. Store the album horizontally so that all the weight is supported.

A 1920s folding camera

TAPA AND BARK CLOTH AND PAINTING ON BARK

Tapa or bark cloth is a type of paper-like fabric which is made from the fibrous material of trees, particularly from types of mulberry tree. It is not very durable and is usually produced by people who do not have ready access to woven cloth. It is made into clothing and hangings and can also be used as a background for paintings. Travellers have been returning with tapa from the South Seas, Africa and South America since the early nineteenth century.

Tapa is made by continuously beating the inner layers of bark of various trees – not the bark itself – into long strips resembling a thin, strong felt. It does not have any weave. It is usually decorated with paint or dyes with symbolic or decorative patterns.

INSPECTION

Bark cloth is more like paper than a textile. It can be damaged by light, damp, pests, mould, dirt, dust and too high or too low relative humidity. If it becomes very dry it will become brittle. If it is very damp mould will grow on it. Check for insect attack, particularly silver fish. If tapa has been stored rolled up it may be stiff. Do not unroll without relaxing the fibres (*see*Handling).

Like paper and wood, tapa is affected by the amount of moisture in the air. It swells and contracts as the humidity fluctuates. The paint on the surface will not move in the same way. This difference is likely to make the paint flake and come off, so keep tapa in a constant relative humidity.

HANDLING

Handle a piece of tapa as you would Paper.

Do not attempt to unroll tapa when it is very dry. It will crack as you open it.

If it has been stored rolled up and is stiff, place it in a steamy bathroom for a few hours. Or if your bathroom won't stay steamy for long enough place the roll in a sealed polythene bag or box with a container of hot water. This will relax the material and allow

it to be unrolled. Ease it open, don't force it. It can then be dried flat. Lay the tapa on a soft board covered with polythene or polyester terephthalate (Melinex, Mylar) sheet. Cover the tapa with a piece of nylon net which is slightly larger than the object. Stretch the net taut over the tapa and secure the net with weights or pins. If you pin the net the pins should be at a slight angle with the head pointing away from the centre of the object (*see*Textiles). Allow the tapa to dry naturally.

Do not let the tapa stay damp for long because it is very likely to develop mould.

Old tapa may be valuable and will be very fragile. Handle with great care and always seek advice from a paper conservator.

CLEANING

Clean tapa regularly so that dust and dirt does not collect on the surface. Brush it with an artist's soft paint brush, holding the nozzle of the vacuum cleaner in your other hand to collect the dust. Alternatively, you can clean it with a vacuum cleaner set on a low setting as described in Textiles: Cleaning, protecting the bark cloth with a piece of nylon net. Do not let the vacuum nozzle touch the surface of the painting as this can damage the paint layer as well as the fibres. If the paint is flaking, do not vacuum the object. It should be conserved and cleaned by a conservator.

Bark cloth should never get wet so do not wash it. The water will dissolve the binding adhesive in the cloth and in any painted decoration.

Do not apply any kind of varnish to tapa.

DISPLAY

Light, heat and moisture affect tapa. It is important that the conditions

should be correct, *see* Textile: Display.

Do not hang tapa on outside walls which could be damp, or where direct sunlight could fall on it. Like paper, tapa will survive better in low light and when it is framed as this protects if from dust and dirt.

Tapa can be mounted on acid-free board and framed like a drawing. It can be hinged to an acid-free mounting board in the same way as a drawing. Use an acid-free card mounting frame to create an air gap of about 0.25cm (⅛in), to prevent the paint layer sticking to the glass.

Small modern bark paintings look very good mounted on board covered in hessian. *See* textiles: Mounting a textile. Attach the bark painting to the hessian using a PVA emulsion (Vinamul 6815 or Mowilith DMC2 or Evostik Resin W). Put a small amount of adhesive in a line around the edge of the tapa about 1.5cm (½in) in from the edge. Make sure that you do not

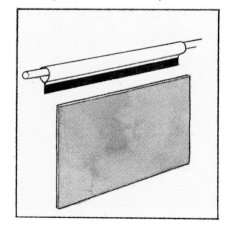

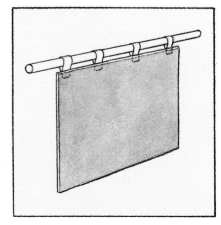

above *Make a cotton sleeve and use iron-on material to attach the taps*

right *Make small loops to hang valuable tapa*

use too much adhesive otherwise it will squelch out and look horrid. Lay the tapa in position on the board, cover it with silicone paper or white blotting paper and press it flat with a weight. Leave for twenty-four hours.

Large tapas can be hung using the same principle as tapestries, *see* Tapestries. A cotton sleeve should be made the same length as the width of the tapa. The hanging rod will go through this. The sleeve is attached to the tapa with iron-on tape. First sew the sleeve to the tape and then fix the tape to the tapa by ironing it on along the top of the tapa on to the reverse side. Valuable, rare or old tapa should not be hung like this as it is not yet known whether the adhesive on the iron-on tape will be harmful to the tapa. If a valuable tapa has to be hung make small loops at 15cm (6in) intervals held in place with the iron-on tape in a similar way to tapestries.

STORAGE

The ideal storage condition for tapa is a cool, dry, dark and clean area, free of pests, with good ventilation and a constant temperature and relative humidity. Never put tapa in an airing cupboard which is usually warm and fluctuates from moist to dry. Basements are normally too damp and the relative humidity fluctuates too much in an attic.

Dichlorvos insecticide strips (Vapona) should be hung in the storage area to help protect tapa against insect attack. The strips must not touch the tapa.

Never allow pins, tacks, sellotape or rubber bands to come into contact with tapa. They should always be removed before the tapa is stored.

Never fold a piece of tapa as folds will soon become creases under the weight and then they will break and tear. Tapa should be rolled round a tube covered with acid-free tissue. *See* Textiles: Rolling a textile. If necessary, wads of acid-free tissue can be used instead of a tube. Once rolled the tapa should be loosely tied with 5cm (2in) wide white cotton tape and rolled in washed calico or an old, clean sheet. Tie with cotton tape.

Lay small pieces of tapa flat and separate each one with sheets of acid-free tissue, (*see* Paper).

IDEAL CONDITIONS

Household: Normal household conditions but avoid damp or very dry areas Keep out of sunlight.
Exhibition: Relative humidity between 50–60 per cent constant. Temperature about 15°C (60°F). Light levels 50 lux.
Storage: Relative humidity 50–60 per cent constant, not below 45 per cent nor above 65 per cent. Temperature 13°–15°C (56°–60°F), constant.
Light levels as low as possible.

REPAIR

If a tapa is torn it can be mended in the same way as Paper.

PAINTING ON BARK

Painting on bark is an Australian aboriginal art. The bark is taken from trees at certain times of the year and then scraped to get a smooth surface. Next it is heated and held down with rocks to flatten it. The surface is then prepared for painting by using natural resins from plants. Originally the aborigines decorated the treated bark with charcoal, clays and other earth colours but now they usually use modern paints.

The main difference between tapa and painting on bark is that tapa is manufactured and has no definite structure. The bark used for painting on bark still has its original structure.

Painting on bark behaves in a similar way to tapa except that it is even more sensitive to relative humidity. If it is allowed to get damp it will curl in an attempt to get back to its original shape. If it gets too dry it will shrink and split. Because bark paintings change shape according to the amount of moisture in the air it is essential not to fix them rigidly to a mount, for instance do not use pins and nails. Allow them room to move naturally.

The conditions for display and storage are the same as for tapa but it is even more important that the relative humidity does not fluctuate.

See Panel Paintings for further information.

STONE

Most types of stone have been used for statues, friezes, carvings, decorative objects, lamps, fireplaces and a huge range of other objects. Some stones such as granite are very hard and almost indestructible, while others like alabaster or soapstone are extremely soft and fragile. The colour of stones can range from the snow white of some marble to the beautiful jade green or black and blood red of granite. The texture of stone can be very open and coarse or close and smooth.

Stone objects can be very plain or highly carved and ornate. They may be decorated with paint or gold leaf or inlaid with other materials.

INSPECTION

Stone objects kept inside usually survive very well. Their greatest danger is from breaking, cracking and chipping. However, stone objects displayed in the open suffer from weathering in the same way as natural stone. The surface can be worn away by rain water and corroded by pollution in the air. Frost can cause a great deal of damage because water penetrates the stone, then freezes and expands which causes the stone to break up. On some stones such as limestone, weathering causes a 'skin' to form on the surface. If this skin is removed or broken the stone underneath will be powdery and the surface detail will be lost.

Mould, algae and lichen can grow on the surface of stone which is damp for any length of time, whether inside or outside. When the stone is outside it grows particularly on the north-facing side of the object. Occasionally algae and lichen can enhance the appearance of an indifferent object but often it is disfiguring.

Check stone for blistering, flaking or crumbly surface, for old repairs, cracks and chips.

If the stone has a painted surface, for instance on heraldic coats of arms, make sure that the paint is sound and not flaking and lifting or powdery.

Stone sculpture has often been painted in the past. Any remaining paint should not be touched but should be cleaned and conserved by a conservator.

HANDLING

Handle stone with clean hands as greasy marks will show. Stone also cracks and chips surprisingly easily.

Smaller statues and objects can be carried but take care that your belt buckle does not scratch the object or its base. Use both hands to carry a piece, place one under the base and use the other to support the object about two-thirds of the way up. Never carry objects by the handle, rims, limbs or other projections. Never lean over objects to pick up another one and make sure long necklaces, lockets and objects hung around the neck such as spectacles and pens do not hit or catch on anything. Before picking up a stone object check if for repairs or pieces which could easily be knocked off.

Do not be fooled by the size and weight of the object you are moving. Large and heavy does not equal strong. A stone object is likely to be less strong than you think. Do not push or drag an object made from stone but always lift it.

If you are moving a large piece of sculpture, always carry it on a truck or barrow well padded with clean, soft blankets. Tie the statue to the barrow with webbing or rope. Put padding between the statue and the webbing or rope to prevent it marking the object. Take into account arms, legs, necks, hands, fingers and any other projections so that they do not bang into

left *Algae and lichen can grow on the surface of stone which is damp*

Pad and evenly support sculptures that are lying horizontally

doors or pieces of furniture on the way.

It is usually safer to move a very fragile stone piece standing upright, but lie it horizontal if this is impossible, for instance if the doorways are too low. If you have to lie a sculpture horizontal make sure that the object does not rest on any projections, that it is very well padded and that the weight is evenly supported.

Statues or busts on bases or pedestals can either stand on the base without any special fixing, or can be securely bolted or stuck to the base or, somewhere between the two, have pins which fit into the base but which are not actually stuck in. This last type applies particularly to small statues and busts.

If a statue or bust is not permanently fixed to the base or pedestal always move them separately. The base may appear to be firmly stuck on but check it carefully because if it is not it may, after a short distance, cause a lot of damage by dropping off and falling on to something else.

If a statue or bust is permanently fixed to a base they will both have to be moved together. It is advisable, if at all possible, to move them in an upright position. If you try to lie them down you may put stress on weak areas, such as ankles, with disastrous results. If in any doubt, and if the statue is of importance, consult a fine art shipper.

Move one object at a time and do not carry pictures and sculpture on the same trolley, if the trolley lurches or jolts you are likely to have a picture with a piece of sculpture through it.

If an object should become damaged during moving make sure that even the smallest pieces are collected and put in a safe place until it can be mended. When the object goes to be restored it is much easier for the restorer to use the original material, no matter how small the bits, than to have to make up missing areas.

CLEANING

Never clean rare, old, precious or fragile stone objects. This should be done by a stone conservator.

INDOOR STONE
Alabaster must not get wet (*see* Alabaster). Do not attempt to clean a stone object if the surface has deteriorated as you may remove the small amount of remaining detail.

Remove general dust by using a dry, clean, white hogshair artist's paint brush. Gently brush the dust off the surface holding the nozzle of a vacuum cleaner in the other hand. The end of the nozzle should be wrapped with foam plastic.

If the object is in good condition and it is still rather grubby it can be washed using warm water containing a few drops of a non-ionic detergent (Synperonic N), not household detergent. First wet the whole surface of the object with clean water, then lightly scrub the surface with the soapy solution using a bristle brush such as a toothbrush or soft nail brush. Rinse well with clean water and allow the object to dry.

To clean stone that has a sound painted surface, such as a coat of arms, it is possible to use spit, but do not attempt to clean paint that is powdery, flaking or lifting. Spit contains a 'surface active agent' which acts as a natural detergent. Using a cotton bud, dampen the end with spit and test clean a small inconspicuous area. If dirt and no pigment comes off, clean the paint, turning the bud as you go. Discard the buds when they are dirty. *See* Painted Stone.

OUTSIDE STATUARY
Regularly remove leaves and debris that have caught in the crevices of the statue, otherwise they will hold water and speed up the deterioration of the stone.

Never clean a statue that has a deteriorating surface. It is not always easy to tell how sound the surface of limestone and sandstone is because the 'skin' formed by weathering will actu-ally appear sound but if you tap it it will sound hollow. Never clean limestone or sandstone in this condition and take care not to knock the surface or it will break off. Get help from a stone conservator.

If outdoor sculpture is sound and does not have a deteriorated, sugary or rough surface, it can be cleaned by spraying with water. You need to set up a hose pipe so that you can continuously spray the statue with a fine spray of water. Use a lawn sprinkler attachment on a fine spray setting or the spray attachment of a hand-held, pressurised garden spray which you can attach to the end of the hose.

You will have to turn the statue or the hose to ensure that all sides of the object are cleaned. Spray a fine mist of water over the sculpture until the dirt can be brushed away with a soft bristle brush such as a very soft toothbrush. The amount of time it takes for the dirt to soften varies, it may be anything between one hour and twenty-four hours. Do this on a warm sunny summer's day when there is no danger of frost.

If a stone object is covered with lichen or algae these can be killed with a fungicide. Brush a 1 per cent solution of dichlorophen (1gm dichlorophen to 100ml water) dissolved in water over the surface. Do not do this near a pond or waterway as it will harm the flora and fauna.

DISPLAY

INDOOR DISPLAY
Do not display stone above fireplaces, radiators and other heat sources. The rising heat will deposit dirt on the surface.

Stone reliefs can be displayed on a wall but they must be prepared with suitable fixings by a stone conservator. The object may also need to be supported from underneath. Use either stainless steel brackets covered with plastic tubing or chamois leather to prevent the metal staining or scratching the stone. Make sure that the wall is not damp and that it is strong enough to carry the weight of the stone.

OUTSIDE DISPLAY
Stone objects that are displayed outside will deteriorate more quickly than those that are inside; however,

under the right conditions they should not come to a lot of harm. Marble may deteriorate quite rapidly and should not be displayed outside (*see* Marble). Never put alabaster outside (*see* Alabaster).

If you need to make a new plinth for a statue it should have damp proof membrane built into it to prevent damp rising through the plinth. In addition, dig a small trench round the plinth and fill it with small stones to prevent weeds and grass growing up to the base and to improve drainage.

It is essential that statues are mounted at the correct angle to the base or plinth. Leaning statues produce stresses that can be damaging to the sculpture over a period of time. If a plinth is unstable or has moved due to soil subsidence it should be rebuilt on an appropriate foundation.

Carved stone benches should be raised several inches off the ground and should be insulated from rising damp by placing damp-proof membranes under their feet.

Do not place stone sculpture too close to trees and bushes. Over-hanging branches can scratch the surface of a sculpture. Keep an eye on the length of the branches and trim them back if necessary. Do not place stone sculptures under trees as water dripping off the leaves and branches will cause uneven staining on the piece. Do not place stone sculptures where overhanging ivy and trailing plants can create a tent-like effect as this encourages algae growth. Do not let ivy grow up stone objects as it will destroy the surface.

Spray from lawn sprinklers can be harmful if the water contains fertilisers or other such chemicals. Remember

A new plinth showing the damp proof membrane

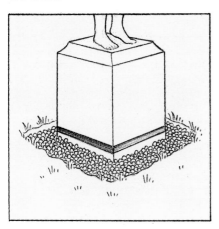

that the spray travels further than you think. If you do spray your lawn, temporarily cover your sculpture with a sheet of polythene.

STORAGE

Store stone objects in a dry place where the temperature does not fluctuate too much. Wrap small objects in acid-free tissue and, if possible, pack objects singly in acid-free boxes. If you have to use polythene boxes make sure that the lids are well perforated to avoid condensation. Never put stone objects in polythene bags or wrap them in sealed polythene. Large objects can be covered with a clean white dustsheet.

Keep outside stone sculptures and objects under cover when they are not on display. Outbuildings, sheds and garages are suitable if they are dry and clean enough. Put the sculpture far enough back in the storage area and not too close together, so that you do not have to keep moving them to get at other things. Cover the sculptures with perforated polythene or, even better, a clean dustsheet to keep off the grease, grime and bird droppings. Set up a barrier around them of unimportant objects such as boxes. Remember the lawn mower is always rather bigger than you think and can easily knock into an ill-stored sculpture. Stand stone objects on wooden slats or polythene sheeting to prevent them being affected by any rising damp from the floor.

Do not store stone objects in damp cellars or outbuildings

Outside stone objects which are too difficult to move into storage should ideally be covered for protection during the winter. Purpose-built wooden covers are ideal. It is essential that the covers have ventilation holes in the sides to prevent condensation. Put the covers on while the object is completely dry.

Before winter sets in, remove soil from stone urns and troughs. This reduces the likelihood of their being split by frost and ice. Ensure that any drainage holes are clear.

IDEAL CONDITIONS

Household: Normal household conditions.
Exhibition: Relative humidity 50–60 per cent. Temperature about 18°C (65°F).

Light levels not critical. Painted stone not more than 150 lux.
Storage: Relative humidity 50–60 per cent. Temperature 5–15°C (41–60°F), no lower or higher. Light levels not critical.
Painted stone kept in low light levels or dark.

REPAIR

Do not repair old, rare or precious sculpture. If small pieces such as fingers, are broken off an outdoor stone statue they can be stuck back into place using a quick-setting epoxy adhesive (5-minute Araldite or Devcon). Do not use too much adhesive or it will squelch out. Hold the piece in position until the adhesive has set. Remove any excess adhesive from round the join with a sharp knife or scalpel. Take care not to scratch the stone. You should stick a piece back only when the object is completely dry, so do not try to repair a statue in winter. If a larger piece such as an arm or leg is broken off do not attempt to stick it back yourself. It is a skilled job to repair stone to make it strong and safe.

Stone objects kept indoors, particularly alabaster and marble, should not be repaired with epoxy adhesive as it may stain the stone in the future. To repair small pieces use an easily reversible adhesive (HMG or UHU All Purpose Clear Adhesive). Any more serious damage should be repaired by a conservator.

TYPES OF STONE

MARBLE

Marble is a hard crystalline rock which can be highly polished. The lustre of polished marble is caused by the light penetrating the surface of the marble and then being reflected back by the deeper lying crystals. There are many varieties of ornamental marble ranging in colour from black through green, yellow and almost all colours of the spectrum. Some of the great Greek sculptures, including the Elgin Marbles, were made with marble from Mount Pentelicus in Attica. The marble used by Michelangelo and Henry Moore comes from Carrara in Italy.

Marble is used for sculpture and buildings, for fire surrounds, for floor and wall tiles, for tops of tables and washstands and for decorative friezes, pedestals, vases and urns. The Romans used it for sarcophagi and monuments. It was also used to build the Taj Mahal. Marble can be carved and polished, painted, inlaid with other marbles or precious and semi-precious stones and with gold or silver.

INSPECTION
Marble is porous and will stain and discolour easily. It can be damaged by chemical and physical action and stained by rust, algae and lichen, and by smoke from fires and by oil. Marble will also absorb dirt from handling and colour from unsuitable packing material, cosmetics and wine. Fruit juices and some foods can etch and stain marble. Marble cracks, chips and breaks.

Marble displayed outside will have the surface worn away by rain and corroded by atmospheric pollution. The surface will become rough and uneven and detail may be lost. In badly polluted areas the corroding surface will become blackened by soot and general grime. Water will penetrate the surface, particularly a corroded surface, either as rain or as water drawn up from the ground. This water can then freeze and expand. The marble may split and the surface spall off.

The surface of marble can develop a sugary appearance which indicates that the surface is deteriorating. This often occurs on the underside of

opposite *Regularly remove leaves and debris from the curves and the base of a statue*

above *Overhanging greenery encourages algae*

below *Iron dowels frequently secure arms and legs onto the body of a sculpture*

carving, the surface will feel rough and granular to the touch. There may even be loose crystals like granulated sugar.

Salt-laden air near the sea accelerates the deterioration. Salt can be carried a distance of about thirty miles from the sea so if you want to put marble sculpture outside make sure you really do live inland.

Arms and legs on marble statues

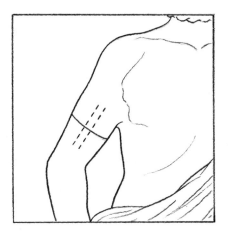

were almost always pinned on to the main body of a marble figure with iron dowels. Check for rust-coloured staining on the surface of the marble which could be iron staining from corroding iron dowels, clamps and pins. As the iron corrodes it expands and will eventually split the marble. If you see iron staining and cracking in the marble, get help very quickly from a stone conservator.

Marble pedestals are often made by boxing together pieces of marble so that the pedestal appears to be made of a solid piece. With time the adhesive used to stick the marble to the core can give way and the veneer of marble can come off. Check that the veneers are sound.

Check that the 'jointing' material used in fire surrounds has not dropped out. A stone mason or very good builder should be able to put this right for you.

Sometimes marble can have a painted surface, for instance on heraldic coats of arms, *see* Stone and Painted Stone.

HANDLING
Marble is a hard and brittle substance and will break or chip very easily. *See* Stone.

Clean hands are essential for handling marble objects, particularly white marble. If the piece is not highly polished it is advisable to wear clean white cotton gloves, however, if the surface is highly polished, gloves will be too slippery.

If you place a marble piece down heavily on to a hard surface it can shatter.

When you tie a marble statue on to a barrow make sure you put clean padding between the webbing and the stone as marble marks very easily.

CLEANING
Do not clean ancient, rare or precious marble pieces or marble that has a deteriorating surface. It is possible that some ancient or antique marble objects may have traces of pigment on them. This is not always easy to see but is very important and can be completely lost by cleaning. Always ask for advice from a stone conservator.

Indoor Sculpture Do not allow marble to become very dirty but never use cloths or dusters, particularly not coloured dusters, for cleaning as they tend to rub the dust into the surface and may smear greasy dirt. Do not use feather dusters because the feathers break and the broken ends of the spines will scratch the marble.

Dusting marble Remove general dust by using an artist's dry, clean, white hogshair paint brush. Gently brush the dust out of the detail and off the statue holding the nozzle of a vacuum cleaner in the other hand. Take care not to knock the marble with the end of the nozzle; if necessary tape some foam plastic round the end.

Washing marble Before washing a marble sculpture make absolutely sure it is neither alabaster nor painted plaster. To check, lie the sculpture on its side and with a sharp knife or scalpel very carefully scrape a tiny area on the underside. If the sculpture is made of plaster it will be soft, white and powdery. If it is alabaster it will be soft, but not as soft as plaster.

Washing marble can drive the dirt further into the surface as marble is so porous. Household detergents may discolour the surface. Acids, no matter how dilute, attack marble and should *never* be used. Never use proprietary stone or marble cleaning agents which do not say exactly what their contents are. If they contain any acids they will damage the surface. Iron stains are virtually impossible to remove from marble.

It is possible to clean an ordinary marble object, in sound condition, by wiping the surface with swabs of cotton wool dampened with a mixture made up of 300ml (½ pint) white spirit, 300ml (½ pint) distilled or de-ionised water and one teaspoon of a non-ionic detergent (Synperonic N). The mixture can be kept in a screw-top jar to be used when necessary. Do not use a metal container. Shake the mixture well before using it.

Use both sides of the swabs and discard them as soon as they become dirty. Wipe in one direction only and do not rub the surface. Always work from the bottom of a piece of sculpture upwards. This is because if any of the cleaning fluid should run down on to a still dirty area it will 'set' the dirt and make it almost impossible to remove. But the swabs should not be that wet.

Clean a small area at a time and rinse as you go by wiping over with clean swabs of cotton wool dampened with distilled or de-ionised water. There may well be areas of a statue that will not clean as well as the rest. To prevent over cleaning some areas and the marble looking patchy, lightly clean the statue all over once and then, if necessary, go over it again. The result will be much more satisfactory than 'thoroughly' cleaning the first time and perhaps being left with a blotchy object.

If the object is very small or has intricate carving use cotton wool buds or a few fibres of cotton wool wrapped around a cocktail stick to clean in the details. Turn the bud as you go and discard it when it is dirty.

Cleaning very dirty marble If you have a very dirty but sound piece of marble or one that has old wax or varnish on it, it can be cleaned by using a dichloromethane-based paint remover (water washable Nitromors in the green can). Should there be any spots of paint, wax or other dirt on the surface of the marble, scrape off as much as possible with a plastic picnic knife but take care not to scratch the marble surface. Wear rubber gloves and take care not to get any remover on your skin. If you do, wash it off immediately. Work in a well-ventilated room with all the windows open, or, if possible, outside.

Apply the paint remover to a few square inches of the sculpture with a clean, long-handled paint brush. Brush the remover on lightly so that the dirt is not pushed into the pores of the marble and leave on the surface for only a few minutes. Wipe off the remover with clean cotton wool swabs dampened with acetone or white spirit. Then wipe the area again with clean dry swabs. Do not allow the paint remover to dry out on the surface. Apply the paint remover to the next area and repeat the procedure. Place the dirty swabs in a lidded container and allow them to evaporate outside before putting them in the dustbin.

Poulticing After you have cleaned the surface of the sculpture with the paint remover, you can remove any dirt that remains engrained in the pores by cleaning with a poultice. This works by drawing the dirt into the poultice as it dries.

The poultice is made from clean white blotting paper and distilled or de-ionised water. Tear the blotting paper up into small pieces and place it in a clean bowl. Add enough water so that you can mash the paper and water to make a thick pulp. Apply the pulp all over the surface of the object as a coat about 25mm (1in) thick and leave it to dry for about twenty-four hours. At this stage the poultice will not be completely dry but the top surface will have formed a crust. Do not allow the poultice to dry out completely. The poultice is ready to come off when it can be pulled away cleanly from the surface.

If you are interrupted and cannot remove the poultice when it is at the

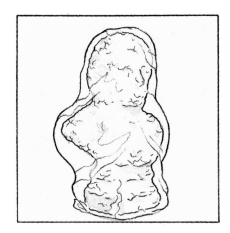

Poulticing a bust

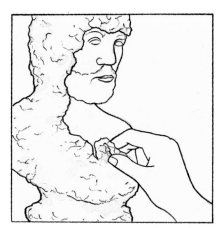

Removing the poultice

correct stage, cover the sculpture with polythene to prevent the poultice from drying out.

Peel off the poultice and wipe the exposed surface with cotton wool swabs wetted with distilled or de-ionised water. Do not allow the exposed surface to dry out before you have wiped it as otherwise the dirt and any remaining fibres from the poultice will dry very hard and become difficult to remove. Make sure all traces of the poultice are removed.

If further cleaning is still necessary apply another poultice.

Cleaning marble with a mild abrasive Some marble sculpture does not always clean using the above methods but a mild abrasive may clean the surface. Use a mildly abrasive chrome cleaner (Solvol Autosol). Rub it evenly over the surface of the marble using a circular movement with an artist's clean, white stencil brush. Wipe off the cleaner with swabs of cotton wool dampened with white spirit and polish the surface with a soft, clean white cloth. Never use any other abrasive, particularly not household scouring powders and creams (such as Ajax and Vim) because the chemicals they contain can harm and discolour the marble and the abrasive will scratch the surface.

Waxing and finishing a marble sculpture When you have finished the treatment and the statue is dry the surface may appear a little dull. Apply a light coat of microcrystalline wax with a bristle brush and polish with a soft, clean white cloth. Finally dust over the surface with some pure talc. This fills the pores of the marble so that dirt will not become engrained in the future and it prevents dirt from being attracted to the wax.

To clean painted marble *see* Stone.

Outside Sculpture It is rare for marble statues to be displayed outside. If you do have one in your garden clean it exactly as for Stone. *See also* Cleaning Indoor Marble.

DISPLAY

Indoor display There is a tendency to think that because marble is heavy and dense it can be displayed anywhere. However, marble objects, particularly those that are pure white can be damaged by damp even when they are displayed indoors. Damp air can cause iron staining and permanent discolouration of the surface as well as etching it. Be aware that this is a danger if you place marble statues in bathrooms, near frequently opened windows, by indoor swimming pools or in conservatories.

Do not display marble above fireplaces, radiators and other heat sources. The rising heat will deposit dirt on the surface.

If you have houseplants near marble objects or on marble table tops make sure that wet leaves do not rest on the marble surface as they can mark it. Do not spray houseplants with water if they are standing on or near marble as the fine mist may eventually cause staining in the marble.

See Stone for display.

Outside display Marble objects that are displayed outside will deteriorate very much more quickly than those that are inside. It is rare that a marble piece will remain unscathed from the elements outside so if you have a statue and wish it to remain in good condition, it should be kept inside.

If you insist on displaying marble outside *see* Stone for the most suitable conditions.

STORAGE
Store marble as described in Stone.

IDEAL CONDITIONS
See Stone.

REPAIR
See Stone.

MARBLE FIREPLACES
Marble fireplaces that are in use tend to accumulate a layer of sooty, slightly tarry dust, particularly on any mouldings or details. If the fireplace is made of white marble the dust should be removed by vacuuming as described above as the marble marks very easily. If the fireplace is made of black marble the dust can be removed by using the brush attachment of the vacuum cleaner.

Having removed the dust, clean the fireplace with white spirit and water mixture as described above. If this is not effective, use the paint remover as described above. Take particular care that the paint remover does not dry on the surface of the marble and that when you wipe it off you wipe it all off. If paint remover dries on the dirty marble the dirt will become virtually impossible to remove.

It is difficult to apply a poultice to a fireplace so if the marble needs a little more cleaning use the mildly abrasive chrome cleaner (Solvol Autosol) as described above.

Once your fireplace is clean, wax it with microcrystalline wax to seal the surface. If the fireplace is white, apply talc as above. Maintain the condition of the fireplace by dusting regularly. Occasionally wipe the surface with a damp cloth. Once or twice a year re-wax the fireplace but use only very little wax.

If you have a marble fireplace which has been painted or one with peeling lacquer, remove the paint or lacquer with paint remover and clean as above. Do not use a blowlamp or hot air stripper as it is easy to scorch the marble. Take care not to damage any applied decoration with the paint remover.

Some fireplaces have an original decorative paint surface. If the paint is in sound condition these should be cleaned as for Painted Slate. If the painting is fragile it is better to leave it alone or ask a conservator for advice.

MARBLE FLOORS
Never use patent floor cleaners or household cleaning agents, particularly not creams or scouring powders, to clean marble floors. Only use water, either on its own or containing a few drops of a non-ionic detergent (Synperonic N) or a mild household detergent (Fairy Liquid). Wash and ring the mop out regularly in the soapy water to remove the dirt. Change the water in the bucket before it becomes very dirty. Then rinse the floor well with clean water. Clean the floor regularly so that the dirt does not build up.

Do not make the floor too wet nor slop water on skirting boards, furniture legs or rugs. Wipe the floor round and under furniture by hand with a floor cloth.

ALABASTER

Alabaster is a form of gypsum. It is usually white but can be yellowish, orange or even red, often with darker veins running through it. When alabaster is cut into sheets it is translucent. In some houses in North Yemen and in churches in Ravenna, Italy, alabaster is still used instead of glass in the windows. It gives a beautiful soft light.

Alabaster is very soft and can be scratched with a fingernail. It is also easy to carve and equally easy to break. Alabaster is used for clock cases, lamps and vases, pedestals, tourist souvenirs, effigies on tombs and figures in churches. Church figures were often painted. It can be distinguished from marble because it is so much softer.

Handle alabaster very carefully. Do not set it down hard or it will crack or crumble. *See* Stone.

Alabaster will slowly dissolve in

Never display alabaster objects outside or in a damp room. *See* Marble.

For ideal conditions, storage and repair, *see* Stone.

BLUEJOHN

Bluejohn is a highly decorative translucent fluorspar. It has beautiful bands of colour ranging from blue/violet to light brown and yellow. It is found in Derbyshire and is also, not surprisingly, known as Derbyshire Spar. Although bluejohn has been known since the time of the Romans it only became extensively used in the late eighteenth century when it was used for making vases, boxes, jewellery and other objects, often with intricate metal mounts made of ormolu or bronze. Bluejohn is not usually found in large pieces so often a number of lumps were joined together with shellac or animal glue to make a large object. A bluejohn object was particularly popular in France which imported large quantities of it calling it 'bleu-jaune' hence the English name of bluejohn.

The surface of the stone can be quite soft and scratch easily so take care not to knock it or catch it with your belt buckle. Bluejohn should not be cleaned by immersing it in water as it may be made of several pieces which will come apart. Clean it by wiping the surface with cotton wool swabs or buds moistened with warm water containing a few drops of a non-ionic detergent (Synperonic N) or a mild household detergent (Fairy Liquid). Use both sides of the swabs. Take care not to rub or wet the ormolu (*see* Ormolu). Rinse with swabs or buds dampened with clean water and dry with a soft clean cloth. If the surface is dull, apply a light coating of microcrystalline wax with a piece of cotton wool and polish with a soft clean cloth.

Bluejohn should be repaired with an easily reversible adhesive (HMG or UHU All Purpose Clear Adhesive).

water, particularly tap water, so never immerse alabaster objects in water nor use a blotting paper poultice as described in Marble. Remove dust before doing any wet cleaning otherwise the dirt will be absorbed by the alabaster. Remove dust as described in Marble.

Clean alabaster with the white spirit and water mixture described in cleaning Marble. Merely dampen the cotton wool swabs so as not to wet the surface of the alabaster too much. Rinse off with swabs of cotton wool dampened with white spirit on its own. Dry with a paper towel or a soft, clean white cloth.

If the surface of the alabaster looks dull, apply a little microcrystalline wax and buff gently with a clean, white soft cloth.

If the alabaster is still not clean, clean it with paint remover or a mildly abrasive chrome cleaner (Solvol Autosol) as described in Marble but always test an inconspicuous area first.

Alabaster urns are sometimes used as lamps by placing a light bulb inside them. If too much heat is generated by the light bulb the alabaster will deteriorate, so always use a low wattage bulb and check that the alabaster is not cracking or starting to become crumbly.

BRECCIA

Breccia is a naturally occurring type of marble which is composed of angular fragments cemented together in a matrix. It can be used for table tops and other flat surfaces and should be cleaned as for Marble.

CHALK

Chalk is used as a material for carving. It is extremely fragile and friable, damages very easily and readily absorbs water and dirt. Treat as for Plaster of Paris.

GRANITE

Granite is one of the hardest and toughest rocks. It is very dense and heavy and it is better able to survive the ravages of time than most other stone. It can be red, white, dark grey or almost black. It can be carved and polished to a hard shine. The Victorians used it extensively for tombstones, monuments and garden urns, although it has also been used for table tops and fire surrounds.

Clean granite in the same way as Marble but as it is much tougher it can be scrubbed with a bristle brush. Do not use a wire brush.

JADE

Jade is loosely used to refer to jadeite and nephrite which are different minerals but very similar in appearance. Jade is a very hard, smooth and translucent stone which ranges in colour from dark spinach green through brown to the white which is known as 'mutton fat' jade because of its lardy appearance. Jade can be highly polished.

The Chinese used jade for carvings and amulets, the Moguls in India used it for dagger handles and bowls which they inlaid with rubies and gold, and in Mexico the Aztecs made knives from it for cutting out the pulsating heart of human sacrifices.

Jade is as brittle as glass and will break just as easily. *See* Glass.

For cleaning, *see* Bluejohn. Unless the jade has stones set in it or metal inlay, the object may be immersed in the washing solution. A light coating of microcrystalline wax will revive the surface if it has lost its shine.

For Display, Storage and Ideal Conditions, *see* Glass.

Rare, precious or old jade should only be repaired by a conservator. Small repairs, however, can be carried out using an easily reversible adhesive (HMG or UHU All Purpose Clear Adhesive). Do not use epoxy resin adhesive.

LIMESTONE AND SANDSTONE

Limestone is a comparatively soft stone varying in colour from grey to brown and has been used extensively for architectural carvings on buildings.

Sandstone is very similar to limestone but is more of a sandy, pale golden colour. It has been used extensively for sculpture, particularly in the eighteenth and nineteenth centuries, when garden ornaments became available for the general market. Urns, sculptures, sundials, fountains, garden seats, tombstones and monuments were all made from sandstone.

Both limestone and sandstone are affected by atmospheric pollution which weakens the surface so badly that it will eventually flake off exposing a soft crumbly layer underneath. When this happens the surface detail is lost. There is as yet no completely satisfactory way of dealing with this problem. Do not clean sandstone or limestone which is not in sound condition. Both types of stone can be quite porous and pick up grease and dirt easily. Handle, clean, display and store as in Stone.

ONYX

Onyx is a striped agate and comes in several variegated forms. The most usual colour is green but it can also be white, a yellow ochre colour and reddish. Onyx is used extensively for lamp bases, ashtrays, desks sets, Art Deco figurines, table tops and other small carved ornaments. Onyx is a comparatively soft stone so check carefully for cracks and chips. Handle, clean, display and store as in Marble.

PIETRE DURE

The term pietre dure applies to objects such as ewers, busts and vases which are made from hard or semi-precious stones such as lapis lazuli and agate. These objects can either be made from one stone or several different types of stone and often have elaborate ormolu or other metal mounts.

Comesso di Pietre Dure or, as it is known in English, Florentine mosaic, are decorative panels made by setting hard or semi-precious stones into a stone base to produce a design. These designs are often highly elaborate, depicting flowers, birds, fruit and insects rather in the same way as marquetry. The most impressive panels come for Florence and show scenes, landscapes and portraits. The panels are used to make tabletops, boxes, pictures or to decorate the front of cabinets.

Objects made from pietre dure or Florentine mosaic can be cleaned in the same way as bluejohn. To protect the surface from stains wax it lightly with microcrystalline wax applied on a soft, lint-free cloth.

If any of the stones are loose they can be relaid using an easily reversible adhesive (HMG or UHU All Purpose Clear Adhesive).

ROCK CRYSTAL

Rock crystal is a very hard, transparent, glass-like, naturally occuring material made of quartz. It is used to make objects such as dagger handles, small bowls, small carved ornaments. Occasionally, large pieces of rock crystal have been found and have been carved into vases and bigger objects.

Clean and treat rock crystal objects in the same way as bluejohn and jade. Handle as for Glass. It is sometimes difficult to differentiate between rock crystal and glass. Do not expose rock crystal to sudden changes in temperature.

SCAGLIOLA

Scagliola is an imitation marble made from a composition of gypsum, fish glue and coloured marble powder and chips. When scagliola is polished it looks like a natural marble and was much used for table tops, columns, pilasters and other interior architectural features. Scagliola is very soft and scratches, chips and bruises easily.

It is not easy to differentiate between scagliola and marble but it is much softer. If in doubt, make a small scratch in an unobtrusive area; scagliola will scratch very easily and the exposed surface will be powdery.

Clean scagliola in the same way as bluejohn. If the object is large, use a cloth rather than cotton wool swab. *Never* use paint remover to clean scagliola because it will destroy it. If the surface looks dull, a light wax with microcrystalline wax will improve and protect the finish.

SLATE

Slate is a dense rock which splits easily into thick or thin sheets. Slate can vary in colour from grey to red and green. It is used for roofing, for writing on, for fire surrounds and as a base for carving inscriptions on. Slate can be painted and used for table tops or pictures. It is easily chipped and broken and is particularly susceptible to frost.

Clean slate as for Marble. If a slate surface looks dull after cleaning rub in a 1:1 solution of boiled linseed oil and white spirit. Only use a small amount and rub it in well.

Painted slate table tops should be cleaned in the same way as painted furniture. Do not use organic solvents such as white spirit, acetone, or alcohol on the paint and do not rub the surface hard. Do not leave the paint wet or damp for any length of time. Take particular care when watering plants on a painted slate surface and mop up any spills immediately.

Do not put anything hot directly on to a painted slate surface or the paint may lift off.

Small, painted slate objects can be cleaned with spit, *see* Stone.

Slate pictures should be dealt with by a painting conservator and should be framed and unframed by a framer.

SOAPSTONE OR STEATITE

Soapstone is rather like alabaster but is very much softer. It comes in a variety of colours ranging from white and yellow to a bluish grey or green colour and it feels rather soapy, hence its name. Soapstone is used to make small carvings, particularly for the tourist industry; a great deal of Eskimo art is carved in it.

Clean as for Alabaster.

COMPOSITION OR ARTIFICIAL STONE

Composition stone is made of stone dust and fragments mixed together with cement. The first objects were produced in the eighteenth century by Eleanor Coade who manufactured vast quantities of garden sculpture and ornaments. Nowadays, stone dust is mixed with modern resins as well as cement to produce a very convincing artificial stone.

It can be quite difficult to distinguish between limestone, sandstone and composition stone but if there are any signs of air bubbles in the surface of the piece it is definitely composition stone for no real stone has air bubbles in it. Pieces cast in composition stone often have flash lines from the mould remaining on the surface.

Composition stone can be cared for in the same way as Limestone and Sandstone.

Recently synthetic resin and marble dust and chippings have been used to produce some pleasing statues. These can be displayed outside and should be treated in the same way as marble.

PLASTERCASTS AND MOULDS

Plaster of Paris is basically gypsum which, when mixed with water, sets hard quickly. It is cheap, easy to pour into moulds and takes paint well. It is therefore ideal for mass producing statues and ornaments. Until the advent of modern materials, plaster was used for making moulds. The Victorians used plaster not only for making popular statues but also for making moulds and then the casts of monumental friezes and statues such as those from the Parthenon.

Painted plaster figures were made in their thousands until the advent of synthetic plastics. Plaster was used to make anything from fairground prizes to the original Woolworth's flying ducks. Plaster was also used for imitation bronzes and terracotta statues which are often hard to tell from the real thing.

Some plaster figures were impregnated with wax and other similar materials. This made the plaster appear more like stone or ivory and also made it slightly tougher.

INSPECTION

Plaster is extremely soft and friable and suffers greatly from physical damage. If a plaster object is knocked it will chip and the chalky, white plaster will show through any paint.

Plaster absorbs water and dirt easily. Water can stain plaster and cause it to disintegrate and dirt is almost impossible to get off.

HANDLING

Great care must be taken not to allow plaster objects to knock against each other or anything else. Set them down carefully and take care that your belt buckle does not scratch the surface as you carry an object. Always have clean hands when handling a plaster object. Plaster objects must never be allowed to become wet. *See* Stone.

Plaster moulds are usually made of two or more pieces. In order to protect the inner surface of the mould, carefully tie all the pieces together with cotton tape. Plaster moulds rapidly wear out so if you have an old plaster mould which you want to use you should make a cast from it and then mould the cast. This new mould can be made in plaster or synthetic materials and should be used to cast from.

CLEANING

The only way to clean unpainted plaster is by dusting it. It cannot be washed. Do not, however, use a duster as this will rub the dust into the surface and may smear greasy dirt. Brush the dust off with a clean, white hogshair brush as described for Marble. Plaster statues which have not been painted or otherwise treated are very soft and it is easy to rub the edges off any detail when cleaning.

Painted plaster statues or plaster objects that have had the surface treated with wax or shellac can be cleaned by dusting and then wiping the surface with swabs of cotton wool barely moistened with warm water and a few drops of a non-ionic detergent (Synperonic N) or a mild household detergent (Fairy Liquid). If the paint surface is damaged use a cotton wool bud and avoid getting water into the plaster. Before cleaning, test in an inconspicuous area that the paint will not come off with the washing solution. Use both sides of the swabs and discard them as soon as they are dirty. Work from the bottom up. Rinse with swabs of cotton wool moistened with clean water then allow the object to dry naturally. If you are cleaning a large statue clean and then rinse a small area at a time.

DISPLAY

It is important that plaster is protected from dust as much as possible. Do not place plaster objects over direct heat sources such as open fires and radiators as the heat will carry dirt upwards and deposit it on the object. Keep plaster objects out of damp areas such as bathrooms and conservatories and do not place painted objects in direct sunlight. Check that wire fixings on wall ornaments are not rusting and weakened. Do not hang plaster figures on a damp outside wall as the plaster will absorb the moisture which will weaken the plaster and cause any metal fixings, particularly iron, to corrode.

STORAGE

Store plaster objects in a cool, dry area. On no account keep plaster objects in a damp cellar, loft or outhouse.

Wrap small plaster objects in acid-free tissue and place them where they will not get knocked. Larger plaster objects should always be covered with a dustsheet to protect them from dust and dirt.

IDEAL CONDITIONS

Household: Normal household conditions. Avoid damp rooms.

Exhibition: Relative humidity 45–60 per cent. Temperature about 18°C (65°F). Light levels not critical. For painted statues about 200 lux.

Storage: Relative humidity 45–60 per cent. Temperature about 15°C (59°F). Low light levels.

REPAIR

Plaster can be mended using a PVA emulsion (Evostik Resin W). Paint both sides of the break with water which prevents the water in the adhesive being absorbed by the plaster which would make the adhesive dry too quickly. Then paint a thin layer of adhesive on to both break edges. Join the pieces together and allow the adhesive to dry thoroughly. Wipe off any excess adhesive from the surface with a damp cloth before it dries.

If the metal fixings are rusted through you can replace them with thick brass picture wire.

PLASTER MOULDINGS

Many ordinary Victorian and Edwardian houses have decorative plaster cornices, ceilings and ceiling roses. If the decoration is filled with the accumulation of years of white wash and paint, the detail can be revealed by picking out the old white wash and paint. First vacuum the moulding. Remove any objects that are underneath the area to be cleaned and cover the floor with dustsheets. Use an artist's white hogshair brush or a decorator's paint brush to remove dust from deep carving and moulding. Wear goggles and a dust mask. Fix a strip of foam plastic round the end of the nozzle of the vacuum cleaner and hold it in the other hand to catch the dust as you brush it out.

Using a sponge or paint brush dampen the surface with water containing a few drops of a non-ionic detergent (Synperonic N) or a mild household detergent (Fairy Liquid). The paint and white wash will soften before the plasterwork, pick it out with dental tools and wooden picks. Wash off remaining bits and pieces with a damp sponge, rinsing it regularly in clean water. Do not get the plasterwork too wet. It is a time – consuming, dirty, back-breaking job but the end result can be amazing.

TEXTILES

Textiles are materials which are produced from interlacing yarns or thread. These include fabrics made by lace making, crocheting, knitting, weaving, braiding, knotting carpets and embroidery. Other fabrics which are not woven, such as felt, are also counted as textiles. Textiles are usually made from wool, linen, cotton, silk or man-made fibres.

Spun or twisted thread is turned into a woven fabric by criss-crossing the warp and the weft threads. This is usually carried out on a frame or loom. The warp threads are stretched from one end of the loom to the other while the weft threads are passed between them. The most basic type of weave is a simple criss-cross of warp

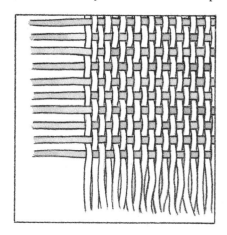

and weft threads (under one, over one), however a pattern can be woven into the fabric by altering how the warp threads interlace with the weft, such as in worsted cloth. Coloured designs can be woven into the fabric by dyeing some of the yarns. Alternatively, patterns can be printed or embroidered on to the fabric after it has been woven. Metal threads are sometimes used for decoration and can either be woven into the fabric or added later.

Textiles have a vast range of uses from clothing, carpets, wall-hangings and bags to lining suitcases and boxes.

INSPECTION

Textiles are harmed by light, heat, dirt, handling, cleaning, dampness, mildew, mould and insects. Ideally, textiles should be kept dry, clean and in total darkness but in everyday life this is unrealistic as they are either in use as carpets, rugs, upholstery and hangings or on display as embroideries, lace and costumes. The

left *The most basic type of weave is a simple crisscross of warp and weft threads*

below *Textiles are harmed by light*

174

main aim of textile care is to keep exposure to light, dirt and damp to a minimum.

Textiles should be checked periodically for signs of decay, particularly when first acquired or brought out of storage. The condition of items that have been on display for years is often assumed to be good but they should also be checked regularly. Look for faded colours, yellowing of cotton or linen fibres, dry, brittle or fraying threads, staining, moth, mould, dirt, tears and localized wear. Textiles framed under glass such as samplers, embroideries and lace should be checked for mould, dust and insects. Check that pins and fastenings are not rusting, rotting or staining the fabric. Look for wear on carpets or rugs at heavy traffic points.

Light fades colours and weakens the fibres, and the higher the temperature the faster the disintegration. Fading is the first indication of light damage but it is also a sure sign that the fibres themselves are weakening. The effect of light is gradual but irrevocable and is rarely noticed until the damage has been done. Compare the back and front of rugs and embroideries, and the hidden parts of upholstery and costumes. Any fading means that the textile will need particularly careful handling. Move carpets and swop curtains from one side of the window to the other to give exposed areas a rest from light.

Decay may also be due to the materials used in the textiles' construction. Some dyes rot the textile itself, this is especially noticeable on patch-work quilts and printed fabrics. Browns in particular are a problem as they are dyed with an iron fixative or mordant which accelerates the decay of the fibres. Unfortunately, it is not normally possible to stop this sort of deterioration except by trying to avoid over exposure to light or moisture. In addition, the chemicals used in finishing fabrics and residues of soap and detergent can be potentially harmful and may cause white fabrics to yellow.

Dust and dirt also cause damage. The grit in dust can physically harm textiles by causing minute cuts in the fibres and will greatly increase the rate at which textiles in use will wear. For example, walking on carpets that have dust and grit in them will wear them out faster than walking on clean carpets.

Dust and dirt are also likely to be acidic which can accelerate decay in the textile. Ensure that no dust is seeping in through gaps in the front or back of frames of embroideries, samplers and lace (see Framing).

The insects which damage textiles are likely to be moths, carpet beetles, silver fish and cockroaches. Usually the damage is caused by the eating habits of the larvae rather than the adult beetle. However, some damage or staining can result from the insects' excrement. Cockroaches are the worst offenders.

Moths and insects rarely attack clean dry fabrics but they are attracted to old food, stains, dirt and dust. Vacuum the edges of fitted carpets and under furniture and other areas where dust collects as this is where insects will breed.

The materials most at risk are wool, fur and feathers. The latter two should always be stored separately from other fabrics because they are particularly prone to insect attack.

MOTH DAMAGE

Moth damage appears as small irregular shaped holes. It is caused by the larvae which hatch from eggs laid by the adult moth. Where there are traces of moths, white cocoon wisps, larvae cases, dead moths or damaged fabric there are probably moth eggs or active larvae. The larvae of carpet beetles feed over a much larger area than the mother so the holes are likely to be further apart.

TREATMENT FOR MOTHS

If you find evidence of moth there will almost certainly be minute eggs, virtually invisible to the human eye, on the piece of fabric. If these eggs drop on to other fabrics the infestation will be spread. It is sensible, where possible, to clean the object outside. In order not to scatter eggs as you go through the house, carry the textile in a polythene bag.

Shake, brush or vacuum the textile to remove the minute eggs and debris (see Cleaning). If the fabric cannot be moved outside, carefully vacuum it as described in Cleaning.

Clean out the storage area to remove dust and dirt. Put a proprietary moth-killer, or dichlorvos strip (Vapona) in the storage area. Paradichlorobenzene is cheap and effective. Follow the packet instructions closely. Remember these moth-

killers are more efficient at discouraging adult moths than killing the larvae so all the eggs must be removed from infected areas. If mothballs are used, make sure that they do not come into direct contact with the fabric as they will damage it. Insecticides evaporate so replace them as directed in the instructions.

An old-fashioned pot-pourri of aromatic herbs may be effective in discouraging moths and more pleasant to live with than mothballs. There are a number of herbs which help protect fabrics from moth, these include mint, sage, rosemary, mugwort, lavender,

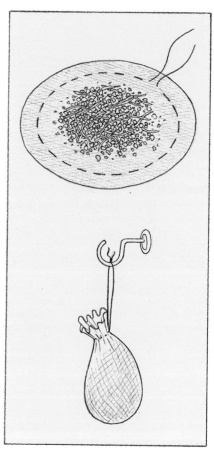

Use herbs to make a moth bag

thyme, santolina, southernwood, woodruff, and sweet marjoram. You can either make a bag from just one herb or from a mixture.

To make a one-herb moth bag put a heaped tablespoon of either mint, rosemary, mugwort, southernwood or woodruff on to a circle of thin muslin about 7.5 cm (3 in) in diameter. Add a few pieces of chopped oris root or a teaspoon of crushed cinnamon stick, gather the muslin and tie the bag with cotton tape. To make moth bags with a mixture of herbs you can either use a tablespoon of sweet marjoram and woodruff and two tablespoons of lavender flowers or mix equal quantities of rosemary, southernwood and sage and add a few pieces of chopped oris root.

Large objects such a tapestries or carpets can be treated for moths but this should be done by a textile conservator.

MOULD

Mould often appears as fuzzy-edged spots – black, grey or white – which can stain and rot fabric. Mould, of which mildew is only one form, is encouraged by poor ventilation and damp conditions. Burst pipes, leaking roofs and damp basements can all start mould growth in previously clean dry fabrics as the spores are always present in the air. Storage in polythene bags can lead to mould growth as a result of condensation inside the bag. Badly framed embroiders, samplers and lace may also suffer, especially if they are hung on outside walls or in humid kitchens and bathrooms where condensation occurs. Mould can start where framed fabrics are in contact with the glass. Stone, brick or terracotta tiled floors may be damp. Check under rugs and carpets that are on solid floors or wherever damp is suspected.

You will need to treat the mould but to prevent it occurring again you will also have to remove the cause of the damp. To get rid of the mould dry and air the affected fabric and then vacuum off the powdery spores, (see Cleaning). Take care not to spread the spores or they will infect other materials. Improve the conditions by repositioning frames, curing damp and improving ventilation of the storage area.

HANDLING

All textiles should be handled as little as possible. Unnecessary handling puts a strain on the fabric and dirt from hands will inevitably get on to the textile. Always have clean hands and make sure that any surface you may lay the textile on is clean and dry.

Use plastic or glass cups under furniture legs (see Carpets and Rugs). Consider having loose covers to protect valuable upholstery but do not use them over velvet upholstery as the pile is easily crushed.

If curtains are closed regularly by hand they will soon develop wear patches. Use pulley strings or a drawing rod for curtains on rings and poles. Lift floor-length curtains well clear when polishing or vacuuming underneath.

Keep textiles away from sharp objects such as watches, jewellery and belt buckles, also avoid smoking, eating, drinking, using ink, felt-tip or ball-point pens near textiles. When laying large objects on the floor always put clean sheets underneath.

If there are small items such as loose buttons and metal pins which go with the textile they should not be left on. Put them in a white envelope and sew it loosely on to the textile. This is safer than pinning things directly on to the fabric.

CLEANING

Very fragile or precious textiles should only be cleaned by a textile conservator.

Dirt and dust not only make the textile less attractive and dull the colours, they also encourage decay. However, over-keen cleaning can do even more damage than dirt and dust.

Dusting a textile does no good at all, it only rearranges the dirt. Gentle vacuuming is the safest form of cleaning for strong textiles. Very fragile fabrics should not be vacuumed.

Use a small hand-held vacuum cleaner such as a Moulinex Petivac, Black and Decker rechargeable Dustbuster, a Hoover Dustette, or the lowest power setting on a cylinder model. The danger of vacuuming is that tassels, fringes and loose threads or even the textile itself can be sucked into the vacuum cleaner. This danger is reduced by covering the nozzle with

nylon or terylene net. A piece of nylon tights or stocking held over the end of the nozzle with an elastic band will do. Gently move the nozzle of the vacuum cleaner over the surface of the textile. Hold the nozzle so that the end is about ½ cm (¼ in) above the textile and take care not to rub the nozzle against the fabric. Make sure you go over all the surface.

Smaller pieces of textile such as samplers or lace, can be protected from the vacuum cleaner by laying them flat on a soft, clean, acid-free board and covering them with terylene net or nylon filament net. Pin the net down around the textile, not to it, and

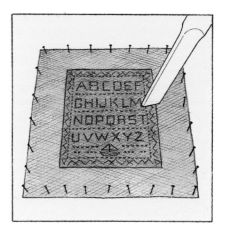

Protect small pieces of textile from the vacuum cleaner by covering them with nylon filament net

vacuum as above.

If the fabric is strong enough, lightly brush it or pat it before vacuuming to loosen some dust and make the vacuuming more effective. Never beat carpets or upholstery (see Carpets and Rugs).

WASHING

There are two types of washing, washing with water – wet washing, or 'washing' in a dry cleaning solvent – dry cleaning. They are used to remove any dirt and stains that remain after vacuuming. Strong fibres can be wet washed if the dyes are colour fast and most types of fabrics can be dry cleaned.

The two types of cleaning remove different sorts of stains. Dry cleaning removes grease-and oil-based stains but has little effect on water-carried stains such as perspiration. Wet

Cover the end of the vacuum cleaner with nylon net or stocking

washing has little effect on oil-based stains.

Most dyes will not run in dry cleaning solvents nor are special finishes such a glazed chintzes affected. Dry cleaning solvents are less harmful to pile fabrics such as velvets and do not remove pleats or tucks set in with heat and steam. Dry cleaning firms will always clean 'at the owners' risk' so only send strong textiles and then only use specialist firms and explain that the piece is old. As some dyes and finishes can be affected by dry cleaning solvent try to find a dry cleaner who uses Arclone rather than Perclone as it is safer. Do not send valuable or antique textiles to a commercial dry cleaner. If in doubt ask a textile conservator to advise you.

Do not wash textiles that have metal threads, metal fastenings or decoration or textiles that have been repaired. Never wash a textile unless you are absolutely sure that it is a suitable material, strong enough and that all the colours are fast (see below). If you have any doubt about whether you should wash a textile, don't. Consult a qualified conservator. A mistake can cause irreparable damage.

For plain cotton and woollen items these are some basic rules for hand washing:

Remove as much dust and loose dirt by vacuuming prior to wetting. Test all colours for fastness paying special attention to repairs (see Colour fast test). Never machine wash.

Use soft water or pre-treat water with sodium hexametaphosphate (Calgon) water softener, (see below).

Water should be no warmer than lukewarm but cold water is less likely to make colours run.

Use a non-ionic detergent (Synperonic N) or Stergene or Woolite as a detergent.

Never use commercial detergents including biological washing powder which, although suitable for everyday clothes, contaminate fabrics with additives that can speed yellowing and decay. Never use bleach as this weakens the fabric.

Whenever possible separate the lining and interlining and wash them separately.

Support the fabric on a piece of net and dab it gently with a sponge

Never wash silk or satin, banners, flags, tapestries or embroideries or where there is any sign that the base fabric has weak areas.

COLOUR FAST TEST
Lay the textile on white blotting paper. Mix up a solution of water with a few drops of the deteregent you intend to use. Place small swabs of cotton wool soaked in this solution on top of the textile in places as inconspicuous as possible. Do the test for each individual colour, including the colour used for restoration. Leave for about twenty minutes. Examine the blotting paper and the cotton wool carefully. If there is any trace of colour the textile should not be washed.

WASHING TEXTILES
Use a large, shallow container, not a metal one. Plastic ones from garden centres and photographic shops are excellent. Alternatively, use a bath for larger objects. Fill the bath or container with soft or softened water which is cold or no more than lukewarm. Hard water can be softened by boiling, allowing it to cool slightly, adding a small quantity of water soft-

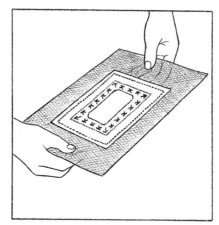

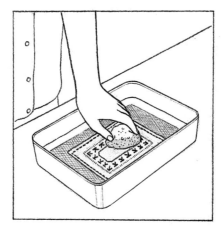

ener such as sodium hexametaphosphate (Calgon) and then allowing the water to cool further. Use enough water to allow gentle dunking so that dirt can float out rather than be squeezed out. Add a few drops of a non-ionic detergent (Synperonic N) or a detergent produced for delicate fabrics such as Stergene or Woolite. Do not use too much otherwise you will need to rinse the fabric a great deal.

Textiles are at their weakest when wet. Anything other than the most robust textiles must be laid on a piece of nylon net to act as support when it is lifted in and out of the water.

Cut a piece of net rather larger than the size of the textile, lay the textile on it and lower it carefully into the water. When the textile is completely wet gently dab the fabric with a sponge. This will encourage the dirt to come out. Do not squeeze or rub the textile with your hands. Press and release the sponge along the whole length of the textile.

When the whole textile has been washed lift it out of the dirty water. Use two hands and hold each end of the net so that there is no strain on the textile. If it is a large textile use two people, one at each end of the net. Always lift the textile out of the water before tipping the water away.

If the textile is very dirty wash it once again. Rinse very thoroughly with two to three changes of clean, warm, soft water and then give a final rinse with distilled or de-ionised water from a chemist (not a garage). Some rust spots which are found on textiles are thought to be caused by iron impurities in ordinary tap water so it is important to use distilled or de-ionised water for the final rinse.

Lay the net and the textile on a clean white bath towel, lay another towel on top and press down gently to absorb the excess water.

Dry the textile by laying it flat on a sheet of Formica or glass or on a board covered with polythene or polyethylene terephthalate (Melinex, Mylar). The textile should be dried with the right side facing upwards and smoothed into shape as much as possible. Dry naturally away from sunlight and artificial heat. Good ventilation speeds drying, an electric fan which is not heated may help. Avoid or minimize ironing by smoothing out the fabric before it dries.

To dry lace and small fine objects, *see* Lace.

Any stains and spots that remain after cleaning are best left. In general, more harm is done by trying to remove them than by leaving them alone.

DRY CLEANING
It is dangerous to use solvents in any quantity without excellent ventilation and fire precautions. It is also very difficult to dispose of dirty solvent. Dry cleaning using solvents should not be carried out by the amateur. If a textile cannot be washed take it to a textile conservator for cleaning.

POWDER CLEANING
If a textile cannot be washed you can sometimes remove some dirt and improve its appearance by cleaning with kaolin. Do not use this method on satin as the surface threads are easily damaged. Sprinkle a little kaolin on the surface, work it gently into the material with an artist's soft brush. Leave it for about fifteen minutes. Vacuum the kaolin away as described above.

Fluff sometimes sticks to textiles, particularly velvet and velour and it is difficult to remove from the fabric without damaging the pile. Self-adhesive tape will take it off if pressed gently against the textile. '

IRONING
Heat and moisture accelerate decay so that ironing should be avoided whenever possible. Arrange textiles so that they dry in the correct shape flat against a smooth Formica, glass or polythene surface. Creases in wool and silk textiles often drop out if they are allowed to hang for a few days.

If an iron has to be used it should be on the lowest setting.

Never iron an uncleaned textile because heat fixes many stains and seals in dust and dirt. Pile fabrics such as velvet should be ironed as little as possible. Often the creases will drop out if you hang the object in a steamy bathroom. If you have to iron velvet, iron it on the wrong side with the pile lying against another piece of velvet.

Always use a lightweight iron at its lowest heat setting (about 100°C), at this temperature the iron will not hiss when you spit on it. Do not trust the thermostat on the iron. Use a pressing rather than a rubbing action. A clean white linen tea-cloth placed between the textile and the iron will give further protection.

STARCH
Avoid using starch as this is a food for insects. It also causes damage as stiffened fabrics are brittle and can be easily cracked. Old-fashioned rice starch (Robin starch) is permissible for christening dresses or wedding veils. However, always wash the starch out before storing them again. Never use spray-on stiffeners or plastic starch because they contain silicone which cannot be washed out.

DISPLAY

All cleaning puts a strain on fabrics so whenever possible display textiles so they will not get dirty, for instance keep them under glass.

Light is a textile's greatest enemy. Hardly any tapestries or upholstery have survived unfaded and without deterioration. Only those rare pieces that have been stored in darkness for most of their existence show their original colours.

The low light levels insisted on by museums for permanent and temporary exhibitions cause frequent comments from visitors but are necessary for the long-term survival of the items on display. However, the human eye soon adapts to dim light and what at first appears as poor lighting of an exhibition is quite adequate after a few minutes. The ultra-violet radiation in daylight and most fluorescent lights damages all textiles, not only can their colours fade but the structure of the raw materials, both animal and vegetable fibres, is also attacked.

Position textiles and hangings so that they receive the minimum light. Corridors and halls often have poor lighting so are better for textiles than living rooms. Window walls get much less light than other walls in a room but check that they are dry, often outside walls are slightly damp which could be harmful to the textile.

Blinds are very useful for cutting out light. In particular they help to protect curtains. Roller blinds made from plain calico can reduce the light level effectively without plunging the room into total darkness. Sometimes it is not necessary to pull the blinds down completely. They can be effective if only pulled down far enough to cut out direct sunlight.

Ultra-violet screening films can be applied to windows, picture glass and fluorescent tubes but their effectiveness varies and probably leads to a false sense of security. Do not apply UV filters to stained or painted glass or early leaded glass. Get expert advice from a conservator rather than the manufacturers before buying ultra-violet screening (*see* Light).

Draw curtains and close shutters when rooms are not in use. Dustsheets protect objects from light. Move rugs and carpets around to avoid one area getting much more light than another.

As well as light, textiles must be protected from heat, moisture, dirt and dust. If they are framed under glass the framing must be properly done (*see below*). Textiles should be displayed away from dust-carrying draughts and never above radiators and fireplaces.

If a fabric is displayed without adequate support it will give at the weakest points. Tapestries often have horizontal tears and breaks because they were woven horizontally but have been hung vertically. The weight should be taken by the warp. Fragile textiles should be supported with a lining fabric. These sorts of repairs are beyond the scope of this book.

Do not display antique embroideries or other textiles on a stretcher frame. They put too much strain on the fabric and do not support the centre. They also allow dirt to penetrate from both sides.

Never use pins, drawing pins, tacks, wire staples or any other metal fixings to secure textiles. They are very damaging.

Ideally, flat textiles should be displayed horizontally or slightly inclined. Unfortunately, this is not usually practical but very fragile textiles should never be displayed vertically.

TO MOUNT AND FRAME A TEXTILE
The support can be made of hardboard, blockboard, wood or thick acid-free card or Gatorfoam. Use the smooth side of hardboard or sand the wood or blockboard smooth. Cover the surface with acid-free card or polyethylene terephthalate sheet (Melinex, Mylar). Do not attempt to mount an object on a board that is too small. The board should be at least 2 cm (¾ in) wider all round than the textile to be displayed. Cover the board with a fabric such as linen or

heavy-duty cotton.

A beige colour is often effective with textiles but some, such as lace, show up more dramatically against a dark background. If the fabric is coloured, test that it is colour fast. If it is a very fine fabric it will be necessary to put some padding underneath. Cotton flannelette or polyester quilt padding are the best materials to use as they will attract moths less than felt or wool.

Cut the mounting fabric so that there is about a 7.5 cm (3 in) margin all round. Stretch the mounting fabric over the board and secure it at the back. It is important to keep the weave of the mounting fabric as straight as possible and parallel to the edges of the board. Use polyvinyl acetate emulsion for sticking it to the board. Do not use rubber-based contact glue. Staples may also help if the board is thick enough. Do not stick the fabric to the front of the board.

First hold the textile to be displayed temporarily in position using fine stainless steel pins. Take care not to cut any threads with the pins, make sure they go through the spaces between the threads. Do not start pinning from the top or bottom but work from halfway down to the corners. This will help keep it straight. Make sure the textile is aligned with the edges of the board and that the threads are parallel with the threads of the mounting fabric. Positioning is tricky so take it slowly. Always remove pins before altering the position of the textile and do not try to force it into place. Do not stretch the textile too much but make sure it is firm enough so that it will not sag when it is hung up.

Use a fine curved needle and fine thread to sew the textile in place. Do not use monofilament nylon thread as it will cut the textile. If possible use a thread made of the same material as the textile. Sew around the edges, again starting from the middle rather than the top or bottom. Use fairly small stitches quite close together. Do not pull them too tight but they should be tight enough not to allow the textile to drop.

Ideally, the textile should be framed. The frame can be wood or metal and glazed with either glass or acrylic sheet (Perspex, Plexiglas). Box frames made from acrylic sheet can also be very effective. It is essential that the 'glass' and the frame are well

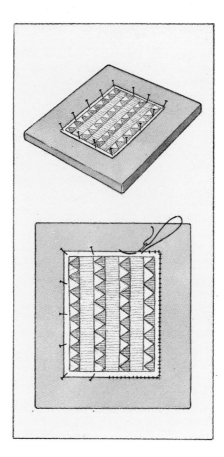

Pin the textile into position starting from the centre of one of the sides. Then use a curved needle and fine thread to sew it in place

sealed to prevent dust getting in. Seal the glass into the frame with gummed paper. The textile must not touch the glass so the rebate must be deep enough. It may be necessary to use a fillet or sub-frame of acid-free board or wood between the mounted textile and the 'glass', (*see* Framing Prints and Drawings). Cover the back of the mounting board with another board and hold it in place with small tacks used in picture framing. Seal the edges with gummed tape to prevent dust from entering the frame from the back. Some objects such as stumpwork or heavy embroidery are almost three dimensional. They will need a box frame which should be made by a frame maker.

For hanging larger textiles, *see* Carpets and Tapestries.

For displaying clothing, *see* Costumes.

STORAGE

The ideal place to store textiles is a cool, dry, dark, clean area, free of pests and with a steady temperature and relative humidity, i.e. in the dark and away from heat and moisture. Do not store textiles in or near wood which has been treated for woodworm as the chemicals used can affect the textile.

Never put textiles in an airing cupboard which is usually warm and fluctuates from moist to dry. Basements are too damp and attics are unsuitable because the temperature and relative humidity fluctuate too much.

Items should be cleaned before storing to avoid attracting insects. Remove any steel pins, brooches, staples or metal fastenings and trimmings they can damage other textiles and corrode, stain and rot the fabric. If you are storing a number of textiles you should keep those with metal fastenings away from the others.

Keep any labels, bills or notes with the fabrics as they often add to their historical value but do not attach them with pins. Place them in a good quality white envelope and stitch them to the outside container or cover.

Use acid-free tissue for padding and wrapping. Never use coloured tissue or old paper packing that is yellowing or becoming brittle. Newspapers are very acidic and particularly lethal and should never ever be used.

Avoid folding textiles, damage often occurs along fold lines. Squashed folds become permanent creases which will in time crack and tear. If items must be folded, lay wads of acid-free tissue along the fold lines to lessen creasing.

Where several small textiles are stored together, label the box clearly showing the order of packing. Use lidded storage boxes, preferably made from acid-free card. If you used lidded polythene boxes make perforations in the lid or the sides to allow air to circulate to prevent condensation forming inside the box. Always line boxes with acid-free tissue.

Clean fabrics are rarely attacked by moths but it is always a good idea to use proprietary moth repellents. Do not place mothballs directly on to the fabric. Paradichlorobenzene crystals placed in storage areas and boxes help prevent mildew, mould and moths. Do not let them touch the object as they will cause it to rot. You can also

Sew an envelope containing any labels etc onto the garment or container

place dichlorvos strips (Vapona) in the room itself.

Do not store coloured and white fabrics together in case they become damp by accident and the colours run.

Large textiles, including rugs and tapestries which cannot be stored flat, should be rolled rather than folded.

ROLLING A TEXTILE
Large textiles must be rolled around a reasonable sized tube. Ideally, the tube should be made from acid-free cardboard. If this is not possible you can use PVC drainpipe or cardboard tubes but they are acidic and can cause harm to the textile in the future. Cover these tubes with several layers of acid-free tissue. If you are going to store the object for a long time wrap the tubes in polyethylene terephthalate sheet (Melinex, Mylar). The larger, thicker and stiffer the textile, the greater the diameter of the tube must be. Most textiles can be rolled on a tube with a diameter of between 10 and 12 cms (4–5 in), very fine fabrics may be rolled on a smaller tube, but never less than 5 cm (2 in) diameter. The tubes should always be longer than the length or width of the object being rolled so that there is at least 5 cm (2 in) of the tube protruding beyond the edge of the textile to prevent the edges of the object from being damaged.

Roll all items with the right side outwards. If the textile has any pile it must be rolled in the direction of the pile. Similarly kelims, carpets and tapestries must be rolled in the direction of the warp. Cover the right side with acid-free tissue as the rolling proceeds and smooth out creases and folds as you go. If two people are

rolling make sure that they both roll at the same speed.

Secure the roll with wide, white cotton tape or Velcro. Cover with acid-free tissue, washed calico or an old, clean sheet. Do not use polythene as condensation may form inside the polythene.

The rolls must be kept horizontal and should, ideally, be suspended so that there is no weight crushing the underside of the textile. This particu-

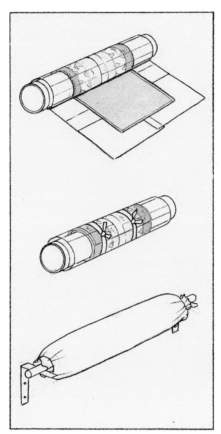

Rolling a textile for storage

larly applies to heavier textiles such as carpets but if possible every rolled textile should be stored in this way. To suspend a rolled textile, fix a couple of brackets securely to the wall. Push a pole through the tube and rest the ends of the pole on the brackets.

IDEAL CONDITIONS

Household: Normal household conditions, keep dust-free and away from direct sunlight.

Exhibition: Relative humidity 50–60 per cent, ideally 55 per cent. never below nor above 65 per cent. Temperature about 18°C (65°F) Light levels low 50 lux.

Storage: Relative humidity about 55 per cent. Temperature between 5°–15°C (40°–60°F) Low light/dark.

REPAIR

To repair textiles well is a difficult and skilled job. Rare and precious items should always be restored by a textile conservator.

Never use adhesives on textiles, they look ugly, are difficult to remove and cause irreparable damage. Any repair must be done by sewing.

Never darn or sew up tears as the stitches may cause more damage to the textile.

Textile conservators will strengthen torn and weak fabrics by carefully sewing them on to a suitable backing material. This is the safest and most satisfactory way of restoring textiles but it is beyond the scope of this book.

TYPES OF TEXTILE

BEADWORK

Beadwork is the decoration of textiles with beads, which can be used to great effect on their own or with silk or wool needlework. They can be strung on a single thread in a definite order, which can then be knitted, plaited, woven or even crocheted into the fabric as it is made. Alternatively, they can be woven into the fabric or they can be stitched on to a backing material.

They were used as long ago as the Pharaohs, who wore beaded collars. In the sixteenth and seventeeth centuries it became popular in Europe to decorate dresses, looking glass frames and small caskets with beads. The Victorians used beadwork extensively for pictures, cushion covers, footstools, chair covers, tea cosies, purses and jewellery, and in the 1920s they were again used to decorate dresses. Some modern evening bags, particularly those made in Italy, are beaded.

INSPECTION
Check to see that the threads holding the beads are not broken and that the beads themselves are not cracked. Beads are suprisingly heavy, so that it is important to make sure that the material on to which the beads are sewn is strong enough to support their weight.

HANDLING
When carrying beaded dresses make sure that the weight is evenly supported. Do not carry them by one small area such as the shoulders. Beaded dresses often have a chiffon base which is likely to shred. All beadwork should be handled with care because if the threads holding the beads are fragile and break, then disaster strikes.

When transporting beaded chairs or stools take care not to press your fingers or thumbs into the beadwork as you lift them, as the pressure may break the threads holding the beads. If possible, lift a stool by holding the legs and lift a chair by placing your hands under the seat on each side.

CLEANING
Dust, which is abrasive, is very bad

for beadwork as it tends to damage the threads holding the beads. If beadwork is very dusty use an artist's soft paint brush and brush gently over the beads holding a vacuum cleaner in the other hand to take the dust. Cover the end of the vacuum cleaner with nylon net or part of an old pair of tights or

above The threads holding the beads will break easily

opposite Rolling a large carpet

stockings held in place with an elastic band. Take care not to knock the beads with the end of the nozzle as this can either break or crack the beads or snap the threads holding them. Never vacuum beadwork directly as you are more than likely to suck the beads off.

Never wash beadwork. If it needs further cleaning take it to a textile conservator.

DISPLAY
Do not display beadwork objects in direct sunlight or close to a heat source. Sunlight and heat will fade and damage the supporting material and the threads. Do not display beaded dresses unless they are well supported from the waist. *See* Textiles: Costume display.

STORAGE
Keep beadwork in a cool, dry, clean, well-ventilated and dark area. Wrap smaller objects in acid-free tissue and preferably keep them in an acid-free box. Pad small objects such as evening bags with acid-free tissue to keep their shape. Do not store objects in sealed polythene bags or boxes. Store beaded dresses flat (see Textiles: Costumes). Cover firescreens and larger objects with a clean dustsheet to keep the dust from settling on the object.

IDEAL CONDITIONS
See Textiles.

REPAIR
Beadwork is very difficult to restore and should be carried out by a conservator. If you have a 1920s beaded dress that you want to wear make sure that the beads are secure and the chiffon is strong enough to support them. If it is not, the whole of the dress should be supported by sewing it on to a lining of silk crepeline or very fine nylon net. You need to be an accomplished seamstress to do this.

If the beadwork is unravelling, make sure you secure the end of any loose threads either by stitching through several beads or by tying the ends in order to catch the beads which are loose.

CARPETS AND RUGS

There is no real difference between carpets and rugs except that the term 'rugs' tends to be used for tribal pieces whereas classical pieces are referred to as carpets. However, most people when referring to rugs think of them as being smaller than carpets.

Carpets and rugs can be made either with a knotted pile or they can have a flat weave such as is found in kilims and Indian dhurrys. Carpets can be made of natural animal fibres such as wool, silk, goats' hair, natural fibres of vegetable origin such as cotton, jute, linen, or of a mixture of different fibres, including metallic threads. Nowadays they can also be made of man-made synthetic fibres. Whatever materials are used to make them, the basic care of carpets and rugs is the same.

INSPECTION
Look for wear on carpets at heavy traffic points, for example in doorways, by telephones or much used cupboards and the route to the television.

Check whether the legs of furniture are causing dents in the carpet. Uneven underlay or small bits of underlay, if not butted closely together, will produce worn ridges on a carpet. Deteriorating rubber underlay will stick to the carpet and damage it. Rucked carpets will wear along the top of the ridge.

Check that the carpet is not fading unevenly, for instance where a table covers some of the area and so prevents light falling evenly on the whole. Check underneath carpets and rugs for signs of moth or carpet beetle. If carpets are on solid floors check for damp as this encourages mould growth and insects.

See that the side cords on the edges of the carpets and rugs are not unduly worn. As the side cords are thicker than the rest of the carpet they tend to wear quicker. See, too, that the fringes of carpets have not broken off, causing the pile to start to push off and the weave to unravel.

HANDLING
When moving a large heavy carpet, rather than straining it by trying to pull it around, it should be rolled, carried and then unrolled. Lift carpets rather than drag them otherwise weakened threads may give way.

Do not fold carpets as creases are likely to form which will cause the carpet to wear unevenly when in use. Always roll carpets with the right side outside. This stops the pile from being squeezed against itself.

Small carpets can be turned over before being rolled but very large carpets should be pulled back on

themselves before being rolled round a cardboard or plastic tube (*see* Textiles). This operation will involve at least two people and you should take your shoes off before you begin.

Stand side by side on one end of the carpet facing the end. Pick up the end of the carpet and walk backwards pulling it with you for several steps. Place the tube covered in acid-free tissue or polyethylene terephthalate (Melinex, Mylar) on the wrong side of the carpet at the end you are holding and start to roll away from you. Cover the right side of the carpet with acid-free tissue as you roll. Then walk back another few steps carrying the tube with the carpet rolled round it and

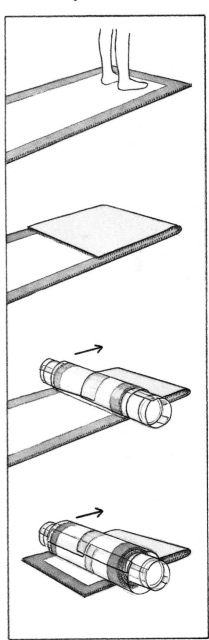

then roll up the next bit of carpet. Carry on in this way until the end of the carpet is reached. This will give you a carpet rolled in the correct way without actually having to turn the whole carpet over before you start.

CLEANING

Grit and dirt can physically damage carpets by working their way down through the pile and causing minute cuts in the fibres. Dust and dirt are likely to be acidic which will accelerate decay in the carpet.

Carpets should be vacuumed regularly – once a week for the average sitting room, more often for halls, passageways or stairs. Once a month vacuum the back of the carpet and the floor under it as this is where the dirt and grit collect. Regular vacuuming should make the need to beat a carpet unnecessary. Beating may damage the carpet.

Vacuum the carpet in the direction of the pile, not against or across it. However, if a carpet is very dirty you can occasionally vacuum against the pile but this should not be a regular practice. It helps to loosen dirt if a rug or carpet is shaken before vacuuming. Carpets with a pile can be turned upside down, patted on the back and then the dust which comes out can be vacuumed up.

Very good rugs should be vacuumed through nylon net (*see* Textiles). Otherwise use the vacuum cleaner with a smooth nozzle on the lowest setting. Make sure that the edges of the carpet are well secured when vacuuming so that they do not get sucked into the machine. Do not use vacuum cleaners that 'beat as they sweep as they clean' such as upright ones.

Make sure that there are sufficient and big enough doormats at strategic entry points in the house to take up the worst of outside dirt.

If you spill liquid on a carpet mop it up as soon as possible using a dry cloth or paper towel. Avoid rubbing the carpet as this may disturb the pile. Put the paper towel or cloth over the spillage and press it with your hands or, if it is a very large amount of liquid, stand on it. Replace the towel when the first one is damp. Repeat until no more liquid is absorbed by the towel.

Carpets also suffer from having old chewing gum, candle wax, glue and many other horrors dropped on them.

Mop up spills by pressing on a cloth or towel rather than by rubbing

If candle wax has dropped on the carpet scrape as much of it off as you can with a blunt knife or palate knife. If the wax has gone right into the material what remains after the scraping can be removed with blotting paper and an iron. Place a sheet of blotting paper or paper towel on top of the wax and another under the carpet. Go over the surface with a warm not a hot iron. The wax will melt and be absorbed by the paper. Change both sheets of paper continually until no more wax appears on either sheet. There is always a danger of this method driving the wax further into the carpet so it is important to scrape off as much of the wax as possible first. Any wax you cannot get off can be removed with white spirit. Carefully dab the wax with a cotton wool swab dampened with white spirit. Finally dry the patch by gently pressing it with a paper towel. This way the wax should not be driven into the material.

Modern adhesives leave a residue when dropped on to fabric, which then becomes impossible to remove. Sometimes, if you go over the area with white spirit or lighter fuel the adhesive may swell and become stretchy and then you may be able to pull some off. Make sure you do not pull up any threads of the carpet. You will probably not be able to remove all the adhesive.

Chewing gum can be removed by freezing it. Put an ice cube in a polythene bag and hold it against the chewing gum until it becomes brittle. When it does, it can be removed with a blunt knife or a palate knife.

Do not use commercial carpet cleaners, machines which generate steam or shampoo to clean carpets. All of these can cause damage. If your carpet really needs washing ask the advice of a textile conservator.

DISPLAY

Most floor surfaces that are smooth, dry and clean are suitable for carpets. Always make sure that a carpet sits flat otherwise the top of the wrinkles will soon be vacuumed bare.

All carpets need some form of underlay, as it reduces wear of carpets by cushioning them from the unevenness of the floor. Underlay should be of natural fibres and not made of synthetic rubber as this tends to disintegrate and then sticks to the carpet and to the floor. The underlay should always come to the edge of the carpet and should preferably be in one piece. If it is necessary to use two or more pieces of underlay make sure that they are butted closely together but not overlapping, then fix them in position on the underside with carpet tape to prevent them from 'walking' apart. Trim the underlay with scissors to fit irregular rug shapes. Underlay will spread with time, so trim it again when necessary. It is sensible to fit anti-creep tape on the underside of the underfelt for carpets that are on slippery floors or use non-slip underlay. The non-slip underlay may not be thick enough and you should put ordinary underlay on top of it.

On stone or wooden floors, a heavy-duty, damp-proof paper, available from carpet shops, should be put down between the floor and the underlay. This helps to protect the carpet from rising damp and from the dust that rises between floorboards.

Avoid placing carpets in direct sunlight and turn them regularly to avoid uneven fading and wear. If possible, keep the curtains drawn or partially drawn on very sunny days or fit a blind or ultra-violet screening on the window (*see* Textiles).

Silk rugs should never be placed where there is a lot of traffic and should never be vigorously cleaned as the silk pile will be vacuumed out very quickly. They should be vacuumed as for Tapestries. If possible, display them as wall-hangings.

If a carpet is too long for a room never turn it in under itself. Roll the excess, right side out, on to a tube covered with acid-free tissue.

Carpets that are placed on top of fitted carpets have a tendency to 'walk' in the direction of the pile of the fitted carpet. Fit anti-creep tape to the underside of the carpet.

If furniture is placed on a carpet, particularly if it has metal casters, place furniture cups underneath the legs. This will help to spread the weight and so minimize the denting in the carpet. The cups can be made of plastic or glass or you can cut out small circles of hardboard about 5cm (2in) in diameter which can be painted to match the carpet. Move the furniture from time to time to give the carpet a rest.

Dining areas are an unsatisfactory place for carpets as apart from the risk of staining from food and drink, the table and chairs concentrate wear on small areas and the pushing back of chairs at the end of a meal causes great strain.

Sparks and falling embers will damage a fireside carpet so always make sure that there is a good fireguard in position.

Stair carpets should be moved a few inches from time to time to change the area of wear. If the underlay on the treads is very compacted it should be renewed. This will greatly prolong the life of the carpet.

Carpets can also be used as table coverings but the edges of the table must be padded with a blanket or felt underlay to prevent the edges biting through the carpet.

Small, light carpets make ideal wall-hangings. However, never hang carpets in direct sunlight or over direct heat sources such as fireplaces or radiators as the heat will cause the fabric to dry out and become brittle. The heat will also cause dust to rise and settle on the carpet. Do not hang carpets on outside walls that may be damp.

Carpets can be hung either by being backed on to a board covered in a suitable material or by being hung from the top using a sleeve for a hanging pole or they can be fixed using Velcro.
Hanging a carpet To mount a carpet on a board, use a strong board such as blockboard, or ideally, as it is acid-free, Gatorfoam.

Cut a piece of board about 4cm (1½in) wider all round than the carpet

to be mounted. Cover the board with a suitable material such as linen or cotton sateen curtain lining. Cut the mounting fabric so that there is about 7cm (3in) margin all round. Stretch the mounting fabric over the board and secure it at the back. It is important to keep the weave of the mounting fabric as straight as possible and parallel to the edges of the board. Use polyvinyl acetate emulsion for sticking it to the board. Do not use rubber-based contact adhesive. Staples can also be used to secure the fabric. Do not stick the fabric to the front of the board (*see* Textiles for illustration).

Place the covered board horizontal and lay the carpet on top. Smooth out all wrinkles and creases until the carpet is completely flat and then make sure that the warp and weft threads of the carpet are running as near parallel to the edges of the board as possible. If you feel it necessary, pin the carpet at about four-inch intervals using stainless steel pins between the threads not through them, to secure it in position. Do not start pinning from the top or bottom but work from half way down to the corners. Using buttonhole thread and a curved upholstery needle, carefully

sew the carpet round the edges to the backing material using an oversewing stitch. Sew between the threads and not through them to avoid splitting the threads.
To make a sleeve A sleeve can be used to hang a carpet from a pole. Using carpet binding or soft webbing about 5cm (2in) wide, cut a strip that is slightly longer than the width of the carpet. Turn the ends of the webbing in and hem them. Stitch the top edge of the webbing about 2cm (¾in) below the top of the carpet. Use buttonhole thread and a curved upholstery needle. In order to know where to sew the bottom edge of the webbing, place a suitable hanging pole on the carpet inside the webbing and see where the bottom edge of the webbing will come to on the carpet. Make sure there is enough slack to be able to slip the pole easily in and out. Sew the bottom edge of the webbing straight across the carpet. The pole must be at least 10cm (4in) wider than the carpet. Insert the pole and, using the protruding ends, hang it up with chains.

Velcro can be used for hanging smaller carpets. It can support a surprising amount of weight.

Sew along both edges of the soft

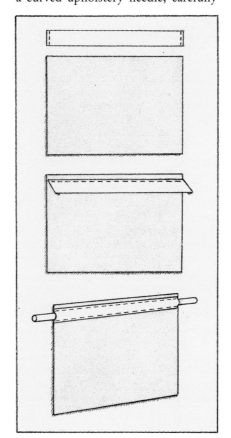

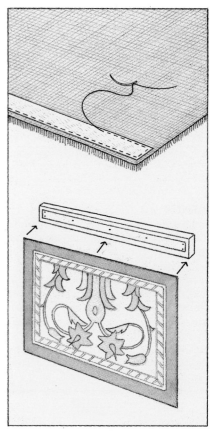

right *Making a sleeve to hang a carpet*

far right *Using Velcro to hang a carpet*

half of the Velcro to the top of the carpet about 1.5cc (½in) from the top. Use buttonhole thread and make sure you sew between the threads of the carpets and not through them. Fix the stiffer half of the Velcro to a wooden batten with tacks. Secure the wooden batten to the wall and press the two halves of Velcro together.

STORAGE

Carpets should always be stored in a cool, dry, well-ventilated and dark area. Storage areas should be kept clean to discourage insects.

Never fold carpets no matter what the carpet dealer says. They should be rolled. *See* Textiles: Storage.

Ideally, carpets should be rolled and suspended from brackets as in Textiles. If this is not possible, carpets should always be stored lying down horizontally so that they are evenly supported. The rolls should never be allowed to stand upright on their ends.

Do not place carpets directly on to a stone, brick or concrete floor. Always place wooden battens or some polythene sheeting under them to protect them from rising damp. *See* Textiles for storage conditions.

IDEAL CONDITIONS

Household: Clean, cool, dry, dark. Away from heat and moisture.

Normal household conditions but avoid bright sunlight.

Exhibition: Relative humidity between 50–60 per cent ideally 55 per cent, never below 40 per cent nor above 65 per cent. Temperature about 18°C (65°F). Light levels 50 lux.

Storage: Relative humidity about 55 per cent. Temperature between 5–15°C (40–60°F). Low light/dark.

REPAIR

Old, rare and precious carpets should not be mended by the amateur. Ask for advice from a textile conservator or a reputable carpet dealer.

Worn or fragile areas of a carpet can be strengthened by stitching patches of linen to the underside. The patch should be larger than the weak area. Using buttonhole thread of an appropriate colour, stitch the linen to the carpet between the threads, not through them.

When the fringes of carpets break off the pile starts to push off and the weave to unravel. This can be secured

Use linen to patch the underside of a worn area

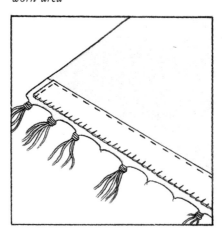

Sew tape along the edge of the carpet to strengthen it

by stitching tape or webbing along the edge on the wrong side of the carpet. This will give support to the worn area and prolong the life of the carpet. Never use any adhesives, adhesive tape or iron-on binding on carpets.

Side cords The side cords of capets usually wear through before the carpet itself because they are thicker than the rest of the carpet. They are the 'selvedge' of most hand-made carpets. When the carpet is being made the weft thread, at the end of each row, goes round and back over several warp threads. When the carpet is finished this edge is usually oversewn as well.

Once the oversewing on the side cords is worn away the core of warp threads will begin to wear too. If you see that the oversewing is beginning to wear you should replace it as soon as possible. This will prevent the core threads from becoming worn. This is one occasion where a 'stitch in time' really will save nine.

Strengthening worn oversewing Use a

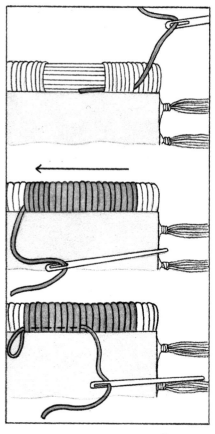

Strengthening worn oversewing

Oversewing a double-sided cord using figure-of-eight stitches

straight needle, such as a carpet or tapestry needle, and an appropriate coloured silk or wool thread. You should start sewing 1cm (½in) or so from the worn area. To hold the thread in place run the needle under the binding for about 2cm (1in) starting from the damaged area. Oversew back along the damaged area and about 1cm (½in) beyond. Do not make the stitches too tight. Finish off by running the needle back through

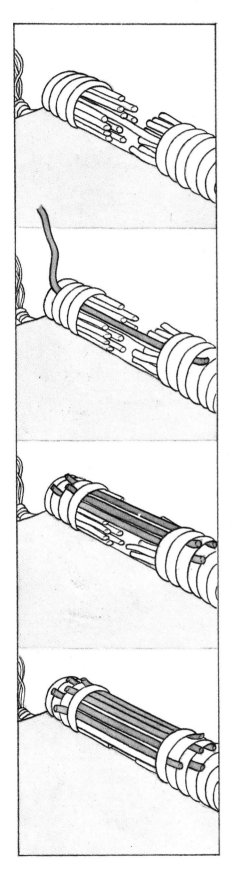

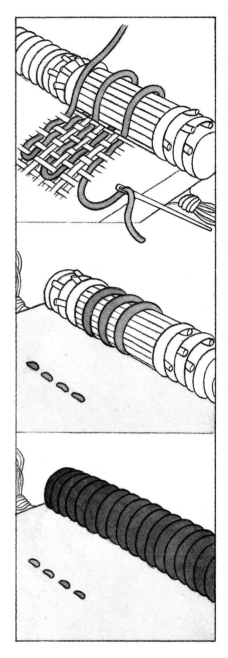

Repairing the core of the side cord

use figure of eight stitches to oversew it.

If the core of the side cord is broken and some threads are missing you will have to strengthen it by sewing in some new threads. Do not cut off the broken threads. You will need to run some new threads parallel to the edge of the carpet in line with the existing core threads.

Repairing the core Use a cotton, linen or wool thread of an appropriate colour and thickness.

Repairing the core Use a cotton, linen or wool thread of an appropriate colour and thickness.

Insert the needle into the undamaged oversown cord about 2cm (1in) from the damaged area. The needle should be in line with a damaged warp thread.

Pull the needle across the damaged area and insert it into the cord in line with the same warp thread. Leave a small tail of thread sticking out of the cord.

Pull the needle across the damaged area and insert it into the cord in line with the same warp thread.

Run the needle into the undamaged oversewn cord and take your thread along for 2cm (1in). Come up through the oversewing and cut the thread leaving a tail. Continue by repeating this procedure until the core is an appropriate thickness. It is important that the tension of the threads is correct and does not distort the line of the side cord. Too tight and the carpet will bunch, too loose and the cord will be misshapen.

Then the weft threads have to be replaced. Run the needle into the carpet directly in line with the missing weft thread. Bring the needle out about 2cm (1in) into the edge of the carpet leaving a tail of thread. Pass the needle back through the carpet so that it comes out with the next missing weft thread and parallel to the first thread, leaving a small straight stitch on the surface of the carpet.

Loop the thread round the warp threads you have just replaced. Run the needle back into the carpet through the next weft thread and repeat the operation. The warp threads should be neatly bound by the replacement weft threads. Finally oversew the whole replaced cord.

The fringes of carpets are the ends of the warp threads. When they wear and break off the weft threads and the

Repairing the weft thread

pile will begin to unravel. The fringes can be replaced. The technique used is similar to replacing the weft threads as described above. Instead of wrapping the tread round the core, a long loop is left which is later cut to form the fringe. The loop should be longer than the original fringe so that it can be trimmed to size. The replacement fringe should be knotted if necessary.

KILIMS

Kilims are rugs without a pile. They are in many ways similar to a tapestry. The Indian equivalent is a dhurry.

the oversewing for about 2cm (1in). Cut off the thread.

If the carpet has a double-side cord

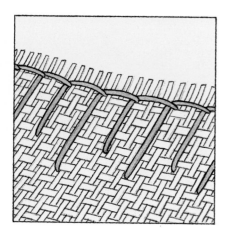

Strengthening the fraying end of a kilim using blanket stitch

When the end of a kilim wears, the weft threads begin to break and unravel. Secure these threads to prevent the kilim from unravelling any further.

Using blanket stitch sew along the whole of the edge of the kilim; each stitch should be about four warp threads wide. Vary the length of the stitches into the kilim to avoid disturbing the weft along one line. The needle must go through the spaces between the warp threads and not through the threads themselves. Use a buttonhole thread of an appropriate colour and sew from behind so that the stitching shows as little as possible from the front. Make sure that the stitches are even and not too tight.

RAG RUGS OR MATS

These were the poor man's carpet and were made by hooking pieces of any fabrics that were available such as old bits of trousers, shirts and vests into a sacking type of material or indeed into an old sack. Because every sort of colour and type of material was used it is impossible to say whether a rag rug is suitable for washing or not. They should therefore always be dry cleaned.

COSTUMES AND CLOTHING

Costumes and clothing present special

right *Hang clothing on padded hangers, and sew cotton tapes to waist bands to suport the weight of skirts*

far right *Hanging a high-collared garment*

problems of display and storage. Old, rare or precious clothing should never be used for amateur theatricals. Make-up, perspiration and handling quickly destroy fragile fabrics. Use old costumes and accessories as models to make replicas instead of wearing the originals. If items are to be worn for photography insist that they are professionally cleaned afterwards to remove acid perspiration (*see* Cleaning).

Costumes and clothing must be clean as perspiration rots fabric and old food stains encourage moths.

Only very simple cotton or linen costumes should be washed (*see* cleaning). Other costumes should be professionally dry cleaned (*see* Cleaning).

Whether displayed or in storage, costumes must be well supported or they can gradually loose their shape and split at the seams. Tailors dummies of the appropriate size should be used where possible for displaying costumes. However, some people do not necessarily want a tailor's dummy in their sitting room, but they may want to display garments they own such as embroidered clothing bought back from South America or the Middle

East. This type of object can be mounted on a board in the same way as described in 'to mount and frame a textile'. Never use metal pins for display nor pin the object directly on to the wall.

All costumes ought to be stored flat, this is not always practical but those which are in bad condition, heavy, knitted, heavily embroidered or decorated must be stored flat if they are to survive.

Avoid folding costumes as damage often occurs along fold lines. If items must be folded soften the effect with wads of acid-free tissue laid along the fold lines (*see*: Storage Textiles).

Costumes that are too large to be packed flat should be hung on padded hangers. Never hang clothing directly on to ordinary hangers, and in particularly on to wire hangers. Pad out the hanger with acid-free tissue or cotton or polyester padding. Make sure that the hanger is not too long otherwise it will damage the sleeves.

Where possible, sew cotton tape loops on to the waistband and hang them over the hanger to give addition support. The waistband should always be horizontal when the costume is hanging. The costume also ought to be padded out with crushed acid-free tissue to help keep its shape. Garments must be hung so that they do not touch the floor. Beaded dresses should, ideally, always be stored flat but if this is not possible they must be supported from the waist.

The wire hook on a hanger should not come in contact with the fabric, so wrap acid-free tissue or some white cotton tape around it. If the garment has a high collar wrap extra layers of acid-free tissue round the hook in order to keep the collar in shape. Make sure the hanger hook is long enough and that the top of the collar

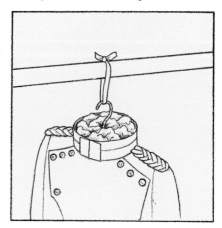

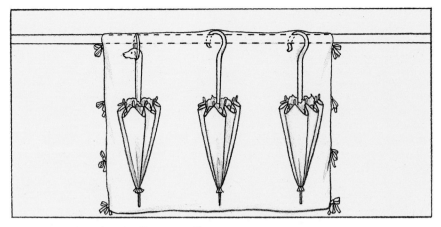

Hang parasols and umbrellas vertically. Drape them with a cotton sheet for protection

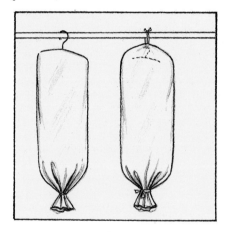

Protect costumes in storage with calico bags

is not pressing against the hanging rail. If necessary, you can use a piece of cotton tape tied to the rail to extend it. Do not squash costumes together on the rail.

Costumes in store should be protected from dust by covering them with closely woven cotton bags. These give the best protection from dust without reducing ventilation. They can be made from washed calico or old sheets and tied with white cotton tape. Do not use polythene bags as they attract dust and condensation can form inside which may cause mould growth.

Hats, shoes, gloves and bags should be padded into the correct shape with acid-free tissue. Parasols and umbrellas must stand or hang vertically with the handle uppermost and should be left slightly open. Pad the folds with acid-free tissue to prevent them from being creased. Make sure they do not touch each other. Drape

acid-free tissue, washed calico or an old, clean cotton sheet over them to protect them from dust. Make sure there is no extra weight on the wire frame.

Cardboard boxes used for storage should have lids and be lined with plenty of acid-free tissue. Boxes from florists are often a suitable shape though, ideally, storage boxes should be made from acid-free card. Always put a final layer of acid-free tissue in the box before you put the lid on. Drawers should be similarly lined since most woods give off acid vapours – oak is particularly bad.

Be warned, packing costumes properly requires an amazing quantity of acid-free tissue.

See Textiles for further information on display, storage, ideal conditions and repair.

FANS

The Chinese are thought to have developed the first fold up fan; before then fans were usually paddle shaped and attached to the end of a stick. This paddle type of fan is still used in countries such as Thailand.

By the early seventeenth century fans were becoming essential fashion items for the rich. The shape of the fans developed from being a small arc to a full semi-circle with supporting sticks made of tortoiseshell, ivory or mother of pearl, among other materials. The fans themselves were made of silk, lace, paper or ostrich feathers and were sometimes encrusted with jewels and gold and silver. They could be painted or embroidered.

Fans were sometimes used to commemorate events and carry portraits or information. When Charles II returned to England as

king, fans with oak leaves and crowns inscribed 'The Happy Restoration' were a must. Other fans opened up with instructions on the latest dance steps or acted as prompts for those in church who could not remember their prayers.

Ordinary people used fans with sticks made from bamboo, wood, bone or plastic and fairly simple coverings of paper or fabric.

INSPECTION
Check for cracked or broken sticks and rotten ribbon which, when it disintegrates, will let the fan over-extend. The material used for the fan itself may crack and split where it folds. Feathers may be attacked by insects, silk may rot and vellum may grow mould, so refer to the relevant chapter for each material used.

The spindle which holds the base of the sticks together may break or work loose and leave the sticks to hang free. This will do terrible things to the fan.

HANDLING
Fans have nearly always been made to be used and so were designed to be opened and closed. This puts strain on the fabric and wears it out so that fans of any age or value should be opened and closed as little as possible.

The sticks are often very fragile and easy to snap and are difficult to mend.

CLEANING
If a textile fan has painted decoration on it do not try to clean it as the paint will more than likely come off. Refer to the chapter concerned with the individual materials used in the construction of the fan.

DISPLAY
Display fans away from heat and direct sunlight or bright lights. For general conditions for display refer to the chapter relevant to the material.

In order not to have to keep opening them, decorative fans should be displayed open. When a fan is lying open it does not lie flat – the right-hand side will be higher than the left-hand side. The fan should therefore be supported or it will eventually distort as strain is put on the unsupported sticks.

Fans on display should be framed to protect them from dust. As they are three-dimensional they will need a box frame. This should be made by a frame maker.

Do not attempt to mount and frame a fragile, rare or precious fan yourself. This should be carried out by a textile or paper conservator.

STORAGE

When fans were in use they were stored closed in a purpose-made box. As a result of being folded many fans have cracked along the folds in the material. It is therefore recommended that, if you have the space, fans be stored open.

A storage support can be made by padding a board with acid-free tissue or polyester wadding. You will need more padding at the right-hand side of the fan in order to support it. If you have more than one fan they can be stacked on top of each other by tacking some equal sized wooden blocks to the corners of each board. These blocks will separate the boards and they can then be stacked in a drawer.

If the fan cannot be stored open, wrap it in acid-free tissue and store in a cool, dry, clean, dark place, preferably in an acid-free box.

The storage conditions vary slightly depending on the materials used in the construction of the fan. Refer to the chapters relevant to the materials.

IDEAL CONDITIONS

These will depend on the materials used in the construction of the fan. Refer to the chapters relevant to the materials.

---

opposite Costumes and clothes can be displayed on a tailor's dummy

right Rethreading a fan with three slits in each stick

below Rethreading a fan with one slit in each stick

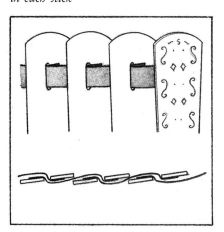

REPAIR

Old, rare and precious fans should only be restored by a conservator.

The spread of the top of the sticks of many fans is controlled with a ribbon. If the ribbon is weak or missing it can be replaced. Choose a ribbon of a suitable colour and width.

There are two different ways of threading fans. They have either one or three slits. If the sticks have three slits the ribbon is in one length.

Open the fan and measure a piece of ribbon slightly longer than the outside edge of the fan. Glue one end of the ribbon on to the inside of the right-hand guard with PVA emulsion adhesive (Evostick W). Snip the other end into a point. On the first stick thread the ribbon from the front to the back through the first slot and then back through the second slot and then back again through the third. Pass the ribbon through the slots in the next stick in the same way, starting from front to back. Make sure that the first stick just overlaps the second stick as you pull the ribbon taut. Continue through all the sticks in the same way. Before sticking the ribbon to the left-hand guard check that the fan will open and close and that all the sticks are overlapping each other evenly.

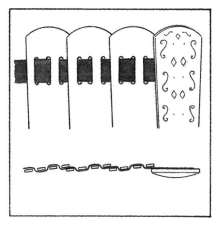

You may have to slightly adjust the ribbon.

If the sticks have only one slit rethreading them is slightly more complicated. You will need two more small lengths of ribbon than there are sticks, i.e. if there are eight sticks you will need ten pieces of ribbon. Cut the ribbon approximately the same length as the width of two sticks. Starting from the right-hand end fix one end of a piece of ribbon to the back of the guard with PVA emulsion or an easily reversible adhesive (HMG or UHU

All Purpose Clear Adhesive). Fix the second piece of ribbon to the front of the first stick and the third piece of ribbon to the front of the second stick, carry on to the end.

Once the adhesive is dry, return to the right-hand guard. Thread the ribbon attached to the guard and the ribbon fixed to the first stick through the slot in the first stick, from front to back. Position the first stick so that it is slightly overlapped by the guard. Keeping the second piece of ribbon out of the way fix the first ribbon to the back of the first stick and when the adhesive is dry trim off any spare ribbon. Carry on to the end. Make sure you wait long enough for the adhesive to dry or all the pieces of ribbon will come unstuck.

FLAGS, MILITARY COLOURS, BANNERS, PAINTING ON TEXTILES

Over the years, flags, military colours and banners have been displayed so that both sides could be seen, usually by being hung from a wooden pole slipped through the sleeve that originally supported them. Eventually the textile rots and shreds.

It is possible for flags, military colours, and banners to be lined almost invisibly with very fine net but this should only be done by a textile conservator.

If you have an old flag that has been hanging in a hall or a church for some considerable time, do not take it down without first consulting a conservator as a great deal of damage can be caused very quickly by bad handling.

Antique flags, military colours and banners should only be cleaned, conserved and displayed by a textile conservator.

Ideally, flags, military colours and banners should be displayed in a glass case or frame. If possible, this frame should lie flat. Otherwise they should always hang from horizontal poles and should never be allowed to hang in diagonal lines from an upright or diagonal pole.

Flags, military colours and banners should be stored as for Textiles.

Modern or reproduction flags and banners should be cleaned and looked after as for textiles.

PAINTING ON TEXTILES

Painting on textiles is another specialist area where work should only be untaken by a textile conservator.

Painted textiles must always be stored flat. Sandwich them between layers of acid-free tissue and store them in a cool, dry, clean, dark area. Never roll them because the painted surface may be hard and inflexible and will pull out of the textile when you attempt to roll it.

METAL THREADS

Metal threads can be found in embroidery, tapestries and carpets or can be used for decorating uniforms and other clothing. These metals threads are usually made of thinly beaten metal wound round a core of silk or cotton thread. They can be made from alloys of gold and silver but are more usually made from silver gilt or brass or copper which is gilded or silvered. Occasionally the silver is coated with a yellow lacquer to make it look like gold. Care should be taken not to remove this lacquer. Strips of metal and metal wire wound round in a spiral as well as metal sequins can also be found in textiles. An object can be heavily encrusted with metal threads or only have a few strands running through it.

Textiles containing metal threads should not be washed. Vacuuming using nylon net for protection, will remove dust and dirt (*see* Textiles: Cleaning).

The metal is often dull from tarnish. Never use a proprietary metal cleaner or clean metal threads with a glass bristle brush even though it may make the metal nice and shiny. The bristles will scratch the metal and damage the thread by scatching off gilding or silver.

The most you should do is wipe over metal threads with a cotton bud very slightly dampened with warm water containing a few drops of a non-ionic detergent (Synperonic N) and a few drops of ammonia. Rinse thoroughly with a clean bud dampened with clean water and allow to dry. Do not allow the threads to become very wet. If necessary dry with a hairdryer set on *Cool*. Make sure that no liquid gets on to the surrounding material.

The cleaning of metal threads is very difficult. Damage can easily be done to the textile or the thread. Cleaning should only be carried out by a textile conservator who may try to persuade you not to have it done at all because in many cases cleaning the metal may cause damage.

Where possible textiles with metal threads should not be rolled but if they have to be, use a cylinder of greater diameter than you would normally use. Place a layer of polyester wadding between the interleaved sheets of acid-free tissue. This will take up some of the differences between the raised metal decoration and the flat textile. It will also allow the object to be rolled more evenly and prevent strain being put on a few small areas (*see* Rolling a textile).

See Costumes and textiles for display and storage.

SAMPLERS AND OTHER EMBROIDERIES

CLEANING
When vacuuming samplers and flat textiles lay them on a board and cover them with nylon net. Pin this around the sampler not to it. Vacuum as described in Textiles.

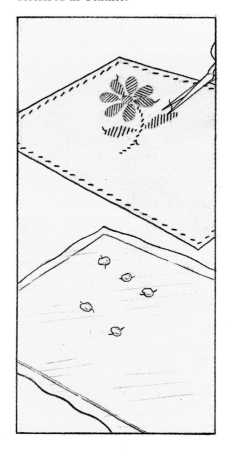

Only wash a sampler or an embroidery after a thread of each colour has been tested for colour fastness as the colours are very likely to run. First examine the sampler carefully for any signs of colour bleeding, perhaps from earlier washings. At the same time check for repairs as these may be less colour fast than the original threads, they are often more obvious on the reverse. Do not attempt to wash silk and satin embroideries or others where there is any sign that the base fabric has weak areas.

When testing the colour fastess of threads on a sampler or embroidery examine the back for loose thread ends of each colour and any repairs. With tweezers and sharp scissors, snip off tiny samples of each colour about 0.25 cm (⅛ in) long. Place them on a sheet of clean white blotting paper, the same size as the sampler, in the position corresponding to where they are on the back of the sampler. Mix up a solution of water and a few drops of a non-ionic detergent (Synperonic N). Place small swabs of cotton wool soaked in this solution on top of the threads. Cover with a sheet of polythene and leave overnight. Remove the polythene and the swabs of cotton wool and examine the sheet of blotting paper and the swabs of cotton wool carefully with a magnifying glass for any signs of colour bleeding. If there is any sign of colour then cleaning can only be continued by an expert.

See Textiles for washing.

Dry the sampler on a sheet of glass or a clean Formica surface. On no account dry it with artificial heat or in bright sunlight. Dab the wet sampler with a clean white towel to absorb excess water. Arrange the sampler on the glass or Formica while it is wet so that it dries with square corners and straight edges. The sampler should not need ironing if it is dried like this. Any ironing that is necessary should be done with a lightweight iron at the lowest heat setting (*see*: Ironing Textiles). Use a clean white towel between the iron and sampler to prevent any raised stitching from being crushed. Use a pressing rather than rubbing action. Should any bad creases remain in the sampler, use a steam iron to avoid pressing heavily with the iron. Make sure the steam does not cause the colours to run.

Testing the colour fastness of threads

SCREENS

Once fabric-covered screens begin to split and tear very little can be done by the amateur. The torn or split fabric should be patched from behind and not sewn. This means that the covering fabric attached to a frame would have to be undone. This restoration work should only be carried out by a professional conservator.

TAPESTRY

Tapestries and canvas work are often confused because of the similarity of appearance. Tapestry is a handwoven fabric usually made of wool, silk or linen or a combination of these fibres. Canvas work, known as needlepoint in America, is embroidery done with a needle and threads of wool or silk on an existing cotton or canvas base.

The pattern or picture of a tapestry is made by the weft thread as the tapestry is being woven, and so is part of the structure of the tapestry. In canvas work the structure is already there in the form of a linen, cotton or canvas base and the pattern or picture is added to it. Tapestries are made on a loom and are usually used as wall-hangings.

Canvas work is most often found on chair seats, backs and arms and on stool tops.

INSPECTION

Tapestries attract dirt from the atmosphere because of their rough texture. Most tapestries will be dirty, dusty and often brittle as a result of light and pollution damage. Areas woven in silk deteriorate more quickly than those woven in wool. However, brown wool, especially used in outlines, deteriorates quickly because of the dye used.

The sheer weight of a tapestry is one of its greatest problems. The top part of the tapestry is the weakest area because all the weight is hanging from it. The slits which occur when two colours in the design meet are another weak area. These slits were usually sewn up with cotton or linen thread but when this rots and the stitching gives way, the weight of the tapestry causes the slits to pull apart. These slits should be sewn up as soon as possible to avoid the tapestry becoming mishapen. Some tapestries have small slits woven into the design to emphasize certain features. These were not sewn up originally and should be left unsewn.

Tapestries are often lined to protect the back from dust and to help them hang better. The lining may shrink over the years. Check that the tapestry is hanging square and flat. If it is not, this may be due to the lining having shrunk or because the tapestry is incorrectly hung. Deal with the problem before further damage is caused.

Check tapestries for moth and mould (see Textiles). Check them for damage caused by furniture being pushed back against them.

HANDLING

Always have clean hands when handling tapestries. Tapestries are often very brittle, split and tear easily and are surprisingly heavy. The less you handle them the better. Tapestries should never be folded, they should always be rolled round a tube. Roll them with the right side, i.e. the design side, outside, see Textiles). If a tapestry is to be taken down or hung up ensure that there are enough people available to support the tapestry as a great deal of damage can be caused if the weight is not evenly supported. To take a tapestry down off a wall, loosely concertina the tapestry along the top, working from one side to the other, or with one person at each end, and work towards the middle. Unhook the tapestry as you go. Lower the tapestry to the ground and lay it gently on the floor, preferably on a clean sheet, right side down. Open the tapestry out by holding one side firmly at each corner and easing the tapestry flat. This operation is harder than it sounds. Make sure that there are enough people around to help and enough, stable, long ladders. The tapestry can then be rolled. See Carpets and Rugs.

CLEANING

Never attempt to clean an old, rare or precious tapestry or one in bad condition. This must be done by a textile conservator.

It is possible to remove surface dirt and dust from a hanging tapestry that is in good condition by vacuuming through nylon net. See Textiles: Cleaning. Before rolling a tapestry for moving or storage, vacuum the back and the front while it is flat.

DISPLAY

Tapestries are very sensitive to light so never hang them in direct sunlight. The light not only fades or changes the colours, which can completely change the balance of the picture, it also breaks down the fibres. Many of the old tapestries we see today were originally very different colours, especially the foliage which loses its green and turns blue. Blinds are a very good way of keeping light levels down.

Never hang tapestries over heat sources such as radiators or fires or on outside walls that may be damp. Wide corridors are a good place to hang tapestries but do not hang them where they will be constantly moved by draughts or where passing people or small children with sharp toys will rub against them. See Textiles and Carpets.

STORAGE

Tapestries should always be stored in cool, dry, well-ventilated, dark areas which should be kept clean to discourage insects from breeding. Remove any metal rings or other fixings before storing. Tapestries should be stored rolled up. Roll them in the direction of the warp with the right side outermost. The lining must be on the inside otherwise damage can be caused. See Textiles: Storage. Before storing tapestries make sure that they are clean and moth-free. Use proprietary moth repellents but do not place them directly in contact with the tapestry.

IDEAL CONDITIONS

Household: Clean, cool, dry and dark. Away from heat and moisture. Normal household conditions but avoid sunlight.

Exhibition: Relative humidity between 50–60 per cent, ideally 55 per cent never below 40 per cent nor above 65 per cent. Temperature about 18°C (65°F). Light levels 50 lux.

Storage: Relative humidity about 55 per cent. Temperature between 5°–15°C (40°–60°F). Low light/dark. Constant conditions should be maintained.

REPAIR

The slits on tapestries where the colours meet sometimes become unsewn as the thread rots. Do not attempt to resew these slits on old,

left *Canvas work and other embroidered textiles should be framed*

below left *Sewing up a slit in a tapestry*

opposite *A whitework cushion damaged by age and use*

thread too tight and keep the tension even. Finish off by sewing twice round the warp thread at the other end of the slit.

UPHOLSTERY

Furniture has been upholstered since the late seventeenth century but very little has survived from that date. Original upholstery on antique chairs is rare and both the surface fabric and the total structure of the upholstery may have historical importance so it should be preserved. Not only does upholstery wear out quickly but it is often altered to suit changing tastes. As a result furniture is seldom covered in its original upholstery. *See also* Leather.

INSPECTION
Upholstery has a lot to withstand. It is continually under strain from the springs and padding, is subjected to dust, dirt, spillages, jumping children, dirty dogs, bottoms, moths, mildew and is exposed to the harmful effects of light.

Look and feel for loose joints in the chair or sofa. A weak framework puts a strain on the covering fabric which is only the outer skin of a complex arrangement of webbing, springs, stuffing and wadding all sewn together with twine. Any fault below the surface will eventually affect the covering itself.

Minor damage, such as small tears and loosened braid or fringes, should be stitched up before fraying makes neat repairs impossible. Worn piping around the edges can be oversewn or re-covered. Always sew, never stick. Adhesives make future restoration much more difficult and are impossible to remove.

If the frame has woodworm it should be treated. If the upholstery is still on the piece of furniture you cannot use liquid woodworm killer. The furniture will have to be fumigated. If, however, you are having the furniture re-upholstered, the wood can be treated with a liquid woodworm killer while it is stripped of

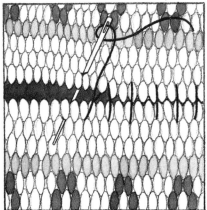

rare, precious or fragile tapestries. These must be dealt with by a textile conservator. However, on a more recent tapestry it is permissible to sew

the slits up yourself.

To sew a slit in a tapestry As you are going to sew up the slits of a tapestry in good condition this can be done while the tapestry is still hanging on the wall. Use buttonhole thread or an appropriately coloured polyster thread with a count of thirty. It is better to use a tapestry needle because it has a blunt end but you may need to use a curved needle if the slit is very difficult to get at. Make sure that you sew between the threads not through them, particularly not round the warp threads. To secure the end of the thread sew it twice round the warp thread at the end of the slit. Continue to sew along the slit so that the stitch will be straight on the front and diagonal on the back. Do not pull the

upholstery. Make sure that the liquid does not get on to a polished or veneered surface. Allow several days for the liquid to dry out completely before re-upholstering.

HANDLING

Take care when moving upholstered furniture because the upholstery is easily damaged. Sharp edges of tables, door handles, keys in doors or even light switches can catch and rip fitted upholstery, particularly the backs of chairs and sofas.

Loose covers should always be well tucked into the furniture so that there is no danger of the cover hanging down and the castor running over it causing that terrible tearing sound.

If you are having covers made it is always worth having additional separate arm and back pieces made at the same time. This will double the life of the cover as these are the areas which always get dirty and wear out first.

Before re-covering drop-in seats always remove the old covers. If you do not, the seat will be slightly bigger than it was before and when dropped back into the chair and sat on, it is likely to force the seat rail joint apart.

If you have antique furniture with its original upholstery take great care when moving it. Upholstered antique stools and chairs should be carried by the legs, particularly if they have tassels or braid round the edges. Larger pieces of furniture, such as chairs, should be carried by two people, lifting from under the seat, not by the arms.

CLEANING

Keep upholstery clean to protect it from damage caused by dirt and insects. The main insects that will attack upholstery are clothes moths and carpet beetles. Insects are partial to the stuffing of upholstered furniture. If it appears that there are insects inside the upholstery then have the piece fumigated.

Vacuum upholstered furniture regularly to remove the larvae and the eggs of moths and to keep it clean. Use a vacuum with a nozzle attachment, not a brush. Make sure the nozzle is clean and smooth. Keep the suction head away from fringes which can easily unravel and always use netting over the nozzle. Clean particularly in crevices and down the backs and sides of chairs and sofas and under furniture where moths can breed.

Protect antique and fragile upholstery from being damaged while vacuuming by either placing nylon net over the upholstery or by covering the nozzle of the vacuum cleaner with net. *See* Textiles: Cleaning.

After vacuuming, some upholstery can be wet cleaned but never attempt to wet clean antique, fragile or precious upholstery. Ideally, the upholstery should be removed to clean it properly but for most of us this is out of the question.

If you are going to wet clean upholstery while it is on the piece of furniture the whole cover should be cleaned at the same time. It is usually better, particularly on plain fabrics, not to try to remove individual dirty spots. You are likely to end up with the stain, an over cleaned area and a dark ring around it and you will wish you had not started.

Good quality cleaners, if you follow the instructions carefully, can be used to wet clean modern fabrics. Do not allow the upholstery to become very wet because the liquid will draw the dirt up from the stuffing and make an even worse mess.

Do not be tempted to use special finishes that can be sprayed on to upholstery to make it 'dirt and stain resistant'. They may make future cleaning more difficult. They should never be used on antique fabrics.

A lot of upholstered furniture has exposed wood which needs polishing from time to time. Wherever possible only dust the wood as furniture polish will stain textiles and is nearly impossible to remove. When you do polish the wood take great care not to get the polish on to the upholstery. Remove drop-in chair seats before polishing the frames.

Remove the dust from around the buttons on button-backed chairs and sofas with a hogshair bristle brush. Have the vacuum cleaner nozzle held in your other hand at the ready to catch the dust as you brush it out.

Upholstery in damp houses can suffer from mould. It often appears as fuzzy edged spots – black, grey or white – which can stain and rot the fabric. The musty smell of mould is very familiar to most people. It is impossible to cure mould if the cause of the damp cannot be eradicated.

To clean off the mould, the upholstery must be completely dried out and aired. Vacuum off the powdery spores. Take care not to spread the spores or they will infect other objects.

To remove chewing gum and wax, *see* Carpets.

Very fragile antique and valuable upholstery should be cleaned and restored by a textile conservator.

DISPLAY

Avoid placing upholstered furniture near windows or bright lights. The upholstered seats of dining chairs are often in surprisingly good condition because they are kept under the dining table in relative darkness. Canvas work panels, often used for seats and chair backs, are stitched with dyed wools or silks that are particularly susceptible to light.

See Textiles.

Almost more than any other sort of

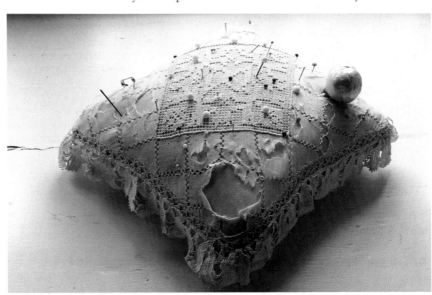

upholstery, beadwork upholstery will deteriorate from wear and tear. Because of its age and structure it is extremely fragile and should never be sat on. If the beads are coming loose, secure them as soon as possible. Handle beadwork upholstery with particular care. *See* Beadwork.

STORAGE

If upholstered furniture is put in store it should be in a cool, clean, dry and dark area. Avoid basements and outhouses which may be damp and lofts or attics which can get very hot or cold. Make sure the furniture is really well covered by dustsheets to prevent unnecesary dirt falling on the upholstery. Hang dichlorvos strips (Vapona) in storage areas to minimise moth and furniture beetle attack.

Do not put heavy dustsheets or loose covers over velvet upholstery as the pile of the fabric is easily crushed.

If upholstery becomes damp, make sure that it is thoroughly dried out before storing since the stuffing holds moisture and encourages mould growth. Attach cotton or muslin bags containing mothballs to legs of furniture but do not allow mothballs to come into contact with the upholstery.

If rooms are not in use for long periods cover furniture with clean cotton dustsheets. They are also essential when decorating or building work is in progress. If necessary, use polythene over the dustsheets but not in direct contact with the upholstery since it attracts dust and condensation.

IDEAL CONDITIONS

Household: Clean, cool, dry, dark. Away from heat, moisture. Normal household conditions but avoid bright, sunlight.

Exhibition: Relative humidity between 50–60 per cent constant, ideally 55 per cent never below 40 per cent nor above 65 per cent. Temperature about 18°C (65°F). Light levels 50 lux.

Storage: Relative humidity about 55 per cent. Temperature between 5°–15°C (40°–60°F). Low light/ dark. Constant conditions should be maintained.

REPAIR

Repair work to valuable upholstery should only be carried out by a textile conservator.

WHITEWORK

Whitework, as the name implies, are textile objects made only from white threads. The yarns used are usually linen or cotton. Whitework objects are often decorated, although the decoration is always carried out with white threads. The most commonly known whitework objects are lace, tablecloths, christening dresses, wedding veils and decorative pillow cases.

CHRISTENING DRESSES

Old christening dresses are usually made of cotton and often have embroidery, cutwork or drawn threadwork on the upper part and around the bottom edge. Christening dresses along with wedding veils and some of the few antique costumes that are expected to be worn occasionally, although it should be remembered that using them can expose them to damage.

INSPECTION

After the christening dress has been worn, check to see that no snags or tears have occurred, particularly round the bottom edge. These can be repaired with a matching cotton thread.

CLEANING

After use a christening dress must be washed. *See* Textiles: Washing.

Hang the christening dress to dry on a small hanger padded with polyester wadding or nylon stockings covered with clean white cotton cloth or washed calico. Do not use heat to dry it. While the christening dress is drying, smooth out the creases and ease it into shape. Make sure that the dress is completely dry before it is stored.

When the christening dress is next needed and brought out of storage it should be allowed to hang from a small padded hanger for a few hours and any small creases will probably fall out. It may help the creases to drop out if you hang it in a steamy bathroom. If you want to starch the dress use a thin solution of rice starch or old-fashioned Robin starch. If it is necessary, iron the christening dress with a lightweight steam iron on its lowest setting.

When the christening is over wash and store the dress again.

STORAGE

Pad the sleeves with crumpled acid-free tissue. Place several layers of acid-free tissue in the skirt and, if the dress has to be folded, make sure that wads of acid-free tissue are placed along the folds. Place the dress in an acid-free storage box lined with more tissue paper. *See* Costumes.

LACE AND CROCHET

Lace and similar fabrics such as fine crochet need to be held flat to keep them in shape while drying. After washing, place the lace on a piece of soft board larger than the object, which is covered with polythene, polyethylene terephthalate film (Melinex, Mylar) or white blotting paper. Gently smooth the object into shape starting from the centre. Cover the lace with a piece of nylon net which is several inches larger than the object. Stretch the net taut over the lace and secure it with weights or pins. If you pin the net the pins should be at a slight angle with the heads pointing away from the centre of the object. To get the best result the pins should be quite close together. The net holds the lace to the flat surface and dries it flat. If you are going to use weights to hold the net, place them closely around the edge of the lace but not on it. Weights from old-fashioned kitchen scales are suitable.

Stretching net over the lace is better than pinning the lace itself as some lace is likely to shrink a little as it dries. This may put strain on the threads as they pull against the pins.

Allow the lace to dry naturally.

For display, storage and ideal conditions, *see* Textiles.

WEDDING VEILS AND LARGE LACE TABLECLOTHS

A great many wedding veils are passed down the family from generation to generation. These are usually made of cotton or lace, although they are often now made of man-made fibres.

INSPECTION

After the veil has been used it should always be repaired and washed before it is stored. Carefully examine it for any weak or damaged areas. If it is a very precious veil or a great deal of repair is needed then a textile conservator should be consulted. If there are just a few snags and weak areas minor tidying up can be carried out.

In order to examine the veil satisfactorily you will need a clear area larger than the veil itself so that the veil can be laid out flat. You may need to move the furniture to make some floor space. Cover the area with a sheet of clean polythene.

Carefully go over the veil looking for damage. You can patch weak or torn areas with fine net which looks similar to the veil. Using a fine needle and polyester or cotton thread of a similar thickness to the threads of the veil, sew the net on to the veil. Take care to get the tension of the stitching right and even. If the stitches are too tight they may cut into the old fabric and if they are too loose they will allow movement between the support and the veil and be ineffective. Make sure you pass the needle through the holes in the lace and not through the threads.

The edges of the veil are the areas most likely to be damaged. If they are, you can strengthen them by sewing an edging of fine net around the edge. If this is not possible oversew the edge.

HANDLING
The size of a wedding veil makes it difficult to handle. Make sure when you are moving it about that the ends do not trail on the ground or become caught on sharp edges.

CLEANING
Whitework objects should never be stored dirty as the dirt will attract insects and mould. Any repairs that need doing should always be carried out before the object is washed.

The problem with washing wedding veils and other large whitework objects is their size. They are hard to handle and can be easily damaged when they are wet so they should

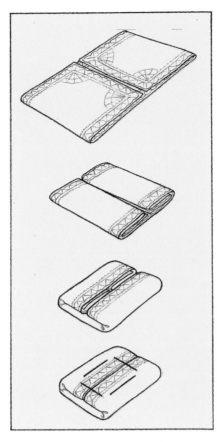

Folding a large whitework object

always be folded up before being washed.

Folding a large whitework object After examining and repairing the object spread it out again so that you can fold it up.

Fold the left- and right-hand edges to meet at the centre. If the veil is rectangular you may need to fold it again in the same way to make it squarish.

Fold the top and bottom edges to meet at the centre. Continue folding the left- and right-hand edges and then the top and bottom edges until the veil is the right sized parcel to be washed in your bath or basin. Stitch loosely through the parcel several times with white cotton thread to secure it. When the veil is secure it can be washed as described in washing a textile.

When you have finish[ed] the object place the parcel [in the] centre of the sheet of poly[thene] the white cotton thread se[curing the] parcel and unfold the v[eil in the] reverse order to which it [was folded] up. This is made easier if yo[u have a] person to take each side o[f the veil.] Carefully smooth the veil i[...] pat dry with a clean white [...] leave to dry naturally and th[...] Lock the dog and cat out of [the room] while it dries.

If necessary, iron the vei[l with a] lightweight steam iron set [...] but take it off the polythene f[irst. It] is easier to iron it on the flo[or with] the veil on a clean white sheet.

STORAGE
To store a veil or other large whitework objects either roll or fold them. *See* Rolling a textile.

If you have to fold the veil, fold it as described above for washing. Put rolls of acid-free tissue along the folds so that they do not become sharp creases. Cover the object with acid-free tissue, washed calico or a clean sheet. Do not use polythene bags as condensation may form inside the polythene. Keep whitework in an area that is cool, dry and dark.

IDEAL CONDITIONS
See Textiles.

TRIBAL ART AND TEXTILES

Most tribal art, be it textiles or objects, is coloured with vegetable dyes which fade or change colour very quickly. Be ultra careful when displaying tribal textiles that they are well away from any sources of direct light. The dyes on tribal textiles and the colours on objects are not fixed. They will run or streak very easily if they get wet or damp.

It is important to check tribal art for insect infestation to which they are also prone. Imported insects can be very voracious *see* Wood: Sculpture.

WOOD

Wood is a very versatile material and has been used from the earliest times for buildings, weapons, eating utensils, furniture, musical instruments, walking sticks, statues and carts and carriages. In fact almost anything can be made out of wood. Wood can be sawn, cut, turned, whittled, carved, sanded and polished. It can be inlaid with other woods, metal, tortoiseshell, ivory and precious stones and can also be painted, gilded and lacquered.

INSPECTION

Wood is a fibrous substance which is susceptible to changes in relative humidity and extremes of temperature. Excessively dry conditions will cause wood to shrink and crack. Conversely, damp conditions will cause wood to swell, warp and twist and inlays to rise. Sudden fluctuations in temperature and humidity will accentuate these processes. Wood continues to react to the environment no matter how old it is.

It is prone to attack by wood-boring insects, particularly the furniture beetle. Surface mould (mildew), which flourishes in damp and unventilated conditions, will stain the surface of wooden items.

Wood will change colour in strong light; some of the darker woods will bleach and the paler woods may become darker. Spillages of liquid can leave white or dark stains on the surface depending on the type of wood.

WOODWORM OR FURNITURE BEETLE

It is not the furniture beetle that causes the damage to wood but the eating habits of the larvae or grubs. The female beetle lays her eggs in crevices, old joints and hidden corners and cracks. After about four weeks the eggs hatch and the grubs burrow into the wood for food and protection. This tunnelling may continue for between one and five years. When the

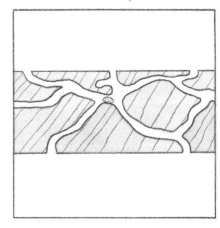

left   *Victorian Schoolroom, now in Armleigh Mill Museum*

above   *schematic drawing of damage caused by wood-boring insects*

right   *Painted ceiling and carved four-poster bed c. 1600*

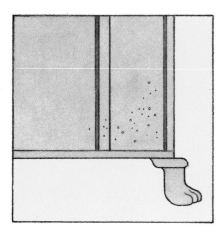

The beetle prefers unfinished or soft wood

grubs are fully grown they change into pupae and, in a few weeks, into fully grown beetles. These beetles then bite their way out of the wood leaving the characteristic round holes. This usually happens between May and August.

New holes will not always be evident on the finished surface of an object. The beetle prefers unfinished or soft wood, such as the backs and undersides of furniture and particularly the soft wood backboards on cupboards and mirrors and the backs of drawers.

Holes in the wood do not necessarily mean that there is active woodworm in the wood, but, if in doubt, assume the worst and treat the wood as though there were. The first indication of the presence of active wood-boring insects is new flight holes which will show up quite clearly as the wood inside the hole will be clean and the edges of the hole will be crisp. Sometimes you can see little piles of wood dust or frass which appear just below the hole. Old flight holes are likely to have darkened and their edges to have become rounded.

Inspect wooden objects, particularly furniture, at least once a year for woodworm infestation. Check drawers and crevices and particularly soft-wood and plywood backboards and other unfinished surfaces. If you acquire a new piece of furniture always inspect if for woodworm before bringing it into the house and, if necessary, treat it.

The best time to treat wood for woodworm is in the spring or early

Schematic drawing of treating wood for woodworm using a syringe and needle

summer when the beetles emerge.

TREATMENT

Do not treat old, rare and precious wooden objects with special finishes or upholstered furniture. These should be fumigated by a furniture restorer or a specialist firm. Fumigation will not harm the special finishes or the upholstery. The treatment is not preventive as the fumigant does not remain in the wood and so will not provide any protection against future infestation.

If you decide that you can treat your wooden object yourself, you will have to use a liquid insecticide. If possible, take the object to be treated outside but if this is not possible make sure you work in a well-ventilated room that is seldom used and have the windows wide open. Wear goggles, rubber gloves and preferably a respirator with a filter for toxic fumes while you are working with the insecticide.

Put polythene sheeting under the object. Take any drawers out of a piece of furniture. Dust and clean objects well, including the inside of drawers, before treating them for woodworm.

Use a clear, low odour liquid insecticide (Cuprinol Low Odour). The insecticide can be injected or painted on to the wood and sometimes you need to do both. It is very important that the liquid insecticide does not get on to any finished surfaces such as lacquered, gilded, varnished, french polished, painted or waxed surfaces. These surfaces can be damaged by the solvent in the insecticide therefore the insecticide should only be injected or painted on the unfinished sides of the wood.

Although small cans of insecticide come with special nozzles with which to inject the liquid, it is much easier,

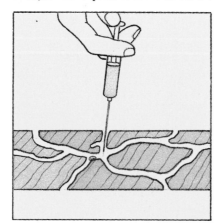

cleaner and more effective to use a hyperdermic syringe and needle which will get the liquid further into the wood where the grubs are. If possible, use a glass syringe. Chemists, doctors and vets who know you will probably supply them.

Inject the fluid into flight holes at about every 5cm (2in) intervals. The tunnels are interconnected and the fluid will run from one to the other. If any liquid gets on to a finished surface wipe it off immediately. The fluid could squirt back at you through other flight holes, therefore always wear goggles. Clean out the syringe when you have finished with the appropriate solvent – it should say what it is on the side of the can.

When painting the unfinished surfaces it is easier to decant some of the insecticide into a smaller glass or metal container, a jar with a screw top is ideal. Apply the insecticide liberally to all the unfinished surfaces with a small, 2cm (½in), paint brush, make sure no liquid gets on to any finished surface, textiles or upholstery.

Allow the object to dry for at least twenty-four hours or according to the instructions on the can. The fumes will take at least this time to dissipate. Do not sit or sleep in a room with newly treated furniture.

The flight holes can then be filled in with a soft wax which matches the colour of the wood. This improves the appearance of the piece and also makes it easier to see if further flight holes appear.

Upholstered furniture can be treated against woodworm when the upholstery has been removed. If you intended to have a piece of furniture re-upholstered this is a good time to treat the frame. Make sure you allow the insecticide to dry well before re-upholstering otherwise it can stain the new fabric.

MILDEW AND MOULD GROWTH

Mildew will grow on wood whenever the conditions are sufficiently warm and damp. The mould will appear as fuzzy grey/white patches which almost always leave a stain when removed. Because the mould feeds off the material on which it is growing it can weaken the object in severe cases. Mould smells musty.

Check poorly ventilated areas such as cupboards, drawers, bookcases, the backs of furniture or pictures next to walls, particularly outside walls.

Removal of mould Any object with mould is likely to be damp so it should be dried out slowly. Move the object to a drier part of the house. Make sure that the object is gradually acclimatized, too fast drying can set up stresses in the object which can cause other problems such as cracking or peeling veneer.

Wherever possible take wooden objects outside to remove the mould. This will stop the mould spores spreading to other objects. Using a soft bristle brush, brush off the mould. Hold the nozzle of the vacuum cleaner in your other hand to catch any mould spores and dust. You can also wipe mould away with a soft damp cloth.

FURNITURE

INSPECTION

Check for splitting and warping, woodworm and mould growth, lifting veneers and loose metalwork and inlay. Check for flaking, cracking and lifting surfaces such as lacquer, gilding and paint. Make sure that joints, legs and rungs are secure. Make sure also that any broken pieces that have come off are put in an envelope or small plastic bag and placed inside the piece of furniture or in a safe place. If you are likely to forget where the pieces have been put, stick a label on the

underside of the furniture telling you where they are.

Do not fix anything such as self-adhesive tape and labels to the finished side of a piece of furniture as they are difficult to remove without damaging the surface.

HANDLING

Only move one piece of furniture at a time and always lift it by the lowest solid part of the main frame. The most vulnerable parts of furniture are the arms and legs of chairs, the top edges and legs of tables and the feet and bases of chests and cabinets.

Never push or pull a piece of furniture across a floor even if it has castors. It puts a great strain on the joints of the furniture and could even tear the legs off. Always lift a piece of furniture.

Do not stack one piece of furniture on top of another, even if it does save a journey. If possible, use two people to carry a piece of furniture. Make

sure that belt buckles cannot scratch the furniture as you carry it. Do not lift chairs by their backs or arms, place your hands under the seat on each side taking care not to apply pressure to the arms. When moving furniture never lift it by projecting parts. The top of a chest of drawer and the over hangs of a table are not made to be useful lifting points, use the top support rail.

If you are moving a cupboard, always lock the doors before you begin. If there is no key, tie the doors closed. If possible, use soft webbing to tie them but if you have to use coarse rope or string make sure that there is padding between the string and the edges of the piece of furniture as string can score or rub the wood.

When moving a chest of drawers, empty the drawers, remove them and carry them separately.

Do not carry heavy pieces through doorways without covering them with something to protect them against bumps and scratches. Once you have

right *A wooden chest in need of help*

far right *Do not lift furniture by the projecting parts, but the lowest solid part of the main frame*

paint from the doorway embedded in the surface, it is very difficult to remove.

Do not turn a piece of furniture upside down unless it is essential. It puts an unnecessary strain on the joints. If you have to turn it over for any reason lift it right up off the floor, turn it over and then put it down squarely on a blanket on the floor. Do not tip it over on its legs.

It is important to remove marble tops, protective glass and other movable tops before moving a piece of furniture. These tops should be carried separately. Raise marble, glass and other movable tops on to their side while still on the table and always carry them vertically as they can break under their own weight if they are carried flat.

If you have to paint a room and it is not possible to move the furniture out make absolutely sure that the furniture is completely covered with a good dustsheet. A little paint splatters a very long way.

When cleaning floors take care of the base (legs, feet, bottom rungs) of furniture. A great deal of damage is done by careless use of vacuum cleaners, floor polishers and wet mops.

Once or twice a year move pieces of furniture away from their usual positions and clean underneath them. The dust that collects is a breeding ground for moths and beetles. Particularly move furniture if it is standing on a carpet as it is one of the favourite places for carpet moths to breed.

CLEANING

DUSTING

Dust is very abrasive and if it is allowed to collect on wooden surfaces it can scratch them when it is dusted off. Dust must be removed and not just pushed from one area to another.

Use a large good quality, soft, clean and dry duster with hemmed edges. These are to prevent dangling threads from snagging on the furniture. Fold over the duster as you go. This will give you several clean surfaces to collect the dust. Shake dusters out after use and wash them regularly.

Never use a duster on inlaid or marquetry furniture or on furniture which has any moulding or veneer missing. The duster will snag on any loose or raised pieces and could pull

them off. Use a wool or fleece mop which is less likely to snag and can also be washed. These mops are on a stick like a feather duster. Do not use a feather duster as the feathers tend to break and the spines can then scratch the surface.

Difficult areas to reach such as corners and deep carving can be cleaned with a hogshair brush.

Candle wax can be removed from a french polished surface by placing an ice cube in a corner of a polythene bag and holding it against the wax. After a few minutes the wax should have become hard and brittle enough to be removed with pressure from a fingernail. Give the area a quick rub with a cloth with a very little polish on it. Then buff it.

POLISHING

If a piece of furniture is old and has been waxed and polished over the years, the shine can be brought up by buffing the surface with a clean soft chamois leather or a clean soft duster without applying any more wax.

WAXING

Furniture is waxed to give a protective coating to the original finish and to provide a hard shiny surface that dirt and dust will not cling to as well as giving the piece of furniture a well cared for look.

French polish, shellac, varnish, paint or lacquer finishes ideally should not be waxed but when furniture is being used rather than just being displayed a thin coating of wax will

help protect the surface from the hazards of everyday life. The wax will help prevent spills of liquid and small scratches irreparably damaging the surface. If too thick a layer of wax is allowed to build up it will eventually dull the surface. Only wax a piece of furniture if it really needs it. Waxing is necessary when the surface has become worn and dull and will not shine when buffed.

Never polish furniture that has lifting or cracking veneer or inlay. It is very difficult to prevent the polishing cloth from catching on the edges of the lifting wood and pulling them off. Also if wax gets under the veneer it will make it much more difficult to stick the missing bits back.

Apply a thin coat of solid wax polish containing beeswax (Antiquax, National Trust wax), with a soft duster using a circular movement. Do not let the wax dry for too long or it may become difficult to polish and will remain streaky. Polish the wax with a clean soft duster.

Try to match the wax with the colour of the wood. Pale yellow waxes used on a dark wood may show white in cracks and depths of carving when dry. It is better to use a darker wax in this case. Similarly dark wax on a light piece of wood will darken it. One of the great advantages in using a solid wax is that it will fill in any tiny scratches that may have been made on the surface of the piece of furniture.

Apply wax to ornate carving with a soft bristle brush and polish it off with a clean soft bristle brush. Keep one

left *A veneered table damaged by light and by damp from houseplants*

right *An overloaded table will eventually collapse*

for applying the wax and one for polishing.

Never use aerosol polishes of any kind directly on to the wood. The solvent in the polish can cause white marks to appear on the surface of the wood as well as a bloom. Aerosol polishes can also dissolve some applied finishes. If you insist on using an aerosol polish use one containing bees-wax but you must spray the polish on to the duster and not on to the furniture. Dampen the duster with the polish, rub it on itself to distribute the polish and then rub lightly over the surface. Polish the furniture with a clean soft cloth. The furniture will require occasional solid wax polishing as the aerosol wax does not give much protection.

Furniture creams sometimes contain ingredients which can be harmful to a waxed or french polished surface so it is better not to use them

Never use any sort of polish which contains silicone. If you use it the surface of the wood will eventually acquire a bloom which is impossible to remove without stripping the whole surface.

Do not wax furniture that has a natural 'raw' finish or that has been oiled. The surface can be cleaned by wiping it with a clean damp cloth. If there are stains or a great deal of dirt on the surface use warm water containing a few drops of a non-ionic detergent (Synperonic N) or a mild household detergent (Fairy Liquid) on the cloth. Rinse well using a clean cloth dampened with clean water. Never swamp the wood with water.

DISPLAY

Central heating dries out both the air in a room and the furniture. The change in temperature and relative humidity which occurs when the heating goes on and off by day and night can cause a great deal of damage to furniture. Panels can split and warp and veneer lifts off. Valuable pieces of furniture are better placed in a room that is unheated but not damp or in a room which has a constant temperature and which is not too dry. It is possible to buy humidifiers to help

control the relative humidity within a room but effective ones are expensive.

Strong light can damage wood and affect the surface colour. Always try to keep furniture out of direct sunlight. If the sunlight falls unevenly or only on part of a piece of furniture the surface will acquire a patchy appearance. Some woods will bleach and others will become darker. If you have no other choice make sure that you move the furniture from time to time to prevent it discolouring unevenly. If you have ornaments and objects on wooden surfaces, occasionally move them to different positions so that they do not leave patches on the surface of the wood.

See that the bases of objects standing on furniture are not rough and do not scratch the furniture. If they are rough, put a piece of brown felt or chamois leather under them. Avoid coloured felt as the colour could bleed into the wood.

If you have houseplants or vases of flowers on furniture always place them on a waterproof mat. Even cache pots should be placed on a mat. Ideally, vases of flowers and house plants should be removed from the furniture before watering. This is nearly always possible with houseplants but with vases of flowers, particularly large arrangements, more water may be spilt moving the vase than by carefully watering it where it is. Always use a long nosed watering can and if any water is spilt on the furniture mop it up at once so that is does not mark. Make sure that the water has not run under the mat. Do not overfill vases with water. If you tuck the top of your finger over the edge of the vase you are about to fill, you will feel the water when it reaches your fingertip which should be before it reaches the top and spills over.

If you put houseplants on polished furniture make sure that the leaves and flowers do not rest or drip on to the surface. Never spray plants with water if they are standing on wooden furniture.

Never put houseplants or vases on gilded furniture as the smallest drop of water can completely ruin the gilding.

Do not place furniture next to radiators or close to open fires. The heat will dry out the wood and cause warping and splitting. Do not place furniture in a room or hallway where uneven or rapid changes in heating and cooling can occur, such as by outside doors.

Hot or cold things can very easily mark some finishes on wood, particularly french polish. Always place heat resistant mats under hot plates and mugs and make sure you place small mats under drinks glasses, particularly if they contain ice. Make sure that wine bottles, particularly chilled wine, and ice buckets have a mat underneath them.

If you spill anything on a wooden surface, mop it up immediately as it can cause discolouration.

Do not push furniture hard back against walls, curtains, hangings. Always allow a few inches between them.

STORAGE

Furniture should be stored in a cool, dark area with adequate ventilation. Keep the store room clean to help prevent attack by woodworm, mould or moths.

Do not place furniture directly on to a stone, concrete or brick floor, place wooden slats, cork tiles or polythene sheeting under the furniture to prevent it absorbing water from rising damp. Do not place furniture near an outside wall, leave at least 30cm (1ft) between the wall and the furniture to allow a really good circulation of air.

Do not store furniture in a loft or attic unless the roof is insulated under the tiles to prevent rapid changes in temperature and relative humidity. Do not use cellars, basements or outhouses unless they are dry. Do not store furniture in a boiler room as it will be too hot and dry.

Cover furniture with clean dustsheets rather than polythene sheeting which can cause condensation.

Hang dirchlorvos strips (Vapona) in storage areas to help control woodworm.

Do not stack other objects or other pieces of furniture on top of furniture with polished surfaces because the surface is easily scratched.

Check stored furniture at least once a year for woodworm and mould growth.

IDEAL CONDITIONS

Household: Normal household conditions. Avoid fluctuations in temperature and relative humidity. Keep out of direct sunlight. Maximum temperature 18°–21°C (65°–70°F)

Exhibition: Relative humidity 50–60 per cent constant, ideally 55 per cent. Never below 45 per cent or above 65 per cent. Temperature about 18°C (65°F) constant. Light levels not above 150 lux. Painted wood and marquetry 50 lux.

Storage: Relative humidity 55 per cent constant. Temperature about 15°C (59°F). Low light levels.

REPAIR

Old, rare and precious furniture should always be restored by a furniture restorer. The restoration of furniture is an enormous subject and is beyond the scope of this book.

Small, loose pieces of veneer or inlay should be stuck back otherwise they will get lost. Use wood working adhesive such as scotch glue or polyvinyl acetate emulsion. *Never* use epoxy resin adhesives (Araldite) or rubber-based adhesives (Copydex and Evostik Impact) on wood. If the piece of veneer or inlay is completely loose remove the old adhesive from the back of the piece and from the carcass. Place a very small amount of the adhesive on the area where the inlay is to be placed. Holding the piece of inlay in a pair of tweezers, lower it into position. Gently press the piece down with your fingers and then wipe any excess adhesive off with a barely damp cloth. Put a piece of silicone paper over the veneered area and place a weight on top. Leave it overnight. *See also* Silver: Inlay.

If the veneer or inlay is loose and raised but can be pushed down flat, insert a little adhesive under the raised area. Push this down and wipe off any excess adhesive with a barely damp cloth. Place a piece of silicone or

waxed paper over the area and weight it down with a flat object and leave for at least twenty-four hours. Place some hardboard or a piece of card between the weight and the silicone paper so that the weight does not mark the surface.

To replace loose or lifting metal inlay, *see* Silver.

BAMBOO

Bamboo is a giant tropical grass or reed with a hollow stem. It was used in the Far East to make simple household furniture and began to be exported to Europe at the end of the eighteenth century. Some bamboo furniture is lacquered and decorated. The term bamboo is also applied incorrectly to late eighteenth and nineteenth century furniture made of European woods, carved and usually painted to simulate bamboo.

Bamboo is recognisable by the double ridge that appears at fairly regular intervals along its length. In 'fake' bamboo these knuckles are much more evenly spaced.

Check bamboo furniture to make sure that joints are secure. Check particularly carefully for active woodworm which can wreak havoc in bamboo in a very short time.

Bamboo can be cleaned with warm water containing a few drops of a non-ionic detergent (Synperonic N) or a mild household detergent (Fairy Liquid). Dampen a cloth or cotton wool swab with the solution and wipe over the surface. Rinse with clean swabs dampened with clean water and dry with a soft clean cloth. If the bamboo is painted test a small area before you begin cleaning (*see* Painted Furniture). If the bamboo looks a bit dull apply a little microcrystalline wax on a brush and buff with a clean, soft bristle brush or a soft cloth.

BILLIARD TABLES

An English billiard table has eight legs and the table framework is fitted with sections of slate which are secured so that a perfectly flat surface is achieved. The slate is then covered with superfine green woollen cloth which has a strong nap running from the balk end (bottom end), to the black spot end (top end).

Most billiard table manufacturers supply instructions and special equipment to clean the tables. In order to keep a good smooth surface the table must be lightly brushed and ironed regularly. Brush from the balk end to the black spot end to bring up the nap and to keep the surface dust-free. Check for moths and, if necessary, spray the fabric with an anti-moth spray taking care not to get the spray on any wood.

BOULLE FURNITURE

Andre-Charles Boulle was a French cabinet maker to Louis XIV and perfected the art of brass and torto-ishell marquetry which is now known as boulle or buhl work. Boulle is very elaborate with flowers, scenes, scrolls and other ornate designs. Either the tortoiseshell can have the brass inlayed into it or vice versa and the brass was often engraved. Later boulle work was often inlayed with mother of pearl, horn and other materials.

The brass and tortoiseshell can lift from the base wood. This applies particularly to the brass because it does not shrink at all as the wood shrinks, and so it will spring up. It is extremely difficult to re-lay the brass inlay and this should only be done by a furniture restorer who specializes in the restoration of boulle furniture.

It is extremely important that boulle furniture is kept at a suitable and constant relative humidity (55 per cent).

Boulle furniture should *never* be dusted with a duster. If any of the brass or tortoiseshell veneer is proud of the surface it will catch on the duster and be torn out and once the brass is bent it makes it extremely difficult to re-lay it satisfactorily. If the surface of the object is in good condition brush it with an artist's hogshair paint brush or blow the dust off with a photographer's puffer brush. The brass on boulle furniture should never be polished.

Boulle objects should never be restored or tampered with by an amateur or inexperienced restorer.

CANE AND RUSH WORK

The cane used to make seats and backs of furniture is made from split rattan which is a type of palm. It was first imported into Europe from the Malay peninsula in the middle of the seventeenth century.

Rush seated chairs are known to have been made in Europe since the Middle Ages and they have been in use in America since the arrival of the Pilgrim Fathers. Rush has also been used to make carpets, mats and baskets.

Cane and rush are long-lasting materials but they will dry out and become brittle in dry, centrally heated atmospheres. Never stand on a chair with a cane or rush seat with hard heeled shoes on as these will cut through the fibres. If you must stand on it take off your shoes and stand on the edges of the chair along the wooden frame.

Check cane and rush seating for woodworm which can occasionally be found in them but more likely in the wood frame of the chair. Check particularly the wood frame around which the rush is wrapped.

Rushes are prone to damage by gritty dust. Carefully vacuum them from time to time with the vacuum cleaner set on *low*.

Cane and rush work can be washed with warm water containing a few drops of a non-ionic detergent (Synperonic N) or a mild household detergent (Fairy Liquid). Dip a cloth in the water, wring it out and wipe it over the surface. Wipe the rushes in one directtion only in order not to catch the edges of the rushes. Rinse with clean water and allow to dry.

Do not allow the rush to become very wet. As rush is vulnerable to mould leave the piece somewhere warm until it is completely dry.

To liven up the cane apply a little microcrystalline wax on a bristle brush and polish off with a clean, soft bristle-brush.

There is now a great revival in chair caning and rushing and there are numerous good books to show you how to do it yourself. Otherwise take the object to a specialist.

CARD TABLES

Card tables, which usually have a covering of baize or leather, fold in half when they are not in use. The baize is a first-class breeding ground for moths. The table should be opened and vacuumed at least once a year. Use the lowest setting on the vacuum cleaner. If evidence of moth is found take the table outside and brush the eggs and cocoons off with a stiff bristle brush. Spray the felt with an anti-moth spray. Cover the wooden edges of the table with polythene or card before you spray so that the spray does not go on to the polished wood.

CHAIRS

Do not sit back hard on or lean hard against the backs of delicate chairs. Do not lean forward or backwards on the front or back legs of a chair as it will loosen or break the joints. Arms of chairs should not be sat on no matter how sturdy they may appear. When you stand up do not scrape the chair bacwards on the floor as it puts a strain on the joints. Lift the chair backwards holding it by the seat.

CORK

Cork is used to make three-dimensional pictures and occasionally architectural models are to be found made in cork dating from the early nineteenth century. Cork is fairly impervious to atmospheric change but can suffer from woodworm attack. It eventually dries out and becomes crumbly. Cork objects should be kept in a steady temperature and relative humidity away from direct sunlight. They should not be displayed in hot, dry conditions or over open fires, radiators or other heat sources.

Remove dust with an artist's hogshair brush but do not use a duster as it will snag on the rough edge of the cork and tear it.

Cork objects should be kept in box frames or under glass or acrylic domes to protect them from dust and insects.

If the cork is stuck onto a backing the adhesive may weaken in time and the cork will fall off. If this happens replace the pieces using an easily reversible adhesive (HMG or VHU All Purpose Clear Adhesive).

CUPBOARDS AND CHESTS OF DRAWERS

When closing cupboard doors always make sure that the catches on the first door are fastened before closing the second door. Do not push doors back further than they can comfortably go or let them swing back hard as this puts a strain on the hinges.

If a cupboard door does not open and close smoothly it could either be because the hinges are not securely fixed or that the frame is out of true because the piece of furniture is not standing level. Check that all the screws in the hinges are there and secure. If the door still binds on the frame put a small wedge or pack a piece of carboard under one or both front legs and see if that helps.

If a door will not stay closed again, check its hinges. Loose or badly fitting hinges or hinges that have a screw head which is proud will prevent the door from closing properly. Try tightening up any loose screws or replace any ill-fitting screw with one of the correct size. It may be necessary to take off the hinge and plug the screw holes before refitting the hinge.

Always open drawers by pulling on both handles and close them by pushing evenly on both sides. If a drawer is difficult to pull in and out check that it is not overloaded. Do not try to force it if it is sticking. If you run a household candle or some beeswax along the runners of the drawer it may make it run more smoothly.

If the drawer is one of several, for instance in a chest of drawers, and appears to be really jammed try taking out the drawer that is directly above or below it. Reach in with both arms and, if there is room, hook your fingers round the back of the drawer and, with someone else pulling carefully on both handles, pull gently on the back of the drawer. This may help get the drawer out.

DESKS
The flaps of drop-fronted desks should never be fully opened without both the pull-out supports in position or the hinges will tear out. Do not put anything too heavy on an open desk.

GLASS-FRONTED DISPLAY CUPBOARDS AND BOOKCASES
If the glass is not too dirty it can be polished with a dry soft chamois leather or lint-free duster. Take care not to rub the wooden mouldings around the glass, particularly if they are gilded. A little spit on a cotton wool bud will help remove fly blow and other marks.

If the glass is very dirty remove the worst of the dust with a cloth and then carefully wipe the glass with swabs of cotton wool moistened with warm water containing a few drops of a non-ionic detergent (Synperonic N). A few drops of methylated spirits in the water may help remove greasy dirt. Use circular movements and use both sides of the swab, discard them when they become dirty. Never let the swab touch the edges of the wood, particularly if the wood is polished or gilded. Hold a piece of thin card against the inside edge of the moulding to keep the swabs away. Finally rub over the glass with a dry cotton wool swab or soft clean lint-free cloth. Do not clean the glass with commercial glass

cleaners as the chemicals they contain will harm the surround.

Some glass panels in furniture have painted decoration on the inside. Never touch the painted surface. *See* Glass: Painted Glass.

GILDED FURNITURE
See Gilded Objects.

INLAY
Inlaid wood is wood that has had other materials let into it. These materials can either be other, different coloured woods or they can be ivory, horn, mother of pearl, bone, brass, tortoiseshell and other such materials.

MARQUETRY
Marquetry is a decorative veneer which is made up of shaped pieces of wood or pieces of thin sheets of another material such as ivory, mother of pearl, tortoiseshell, ivory, bone or metal. These different materials form geometric patterns or floral and figurative scenes. Dust and polish marquestry with care as the corners of the different pieces of material can easily catch on a duster. If the surface feels at all rough it probably means that the veneer is loosening in which case dust the surface with an artist's hogshair paint brush.

PARQUETRY
Parquetry is inlaid or veneered wood that has a geometric pattern made up of different coloured woods or the same wood laid so that the grains lie if different directions. Wooden (parquet) floors are often made in this way.

VENEER
A veneer is a very thin sheet of wood which usually has an attractive grain or colour which is then glued on to a carcass of an inferior wood or chipboard. Veneers are often made of hardwoods such as mahogany, walnut or bird's eye maple. Veneering a piece of inferior wood is a great deal cheaper than using a solid piece of hardwood. Veneering also make it possible to match and reverse the grain patterns in the wood to form a decoration.

JAPANNED AND LACQUERED FURNITURE
See Japanned and Lacquered Objects.

LEATHER COVERED DESK OR TABLE TOPS AND BUREAU-FALLS
See Leather.

PAINTED FURNITURE
Some furniture is beautifully decorated with different types of painted surfaces. These painted surfaces can simulate marble, tortoiseshell and exotic woods, as well as depicting scenes and landscapes. Painted surfaces on furniture can crack, lift and flake. Fluctuations in temperature and relative humidity make the base wood shrink, swell and twist and this causes the paint layer to detach itself from the wood. In addition, the paint dries out and becomes less elastic and more brittle with time.

Flaking, damaged, rare, old or precious painted furniture should always be cleaned by a conservator.

Before attempting to clean a painted piece of furniture, check that the paint is in good condition and that there are no hairline cracks. If the paintwork is sound, dust it regularly with a clean soft duster. If the surface is still dirty it may be possible to clean it further by wiping the surface with a cotton wool swab barely dampened with warm water containing a few drops of a non-ionic detergent (Synperonic N); do not use ordinary household detergent. First check in a small inconspicuous place that any protective varnish does not come off and that the paint will not be affected by the cleaning solution.

Begin cleaning at the bottom of the piece of furniture and work upwards. If it is a large piece of furniture clean a small area at a time and rinse as you go. Do not overclean areas, which will give a patchy look. It is better to lightly clean the whole piece twice than to have some areas cleaner than others.

Keep an eye open as you clean different coloured paints as some could be affected more than others. Watch out particularly for areas which have been previously restored as that paint may behave differently. If any paint appears to be coming off on the cotton wool swab stop cleaning at once. You will have to consult a conservator.

Do not allow the painted surface to become very wet or the water could penetrate the paint layer and cause damage both to the paint and to the wood.

When you have finished going over the surface with the cleaning solution rinse it with clean cotton wool swabs dampened with clean water and dry immediately with a soft clean cloth.

A thin coating of microcrystalline wax can be applied to the painted surface to help to protect it and to brighten it up. Apply the wax with a soft cloth and polish off with a soft clean cloth.

Never put anything, hot or very cold directly on to the surface of a painted piece of furniture as it could mark it or cause the paint to lift off. Always use coasters under mugs and glasses. Do not leave the painted surface wet or damp for any length of time. Take particular care when watering plants standing on a painted surface and always make sure they are on a waterproof mat.

PAPIER MÂCHÉ FURNITURE
See Papier Mâché.

STRIPPED PINE
Pine is a straight grained wood that ranges in colour from yellow to nearly white. It is often used to make the carcass of a piece of furniture which is then veneered. It has also been used extensively to make household furniture which was almost always painted. It has now become very fashionable to strip the paint off and to display the piece of furniture with the raw stripped pine finish. Pine doors, skirting boards and shutters are also treated in this way.

People who strip pine commercially normally strip the furniture in a tank of caustic soda and then hose it down to remove the caustic soda. One of the great disadvantages of this method is that the caustic soda tends to eat away all the adhesive in the joints of the furniture as well as the paint. This can result in a very rickety object. If you are thinking of buying a piece of furniture that has been stripped in this way check it for stability.

Sometimes stripped pine can look a little 'acid' in colour but it is possible to rectify this by waxing the furniture with a slightly darker coloured wax. Many second-hand furniture shops and particularly shops that specialise in stripped pine sell this. Apply the wax evenly all over the surface and polish off with a soft clean cloth. When you have reached the desired coloured finish continue to wax the piece of furniture from time to time with a neutral coloured wax.

Otherwise dust and clean stripped pine furniture as you would furniture.

TABLES
If you are using a table with a finished surface, particularly a french polished surface, to write letters on make sure you place something under the sheet of paper otherwise the writing will indent into the surface of the wood. If you are using a typewriter or word processor on the table always make sure that they are on something soft such as a felt mat or a magazine or they could scratch the table.

GARDEN FURNITURE

Garden furniture is usually made of teak. If left untreated it will eventually turn an attractive silvery-brown colour and lichen will grow on it. If you wish your furniture to remain a uniform colour bring it in every autumn and when it is thoroughly dried out, paint teak oil all over the surface. Remember to do the undersides and the sides. The teak oil turns the furniture a rich dark brown and if the furniture is annually oiled it should last indefinitely.

If you are storing garden furniture in a shed, cover it with a tarpaulin or dustsheet to keep dirt, dust and particularly bird droppings off it.

Do not store garden furniture standing directly on a concrete, stone or brick floor as rising damp will affect the wood. Place the furniture on wooden slats, cork or polythene.

OTHER TYPES OF WOODEN OBJECTS

WOODEN FLOORS

A polished wooden floor can be swept or cleaned with a vacuum cleaner. It can then be washed by wiping over with a mop dampened with water containing a few drops of a non-ionic detergent. It should then be rinsed with a clean mop squeezed out with clean water. Do not allow the floor to become very wet and allow it to dry naturally. If, for any reason, you need to scrub the floor always do so in the direction of the grain using a bristle brush.

If a floor is polished the surface can be maintained by wiping with a duster soaked in a 1:1 mixture of paraffin and vinegar. The cloth should be made from wool or cotton, soaked in the mixture and then allowed to dry before being used to polish the floor. This will remove superficial dirt and leave the floor shiny.

From time to time apply a little liquid floor wax. Allow it to dry and then polish the floor with a soft cloth or a polisher with clean brushes. It is not a good idea to apply the wax too frequently as a thick layer of polish will build up which will be slippery and will easily mark. The floor can be buffed up between waxing by going over it with a polisher. *Never* use polishes containing silicone.

WOODEN FLOORS IN BAD CONDITION

If a wooden floor has been neglected or badly treated it may be necessary to strip it and re-seal it. Do not attempt to strip floors with a painted decoration of historical significance. Mechanical sanders are difficult for amateurs to use well. Not only are they likely to remove too much wood but they frequently leave whorls in the wood. If the floor is uneven or the planks have warped a mechanical sander will remove the higher areas of wood.

If you have to remove old sealer, varnish or paint, strip the floor using a hand-held sander or water washable dichloromethane based paint remover. If using a hand-held sander work in the direction of the grain and take care that the sander does not cut into the wood or leave marks on the surface. Wear an effective dust-mask with filters. If the paint remover is used keep the room well-ventilated and wear rubber gloves and goggles. Follow the instructions on the tin carefully and only clean a small area at a time.

The floor can then be sealed using a polyurethane floor sealer. Use a floor sealer with a silk or matt finish as the gloss finish is too glossy. For the best finish apply the sealer carefully and rub it down with fine sandpaper between each coat. Follow the manufacturer's instructions. When the floor sealer is thoroughly dry, a layer of liquid floor wax can be applied.

It may only be necessary to remove a build up of old wax from the floor. This can be done using white spirit. Wipe the floor with cotton rags dipped in white spirit. Keep the room well-ventilated and wear rubber gloves and remember that white spirit is flammable. Loose boards should be nailed back down to the joists. Do not use iron nails in oak floors but use stainless steel, copper or brass ones as oak will cause the iron to rust which will stain the wood.

PARQUET FLOORS

Parquet or parquetry floors are made from blocks of wood laid on to a base. The blocks can be anything from 0.3 cm to 1 cm (⅛ to ½ in) thick, although old blocks can be as much as 5–7 cm (2–2½ ins) thick. These thicker bricks were often laid directly on to a bitumen base.

If these floors become wet from too liberal washing or other hazards the blocks will become loose and warp and curl up. If a parquet floor is stripped with a mechanical stripper the machine can lift up the blocks and may also sand through all the wood.

The blocks can become loose particularly in doorways. If a large area of blocks is loose draw a rough diagram of how they are placed and number each block with a paper label. Lift the loose blocks up and clean underneath them, remove any old adhesive and dirt from the floor and the base of the block. Degrease the surfaces with methylated spirits. Fix the blocks back into position with polyvinyl acetate emulsion adhesive. If some of the blocks are lower than others they can be made more even by placing thin strips of wood underneath the appropriate area of the blocks.

If many blocks are loose it may mean that the underfloor is in bad condition. The parquet floor can be taken up and relaid on plywood or chipboard but this should be done by a professional floor layer.

The blocks of parquet flooring often become loose near outside doors because of water brought in off shoes. If this continues to happen the blocks will become loose again so use a good doormat and if this becomes very wet remove it and allow it to dry elsewhere.

Never nail down the blocks of parquet floors as they will be unable to expand and contract with the rest of the floor.

Wooden floors and, particularly wooden stairs are slippery. Use anti-creep tape to prevent rugs from slipping or very good quality rubber underlay.

WOODEN SCULPTURE

INSPECTION
Check wooden sculpture regularly for woodworm. If there is any sign of infestation *see* Woodworm page 198. If you bring wooden sculpture back from far-flung places check them carefully for wood-boring insects. If there is any sign at all seal the sculpture securely in a polythene bag with a dichlovos strip (Vapona) and get expert advice from a local museum or a pest control company. Many foreign wood-boring insects are a great deal bigger and more voracious than our home-grown variety. You certainly do not want them in the house.

Wooden sculpture often crack and warp. This is either as a result of changes in the temperature and humidity or because unseasoned wood has been used. Never fill cracks in wood with a hard-setting filler such as Plastic Wood or Polyfilla as these will not move with the wood and this will set up stresses and could cause cracks to appear elsewhere. If you wish to fill a crack use an appropriately coloured wax.

HANDLING
Always pick up a wooden sculpture by the main part of the object. Support the weight from underneath and hold the object steady with your other hand about two-thirds of the way up. Do not pick up a wooden sculpture by the arms or decorative projections, even thought these may appear to be convenient handles, as they can easily split off. Take care that any pieces of the sculpture that stick out do not knock into doorways when the sculpture is being carried. Take care also that your belt buckle does not scratch the wooden object as you carry it against yourself.

Check that sculptures that are mounted are secure on their mounts, if the base is loose it may well fall on to something when you pick up the object.

Move large wooden reliefs on a well-padded trolley. There should always be two people to hold the relief vertical.

Do not fix anything to the finished surfaces of a piece of sculpture. Self-adhesive tape and labels are difficult to remove and may damage the surface.

CLEANING
See Wood. Do not attempt to clean rare, fragile, old or precious wooden sculpture. These should be cleaned by a conservator. Some old wooden sculpture can be very fragile and worm eaten. It is possible to consolidate this but it should be done by a conservator.

DISPLAY
Do not bring wooden sculpture from a cold damp place into a centrally heated room. Do not place them on or near a radiator or near or above a fire, as the heat will cause the wood to crack and warp. Do not place wooden sculpture where direct sunlight can fall on the piece as this can cause the wood to change colour, or close to houseplants which could be sprayed with water or near those which give off water through their leaves (*see* Furniture: Display). Fluctuating temperatures and relative humidity can cause serious damage to a wooden object.

STORAGE
Store wooden sculpture in a clean, cool, dry, well-ventilated and preferably dark area. It should neither be too dry nor too damp and the relative humidity should be constant.

Wrap small wooden sculpture in acid-free tissue or, if it is a large piece, in perforated polythene. Do not store wooden sculpture in damp basements or outhouses where they will be prone to insect attack and mould growth. Avoid using attics as the temperature can fluctuate wildly if the attic is not insulated under the tiles. You should not place wooden sculpture in a boiler room or airing cupboard or directly on to a stone or concrete floor, but put them on wooden slats, a cork mat or some polythene. Do not place wooden sculpture in metal or wooden cabinets unless they are well-ventilated, as lack of ventilation will cause mould growth. For further information, *see* Wood.

IDEAL CONDITIONS
See Wood.

POLYCHROME OR PAINTED STATUES
Wooden statues are sometimes painted. There may be a layer of gesso on the wood which is painted, or the paint can be applied directly on to the surface of the wood.

Rare, old, fragile or precious polychrome sculpture should be cleaned and conserved by a conservator.

On wooden sculpture where the paint has been applied directly to the wood the paint may be powdery. Remove any dust with an artist's hogshair brush taking care not to brush any paint off. Do not try to clean the paint with water or any other solvent.

Thick layers of paint or paint on gesso often cracks, lifts and flakes. Do not dust polychrome statues with a duster as the edges of the paint can catch on the cloth and be pulled off. Dust very gently with an artist's hogshair paint brush.

If the paint is dirty but in good condition and not flaking or lifting and the piece is not old, rare or precious, it may be possible to clean the paint surface using a cotton bud dampened with spit. Clean the paint by rolling the bud gently over the surface. Discard the bud when it becomes dirty. If there is any gilding on the piece take extreme care that you do not rub it off.

Do not clean polychrome sculpture with patent picture cleaners or other cleaning agents.

See Wooden Sculpture for handling, display and storage.

REPAIR
Small, broken pieces can be fixed into place with an easily reversible adhesive or polyvinyl acetate emulsion. Do not attempt to repair old, rare on precious wooden objects.

GILDED OBJECTS

Gilded furniture, picture and mirror frames and gilded objects are made from wood which is covered with a thin layer of gesso (a mixture of whiting or plaster of Paris and, among other things, rabbit skin glue). Often a colour such as a deep natural red or yellow ochre, both known as bole, is applied to the gesso and then sheets of gold leaf are laid on to the surface and burnished. Occasionally, the bole is applied directly to the wooden surface. Silver leaf is sometimes used but, as the silver tarnishes quickly, it is nearly always varnished. The varnish may be coloured to make the silver look like gold leaf.

Carved and gilded furniture and mirror frames became very popular in England in the eighteenth century, although gilding is a technique which has been used since the Middle Ages. Some very ornate pieces, particularly

those produced in the nineteenth century, are often made from a material called 'composition' or 'compo'. It can be wrapped around an iron armature and modelled or moulded and fixed directly onto a simple wood base. It is then gilded.

INSPECTION

The gilding can wear off an object very quickly and the ground colour or the gesso will show through. If the gesso starts to flake off, this could be because the wood has shrunk or changes in the relative humidity have made the wood expand and contract causing the gesso to crack and flake off. Wire armatures may rust and start to split the compo and push it off. Rust colour may show through the cracks.

HANDLING

Do not rub gilding. Never leave a piece of gilded furniture where people or a curtain will run against it as the gold will soon wear away. Do not knock a gilded surface as the gesso will mark or break. When lifting or carrying gilded furniture or frames make sure you do not scratch them with your belt buckle or sharp objects. Take care not to hit the base of a piece of furniture with a brush or vacuum cleaner when cleaning the floor. Water must never be allowed to get on to a gilded surface, so take care when cleaning other surfaces and when watering plants nearby. Do not allow plants to rest against a gilded frame or object.

CLEANING

There are two types of gilding, one is water gilding and the other is oil gilding. The difference is in the method of application. It is very difficult to tell them apart. Water gilding will come off with water and oil gilding with white spirit and other solvents. It is therefore inadvisable to do anything other than dust a gilded object unless you are absolutely sure what sort of gilding it is.

Do not dust a gilded object with a cloth but brush the dust off very gently with an artist's hogshair brush. If the object is very dusty hold a vacuum cleaner in your other hand to catch the dust. Do not let the nozzle of the vacuum cleaner touch the surface of the object. Use a photographer's puffer brush to get the dust out of intricate detail.

DISPLAY

Gilded objects should be displayed where they will not suffer physical damage from rubbing or knocking. They must be kept in an area with a constant relative humidity and they must not be displayed in direct sunlight.

For further information on display, storage and ideal Conditions *see* Oil Paintings, Frames and Wood.

REPAIR

If the gold leaf is worn away and the gesso is cracking and flaking, the object can be restored and regilded but this should only be done by a gilder. Do not attempt to retouch rubbed areas with gold paint as the paint will look nasty and granular, will tarnish quickly and will make the proper job harder to do when it becomes necessary.

TUNBRIDGEWARE

Tunbridgeware was developed in Tunbridge Wells in the late seventeenth century and consists of small wooden objects lavishly decorated with marquetry patterns by a special method. The design was created by gluing together sticks of various coloured woods, about 6in long, so that the ends of the sticks formed the pattern. The block of sticks was then finely sliced transversely so that about thirty sheets of an identical pattern were made. The woods used tended to be hardwoods such as beech, sycamore, holly, cherry, blackthorn and

opposite *A primitive jack-in-the-box*

above *Gilded and polychromed wood: detail of an altar in Valladolid, Spain*

mulberry. The objects made included small boxes, picture frames, games boards, and sometimes larger objects such as writing boxes and games tables.

The inlays can be damaged by damp which causes in inlay to rise.

Clean Tunbridgeware in the same way as marquetry. If the surface is dull, apply a little microcrystalline wax with a soft bristle brush and polish off with a clean, soft bristle brush.

Do not place where direct sunlight can fall on the object as the colours will fade. Do not place close to plants that are likely to be misted as the water could cause the marquetry to lift.

If the surface is raised and can be pushed down flat, repair as for Wood.

FRAMES

Frames are used to protect paintings or mirrors as well as to enhance their appearance. Old and elaborate frames are often works of art in their own right. Most frames, apart from modern ones, are made from wood which can be decorated in a number of ways. The most elaborate frames are carved, coated with gesso and decorated with gold leaf and sometimes pigments. However, some frames made in the eighteenth century and onwards look as if they are elaborately carved but are in fact made from 'composition'. This is a putty-like material which was moulded in wooden moulds and then stuck on to a simple wooden base. Compo frames are usually gilded.

Gold, silver and other metal leaf are used to decorate frames. Frames can also be painted, japanned, inlaid or covered with, among other things, shagreen, tortoiseshell, mother of pearl or ivory. Metals such as silver and, more recently, aluminium are sometimes used to make frames.

HANDLING
For general handling *see* Oil Paintings.

If the gilding on a frame is flaking or parts of the frame are coming off it will need restoring by a conservator. Keep any loose pieces in an envelope until you can get it restored.

If there is evidence of active woodworm in the frame, the picture must be removed as before any treatment is carried out as the chemicals used for woodworm treatment can harm the paint or varnish. Do not return the picture into the frame for at least three months to allow time for all the solvents to evaporate.

If you treat a gilded frame for woodworm yourself make sure that the insecticide does not get on to the gold. You will have to inject the fluid carefully from the back checking that it is not coming out of another hole or through the front. If there are a great many flight holes it will be safer to paint the insecticide on to the back of the frame. Fumigation is the best method for controlling woodworm under these circumstances but this must be carried out by a specialist. (*See* Furniture).

For handling frames made from other materials see the appropriate section.

CLEANING

Gilded frames are easily damaged. Never get them wet or try to clean them with water or other liquids. Never dust them with a duster, this applies to gessoed or compo frames in particular as the duster will catch rough edges and could pull off pieces. Brush the dust off with an artist's hogshair paint brush and hold the vacuum cleaner with the other hand to catch the dust. Do not knock the gilding with the vacuum cleaner. Make sure you do not brush the dust on to an unglazed picture.

Simple, uncarved frames can be cleaned by dusting gently with a soft cloth. Do not rub too vigorously or the gilding will wear through.

When cleaning the glass in a frame do not use commercial glass cleaners as they contain chemicals which can harm the frame. The glass should be cleaned by polishing it with a clean, dry, soft chamois leather. Protect the edges of the frame by holding a piece of thin card against them so that your leather does not touch the edges accidentally. A little spit on a cotton wool bud will help remove fly blow and other marks.

If the glass is very dirty clean it with a swab of cotton wool barely dampened with warm water containing a few drops of a non-ionic detergent (Synperonic N). A few drops of methylated spirits in the water may help remove greasy dirt. Rinse the glass with a clean swab moistened with clean water then polish it with a lint-free cloth. Make sure you do not touch the sides of the frame as the gilding, paint or varnish will come off. Protect the edge of the frame with a card as before.

It is very important that the cleaning fluids should not touch the frame or run behind the glass.

Never polish the glass protecting pastel, chalk or charcoal drawings because rubbing will cause static electricity to build up and it will pull the colouring from the paper on to the glass.

To clean frames made from other materials see the appropriate section.

DISPLAY

For information on hanging frames *see* Oil Paintings. The conditions for display should suit the picture which is framed. *See* Oil Paintings, Paper, Prints and Drawings and Photographs.

STORAGE

Empty frames can be stored hanging from two brackets on the wall. Keep in a cool, clean, dry area. *See* Paintings. An insect repellent strip hung with stored frames will help protect them from woodworm. To store frames made from other materials see the appropriate section.

Frames should be stored vertically. Remove wire, chains, hooks and rings before storing so that they do not damage other frames. If possible do not leave frames propped up on the floor as they are bound to be kicked or run into by the vacuum cleaner. They are also nearer the dust and insects. If you have to store frames on the floor put slats of wood at least 2.5 cm (1 in) thick underneath them to raise them off the floor or rest them on padded blocks or a piece of carpet. Do not butt frames against an outside wall which will almost certainly be damp. Lean them against an inside wall with the front facing outwards. Separate them from each other with corrugated cardboard, bubble wrap or hardboard. Do not lean more than five frames against each other. If you have several frames to store you could construct a wooden rack similar to a large plate rack. (see p. 135)

IDEAL CONDITIONS

The conditions must suit the object being framed. *See* Oil Paintings, Prints and Drawings, Photographs, and Mirrors.

REPAIR

Ornate, rare and precious frames should be repaired by a carver-gilder or frame conservator. If the frame no longer holds together well it is not protecting the painting and should be taken to a framer or restorer to be repaired. Do not retouch a good quality gilded frame with gold powders or gold paint. These tarnish very quickly and soon look unpleasant. However, if you use gold paint to retouch a cheap frame take care to cover the painting first so that you do not get gold on to it.

Minor repairs can be carried out using an easily reversible adhesive (HMG, UHU All Purpose Clear Adhesive) or PVA emulsion (Evostick Resin W).

GLOSSARY AND DESCRIPTION OF MATERIALS

ACETONE Acetone is a clear solvent which will dissolve most varnishes, plastics and easily reversible adhesives. It is toxic, dehydrating, flammable and should always be used in a well-ventilated area.

ACID-FREE PAPER Since the mid-nineteenth century, paper-making processes have left papers contaminated with bleaches and fillers which gradually become acidic as they age. Any textiles or objects in contact with ordinary paper risk being damaged over a period of months or years. Heat and moisture accelerate the decay. Acid-free paper, which is free of these bleaches and fillers, is available as tissue, paper or card. In time acid-free paper will absorb acid from objects and the atmosphere and it should be replaced every four or five years.

ACRYLIC SHEET Acrylic sheet (Perspex, Plexiglas) can be clear, coloured, transluscent or opaque and is produced as sheet, rods or blocks. It is used instead of glass in some picture frames and showcases and is sometimes used for producing domes for clocks, etc.

ADHESIVES Adhesives which are easily reversible should always be used wherever possible. An easily reversible adhesive is one which can be readily dissolved. For instance, cellulose nitrate adhesive (HMG) will dissolve in acetone, epoxy resin adhesive (Araldite) will not. The adhesive should not be applied too thickly. A great blob of adhesive does not make a join any stronger.
Cyanoacrylate adhesives e.g. Loctite Superglu. These set instantly with pressure. They are virtually impossible to dissolve or soften.
Easily reversible adhesives e.g. HMG or UHU All Purpose Clear Adhesive. These will be dissolved by and can be removed with acetone.
Epoxy resin adhesives – quick setting e.g. Devcon 10-minute epoxy, 5-minute Araldite – slow setting e.g. Araldite.
Before they set they can be removed with acetone. They can be softened by dichlormethane based paint remover when set.
Polyvinyl acetate emulsion adhesive e.g. Evostik W. When wet it can be removed with water. When dry it can be removed with acetone. See Polyvinyl acetate emulsion.
Scotch glue is an animal glue used in woodwork. It can be removed with warm water.

ALCOHOL Alcohols are useful but highly flammable solvents. Methylated spirits is the most easily available alcohol but the purple dye it contains can stain objects. Isopropyl alcohol is a clear liquid which can be brought from a chemist. Industrial methylated spirits (IMS) which is also clear needs to have a Customs' permit before it can be bought. Alcohol will dissolve shellac, french polish and some easily reversible adhesives. It is useful for cleaning some objects when water cannot be used.

AMMONIA Ammonia can be bought in a concentrated liquid form from a chemist. It has a pungent smell and the vapours can be harmful to the eyes, skin and respiratory system. It should never be used in a concentrated form but diluted with water. Always use it in a well-ventilated room and keep it in a brown, screw-top glass bottle or an eye dropper bottle as light can affect it. When we advise adding a few drops of ammonia do not use household ammonia as it contains other chemicals.

BRUSHES An artist's soft paint brush refers to sable and squirrel hair brushes. An artist's hogshair brush is stiffer than a soft paint brush and usually white. A bristle brush refers to a brush made with natural bristles, not nylon bristles. Brushes used to polish one metal should not be used on another metal, i.e. a silver brush should be used on silver only. To clean brushes wash them in warm soapy water and dry naturally. If they have wax on them clean them first in white spirit and then wash.

CALGON A commercially available water softener containing sodium hexametaphosphate.

CARCASS The carcass is the 'body' of a piece of furniture. It may be made of pine or other cheap woods and is usually veneered.

CHAMOIS LEATHER Chamois leather is a very soft, supple leather used for cleaning. It should be washed in warm water containing soap such as Lux Flakes or Fairy Soap, never household detergent including washing-up liquid or washing powders. Rinse the leather well in clean warm water and squeeze out the water, do not wring. Shake to get it into shape and dry away from direct heat and sunlight. When the leather is dry rub it well against itself to make it soft and supple again.

CHROME CLEANER *See* Mildly abrasive chrome cleaner.

COTTON BUD Cotton buds can be brought ready made (Q-tips, Boots Cotton Buds, etc.) or can be made by twisting a few threads of cotton wool round the end of a wooden cocktail stick or a bamboo skewer.

DICHLOROMETHANE Also known as methylene chloride, it is a constituent of paint removers (Nitromors in the green tin). Dichloromethane is highly toxic and must be used with great care.

Always wear rubber gloves and goggles and work outside. If this is not possible work in a very well-ventilated room. *Never* smoke when using dichloromethane.

DICHLOROPHEN Dichlorophen (Panacide) is a biocide which is soluble in water and is used for killing algae, lichen and fungi.

DICHLORVOS STRIPS Insect repellent strips (Vapona, Mafu) used in the home to destroy insects. The strips give off a vapour which is toxic to humans and therefore they should never be hung in rooms where people spend much time.

EASILY REVERSIBLE ADHESIVE *See* **adhesive**.

EVOSTICK RESIN 'W' A polyvinyl acetate (PVA) emulsion adhesive marketed for woodworking. The adhesive can be thinned with water and before it is set it can be wiped off with a damp cloth. Once set the adhesive can be dissolved with difficulty using acetone.

FOXING Brown or orange spots on paper caused by fungi.

FRASS Frass is insect droppings and dust from the object which can range in texture from fine powder to pellets. It is usually brownish.

FRENCH POLISH A highly polished finish on wood, based on shellac.

FRIGILENE A clear cellulose nitrate lacquer used to protect silver. It can be thinned with Frigilene Reducer. Frigilene lacquer can be removed with acetone.

HOUSEHOLD DETERGENT Most household detergents contain perfume, colouring agents, brighteners and other chemicals in addition to the detergent. These chemicals can be harmful to objects. Fairy Liquid contains fewer additives and is the only household detergent that should be used when indicated.

HYDROGEN PEROXIDE An oxidising bleach. It can cause burns and should be stored away from heat and light. It can be bought in a made up solution of twenty vols or thirty vols. Twenty vols is the recommended strength.

INCRALAC A clear lacquer used for copper, brass and bronze. It contains a methyl methacrylate copolymer with a corrosion inhibitor. It can be thinned and removed with acetone.

INSECTICIDE FOR WOODWORM Low Odour Cuprinol or Rentokil and other commercial brands. Make

sure that they do not contain any colouring agent. Read the instructions before using.

INSECT REPELLENT STRIP *See* dichlorvos strip.

JENOLITE and MODALENE A commercially produced rust remover and inhibitor. Always follow the manufacturer's instructions closely.

LACQUER FOR METAL PROTECTION *See* Frigilene and Incralac.

LEATHER CREAMS Bavon, Connolly's Hide Food, Pliancreme.

MELINEX, MYLAR *See* polyethylene terephthalate film.

MICROCRYSTALLINE WAX A hard semi-synthetic wax whose crystals are very small. It gives a shiny surface and helps protect against moisture. When dry and polished it is not sticky and dust and dirt will not adhere to it. Apply the wax very sparingly to a small area and polish it as you go. If you do not polish it immediately it is difficult to get a smooth, shiny surface.

MILDLY ABRASIVE CHROME CLEANER A very mild abrasive cream which contains a minimum of chemicals and does not leave a deposit on the surface (Solvol Autosol). Do not use any other chrome cleaner.

NITROMORS Niromors is a paint stripper which contains dichloromethane. Use the water washable variety only. *See* dichloromethane.

NON-IONIC DETERGENT Non-ionic detergent (Synperonic N) is a wetting agent which when added to water makes the water clean more efficiently without forming a scum. In addition it does not contain any other chemicals unlike household detergents. Non-ionic detergent is very concentrated and should be used sparingly. A 'few drops' really means a few drops.

NYLON NET/TERYLENE NET Smooth weave nylon fabric made from a mono-filament yarn also known as filtration fabric. Used for protecting textiles when vacuuming and washing.

ORTHOPHENYLPHENOL A fungicide used for books and archival materials. It is made into a 5 per cent weight/volume solution with alcohol (i.e. 5 gms orthophenyl-phenol to 100 ml of alcohol).

PARADICHLOROBENZENE (PDB) An insecticide in the form of white crystals. Used to protect against moths, woodworm, etc. Avoid skin contact and breathing the vapour.

PATINA A patina is the surface colour that an object acquires in time as a result of handling, polishing, age, weathering, etc. It is mainly used with reference to metal, particularly bronze, wood and stone.

PERFORATED POLYTHENE BAGS Generally, objects should not be stored in sealed polythene bags as this prevents good air circulation and can cause condensation to form on the surface of the object. Mould is likely to grow under these conditions. Polythene bags should be perforated to allow the air to circulate. Use food bags already perforated or make holes in the bag with scissors or a knitting needle.

PERSPEX/PLEXIGAS *See* acrylic sheet.

PHOTOGRAPHER'S PUFFER BRUSH Very useful for simultaneously blowing and brushing off dust.

POLYETHYLENE TEREPHTHALATE FILM A clear film which is used as a non-stick surface and is available in different thicknesses (12-175 microns). It is resistant to most common chemicals and will not affect materials. (Melinex, Mylar.)

POLYMETHYLMETHACRYLATE SHEET See acrylic sheet.

POLYVINYL ACETATE EMULSION (PVA) A white liquid with the consistency of single cream, which when set is almost clear. It is commercially available as Evostik Resin 'W' although there are other brand names. A purer form of PVA emulsion (Vinamul 6815, Mowilith DMC2) can be bought in larger quantities. *See* Evostik Resin 'W'.

POTASSIUM OLEATE SOAP A concentrated spirit soap soluble in water and white spirit. (Vulpex.)

RUST INHIBITOR Slows down the rate at which iron rusts. *See* Jenolite.

SCOTCH GLUE *See* adhesives.

SELF-ADHESIVE TAPE Includes any tape with adhesive on one or both sides which will stick instantaneously with pressure. It does not need water to make it stick. (Sellotape, Magic tape, Masking tape, etc.)

SHELLAC A resin made from insects. It is the main component when dissolved in alcohol of french polish. It was also used extensively as an adhesive.

SILICONE PAPER Non-stick paper also known as siliconised vegetable parchment or silicone release paper. It is not the same as greaseproof paper.

SODIUM HEXAMETAPHOSPHATE *See* Calgon.

SOFT CLOTH Old Vyella shirts, sheeting and old tea towels all make good soft cloths. Natural fibres are best because they are absorbent. Ideally, the cloth should be lint-free and white.

SOLVOL AUTOSOL *See* mildly abrasive chrome cleaner.

SYNPERONIC N *See* non-ionic detergent.

TALCUM POWDER Also known as french chalk. Unperfumed talcum powder is available from chemists.

THYMOL A sterilizing agent used to protect paper and other materials from mould. The vapour from dry crystals can be used or the crystals can be dissolved in alcohol.

VACUUM CLEANERS To clean most objects a low powered vacuum cleaner or one that has a low power setting should be used. (Moulinex Petivac cleaner, Hoover Porta-power 800).

WALLPAPER PASTE A cellulose-based water soluble adhesive.

WAXING Wax should be applied sparingly to a surface with a soft, lint-free cloth or a soft bristle brush. It should be polished off with a clean cloth or brush. *See* Waxing Furniture (page 202) for more information.

WHITE SPIRIT A clear solvent which softens and dissolves waxes and other materials. It will not mix with water.

List of Materials and Suppliers

MATERIALS

Acetone
Chemists
US: Fisher Scientific, VWR

Acid-free envelopes and folders
UK: C.A. Coutts Ltd
US: TALAS
Aus: Museums Association,
Conservation Resources, S & M
Supply Co.

Acid-free paper, card, board, tubes, tissue
UK: Atlantis Paper Co, Conservation
Resources UK Ltd, Falkiner Fine
Papers Ltd, Lawrence and Aitken,
good stationers, Spicer Cowan Ltd (for tissue)
US: TALAS, Conservation Materials
Aus: Museums Association,
Conservation Resources
S & M Supply Co.

Almond Oil
Chemists
US: Chemical suppliers

Ammonia
Chemists
US: Fisher Scientific, VWR

Anti-creep tape (Standfast)
Hardware stores
UK: Simon Boosey

Artists' hogs' hair brush and paint brush
Artists' suppliers
US: Conversation Materials, Sam Flax

Autosol *see* **Solvol Autosol**

Balsa Wood
Model shops, hobby shops, hardware stores

Bamboo skewers
Oriental (Chinese or Thai) food stores

Bavon
UK: F. W. Joel Ltd
US: Conservation Materials
Australian readers are advised to contact F. W. Joel Ltd in the UK

Beads
Haberdashers
UK: Ells & Ferrier

Black lead see **Zebrite**

Black paint for iron and steel
Good hardware, DIY and paint stores

Blinds
Large department stores, specialist blind shops
UK: Tidmarsh & Sons
US: Plexi U-V screening (UF3)

available from Rohm & Haas
Aus: department stores such as David Jones, Grace Bros.

Blotting paper
UK: Ford's Gold Medal Blotting
Paper – Falkiner Fine Papers, some stationers'
US: Conservation Materials
Aus: Museums Association, some stationers, Tamarisque Fine Art

Borax
Hardware stores

Boxes, acid-free or low acid content
UK: C.A. Coutts Ltd, Conservation
Resources UK Ltd
US: TALAS, Gaylord, Conservation
Materials
Aus: Museums Association,
Conservation Resources, S & M
Supply Co.

Box frames made from acrylic sheet
Plastics suppliers
UK: Acrylic Design, V.T. Plastics

Brass framing plates
Picture framing shops and suppliers,
good hardware stores

Brushes, soft bristle
Good hardware stores
UK: A selection of brushes is available
from the National Trust (Enterprises)
Ltd, F. A. Heffer & Co Ltd, John
Myland Ltd, W. Canning Materials
Ltd.
US: Conservation Materials, Sam Flax

Calico (US: muslin, undyed cotton fabric)
Department stores, fabric shops
UK: MacCulloch and Wallis,
H. Wolfin & Son Ltd, Quarry Bank
Mill Trust Ltd.
US: large fabric supply houses

Cardboard tubes
Stationery, carpet or fabric shops. See
above for acid-free tubes.

Chamois leather
Car accessory shops
US: Hardware and auto supply shops

Cool lights
Good lighting shops
US: Low U-V emission fluorescent
tubes from Verd-A-Ray; U-V filtering
sleeves for fluorescent tubes from
Conservation Resources

Cotton buds (Q-tips, cotton swabs)
Chemists, chemical or medical
suppliers

Cotton gloves
Chemists, medical suppliers
UK: Wilson (Wearwell) Ltd, Anthony
Moor Ltd

Dichlorvos strips (e.g. UK: Mafu,
Aus: Shelltox)
Chemists, hardware stores,
supermarkets: see also Insecticides

Distilled or deionised water
Chemists, soft drinks manufacturer or
supplier, supermarkets

Draft Clean
Good stationers, art shops, graphic art
suppliers
UK: F. W. Joel Ltd
US: Conservation Materials. Opaline
pads and crumbled erasers from
Conservation Materials and TALAS
Aus: Museums Association, S & M
Supply Co

Easi-flow (non-corrosive flux)
Hardware and DIY shops

Epoxy resin adhesives
Hardware and DIY shops
UK: CIBA-Geigy Ltd (Araldite)
US: Conservation Materials (Araldite
AY103, Hyxtal, Ablebond 342)
Aus: CIBA-Geigy Ltd

Eraser, putty type (Staedler Mars
Plastic 526–50 or Rowney Kneadable
Putty Rubber; US: Kneaded erasers)
Art shops, stationers
US: TALAS, art supply stores

Ercalene
UK: W. Canning Materials Ltd, F. W.
Joel Ltd
US; see Incralac
Australian readers are advised to write
to F. W. Joel Ltd, UK

Foam plastic
Local supplier, see Yellow Pages
Aus: Edwards Dunlop

Folders for paperback books etc *see*
Acid-free folders

Frigilene (US: Agateen)
UK: W. Canning Materials Ltd, F. W.
Joel Ltd
US: Agate Lacquer Mfg Co.
Aus: *see* **Ercalene**

Gatorfoam (US: Acid-Free Fome Cor)
UK: Atlantis Paper Co. Ltd
US: Conservation Materials

Glass domes
Glass merchants, clock-makers'
suppliers
UK: H. S. Walsh & Sons Ltd (Perspex
domes: S.C. Designs)
Aus; O'Brien Glass Industries

Glass, non-reflecting
Local glass suppliers
UK: H. V. Skan Ltd

Hessian (US: Linen or jute open-weave
fabric for foundation upholstery)

Department stores, specialist fabric shops and suppliers
UK: Russell & Chapple Ltd

Hide Food
Department stores, leather goods suppliers, saddlers
UK: Connolly Bros (Curriers) Ltd
Aus: Museums Association

HMG
UK: H. Marcel Guest Ltd, F. W. Joel Ltd
US: Conservations Materials. Universal Cement (a cellulose nitrate adhesive) available from Randolph Products Co.
Aus: Museums Association, S & M Supply Co

Humidifiers and dehumidifiers
UK: Current information from Museums Association
US: Information from CAL
Aus: Bestobell Engineering

Hydrogen peroxide (20 vols)
Chemists
US: Fisher Scientific, VWR

Hygrometers
UK: Casella London Ltd, Russell Scientific Instruments Ltd, F. W. Joel Ltd.
US: Conservation Materials, laboration supply houses
Aus: Surgico Pty Ltd, Dobbie Instruments

Incralac (*see also* **Ercalene**)
UK: F. W. Joel Ltd
US: Conservation Materials

Insecticide (Low Odour)
hardware stores
UK: Cuprinol Ltd, Rentokil Ltd
US: See recent CAL publication *Pest Management in Museums* by Keith Story for recommendations

Insecticide strip *see* **Dichlorvos strip**

Isopropyl alcohol, Isopropanol
Chemists
US: Fisher Scientific, VWR
Aus: Ajax Chemicals, Laboratory Supply Pty.

Japanese tissue paper
UK: Atlantis Paper Co; Falkiner Fine Papers, F. W. Joel Ltd
US: TALAS, Conservation Materials
Aus: Museums Association, Tamarisque Fine Art Pty Ltd

Jenolite
Hardware and car (auto) accessory stores

Jewel box makers
Consult Yellow Pages
UK: Wheeler & Oliver Ltd, Johnson, Baker & Co Ltd

Light meters
UK: F. W. Joel Ltd
US: Visible-light meters from photo suppliers; U-V meters from Littlemore

Liners glass fibre for lead cisterns
UK: H. Greg & Sons Ltd

Liquid wax
Hardware stores
see also Wax

Long term silver and copper cleaners (US: Mish's Silver Polish, Aus] Nevr-Dull)
Department stores, hardware stores, jewellery and silver shops
UK: J. Goddard & Co Ltd
US: Mish Products
Aus: Museums Association

Magnesia, magnesium carbonate
Chemists, chemical supply houses

Manders Black Ebony paint *see* **Black paint for iron and steel**

Melinex (US and Aus: Mylar)
UK: ICI, F.W. Joel Ltd, Trylong Ltd, Strand Glassfibre Ltd
US: Conservation Materials
Aus: Museums Association, Conservation Resources

Methylated spirits (US: ethanol)
Hardware and DIY stores
US: Fisher Scientific, VWR

Microcrystalline wax
Ready-prepared paste *see* Renaissance wax

Modalene
UK: Modastic Ltd

Naphthalene (moth balls)
Chemists, department stores
UK: F. W. Joel Ltd
US: *see under* Insecticides

Nitromors *see* **Paint Remover**

Non-ionic detergent
UK: Synperonic N from F. W. Joel Ltd
US: Triton, Orvus WA Paste from Conservation Materials, Igepal from GAF
Aus: Lissipol from Museums Association

Nylon Line (US Monofilament)
Fishing tackle shops, hardware stores

Nylon net, terylene net
UK: Black Brothers and Boden Ltd, Picreator Enterprises Ltd
US: TALAS
Aus: haberdashery shops

Orthophenylphenol
UK: F. W. Joel Ltd
US: TALAS, chemical supply houses
Aus: S & M Supply Co.

Packing materials
UK: Bubble wrap (Polythene air-cap) from Costerwise Ltd (wholesale), Transatlantic Plastics Ltd
US: Local suppliers, check Yellow Pages
Aus: Edwards Dunlop, B. J. Ball

Paint remover
Hardware and DIY stores
US: Nitromors is available from Conservation Materials

Paradichlorobenzene (PDB)
UK: Chemists, F. W. Joel Ltd
US: See under Insecticides

Aus: Ajax Chemicals, Laboratory Supply Pty Ltd

Photograph Albums, acid-free
UK: Atlantis Paper Co Ltd
US: TALAS
Aus: Conservation Resources, S & M Supply Co.

Photographer's puffer brush
Camera shops
US: photo supply stores

Picture chain, cord or wire
Department stores and picture framing shops
UK: J. Shiner & Sons Ltd

Plastic tubing to cover cup hooks and plate racks
Hobby and model shops
US: plastics suppliers

Plastic tweezers
Chemists and medical suppliers
UK: F. W. Joel Ltd, Bell & Croyden Ltd
US: Fisher laboratory suppliers

Plate hangers and stands
UK: department stores and antique shops
US: hardware stores
Aus: department stores

Pliancreme, Pliantene (US: British Museum Leather Dressing)
UK and Aus: F. W. Joel Ltd
US: Conservation Materials

Polyester envelopes
UK: Secol Ltd
US: TALAS
Aus: Museums Association

Polyester padding
Fabric shops, fabric suppliers, large stores

Polyvinyl acetate emulsion
UK: Evostik Resin 'W' – hardware and DIY stores
Mowilith DMC2 and Vinamul 6815 – F. W. Joel Ltd
US: Conservation Materials carries a variety including Rhoplex and CM Bons

Potassium oleate soap, Vulpex
UK: F. W. Joel Ltd, Picreator Enterprises Ltd
US; Conservation Materials

PVC drainpipes for rolling textiles
Builders' merchants and DIY shops, hardware stores
US: Plastics suppliers

Renaissance wax
UK: Picreator Enterprises Ltd, F. W. Joel Ltd, A. Tiranti Ltd
US: Conservation Materials
Aus: Museums Association

Rust remover *see* **Jenolite, Modalene**

Saddle soap
Saddlers, shoe shops, leather goods suppliers, department stores

Safety equipment, fume masks (respirators), gloves, goggles

Safety equipment shops and suppliers, see Yellow Pages
UK: F. W. Joel Ltd
US: Conservation Materials, Fisher, laboratory supply houses

Scalpel handles and blades
Art and graphic supply houses
US: Medical supply houses
Aus: Selby Anax Ltd

Silica gel (US; Art-Sorb [Fuji-Davidson])
UK: Some chemists, Picreator Enterprises Ltd, F. W. Joel Ltd
US: Conservation Materials
Aus: Museums Association, Selby Anax Ltd

Silicone release paper (also called vegetable parchment)
Specialist cookery shops and department stores. Do not use greaseproof paper
UK: Atlantis Paper Co, F. W. Joel Ltd
US: Conservation Materials
Aus: Museums Association

Silk crepeline
Fabric shops
UK: Paul L. G. Dulac et Cie
US: TALAS

Solander boxes
UK: Atlantis Paper Co; Falkiner Fine Papers Ltd, G. Ryder & Co
US: TALAS
Aus: Conservation Resources

Solvol Autosol (Aus: Nevr-Dull)
UK: Car accessory shops, Hunting Lubricants and Specialised Products Ltd
US: Conservation Materials
Aus: Museums Association

Steel wool *see* **Wire wool**

Stoddarts Solvent *see* **White Spirit**

Synperonic N (US: Igepal, Aus: Lissipol) *see* **Non-ionic detergent**

Syringe for treating woodworm
Chemists, doctors
UK: F. W. Joel Ltd
US: Medical and science supply houses

Talcum powder (French chalk) – unperfumed
Chemists
US: Fisher, science supply houses

Tarnprufe - impregnated cloth bags and rolls for silver (Aus: Goddard Non-Tarnish Cloth)
UK: The Tarnprufe Co. Ltd
Aus: Jewellers, hardware stores
US: Suggested alternative: 3M Protector Strips (activated charcoal strips) available from 3M Company

Thymol
UK: F. W. Joel Ltd
US: Conservation Materials, TALAS
Aus: chemists

UHU all-purpose clear adhesive
Stationery and hardware shops
UK: Beecham UHU Ltd

U-V absorbing filters, varnish and sleeves for fluorescent tubes
UK: Bonwyke Ltd, The Morden Co, Solar X Ltd
US: Conservation Resources, Light Impressions
Aus: Hardware and lighting shops

Vacuum cleaners (see Glossary for model)
Electrical shops, hardware stores, department stores
US: Electric appliance shops

Velcro
Haberdashers and department stores
US: Fabric suppliers

Wax polish for furniture
UK: Antiquax, National Trust Furniture wax, any other paste wax made from beeswax (not spray wax) from antique shops, department stores and hardware shops
US: Butcher's Paste Wax, Bowling Alley Wax, Goddards, Bailin and Staple Waxes, from Conservation Materials
Aus: Museums Association

Wax for filling flight holes in furniture
Specialist shops supplying furniture restoration materials, craft shops, some antique shops
UK: J. Myland Ltd
US: Conservation Materials
Aus: Museums Association

Webbing for securing doors and drawers when moving furniture (use heavy duty)
Haberdashers and upholsterers
US: Fabric and upholstery suppliers

White spirit (US: Stoddarts Solvent)
Hardware and DIY shops, builders' merchants
UK: John Myland Ltd
US: Fisher, VWR
Aus: Ajax Chemicals, Laboratory Supply Pty Ltd

Wire wool (US: Steel wool)
grades 0 to 0000 (finest)
Hardware and DIY shops
US: Supermarkets

Zebrite (US Graphite)
Department stores and provincial hardware stores
US: Chemical supply houses

ORGANISATIONS

UK
United Kingdom Institute for Conservation (UKIC)
37 Upper Addison Gardens, London, W14

International Institute for Conservation of Historic and Artistic Works (IIC).
6 Buckingham Street, London, WC2
01-839 5975

The Museums Association
34 Bloomsbury Way
London, WC1
01-404 4767

The Museums and Galleries Commission
7 St James's Square
London, SW1
01-839 9341

Area Museums Service for South East England,
Kenwood,
Hampstead Lane,
London, N1

(AMSEE will supply addresses for Museums Services in other areas)

US

The American Institute for Conservation of Historic and Artistic Works (AIC),
The Klingle Mansion,
3545 Williamsburg Lane, N.W.
Washington, D.D. 20008
(202) 364-1036

Conservation Analytical Laboratory
Smithsonian Institution
Washington D.C. 20560
(202) 287-3700

Australia

Museums Associations of Australia Incorporated

NSW

Museums Association of Australia
NSW Branch
P.O. Box K346
Haymarket 2000
PH. 2170111
and

c/o Historic Houses Trust of NSW,
'Lyndhurst'
61 Dougan Street,
Glebe NSW 2037

Vic

c/o Ministry for the Arts
186 Exhibition Street,
Melbourne
VIC 3000
(03) 669 8666

SA

c/o History Trust of South Australia
122 Kintore Street
Adelaide
SA 5000
(08) 228 5253 Adelaide University

WA

c/o Western Australian Museum
Francis Street,
Perth
WA 6000
(09) 328 4411 or 339 6329

QLD

c/o Queensland Museum
PO Box 300

South Brisbane
QLD 4014
(07) 240 7555)

TAS

c/o Tasmanian Museum and Art
Gallery
PO Box 116M
Hobart
TAS 7001

ACT

c/o Dept of Territory
PO Box 435
Manuka
ACT 2603
(062) 462 714

**The Institute for the Conservation of
Cultural Materials (ICCM)**
GPO Box 3762
Sydney
NSW 2001

SUPPLIERS

UK
Acrylic Design Ltd
697 Harrow Road
London NW10 5NY
01 969 0478

Atlantis Paper Company
Gulliver's Wharf
105 Wapping Lane
London E1 9RW
01 481 3784

Beecham UHU Ltd
11 Stoke Poges Lane,
Slough,
Berkshire SK1 3NW

Bell and Croyden Ltd.,
50 Wigmore Street,
London W1

Black Brothers and Boden Ltd,.,
53 Stoney Street,
Nottingham NG1 1NA.
0602 505772

Bonwyke Ltd.,
18 Silver Birch Avenue,
Fareham,
Hampshire PO14 1SZ
0329 289621

Simon Boosey,
Tun House,
Whitwell,
Hitchin,
Hertfordshire
043 887 563

W. Canning Materials Ltd.,
Great Hampton Street,
Birmingham B18 6AS.

Casella London Ltd.,
Regent House,
Britannia Walk,
London N1 7ND
01–253 8581

CIBA-Geigy Plastics Division
Duxford,

Cambridge CB2 40A
0223 832121

Connolly Bros (Curriers) Ltd.,
Wandle Bank,
South Road
London SW19 1DW
01–542 5251

Conservation Resources UK Ltd
Unit 1
Littleworth Industrial Estate,
Wheatley,
Oxfordshire OX9 1TZ
086 772244

Consortium Conservation Ltd.,
Victoria Dock,
Dundee DD1 DHU

Costerwise Ltd
Protective Packaging Specialists,
16 Rabbit Row,
London W8 4DX
01–221 0666

C. A. Coutts & Co. Ltd.,
Violet Road,
London E3 3QL
01 515 6171

Cuprinol Ltd
Adderwell,
Frome,
Somerset BA11 1NL.
0373 65151

Paul L. G. Dulac et Cie.,
3 rue Romarin,
5 Place du Griffin,
Lyon, France

Ells & Farrier Ltd.,
5 Princes Street,
Hanover Square,
London W1R 8PH,
01 629 9964

Falkiner Fine Paper Ltd.,
76 Southampton Row,
London WC1N 3XX,
01 404 5011 (temp)

Glass Dome Co.,
High Street,
Leigh
Nr. Tonbridge,
Kent, TN11 8RH
0732 833000

J. Goddard & Co Ltd.,
Frimley Green,
Camberley,
Surrey GU16 5AJ
0276 63456

H. Gregg & Sons,
34–38 Snedshill Trading Estate,
Oakengate,
Telford,
Shropshire

H. Marcel Guest Ltd.,
Riverside Works,
Collyhurst Road,
Manchester

W. J. Hagarty & Sons Ltd.,
FL–9490 Vaduz,
Belgium

F. A. Heffer & Co. Ltd.,
24 The Pavement,
London SW4 0JA
01–622 6871

**Hunting Lubricants and Specialised
Products Ltd.,**
Queen's Road,
Morley,
Leeds LS27 0QJ
0532 537211

Imperial Chemical Industries,
Petrochemicals and Plastics Division,
PO Box 6,
Bessemer Road,
Welwyn Garden City,
Hertfordshire AL7 1HD

Frank W Joel Ltd.,
Unit 5,
5 Oldmedow Road,
Hardwick Industrial Estate,
King's Lynn,
Norfolk PE30 4HL.
0553 760851

Johnson-Baker & Co. Ltd.,
Ivy Cross Works,
Shaftsbury,
Dorset SP7 8PU.

Lawrence and Aitken
Albion Works,
Kimberley Road,
London NW6 7SL
01–624 8135

MacCulloch and Wallis
25 Dering Street,
London W1.
01–629 0311

Modastic Ltd,
88–96 Bridge Road East,
Welwyn Garden City,
Hertfordshire AL7 1JW
070 73 24373

Anthony Moor Ltd.,
Bingham Industrial Estate,
Bingham,
Nottinghamshire, NG13 8GG.
0949 38517

The Morden Company,
7 Lytham Road,
Heald Green
Cheadle, Cheshire, SK8 3RQ
061 437 4379

John Myland Ltd.,
80 Norwood High Street,
West Norwood,
London, SE27 9NW
01 670 9161

**The National Trust (Enterprises)
Ltd.,**
Western Way,
Melksham,
Wiltshire

Picreator Enterprises Ltd.,
44 Park View Gardens,
Hendon,
London, NW4 2PN.
01 202 8972

Quarry Bank Mill Trust Ltd.,
Styal,

Cheshire, SK9 4LA,
0625 527 468

Rentokil Ltd.,
Products Division,
Felcourt,
East Grinstead,
West Sussex, RH19 2JY.
0342 833022

Russell & Chapple Ltd.,
23 Monmouth Street,
Shaftesbury Avenue,
London WC2H 9DE.
01 836 7521

Russell Scientific Instruments Ltd.,
Rash's Green Industrial Estate,
Dereham,
Norfolk NR19 1JG.
0362 3481

G. Ryder & Co.,
Denbigh Road,
Bletchley,
Milton Keynes,
Buckinghamshire, MK1 1DG.
0908 75524

S. C. Designs,
24 Derwent Close,
Claygate,
Esher,
Surrey, KT10 0RF
0372 68640

J. Shiner & Sons Ltd.,
8 Windmill Street,
London, W1P 1HF.
01 580 0740

H V Skan Ltd.,
425–433 Stratford Road,
Shirley,
Solihull,
West Midlands B90 4AE
021 744 6791

Solar X Ltd.,
Solar X House,
8–12 Stockport Road,
Stockport,
Cheshire SK3 0HZ
061 477 5040

Spicer Cowan Ltd.,
Central House,
32–66 High Street,
Stratford,
London E15
and local branches
01–519 4600

Strand Glassfibre Ltd.,
109 High Street,
Brentford,
and local branches
01–568 7191

The Tarnprufe Company Ltd.,
68 Nether Edge Road,
Sheffield, S7 1RX
0742 553652

Tidmarsh & Sons
Trasenna Works
1 Laycock Street,
London N1 1SW

Alec Tiranti Ltd.,
27 Warren Street,
London W1P 5DG

Transatlantic Plastics Ltd.,
672 Fulham Road,
London SW6
and local branches
01–736 2231

Trylon Ltd,
Wollaston,
Northamptonshire, NN9 7QJ
0933 664275

V T Plastics,
49 Wates Way,
Micham,
Surrey CR4 4HR
01685 9545

H. S. Walsh & Sons Ltd.,
12 Clerkenwell Road,
London EC1
01–253 1174

Wheeler and Oliver Ltd.,
14a St Cross Street,
London EC1.
01 242 5795

Wilsons (Wearwell) Ltd.,
Universal House,
843–5 Green Lane,
Winchmore Hill,
London N21 2RX
01–360 9366

H. Wolfin & Son Ltd.,
64 Great Tichfield Street,
London W1P 7AE
01 636 4949

US
Agate Lacquer Mfg. Co. Inc.,
11–13 43rd Road,
Long Island City, New York

Conservation Materials Ltd,
Box 2884,
Sparks,
Nevada 89431
(702) 331–0582

Conservation Resources International
1111 North Royal Street,
Alexandria,
VA 22314
(703) 549–6610

Fisher Scientific
52 Fadem Road,
Springfield,
NJ 07081
(201) 379–1400

Flax Artists Materials
(800) 547–7778

GAF
1610 W. 9th Ave
King of Prussia
PA 19406

Gaylord Brothers Inc.,
Box 4901,
Syracuse,
NY 13221
(800) 448–6160

Light Impressions,
PO Box 3012
Rochester,
NY 14614
(716) 271–8960

Littlemore Scientific Engineering,
Railway Lane,
Littlemore,
Oxford,
England

Mish Products,
214 Springfield Street,
Agawam,
MA 01101

Randolph Products Co.,
PO Box 67,
Park Place E,
Carlstadt,
NJ 07072

Rohm & Haas,
Independence Mall West,
Philadelphia,
PA 19105
(215) 592–3000

TALAS,
213 W. 35th Street,
New York,
NY 10001
(212) 736–7744

3M Company,
3M Center,
St Paul,
MN 55101
(800) 328–1449

University Products,
PO Box 101,
South Canal Street,
Holyoke,
MA 10141
(413) 532–3372

VWR Chemicals
(800) 841–0617

Verd-A-Ray,
615 Front Street,
Toledo,
OHIO 43605

AUSTRALIA
Ajax Chemicals,
9 Short Street,
Auburn, NSW

Bestobell Engineering Products,
70 Gibbes Street,
Chatswood, NSW
(02) 406 4655

Conservation Resources International (Australia),
48 Cribb Street,
Milton,
QLD 4064
(07) 369–2566

Dobbie Instruments,
186 Canterbury Road,
Canterbury 2193
(02) 789–6533

Edwards Dunlop and B. J. Ball,
70 Euston Road,
Alexandria, NSW
(02) 550–1155

Laboratory Supply Pty Ltd,
48–52, Syndenham Road,
Marrickville, 2204
(02) 519–6626

Parameters Pty Ltd,
25–27, Paul St North,
North Ryde, 2113
(02) 888–8777

Planet Lighting,
137 Pyrmont Street,
Pyrmont 2009
(02) 660–8244

S & M Supply Co.,
350 Kent Street,
Sydney, 2000
(02) 264 9166

893 Stanley Street,
East Brisbane 4169
(07) 391 8188

18 Barrier Street,
Fyshwick ACT 2609
(062) 80–6344

Selby Anax Ltd
61–65 Epping Road,
North Ryde 2113
(02) 888–7155

Surgico Pty Ltd
302 Victoria Road,
Gladesville NSW
(02) 816 5200

and

246 Hope Street
West Brunswick VIC 3056
(03) 387 6411

Tamarisque Fine Art Pty Ltd
27 Albion Street,
Surry Hills
(02) 212–1223

INDEX